JOSÉ ANTONIO NAVARRO

José Antonio NAVARRO

*In Search of the American Dream
in Nineteenth-Century Texas*

By David McDonald
Foreword by Arnoldo De León

Texas State Historical Association
Denton

This is Number 2 in the Watson Caufield and Mary Maxwell Arnold Republic of Texas Series.

© Copyright 2010 by the Texas State Historical Association.
All rights reserved. Printed in the U.S.A.

Library of Congress Cataloging-in-Publication Data
McDonald, David R., 1941–
José Antonio Navarro : in search of the American Dream in nineteenth century Texas / by David McDonald ; foreword by Arnoldo De León.
(Number 2 in the Watson Caufield [i.e. Caulfield] and Mary Maxwell Arnold Republic of Texas series)
Includes bibliographical references and index.
ISBN 978-0-87611-243-4—ISBN 978-0-87611-244-1
1. Navarro, José Antonio, 1795–1871. 2. Statesmen—Texas—Biography. 3. Businessmen—Texas—Biography. 4. Mexican Americans—Texas—Biography. 5. Garza Navarro, Margarita de la, 1795–1861. 6. Statesmen's spouses—Texas—Biography. 7. Navarro, Henry. 8. Freedmen—Texas—Biography. 9. Texas—History—Revolution, 1835–1836. 10. Texas—History—Republic, 1836–1846. I. Title. II. Series: Watson Caufield and Mary Maxwell Arnold Republic of Texas series; no. 2.
F390.N38M34 2010
976.4'03092—dc22

David McDonald and the Texas State Historical Association wish to thank the following book patrons for their support.

Frost

San Antonio Conservation Society

Jerome Paul Tillotson

Bill and Loretta Huddleston

E. Jeannie Navarro

Sandra J. Salinas

Max and Irene Navarro

Helen Arciniega Garza

Mary Christine Hollan

Elvira Helena Flores Kahlig

Megan and David D. Martinez

Tino and Millie Duran

Sylvia Navarro Tillotson

Friends of Casa Navarro

The Daughters of the Republic of Texas, Alamo Couriers Chapter

For Sister Mary Christine Morkovsky, C.D.P.,
and in memory of Curtis Tunnell

Contents

Acknowledgements XI

Foreword XV

Introduction I

Chapter One: Roots, 1762–1816 12

Chapter Two: Emerging Leader, 1816–22 33

Chapter Three: The Making of a Legislator, 1822–28 62

Chapter Four: Businessman, Land Commissioner,
and Politician, 1828–35 88

Chapter Five: Mexican-Texan, 1835–40 126

Chapter Six: Statesman and Prisoner, 1840–45 161

Chapter Seven: Tejano Spokesman, 1845–53 203

Chapter Eight: Elder Statesman, 1853–71 242

Appendix One: Margarita de la Garza 275

Appendix Two: Henry Navarro Notes 277

Appendix Three: José Antonio Navarro's Will 279

Notes 286

Index 331

Acknowledgments

DURING THE LONG PERIOD of researching and writing this biography, I have accumulated a mass of debts and obligations owed to the many persons from whom I have been fortunate to receive valuable assistance, both as individuals and staff members of institutions.

Several individuals read the manuscript at various stages of its preparation and made valuable suggestions. They include W. Phil Hewitt, the late Jack Jackson, Bill Holloway, Alvin Gerdes, and especially my brother Thomas McDonald, who served as my editor of first resort and consultant for historical legal matters. Jesús F. de la Teja offered significant organizational recommendations. Special thanks to Pierson "Pete" DeVries for his wise counsel and to Sister Mary Christine Morkovsky, C.D.P., and Father Robert Wright, O.M.I, for their guidance regarding religious issues. I appreciate Carol Cieszinski for sharing the results of her extensive Navarro research. Years of conversations with Alvin Gerdes, compiler of a vast Navarro genealogy, provided invaluable insights into the evolution of the Navarro family. Adela and Joe Navarro always provided spirited debates about Navarro history and heritage. Profound thanks to Adán Benavides for having compiled the *The Bexar Archives, 1717–1836: A Name Guide,* which made possible focused searches through the immense resources of the Bexar Archives that were previously impossible. Credit also goes to David Haynes for sharing his expertise on historical photographs.

Key members of many institutions also gave valuable assistance. Special thanks go to Sylvia Navarro Tillotson for her superb organizational and fund-raising abilities that have built a vital Friends of Casa Navarro support group to benefit the Casa Navarro State Historic Site. Thanks to the patrons whose donations made possible the publication of this book and who are a testament to Sylvia's fund-raising skills.

An indispensable resource was the San Antonio Public Library. Its Texana/Genealogy Department, in addition to having an extensive secondary source collection, has an extraordinary collection of archival material on microfilm. Manager Frank Faulkner was a tenacious library detective who tracked down find the most obscure publication. His predecessor, Jo Myler, also provided invaluable assistance from the beginning of this study.

The Institute of Texan Cultures maintains a historical photographic collection of more than two million items. Thomas Shelton was a knowledgeable guide who could find most needed images without consulting anything other than the index of his memory. Dora Guerra, as Special Collections Librarian at the University of Texas at San Antonio, was generous with her time. Sister Eva María Carolina Flores, C.D.P., Director of the Center for Mexican American Studies at Our Lady of the Lake University, provided invaluable guidance and direction in navigating the collections of historical materials she administers.

Texas Parks and Wildlife staff provided groundbreaking research efforts done during the Navarro site's transition into the Texas Parks & Wildlife Department. They include Sue Moss, Zane Morgan, and Jerry Sullivan. Special thanks to Teresa Garza, research assistant for many years at the Casa Navarro, who provided invaluable insights through her first-hand knowledge of traditional Mexican American culture and with her assistance in preparing transcripts and translations.

For locating obscure materials at the Briscoe Center for American History, much credit is due to Kathryn Kenifick, who was always my go-to person. Thanks also to John Wheat.

In addition, I would like to express gratitude to the following:

Tom McGlathery, former TP&W regional director

Galen Greaser, Texas General Land Office

The late Orabel "Pinkie" Martin and many other members of the San Antonio Conservation Society

Martha Utterback, Daughters of the Republic of Texas Library at the Alamo

John Anderson, Archives Division, Texas State Library

George Farías and many other members of Los Bexareños Genealogical Society

The late Kinga Perynska, Catholic Archives of Texas

Brother Ed Loch, S. M., Archives of the Archdiocese of San Antonio

Elsa del Valle and the late Ildefonso Dávila, Archivo Municipal de Saltillo, Coahuila, México

Israel Cavazos Garza, Archivo Municipal de Monterrey, Nuevo León, México

Alfonso Vásquez Sotelo and Miguel Ángel Muñoz Borrego, Ar-

Acknowledgments

chivo General de Coahuila, Ramos Arizpe, Coahuila, México
Michael Hironymous, Nettie Lee Benson Latin American Collection, Rare Books and Manuscripts
Staff members of the Rosenberg Library in Galveston and San Antonio Mormon Family Research Center

Finally, thanks to the staff of the Texas State Historical Association, especially Associate Editor Ryan Schumacher, for their efforts and support that transformed my dog-eared, marked-up manuscript into a book.

My heartfelt thanks to all who contributed in so many different ways. Any errors that may emerge, however, are mine alone.

Foreword

WHEN SCHOLARS REVIEW the current works on Mexican Americans in Texas, they come across excellent volumes on Tejano personalities such as Juan N. Seguín and biographies of Juan N. Cortina, Petra Vela Kenedy, Catarino E. Garza, J. T. Canales, Carlos E. Castañeda, Héctor P. García, Félix Tijerina, Manuel B. Bravo, and a few others. Yet they would be hard pressed to find a full-length work on José Antonio Navarro, arguably the earliest Mexican American to have made a lasting contribution to Texas history after 1836. Why have scholars lagged in giving deserved attention to this public figure?

It would be impossible to divine the answer accurately, but an explanation might be that Navarro's life confounds historians in at least two ways. For one, his political career crossed three sovereignties complicated by wars and revolutions that brought about five changes in government. As a result, one might wonder to which era of Texas history he belongs and which group of historians should write about him. Historians tend to carve out areas of specialization and that is true as well in Mexican American history. If Mexican American history is assumed to begin in 1836 when Mexicans in Texas came under the jurisdiction of the Republic of Texas, then more than half of Navarro's life falls in the domain of the borderlands historians, the group where scholars of Texas under Spain and Mexico are usually classed. The rest of his life fits into the era of those who specialize in Mexican American history.

A second question logically follows: was Navarro authentically "Tejano" or was he Mexican American like the other subjects of biographies mentioned above? Why would such an issue matter? The inclination in Mexican American historiography thus far has been to focus on those personalities who endeavored to improve the condition of their community in the face of Anglo oppression or injustice (as rebels, labor leaders, resolute reformers, and the like). Traditional studies cast Navarro as something other than that. They considered him as an enigma in Tejano history: one of only a few Hispanics to have played a prominent role in the nineteenth century, and one who appeared hesitant to confront white authority on those occasions for the good of his Hispanic compatriots. His career hardly stirs the imagination like those of Juan Cortina, Héctor P. García, or others whose fidelity to their community was unquestionable.

This long-awaited book on José Antonio Navarro settles the conundrum over Navarro's place in both historical eras as well as the question of his ethnic sentiments. It does so by using all available primary materials on the subject and by critically reassessing older sources that unwittingly produced confusion over Navarro's niche in Texas history. This thorough exploration and methodological approach corrects much misinformation about Navarro and offers a more realistic depiction of his life.

As to the first question regarding historical timing, Navarro's lifetime spanned three nations. Born in 1795, he lived during what historians identify as the Spanish colonial period, which lasted until 1821. Between 1821 and 1836, as a citizen of Mexico, Navarro was an important participant in the politics of Coahuila and Texas. After Texas independence and extending into statehood, he continued his political activity under the Republic of Texas, serving one term (1838–39) in the Republic's congress. He maintained a presence in state politics after 1845, serving twice in the legislature. He chose voluntary retirement in the 1850s, but his heart remained focused on his state's well-being throughout the decade and he continued to be influential in public affairs until the time of his death in 1871.

David McDonald's study demonstrates that compartmentalizing Navarro into any one historical period is foolish. Portraying him as belonging to only the colonial Spanish-Mexican period makes no sense, nor does consigning him to the post-1836 era. Historians' existing understanding of such a division is therefore flawed; Navarro's place in Texas history does not belong in this or that age, but as McDonald clearly shows, in the larger narrative.

Regarding the question of ethnic character, Navarro on numerous occasions made political decisions seemingly favorable to Anglo Americans and detrimental to his fellow Tejanos. Historians have puzzled over this behavior. Early interpreters of Texas history viewed Navarro as a hero and patriot who sided with Anglo American liberty beginning in the 1820s, risking life and fortune to achieve political stability for an Anglo Texas. They argued that he placed commitment to the new democracy above allegiance to ethnicity. During the 1970s, on the other hand, some Chicano historians (reflecting the chauvinism of those years) relegated Navarro to traitor status, portraying him as an opportunistic collaborator indifferent to his people's colonized situation. The true heroes for those historians were Juan Cortina, Gregorio Cortez, and others who, by resisting Anglo power, rallied Tejano communities against the oppressive state. Not until the mid-1990s did Navarro's career see some rehabilitation, with the publication of David R. McDonald and Timothy M. Matovina (eds.), *Defending Mexican Valor in Texas: José Antonio Navarro's Historical Writings, 1853–1857* (Austin: State House Press, 1995).

Here, in *José Antonio Navarro: In Search of the American Dream in Nineteenth-Century Texas*, McDonald continues the rehabilitation by demonstrating that stereotyping Navarro politically or ethnically is as frivolous as shelving him in this or that era. The evidence presented here suggests that contrary to the views posited by the two older historical schools, Navarro was consistent in the political stances he advanced for ordinary Texans (both Texas Mexicans and Anglos), and a Tejano comfortable with his "Mexicanness." Several times during his career Navarro took political positions that on first blush appear to implicate him as one in league with Anglo designs to weaken Mexico and incapacitate its people. The two most salient ones include signing the Texas Declaration of Independence in 1836 and accompanying the Santa Fe Expedition in 1841. In 1835–36, Navarro found himself in some difficulty, having to choose between Anglo colonists who advocated federalism and Santa Anna the dictator, but he stood fast against conservative centralism. He was no willing accessory in the ill-fated Santa Fe Expedition either, having rejected initial overtures from President Mirabeau B. Lamar to join. He decided to assist in an effort to prove Tejano loyalty at a moment when Tejano fidelity to the republic was under suspicion. Moreover, Navarro thought his participation would help spare the lives of New Mexicans should they resist the operation upon its arrival in Santa Fe. He suffered dreadfully for his imprudent judgment.

The source material undergirding David McDonald's biography permits him to make the case that Navarro never considered himself anything but an ethnic Mexican. Certainly, he did not undergo any cultural metamorphosis after 1836 to see himself otherwise. Except perhaps for his insensitivity to New Mexicans in 1841, he consistently sympathized politically with (and spoke for) matters concerning Mexicans in Texas and elsewhere. In 1837, he appealed to President Sam Houston to intercede on behalf of the Mexican people of San Antonio who found themselves at the mercy of the Republic of Texas army whose soldiers confiscated their property, stole their draft animals, hurled demeaning epithets at them, and wrongly jailed Bexareños (a term used to describe the inhabitants of San Antonio deriving from "Bexár," the colloquial term for the San Antonio area used extensively during the periods of Spanish and Mexican rule). At the constitutional convention of 1845, Navarro spoke effectively (through a translator) and acted forcefully to defend Tejano lands (whose titles Anglos now contested, accusing their holders of disloyalty in 1836), warded off an attempt to deprive Tejanos of their voting rights, and took umbrage at an insinuation that Mexicans lacked the mental acuity of Anglos. As a state legislator in 1846–48, Navarro spoke for those vulnerable to legal machinations; he made sure that the government protected lands held by Texans born in foreign nations and he labored to guarantee property rights for married women. During the 1850s, he assailed the Know-Nothing Party for its anti-Mexican and anti-Catholic platform. When Texans entertained secession in 1860, Navarro defended the Union, although his sons (as did those of many other Texas Unionists) fought in the Confederate ranks. No other Tejano, across more than three decades, assumed such passionate positions in the relatively conservative climate of nineteenth-century Texas.

Much obtains from McDonald's exceptional research on this historical figure heretofore portrayed as a "gringoized" Mexican who gave preference to Anglo American interests at the expense of his own community. Certainly, Navarro was no Americanized Tejano who rejected his nationality; to the contrary, he affirmed his culture and heritage proudly and consistently. Nor did he countenance an ideology that advanced white supremacy (not even toward persons of African descent) nor, for that matter, a colonial structure conducive to his own personal aggrandizement. In reality, he advocated principles that challenged not only minority persecution, but also policies that unfairly discriminated against all Texans. Further, he took Anglo American authors to task when he thought they discounted the Hispanic contribution to the Texas experience. Based on the evidence it is difficult to contradict David McDonald's contention that Navarro could well be held up as a forerunner to reformers, who championed Mexican American issues in the early decades of the twentieth century.

ARNOLDO DE LEÓN
Angelo State University, 2009

JOSÉ ANTONIO NAVARRO

Introduction

*Perhaps the day will come when some impartial person will write
my history in relation to Texas, and much more, [to show] that
it is my desire that peace will follow and the fraternal links will
again be extended.*—*José Antonio Navarro*[1]

DURING THE 1950s, houses along Laredo Street built in the nineteenth century were rapidly disappearing. The surrounding community, known as Laredito (Little Laredo), had long been a center of
Mexican American culture, with deep roots in Spanish colonial times,
but now it was being pushed aside for modern construction. Among
those threatened were three limestone and adobe buildings that had
sat at the corner of Nueva and Laredo streets for a century. Few knew
that this site was the former home of José Antonio Navarro, once one
of San Antonio's most prominent citizens, but who was now virtually
unknown. Among those who realized the historical value of the Navarro
site were members of the San Antonio Conservation Society.

First, the society saved the site by successfully arranging for it to be
incorporated into an urban renewal project in 1959.[2] The society purchased the site in 1960 and restored it. Further signifying its historical
importance, the Navarro site was placed on the National Register of
Historic Places in 1972. The San Antonio Conservation Society oper-
ated the Navarro site until 1975, then donated it to the Texas Parks and
Wildlife Department to be operated as the José Antonio State Historical
Park.[3] (In the 2000s, the State legislature transferred operation of the
Navarro site, now known as the Casa Navarro State Historic Site, to the
Texas Historical Commission.)

My interest in José Antonio Navarro (1795–1871) began in 1978, when
I became the park superintendent for the Navarro site. I arrived with a
background in Spanish literature, experience in searching Spanish archives, and in preparing English translations of sixteenth-century documents. This background would prove advantageous in compiling information for the present biography, especially considering that Navarro

wrote only in Spanish. An immediate review of the available sources about Navarro immediately showed a limited amount of published information, and much of that turned out to be infested with errors. I had the luxury of time without deadlines to search for primary and secondary sources and to transcribe and translate materials that would provide a solid basis for understanding Navarro's life and times.

In the beginning, I compiled documentation to use for presentations to park visitors. The interpretive programs presented at the Casa Navarro State Historic Site seemed insufficient to promote the recognition of a man of his stature. The materials I collected laid the groundwork for writing an authoritative, comprehensive biography that could reconcile errors, resolve misunderstandings, and utilize newly assembled primary sources. The numerous demands of managing the site, however, prevented the sustained effort needed for writing a biography. Despite these demands, I continued to search for and find more documents, secondary sources, photographs, and other materials. When I retired from the Casa Navarro in 2002, I made copies of the collected documentation and began to write. This biography, therefore, is the culmination of thirty-one years of research on Navarro, one of the most prominent and influential political figures in nineteenth-century Texas.

The seventy-six years of José Antonio Navarro's life spanned the turbulent period that determined the destiny of Texas. For fifty years, he devoted his political energies to the cause of democratic institutions in Texas, and even a short list of his political accomplishments is impressive. He served in Texas legislatures under Mexico, the Republic of Texas, and the state of Texas, and he participated in the constitutional conventions of 1836 and 1845. He held many local offices, and was arrested as a commissioner for the ill-fated Santa Fe Expedition in 1841. And he did all of this while amassing a substantial personal fortune as a merchant and landowner, including fulfilling appointments as land commissioner for two major *empresario* efforts in Mexican Texas.

A consideration of Navarro's life offers a valuable opportunity to analyze the transition of Texas from a Spanish colony, to a Mexican possession, and then to an Anglo-dominated republic and state through the experiences of a true Tejano. A search in libraries for biographies of individuals prominent in nineteenth-century Texas will produce a long list of works on Anglos such as Sam Houston, Moses and Stephen F. Austin, William B. Travis, David Crockett, James Bowie, Edward Burleson, and many others. For Tejanos, however, the shelves are virtually empty. This work is the first Tejano biography of the many that are needed to fill that space.

The story of the Navarros in Texas begins in 1762 when Ángel

Casa Navarro State Historic Site, San Antonio, Texas. Built by José Antonio Navarro around 1850, it served as his town house. Photo by David McDonald.

Navarro, José Antonio's father, ran away from home his home in Corsica at age thirteen or fourteen to work as a servant in various Mediterranean ports. Eventually crossing the Atlantic, he settled in Béxar about 1777, where he married María Gertrudis Josefa Ruiz y Peña. José Antonio was the third of their six children to survive to adulthood, and the story follows his life through the years of war and revolution that eventually brought Texas into the United States.

Navarro's personal and public life was devoted primarily to Béxar, the region surrounding San Antonio in central Texas. Although the area included the presidio of San Antonio de Béxar and the villa of San Fernando de Béxar, it was almost always called Béxar until 1837, when city officials formally named the town San Antonio, and that chronology is generally followed in this study.[4] Because Béxar served as the political and commercial heart of early Texas, a study of Navarro provides a unique perspective on the social, economic, and political networks within which he lived. The key to understanding connections between these worlds is the close-knit family coalition formed by the intermarriage of the Navarro, Ruiz, and Veramendi families. José Francisco Ruiz and Juan Martín de Veramendi, Navarro's uncle and brother-in-law respectively, were important influences on José Antonio Navarro, and his relationship with both of these men is examined. The result is a study that stands apart from other related but substantially different biographical works, such as Ana Carolina Castillo Crimm's excellent study of the De León family of Victoria. That work is a family biography of three generations of Tejanos; however, as important as the De León family was, its focus was largely confined to the Victoria area.[5] The De Leóns lacked the influence of Navarro, whose political reach was felt across Texas and Coahuila, and to some extent in New Mexico. The present work is the first of what should become a gallery of biographies of many similarly prominent nineteenth century Tejanos, including Ruiz, Veramendi, Juan N. and Erasmo Seguín, José Ángel Navarro III, and others.

Biographies of two nineteenth-century figures born in Texas—Ignacio de Zaragoza and José María de Jesús Carvajal—have been published, but their lives and careers were focused elsewhere.[6] Zaragoza, who was the Mexican general whose victory in the Battle of Puebla is commemorated every Cinco de Mayo, was born in Goliad, but his family left Texas when he was seven years old. Carvajal, while born in San Antonio, was most known for his efforts at and below the Rio Grande where he attempted to foment revolution in northern Mexico during a series of border conflicts.

While José Antonio Navarro was an influential figure in Texas, his life has not been understood and appreciated because the means to do so have been scattered and buried deep in archives and libraries. Though Navarro was revered and respected by his Tejano contemporaries and many Anglos, the passage of time diminished awareness of his contributions. Historian Robert Weddle once warned me that "error perpetuates itself," reminding me that part of our job is to identify and correct mistakes that have become generally accepted. Many such errors about Navarro have been published and have taken on a life of their own after being combined and recombined, published and republished.

Brief biographical works on Navarro were published during his lifetime, and they are valuable because they are the based on information provided by José Antonio himself and the recollections of close friends. In 1858, Jacob De Cordova published a book about Texas that included sketches of the lives of several prominent persons, including Navarro.[7] In 1869, Narciso Leal and other friends published historical writings of Navarro from the 1850s, which included a short but authoritative biographical essay. Evidently, Leal had written or was writing a longer account, but said that Navarro's "excessive modesty" would not permit a more detailed biography. After Navarro died in 1871, this consideration was no longer an obstacle and both friends and family wanted a more complete biography written. A biographical booklet about Navarro soon appeared that contained much personal information that could only have come from Navarro himself and persons who knew him well. It was published anonymously in 1876 under the pen name, "An Old

Texan."[8] Comparison with Leal's 1869 sketch indicates that the "Old Texan" was in fact Narciso Leal, who was no doubt assisted by other Navarro friends and Navarro's family members such as José Antonio's son Ángel. Navarro's memory would endure an extended period of neglect after the publication of the 1876 biography.

Naomi Fritz's "José Antonio Navarro," a master's thesis completed at St. Mary's University at San Antonio in 1941, was the first academic study of Navarro's life. Fritz's work established a benchmark that set a course for the historical investigation on Navarro that was to follow and provided materials for authors of secondary sources. The thesis, however, is flawed in several respects. Gaping omissions are evident; she makes no mention of Navarro's role as a land commissioner and only gave scant reference to his historic participation in the 1845 Constitutional Convention. Fritz did not have access to the extensive Navarro correspondence in the papers of Samuel May Williams or other important sources. Some of the newspaper articles she used were erroneous and others she misunderstood. A serious misunderstanding was her conclusion that Navarro encouraged Texas to secede from the United States. This error has been cited repeatedly by subsequent writers, attributing to Navarro a political viewpoint that is false. Fritz made a commendable effort despite the flaws of her thesis, however, and later researchers would sift through her work and build upon it.[9]

Also flawed is a book on Navarro by Joseph M. Dawson, entitled *José Antonio Navarro: Co-Creator of Texas*, which appeared in 1969. Ostensibly a biography, this book's defects in writing, organization, and sources are severe; it is plagued with factual errors and the title itself cannot be justified. Dawson's assertion that Texas was the creation of two individuals is confusing because he never makes clear who the other "co-creator" was, though presumably it was Stephen F. Austin. His title seems to derive from Eugene C. Barker's *Stephen F. Austin, Founder of Texas, 1793–1836: A Chapter in the Westward Movement of the Anglo-American People*. Dawson pursues the Anglocentric implication that the creation of Texas was a result of the founding of Austin's Colony, a shortsighted viewpoint that ignores a century of Texas's Spanish and Mexican history. Many rambling, fictionalized scenarios about what might have happened also mar the Dawson narrative, and historians generally reject it as an unreliable source for Navarro's life. Its value as a biography is further limited because it uses very little of the rich source material that was available in numerous archives or the extensive Texas historiography. Despite such problems, it was the first published writing about Navarro in the twentieth century and, to Dawson's credit, it did foster recognition of Navarro as an important historical figure.[10]

The next major scholarly appraisal appeared in 1976, when James E. Crisp completed his doctoral dissertation on Anglo-Tejano relations during the periods when Texas was under Mexican rule and an independent republic.[11] Crisp's dissertation, which was completed in 1976, was an in-depth study based on an exhaustive collection of sources, and the last two chapters of it are mostly devoted to José Antonio Navarro. One draws a comparison between the lives of Navarro and Juan Seguín; the other describes his crucial participation in the 1845 Constitution that brought Texas into the United States. Crisp returned to his research on Navarro in the recent article, "José Antonio Navarro: the Problem of Tejano Powerlessness."[12] It is a fine essay based on extensive sources that in a few pages presents the highlights Navarro's career as a as a legislator and advocate for Tejano rights. Written independently of the present biography, it presents several conclusions that are parallel to it, most notably that Navarro steadfastly opposed race-based voting credentials. Unfortunately, the article also perpetuates several misconceptions about Navarro, such as that he was the first San Antonio *alcalde* (mayor) elected after 1821, that his mother secured a pardon for him, and that he supported the Confederacy. Although José Antonio did serve as acting alcalde in 1822 as *regidor* (ranking councilman), he was never elected alcalde of the city, and as will be shown later in this biography, Crisp was also in error concerning the pardon and the conclusion that Navarro supported the Confederacy.

The next significant scholarly work to appear on Navarro was a master's thesis written by Anastacio Bueno at the University of Texas at San Antonio, "In Storms of Fortune: José Antonio Navarro of Texas, 1821–1846." Based on a broader historiography than Fritz's work, it is the first well-researched biographical work about Navarro. Bueno's sources are extensive and include many primary documents such as the Samuel May Williams Papers and material from the Bexar Archives. As suggested by the dates in the title, the scope of Bueno's thesis is limited, and the need for a comprehensive and deeply researched biography of Navarro has remained.[13]

Two important works on Navarro have appeared in recent decades, although they too have not given a comprehensive overview of his entire life. The publication of a new translation of Navarro's historical writings, by Timothy Matovina and the present author.[14] *Defending Mexican Valor in Texas* not only brought Navarro's writing into the historiographic mainstream, but also made available the biographical sketch of his life written by friends who knew him well. Ten years later, Andrés Reséndez published a marvelous collection of documents concerning the results of Navarro's participation in the disastrous Santa Fe Expedition. Presented in Spanish and English translation, the documents in *A Texas Patriot on Trial in Mexico: José Antonio Navarro and the Texan Santa Fe Expedition* tell the story of the remarkable events of José Antonio Navarro's prosecution and near execution in Mexico City.[15] With the publication of Reséndez's work, my goal of finding, compiling, and organizing, the essential materials pertaining to the story José Antonio Navarro's life was in large part achieved. As a result, the totality of this body of scholarly work done from 1941 through 2005, in addition to the author's research, established a broad foundation upon which the present biography of Jose Antonio Navarro is built.

Despite these scholarly efforts, awareness of Navarro as a historical figure receded below the horizon of Texas history in the twentieth century. He became an enigmatic figure in the popular imagination who, by the mere mention of his name, triggered praise or condemnation, often based upon little or no understanding of the facts and circumstances of his life. A history of the Texas Senate during the Republic and early statehood eras contains a clear expression of the perceived incongruence of Navarro's life to modern readers: "It remains a mystery why this son of a Corsican father connected by marriage to the most distinguished Mexican families of Texas should have taken as a personal cause the interests of the Anglo-American Texans."[16] The author notes that Navarro's commitment to Texas had begun by 1821 with the initiation of his lifelong friendship with Stephen F. Austin, and adds that the puzzle emerges because Navarro "had nothing to gain for himself and everything to lose" by supporting Anglos. Other writers have concluded just the opposite, supposing that Navarro led his people down the wrong path as a result of self-interest.[17]

Distressing conclusions necessarily follow from the last hypothesis: perhaps Navarro was at best a foolish man who let friendship prevent him from standing up for his best interests and those of his fellow Tejanos; or, at worst, he was a turncoat and a traitor to Tejanos. The latter accusations have dogged Navarro to the present day and marred his reputation. Most of the praise for him as a Texas patriot comes from Anglos, who focus principally on his role as a signer of the Texas Declaration of Independence. Ironically, Navarro's legacy has been tarnished for the very same act because many Mexican Americans believed that he signed the declaration against the interests of his own people. Both views lack depth and perspective, and present mere caricatures of the man. Navarro's commitment to Anglo interests was not his alone, but was shared by other Tejano leaders who believed that Austin's Colony and others like it would help Texas develop to the benefit of all. Thus, the question should be rephrased: why did prominent Tejanos (and many in Coahuila) support Anglo colonization, and later independence? In reality, more than ninety of Navarro's fellow Tejanos elected him as a delegate to represent them at the drafting of the Texas Declaration of Independence once they understood that hostilities with Mexico had progressed to the point where a break was inevitable.[18] These Tejanos knew that Navarro would vote for independence and represent them in the formation of a new government. Thus, a broader community of Tejanos for Béxar sent Navarro to the 1836 Texas Constitutional Convention to act in what they felt was their best interest.

In this biography, I have made a conscious effort to correct such misunderstandings about José Antonio Navarro. I have sought to discover and evaluate the available sources in order to present a truthful biography of Navarro that emphasizes manuscript documents: his letters, letters to him, about him, his historical writing, land records, and other primary sources. Navarro knew little English; all his writings are in Spanish and care has been taken to utilize these sources to maximize accuracy in determining the reasons behind his attitudes, decisions, and actions. Where necessary this writer has unraveled, reinterpreted, and presented the realities revealed by authoritative sources through critical evaluation. Several substantial errors pertaining to Navarro were identified and corrected, including the origins of his forefathers, his marital status, and his views on secession, among others.

Navarro's activities as a legislator are of particular interest and importance and will be discussed in detail. He was elected to the first legislature of the Mexican state of Coahuila y Texas (hereafter referred to as Coahuila and Texas), to the House of Representatives of the Republic of Texas, and to the senate of the state of Texas. In addition, he took part in the constitutional conventions of 1836 and 1845, where he, in the view of some historians, "almost single handedly prevented the possible constitutional disenfranchisement of Mexican Americans."[19] He also developed a deep friendship with Stephen F. Austin, with whom he shared economic and political goals for the development of Texas. Austin urged the Navarro family to apply for land grants and encouraged Navarro's work as a land commissioner. As a result, Navarro's correspondence provides an insider's view of the land grant process through his efforts as a commissioner for the Green DeWitt Colony, his own land acquisitions obtained by grants under Mexican and Texas law, and his purchases.

Among his many accomplishments, Navarro can justly be recognized as the first Tejano historian. (In this book, the term "Tejano" refers to Texans of Spanish and Mexican descent beginning in Spanish colonial times and continuing to the present day, while "Anglo" or "Anglo

American" refers to persons who came from the United States and their descendants.) He wrote two historical essays about the Tejano revolutionary struggle to win independence from Spain from 1811 to 1813 that were translated into English and appeared in San Antonio newspers in 1853 and 1858, These were published in 1869 in a Spanish edition entitled *Apuntes Históricos Interesantes de San Antonio de Béxar* (*Interesting Historical Notes about San Antonio de Béxar*).[20] Navarro's history opposed the accounts, common in the English-language press, that scorned the history and character of Texans of Mexican descent. *Apuntes Históricos Interesantes de San Antonio de Béxar* is also a valuable source that describes the Tejanos' struggles for Mexican independence long before Anglo Americans came to Texas. Navarro's writings display flashes of passion, empathy, and compassion for his people that are lacking in the other histories of Texas from that period, and Navarro's account is the only one that tells the story of that violent period from a Tejano point of view.

An unavoidable fact of José Antonio Navarro's life was that he was as slave owner; therefore, this biography addresses the issue of Tejano attitudes toward race relations and slavery. There is of course only one race—the human race. Nevertheless, the term will be used to distinguish among persons of European, Indian, and African origin. While a thorough examination of race and slavery in Texas with respect to Tejanos is beyond the scope of this study, a preliminary determination from the documentation compiled here supports the thesis that Navarro and other Tejanos as a matter of course absorbed and assimilated values about race and slavery that differed from those of Anglos. These values were shaped by a Spanish-Catholic tradition that recognized the basic humanity of all persons in the community. They were further influenced by the realities of living in a thinly populated frontier region where all kinds of people mixed freely and there was little employment of chattel slavery. Navarro, although he did own slaves, also demonstrated a much more flexible attitude about race than did his Anglo colleagues in the various political forums in which he served. This was especially true in relation to persons of various combinations of European, Indian, and African origin. Perhaps reflecting the Tejano flexibility in thinking on race, one of his slaves, Henry Navarro, became a successful landowner and farmer with the assistance of the Navarro family (see Appendix Two).

Alongside his attitudes concerning race, several of José Antonio Navarro's personal qualities stand out and are especially important for an accurate understanding of his life. He valued education and highly educated himself despite having few resources. Through informal study he attained a superior understanding of law that served him well in legislatures and conventions, and in later years he sent his talented son José Ángel Navarro III (usually referred to simply as Ángel) to study law at Harvard College. While José Antonio is said to have worked as a lawyer, with an office at the present Casa Navarro Historical Site, no confirmation was found for this claim. It is true that he did perform some limited legal representation during the Mexican period, but none was found thereafter, and no record of his employment as an attorney was found in the Bexar County District Court records.

Navarro also valued determination, and it was this determination that allowed him to overcome a disability that might have demoralized others on the frontier where physical vigor was highly esteemed. Most other Tejano leaders had military service or served in the local militia; for example, José Francisco Ruiz had extensive experience as a military man, as did two of Navarro's brothers. Navarro had to make his contributions solely as a civilian because when he was about thirteen his left leg was badly injured in an accident and never healed properly. He was left with a permanent limp and the leg was periodically inflamed for the rest of his life.

It can be said that Navarro achieved a kind of "American Dream" with his accomplishments. James Truslow Adams is credited with coining the term "American Dream" in his 1931 popular history *The Epic of America*. He defined it as a dream of a land in which life would be "better and richer and fuller for every man, with opportunity for each according to his ability or achievement." He added that it was not a dream of acquiring material things, but rather one of a social order in which each man and woman could attain the most of which they are innately capable and could be respected and valued by others regardless of birthright.[21] While Adams may have coined the term, the idea of a world of opportunity began with the opening of America—North, South, and Central—to European settlement. José Antonio Navarro's father, Ángel Navarro, left Corsica to seek opportunities in colonial Mexico that were unavailable to him in European countries. Thus José Antonio's pursuit of what came to be called the American Dream had its origin with his father's journey from Corsica, and the phrase "American Dream" is used throughout this study with that larger scope in mind.

The elder Navarro found success in San Fernando de Béxar and set an example of achievement for his children. More than any of his siblings, José Antonio achieved his own success through self-education, hard work as a merchant and rancher, and an influential political career. He set an example for his own children, among whom Ángel stands out as achieving his own American Dream through formal education. He

José Antonio Navarro. Photo courtesy of Mr. Salim Dominguez Jr.

graduated from Harvard College with a law degree in 1849 and became a successful lawyer and Texas legislator. Three generations of Navarros thus demonstrated the search for and attainment of the American Dream—finding and utilizing opportunities to realize their potential for financial gain, educational advancement, political influence, and the respect of their peers.

An objection may be raised that José Antonio Navarro achieved the American Dream, but thousands of his fellow Tejanos did not. Certainly this is true. Nevertheless, it does not detract from his accomplishments, or from the fact that Navarro led the way toward eventual economic, political, and social integration of Mexican Americans in Texas and their opportunity to work for the same dream. Navarro opposed discrimination against his own people during the 1845 Texas Constitutional Convention, publicly denounced the nativist Know-Nothing Party, and defended Mexican honor in his historical publications. It would be fair to say that in his resistance to discrimination, Navarro was a precursor of the spirit embodied in the progressive reformers who led the struggle for Texas-Mexican equality in the initial decades of the twentieth century. Following Navarro's example, one can look to Henry B. Gonzales, who became a powerful United States congressman, and to Henry Cisneros, another Harvard graduate, who was the first Mexican American mayor of San Antonio since Juan Seguín. These and many others are the heirs of Navarro's legacy as a defender of Mexican American rights, and the rights of all Texans.

CHAPTER ONE

Roots, 1762–1816

JOSÉ ANTONIO NAVARRO'S FATHER, Ángel Navarro, was one of the thousands who have left their native lands over the centuries to search for success in the New World of the Americas. He worked hard to better himself, and his quest for the American Dream was picked up and carried on with particular zeal by José Antonio, his second son. On a spring day in 1792, Ángel Navarro sat at his table and recalled the events of the previous thirty years that had brought him from his Corsican birthplace to a respectable life as a merchant and family man in the frontier community of San Fernando de Béxar (later renamed San Antonio). This recollection came because he was required by Governor Manuel Muñoz to prepare a statement to comply with a royal directive to identify foreigners in the province of Texas as part of a census. Muñoz knew very well that Navarro, despite his Corsican birth, was a respected, loyal citizen. But this bureaucratic requirement nevertheless provides an authoritative summary of Ángel Navarro's life and is the best place to begin a study of José Antonio Navarro.

In his autobiographical sketch, Ángel Navarro said that he was born on the island of Corsica "in the *province*" of Ajaccio, rather than in the capital city of Ajaccio, which might suggest a rustic origin. What his family circumstances were can only be guessed at, but at the time of his birth, a fierce war was raging as Corsicans fought for independence from Genoa, which had dominated the island for more than 500 years. This conflict continued through the years of his youth, ending only in 1770 with the incorporation of Corsica into France. In 1762, when Ángel was about thirteen or fourteen, he took a ship for Genoa "without the permission of my parents." From Genoa he made his way to Barcelona and then Cádiz, "always seeking to serve various persons to earn my keep" as he worked in various ports along the Mediterranean Sea.[1]

Most of the Spanish trade with America passed through the busy port of Cádiz, and it was there that Ángel reached a turning point in his life. He was a youth with much experience working for various individuals

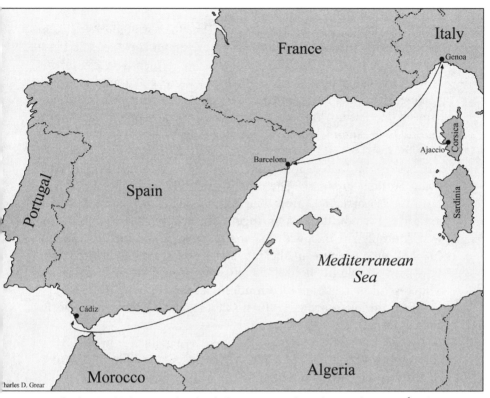

After leaving his home on the island of Corsica in 1762 at the age of 13 or 14, Ángel Navarro worked in the busy seaports of Genoa and Barcelona before arriving at Cádiz, Spain. He traveled from Cádiz to Mexico at around 1768.

(most likely merchants) in major ports and had assuredly learned some valuable lessons about human nature and about trade. While his station in life was still that of a humble servant, he was no longer an ignorant provincial. At this juncture, Ángel must have understood that he had reached the limits of what he could achieve in a place where traditions defined a person's worth and opportunities came more often by birth than by ability. Because there was little future in Spain for a youth not born in the mother country or even in a Spanish territory, he must have seen the tall ships anchored at Cádiz as a solution to his problem. He likely met traders, sailors, and servants who had actually been to Spanish America, and who offered credible accounts of opportunities in the New World for a talented and resourceful young man. He arranged for passage on a ship bound for New Spain—colonial Mexico—where he would seek the American Dream. Indenture is suggested by his saying, "I arrived obligated to seek work with Don Juan Antonio Agustín in the mining district of Vallecillo." After working for eight years in these silver mines between Laredo and Monterrey (evidently to pay for his passage), Ángel made his way to Béxar as a merchant around 1777.[2]

Freed from his obligation to Agustín, Ángel struggled to support himself. He was not the only Navarro to leave Corsica for Texas. A mysterious Juan Antonio Navarro preceded Ángel's arrival in Béxar by at least four years. The 1779 census enumerated Ángel, who owned only a horse, next to Juan Antonio and Juliana Navarro, so he was probably living on their premises. The census confirms the birthplace of both Navarros as Corsica and gives their occupations as merchants; Juan Antonio's age was thirty-two and Ángel's twenty-seven. The two Navarros were probably kinsmen with a shared purpose in coming to Béxar, but Juan Antonio's tenure in the provincial capital was short-lived. The next year, he sold his house and left Béxar. Ángel stayed and became a successful merchant and community leader. He bought the lot and dwelling previously owned by Juan Antonio, and was elected to the city council in 1781.[3]

By the time of his election, Ángel's integration into the Béxar community was almost complete. All he lacked was a family. For marriage prospects, he did not have to look any farther than the other side of Real Street (present day Flores Street), to the home of Juan Manuel Ruiz and his wife, Manuela de la Peña. Among their five children was María Gertrudis Josefa Ruiz y Peña, who at the end of 1781 was sixteen years old. The San Fernando Church marriage records are incomplete and do not show the union of Ángel Navarro and Josefa Ruiz. By the time that Ángel wrote his autobiographical sketch for Governor Muñoz in 1792, he was a well-established merchant, had served on the city council twice, was the father of a nine-year-old son and an infant daughter, and had buried four other children in small graves at San Fernando Church.[4]

In his autobiographical sketch, Ángel's sparse and straightforward style is consistent with a favorite expression attributed to him: "Bread is bread and wine, wine," which was taken to mean that he was impatient with wordy, exaggerated talk. Sparse records make it difficult to document many aspects of Ángel's life. Despite his success as a merchant, scant evidence exists of his acquiring and selling the kinds of goods that were traded on the Texas frontier. He must have bought and sold merchandise such as cloth and crockery, for he operated a store out of his house and clearly had business contacts in Saltillo and Nacogdoches.

Nevertheless, records reveal only one instance of him purchasing ordinary merchandise: one-half pound of thread at an auction of contraband goods. While most of the goods he dealt in remain unknown, the record does reveal that he participated in slave trading. Each census from 1790 to 1803 lists slaves in his possession whose identities vary.[5] Ángel's increasing prosperity was evident in March 1794, when he loaned San José Mission 600 pesos in cash and 145 pesos worth of merchandise.[6] Ángel's status as a merchant was matched by his accomplishments in municipal government. From 1781 to 1807, Bexareños elected him as their *alcalde* or assistant alcalde four times and numerous terms as an alderman.[7] Thus it is clear he had built a solid foundation for his family, which soon included a new member.

At the end of each February in San Antonio, new leaves begin appearing on trees and shrubs. Occasionally, cold fronts pass through dropping temperatures to near freezing, but for the most part the new leaves are a sure sign that the San Antonio winter is ending. During the last days of February 1795, Ángel Navarro and his wife Josefa prepared for the birth of their eighth child. José Antonio Navarro was born on Friday, February 27. His birth must have filled his parents with both joy and apprehension, for disease had already claimed five of their seven children. The newest Navarro joined a three-year-old sister, María Josefa, and an eleven-year-old brother, José de los Ángeles, or José Ángel. On March 6, one week after José Antonio's birth, at least twenty persons, including Navarro and Ruiz family members and friends, gathered at San Fernando Church for the baptism of their newest family member. Ángel and Josefa selected as godparents Juan José Farías, a corporal in the Béxar presidio, and the infant's maternal grandmother, Manuela de la Peña.[8]

José Antonio Navarro was likely born in his father's house or perhaps in the Ruiz grandparents' house across Real Street. As children, he and his siblings were equally at home at their grandparents' house as they were at their own home.[9] Between chores and studies, they would have played such games as *flechas* with toy bows and arrows. Another pastime was *cabestros* (halters), possibly a rowdy game that mimicked the real job of breaking wild horses.[10] Among the neighborhood children living along Real Street was Margarita de la Garza, who was destined to be José Antonio's wife and the mother of their children.

Educational resources were scarce during José Antonio's youth. Instruction at the missions was limited to Indian children, but he may have received some schooling from the parish priest. José Antonio was fortunate to have his mother's brother, José Francisco Ruiz, as a mentor.

Although the government opened a primary school in Béxar in 1803 with Ruiz as schoolmaster, the school only existed for a few months. The city council, responding to an order from the governor, appointed Ruiz as schoolmaster "provided that his minority does not render him incompetent to fill it. His residence . . . is to serve as the school house." Ruiz was nineteen years old at the time of his appointment and had no special educational training. He married the next year and evidently concluded that his income would be adequate to maintain a family. However, a few months later, when the commandant general in Chihuahua reduced the schoolmaster's fees, Ruiz resigned his position.[11] Before Ruiz resigned, eight-year-old José Antonio was most likely one of his best students, and he would continue to benefit from a close, long-term association with his learned uncle. It would not be an exaggeration to say that, after the death of his father, Ruiz was like a "second father" to the young Navarro, and served as his nephew's life-long confidant.

Following his initial education in Béxar, José Antonio was sent to school in Saltillo, which was a mercantile center and also provided educational services for northeastern New Spain. Saltillo, like Béxar, evidently did not have public schools during the Spanish colonial period. Miguel Ramos Arizpe reported that the people "were anxious to be educated, but lacked the resources to attain it."[12] José Antonio had the advantage of family support, since his grandmother, Manuela de la Peña, and other relatives were natives of the provincial capital, and he probably studied under private tutors. Referring to himself and his siblings in his "Autobiographical Notes" written in 1841, Navarro said they received an education that "in those days . . . may have [been] called superior." The quality of Navarro's education is demonstrated by his remarkable proficiency as a writer and orator in his native Spanish.[13]

José Antonio returned to Béxar in the summer of 1808, where his father "placed him in a house of business," probably the Navarro family store. Perhaps it was intended that the younger Navarro would continue his education in Saltillo, but two circumstances prevented that. An accident changed his life at age thirteen when his left leg was fractured "by a blow." The injured leg did not heal properly and he never regained full use of it. He was left with a permanent limp, and the leg was prone to periodic inflammation for the rest of his life. Physical ability was highly valued on the frontier, and Navarro's prowess was diminished at the critical time of his life when he was on the verge of becoming a man. He must have expressed his anguish to his father. In a recollection that could only have come from José Antonio, his father counseled him, saying:

No my son . . . your physical infirmity need have no effect on your mind; the man that possesses moral courage carries more weight, and is more capable of defending his own rights and those of his fellow-citizens than he who possesses merely physical courage. You need not be afraid of being a laughing-stock, if you do not deviate from the narrow path of honor and virtue, for they have a magic and subtle strength which always compels respect.[14]

The second setback came when Ángel Navarro, the Corsican patriarch, died on October 31, 1808, at about age fifty-eight. He was interred the next day in Campo Santo, the new cemetery west of San Pedro Creek—Ángel Navarro was the first to be buried in that sacred ground.[15]

Accepting that he would not be able to live a physically robust life like other boys, José Antonio devoted extra effort to his studies, a devotion that became a lifelong practice. While working, he began an informal study of law, probably under the guidance of his uncle and mentor, José Francisco Ruiz, who had been elected to the city council as *síndico procurador*—city attorney and prosecutor and voting member of the city council. This personal relationship with a council member offered an opportunity for José Antonio to study municipal government and its legal processes from an insider's point of view. He learned enough law to represent several clients during the next few years, but contrary to opinions expressed in later years, he was not a lawyer by profession.[16] Nevertheless, his modest legal study provided a foundation for his effective service in two Texas constitutional conventions and in legislatures for Mexico, the Republic of Texas, and the state of Texas.

Navarro's legal study completed the process that made him a well-educated man. His articulate expression, large vocabulary, and references to historical persons and events demonstrate that he read widely and was acquainted with works of law, history, and classical literature. For example, he was familiar with the great foundation of Spanish law, the *Siete Partidas* (Seven Sections). This compilation, originally prepared in the thirteenth century, remained in force in Mexico, at least in part, through the nineteenth century. In addition, Navarro showed familiarity with the *Recopilacion de Leyes de las Indias*, which formed the basis of government in Spanish America. In his "Autobiographical Notes," Navarro compared the cruelties of the French Revolution to those perpetrated by General Joaquín de Arredondo at Béxar after he defeated the insurgents at the Battle of Medina in 1813. Navarro's reading probably also included Enlightenment writers, as copies of their work are known to have been available to him. Navarro knew some medieval history as well, and compared the executions of Mexican revolutionary leaders to the Sicilian Vespers, a reference to an uprising that began at vespers on Easter Monday in 1282, when Sicilians slaughtered the French who occupied their island. Finally, Navarro was familiar with Greek literature, referring to himself as the "local Socrates" in a letter to Stephen F. Austin. He also mentioned the *Coryphaeus* (chorus leader in Greek theater) in discussing revolutionary leaders who did not recognize the danger to themselves after overthrowing the Spanish government of Béxar in 1811, and he described the Gutiérrez-Magee Expedition as the North American "Band of Leónidas."[17] Given the frontier conditions and his lack of formal instruction, Navarro's education was a great accomplishment and one that led to his other achievements.

José Antonio's formative years were passed during turbulent times for Texas—and the entire hemisphere. During the years between 1803 and 1821, three momentous events occurred that shaped the destinies of the United States and Mexico: the Louisiana Purchase in 1803, Napoleon's invasion of Spain in 1808, and the Mexican Revolution that began in 1810 and ended with Mexico's independence in 1821. Those were precisely the years when José Antonio Navarro grew from boy to man. Throughout these impressionable years his character and personality were shaped by a need to rebuild his family's diminished fortune while coping with not only his physical disability and the death of his father, but also scarcities, revolutionary violence, exile, and even imprisonment.

Despite these obstacles, Jose Antonio's bond with his family remained strong. The Ruiz-Navarro family union was further strengthened in 1810 by its joining with the Veramendi family through the marriage of José Antonio's older sister, María Josefa, to Juan Martín de Veramendi.[18] Dynastic and propitious family unions were important even on the frontier as a way of enhancing a family's status and economic well-being. Obviously, such unions could provide political access as well as assist in developing business and social relationships. The Navarro, Ruiz, and Veramendi families were united not only by kinship and marriage, but also by shared political ideals and economic ambitions for Texas.

Veramendi was the son of a prominent and successful Spanish merchant. His multiple achievements have been overlooked or even maligned by Mexican historians, eventually reducing him to being known only, if at all, as the father-in-law of James Bowie. Following family tradition, Juan Martín entered Béxar politics and became a successful merchant. At the time of his marriage, Juan Martín was a rising star in local politics and would work his way up from various municipal positions to the highest levels of state government. José Antonio Navarro was seventeen years younger than his "political brother," as he referred to Veramendi. If Ruiz was like a second father to Navarro, then Veramendi was apparently like another older brother—one who also became a trusted and experienced confidant. That the two men were close is evidenced by the fact that Veramendi later gave Navarro a power of attorney to represent him before authorities up to and including the Pope.[19]

While José Antonio Navarro grew closer to Ruiz and Veramendi, he drifted away from his older brother José Ángel. After the death of Ángel Navarro, his oldest son became head of the family. As time passed, José Antonio became displeased with his brother's performance in family affairs. For example, José Ángel lost the investment the family inherited upon the death of the Navarro patriarch at the annual fair in Saltillo in 1810. Years later, José Antonio's memories of José Angel's deficiencies were still vivid:

> Under the inexperient [*sic*] tutelage of my oldest brother José Angel
> we could make but the little progress in promoting our interest and
> much less could we apply ou[rselves] to a more perfect education than
> we could if o[ur] f[ather had] lived.[20]

This statement may help explain why Navarro was unable to continue his formal schooling: he had to work to support the family due to José Ángel's mismanagement of its affair. And given José Antonio's even-tempered nature, it was a strong condemnation of his brother. Other factors probably contributed to Navarro's resentful attitude toward his older brother, including differences of personalities and politics. José Ángel was a man of action and military status and may have lorded over his physically impaired younger brother. Political differences would later emerge between the two—José Antonio supported an independent Mexico, but José Ángel was a dedicated royalist. As an officer in the Spanish Army, he evidently fought against fellow Tejanos at the Battle of Medina in 1813.[21]

While learning the family business and studying law, José Antonio observed with keen interest the dramatic, revolutionary movements that battered San Antonio from 1808 to 1813. Because he was blessed with an extraordinary memory and these events made such indelible impressions on him, years later he incorporated them into his *Apuntes Históricos*. In 1808, at age thirteen, he witnessed the sensational arrival in Béxar of French agent Octaviano d'Alvimar, whom Spanish officers had arrested in Nacogdoches. The government of Napoleon had sent

d'Alvimar to foment revolution in northern New Spain.[22] Navarro recalled the exact date, September 8, 1808, and remembered with amuse-
ment the elaborate attire of the French general:

> We saw him enter the plaza of San Antonio with his flamboyant uni-
> form. Covered with insignia and brilliant crosses it challenged the
> genial sun—which nevertheless continued to illuminate the plaza of
> San Antonio until its decline in the west.[23]

As Navarro described it so well, the d'Alvimar incident was a spectac-
ular event; however, the ostentatious French intruder, who was sent
under arrest to Mexico City, was a mere precursor of what was to come.
Napoleon's bold action accelerated a crisis that would lead to revolution
in Mexico and eventually the liberation of most of Spanish America.

The excitement of the d'Alvimar incident had hardly died away when
the people of Béxar began anticipating another celebrated arrival: that of
newly appointed Governor Manuel María de Salcedo. Raised as a *cabal-
lero,* or Spanish gentleman, Salcedo came from a distinguished family
of Málaga. His father had been governor of Louisiana for Spain until
1803, and the younger Salcedo served under him as a military officer.
He regarded the activities of the people of Béxar with a critical eye and
saw little that met with his approval. His decrees displayed a decidedly
puritanical attitude. In particular, he disapproved of the rambunctious
Bexareños' fiestas and issued a decree ordering them to show restraint.
The decree banned men and women from riding a horse together
and prohibited riding at a gallop through the town. He admonished
the people that "Public diversions must not offend God." Many Bexareños surely viewed Salcedo with resentment and animosity as a result
of the restrictions placed on their traditional festivities and his other
overbearing intrusion on their lives. This may have paved the way for
his future ouster.[24]

Despite his heavy-handed moralism, Governor Salcedo did, in fact,
introduce numerous innovations with a beneficial and lasting impact.
For better administration, he divided Béxar into four *barrios,* or sectors,
and appointed a commissioner for each to oversee its cleanliness and
good public order. Hygienic regulations were instituted, such as requiring teamsters to park their carts and draft animals west of the town,
ordering residents to butcher cattle at the slaughterhouse, and mandat-
ing the registration of approved midwives. In addition, he affirmed the
very name of the town. Obviously objecting to the ubiquitous use of the
name Béxar, Salcedo decreed that the name San Fernando de Béxar was
to be used in official and personal written communications.[25]

The Casas Reales, the seat of Spanish government in Texas, was located on the east side of Main Plaza. It was the scene of dramatic events, which Navarro described in later years, during the revolution of 1811–13. Courtesy of the Witte Museum, San Antonio, Texas.

In late 1810, two years after Salcedo's arrival, news reached Béxar of a bloody uprising far to the south instigated by Father Miguel Hidalgo. Rebellious ideas began percolating through the town, and by the end of the year revolution-minded soldiers and civilian leaders began plotting to overthrow Salcedo. José Antonio Navarro must have been aware of the growing revolutionary sentiment, for among the conspirators were his mentors, Ruiz and Veramendi. To lead the insurrection, they and others selected Juan Bautista de las Casas, a retired militia captain from the province of Nuevo Santander (present-day Tamaulipas). The choice of an outsider and newcomer suggests a strategy that would allow responsibility to be shifted to Casas as a scapegoat if the revolt failed. As it turned out, that is essentially what happened. Writing years later, José Antonio damned the revolutionary leader with faint praise, describing Casas as an honorable man, but only moderately talented and easily influenced. At the same time, Navarro criticized the uprising led by Casas as a spontaneous eruption of pent-up, disorganized rage lacking any clear purpose other than retribution and a settling of scores.[26]

From his house at Real and Presidio streets, fifteen-year-old José Antonio had quick and easy access to Main Plaza, where he could observe the dramatic events that took place there in January 1811. Navarro twice referred to himself as being with a group of youths who were captivated by the important events that were occurring in the town, but only Navarro recorded his recollections. Writing as an eyewitness and as one who heard firsthand accounts, Navarro recalled the events of the coup. Casas, accompanied by various citizen-representatives, marched the militia at dawn to Main Plaza. He then entered Casas Reales, the governor's quarters, and made prisoners of Salcedo and other sleeping Spanish officials.[27]

The bloodless coup was over before breakfast. Casas proclaimed himself the new revolutionary governor of Texas. His subsequent actions were predictable. He confiscated the property of Europeans and royalists and jailed them. He sent supporters to spread the revolution to Nacogdoches. He put Governor Salcedo, Lieutenant Colonel Simón de Herrera, and other officers in chains, and then, in a humiliating spectacle, displayed them in Béxar before sending them under guard south of the Rio Grande. As a witness to these dramatic events, Navarro shared the wonderment and admiration of Bexareños toward those rebels who dared to put the Spanish oppressors in chains. These events seemed to confirm that the triumph of Mexican independence was assured. Yet the duration of Casas's revolutionary rule was brief, lasting just thirty-nine days.[28]

It appears that Casas did nothing out of the ordinary for the leader of a successful rebellion. What then brought about the sudden failure of his authority? Historians have offered several explanations for the opposition that arose so quickly and toppled Casas. He ruled arbitrarily and rashly confiscated property; he ignored certain army officers and prominent leaders of Béxar who had helped with the uprising; and he cordially received Hidalgo emissaries who behaved obnoxiously while in town. Navarro noted two additional and persuasive reasons for Casas's failure. First, his movement was seriously flawed because it was an undirected emotional eruption based on rage. Second, there were disturbing reports coming from the south that undermined the insurgents' confidence.[29]

Hidalgo's revolution began spectacularly. His peasant army swelled to as many as 80,000 and he laid waste to Spanish interests in towns and haciendas between the central Mexican town of Dolores and Mexico City. An effective response by royalist forces, however, was not long in coming. General Félix María Calleja del Rey, at the head of an army of professional soldiers, decisively defeated and dispersed Hidalgo's followers at the Battle of Calderón Bridge, five days before Casas arrested Salcedo. News of Hidalgo's setbacks created a desperate situation for Casas, and being an outsider certainly weakened his position in the face of adversity.[30] All these factors combined to create an opportunity for a counterrevolution.

Counterrevolutionary sentiment coalesced around the leadership of Juan José Manuel Vicente Zambrano, the controversial subdeacon of San Fernando Church in Béxar. Zambrano had only recently returned from exile—a consequence of angry confrontations with Alcalde Ángel Navarro and Governor Salcedo, among others. The subdeacon had a record of arrogance and belligerence toward his fellow Bexareños, many of whom had filed petitions demanding his ouster from the province. In 1811, however, burdened by the millstone of Casas's rule, Bexareños evidently found Zambrano's combative nature useful in their effort to restore royal rule in Béxar. Perhaps the supporters of the counterrevolution preferred to keep a low profile and were happy for the flamboyant Zambrano to take the lead. In any case, once sparked, the opposition to Casas grew rapidly, and Zambrano, assisted by his two brothers, assumed control of the counterrevolutionary movement. As events unfolded, José Antonio again watched and listened with an insider's point of view, for two of the principal conspirators were Ruiz and Veramendi. Other prominent citizens joined the cause, forming a governing junta that swore loyalty to King Ferdinand VII of Spain.[31]

On March 3, military leaders and the counterrevolutionary junta members entered the Casas Reales and took Casas prisoner in the same rooms where he had captured Governor Salcedo only a few weeks earlier. José Antonio joined the crowd that gathered in Main Plaza to watch. At the news that Casas was in chains, people cheered and shouted, and the church bells pealed, but Navarro shrank from the clamor of the mob. Years later he recalled with disquiet the jubilant celebration following the capture of the revolutionary leader, and he considered Casas to be a sacrificial victim. He could barely restrain his anger at the misguided counterrevolutionaries who doomed the Casas rebellion and delayed Mexican independence for many years:

> It is not my intention to rebuke the conduct of those who took part
> in this counter revolution that hastened the unfortunate Casas to the
> execution block; but rather to deplore and pity the errant reasoning of
> those who, imbued with the false honor of being faithful to the most
> detestable tyrant of Europe [Ferdinand VII], made an ostentatious

show of plunging the fratricidal dagger into the heart of their Mexican brothers. Thus they hammered the rivets of their own chains, condemning themselves to trudge sorrowfully behind the plodding Spanish ox to earn their daily bread.[32]

Casas's fate was indeed sealed. Executed in Monclova, his head was returned to Béxar and displayed on a pole in Military Plaza.

Although the counterrevolution had succeeded, government in Texas lacked stability. At first, the Béxar junta led by the quarrelsome Zambrano governed the province. Governor Salcedo was absent, having joined the troops accompanying Hidalgo and other rebel prisoners to Chihuahua, where the revolutionary leaders were tried and executed. Salcedo returned to Béxar in December to find his authority substantially diminished. During his absence, gubernatorial powers had been exercised first by the junta and then by Herrera, who served as temporary governor. In addition to the dilution of his powers, Salcedo labored under the burden of a sense of dishonor and embarrassment for having been overthrown and chained by Casas. The governor requested a military inquiry that he hoped would clear his name. Not only was his request denied but, adding insult to injury, Zambrano was promoted to lieutenant colonel as a reward for capturing Casas.[33] Zambrano, now possessing both clerical and military authority, became even more overbearing and arrogant.

East of the Sabine River in Natchitoches, filibusters were aware of Texas's military and political weakness and made plans to exploit it. American and Tejano volunteers gathered around the leadership of José Bernardo Maximiliano Gutiérrez de Lara and Augustus W. Magee. Calling their ragtag band the Republican Army of the North, Gutiérrez and Magee led about 130 men across the Sabine on August 8, 1812. They captured Nacogdoches and the presidio at La Bahía with little opposition, and volunteers swelled their ranks to about 300 men. In response, Salcedo, with Herrera, brought his military forces from Béxar and besieged the invaders fortified within the La Bahía presidio. Gutiérrez held them at bay for three months and repulsed two attacks before Salcedo, low on provisions and with depleted troops, withdrew to Béxar. This unseemly retreat demoralized the Spanish troops, many of whom defected to the rebels. Reinforcements from Louisiana joined Gutiérrez, as did some additional Indian allies.[34] Emboldened, Gutiérrez marched to Béxar.

José Antonio related the main events that followed. Taking command, Herrera led 1,200 troops to Salado Creek. On March 29, 1813, at Rosillo, he engaged Gutiérrez's army, which was estimated to be about 800 strong. It was a bloody, one-sided battle. Navarro claimed that Herrera lost 400 men between dead and wounded, while only five of Gutiérrez's men died and fourteen were wounded. The survivors of the royal army fled in disorder back to Béxar. The Battle of Rosillo (also known as the Battle of Salado) was a disastrous loss for the Spanish. The combined effect of Salcedo's precipitous retreat from La Bahía and Herrera's defeat at Rosillo produced chaos and consternation in Béxar. Gutiérrez marched his army to the edge of town and demanded an unconditional surrender from Salcedo and Herrera. The capitulation took place on April 1, when Salcedo, Herrera, and their officers walked to meet the victorious Gutiérrez. Navarro watched the protocol of surrender and the humiliating parade of prisoners that followed. Recalling these events, he had little sympathy for the hapless Spaniards:

> The cowardly surrender sealed the doom of those unfortunate Spanish officers. They surrendered their swords and were placed between two columns. Gutiérrez and his army crossed to the eastern side of the river, compelling their prisoners to march in front to the sound of martial music, and they entered within the walls of the Alamo—the same Alamo which in March 1836 was to become the cradle of the liberty of Texas and the scene of glory and valor.[35]

The next day, Gutiérrez walked into the Casas Reales and presided over the creation of an administrative junta composed of citizens dedicated to Mexican independence and opposed to Spanish rule.[36]

When Salcedo was overthrown in 1811, he suffered disgrace and banishment. Now a death sentence was secretly decreed for him, Herrera, and their officers. The prisoners were told that ships were waiting for them at Matagorda Bay to carry them to New Orleans, but a military escort led them not to the safety of exile, but to their execution place. Navarro provided a vivid description of the death of the unfortunate Salcedo and his fellow officers. The detail in his narrative shows it was based on a firsthand account of someone present in the execution party, probably Ruiz.

> On the fourth day of April, or possibly on the night of the fifth, sixty Mexican troopers under the command of Antonio Delgado led fourteen Spanish prisoners, including four of Mexican birth, out of Béxar and to the eastern bank of Salado Creek, near the spot where the Battle of Rosillo occurred. There they dismounted from their horses, with no other arms than the dull knives that each of those monsters

carried on their belts. After heaping offensive words and insulting epithets upon the prisoners, they cut their throats. With inhuman irony, some of the assassins sharpened their knives on the soles of their shoes in the presence of their defenseless victims.[37]

The next day, eighteen-year-old José Antonio Navarro watched as the execution squadron rode into Main Plaza after carrying out their sanguinary mission:

> One day after the slaughter, I myself saw that horde of assassins arrive with their officer, Antonio Delgado, who halted in front of the Casas Reales to inform Bernardo Gutiérrez that the fourteen victims had been dispatched. On that portentous morning, a large number of other young spectators and I stood at the door of the Casas Reales and watched Captain Delgado's entrance into the hall. He doffed his hat in the presence of General Gutiérrez and, stuttering, he uttered some words mingled with shame. He handed Gutiérrez a paper that, I believe, contained a list of those whose throats had been cut . . . I myself saw the blood-stained adornments that those tigers carried hanging from their saddle horns, boasting publicly of their crime and of having divided the spoils among themselves in shares.[38]

The execution of the Spanish officers disgusted American volunteers in Béxar who had been Gutiérrez's comrades in arms, and many began deserting. For those who remained, relations with the Mexican soldiers were soured.

Royal authorities responded to the news of the executions at Béxar with rage and plans for revenge under the direction of General Joaquín de Arredondo. He ordered Colonel Ignacio Elizondo to advance his army of some 400 men to the Frio River, a position from which he was to observe the invaders and await the arrival of the main army led by Arredondo. Elizondo did not stop at the Frio but continued to Béxar, where he engaged the rebel forces on June 20, 1813, at Alazán Creek, west of town. José Antonio Navarro joined others in the bell tower of San Fernando Church and later recalled: "We watched the clash of flashing weapons through our field glasses and listened to the horrifying thunder of the cannons." Navarro wrote that after four hours of combat, Elizondo was defeated and abandoned the field, having suffered devastating losses. Gutiérrez lost twenty-two men killed and forty-two wounded. Upon returning to Béxar, Gutiérrez learned that Arredondo had left Laredo and was marching north with more than 1,800 Mexican

*San Fernando Church, as it appeared around 1865, by which time it had been renamed
San Fernando Cathedral. Navarro and others witnessed clashes between Spanish royal
authorities and rebels led by Bernardo Gutiérrez on June 20, 1813, from the bell tower of
the church, which was located on the west side of Main Plaza facing the Casas Reales.
From the* San Antonio Light *Collection, Institute of Texan Cultures, University of
Texas at San Antonio, #L-0010-A. Image courtesy of the Hearst Corporation.*

troops, including the fugitives from the fight on Alazán Creek who,
with the defeated Colonel Elizondo, joined them on the road.[39]

Despite the victory at the Alazán, bitterness and resentment toward
Gutiérrez continued to fester, stemming from the brutal executions. The
"President Protector," as he styled himself, was finally undone by the arrival in July of his fellow revolutionary, José Álvarez de Toledo y Dubois.
Possessed of a winning personal style, Toledo quickly gained supporters and undermined Gutiérrez's authority. In early August, Gutiérrez
was ousted from power and returned to the United States. While the
insurgents changed horses in mid-stream, General Arredondo's army

kept up its relentless march toward Béxar on a mission of revenge and retribution. His army had notable advantages over the insurgent forces. Arredondo brought superior leadership, military discipline, and years of experience to the showdown at Béxar. Veteran subordinate officers assisted the General to ensure control of the army. The rebel force, on the other hand, was less an army than a quarreling mix of Anglos, Tejanos, and various Indian allies. On August 15, Arredondo arrived within forty miles of Béxar. That same day, Toledo led the Republican Army of the North south from Béxar across the Medina River. A number of Bexareños with royalist sentiments rode out and joined Arredondo, including José Antonio Navarro's older brother José Ángel. Others, such as Ruiz, remained with Toledo.[40]

The two forces met on August 18, 1813, in a decisive battle that determined the fate of Texas and of the extended Navarro family for many years to come. In terms of historical significance the Battle of Medina ranks behind the Battle of the Alamo and the Battle of San Jacinto in importance in Texas history, which in combination led to Texas independence. However, in terms of its immediate destructive impact on a populace, the Battle of Medina stands first. It was an extremely bloody conflict, with more combatants killed in action and executed than in all the other battles on Texas soil combined.[41] To military casualties must be added the devastating impact of the executions of hundreds of Bexareño civilians, confiscations of property, dislocations of hundreds of Tejanos who went into exile to escape the wrath of General Arredondo, and the ruin of the local economy brought about by the occupying army. The Navarros and their fellow Bexareños experienced repercussions from the battle that lasted for a generation.

Navarro recalled the Battle of Medina clearly in his *Apuntes Históricos*:

> At last General Arredondo arrived, furious and impatient to quiet the spirit of insurrection and to avenge the death of his compatriots, the governors. On the 18th of August and not on the 13th, as it has been previously reported, Toledo offered to do battle in Medina. This general had 1,500 men including 600 American volunteers; Arredondo had 4,000 men. The battle was fought with great military skill on both sides. The American volunteers formed the regiment of infantry and handled the artillery, composed of nine cannons from four to eight caliber. The cavalry consisted of the inhabitants of San Antonio and vicinity, and of some individuals from Tamaulipas and [Presidio del] Rio Grande.[42]

Navarro also described a battlefield ploy that Arredondo used to animate his troops. At one point it seemed that the Spanish effort was flagging. The general, however, had a trick up his sleeve. Arredondo had his army shout "Long live the King! Victory is ours!" At the same time, his band sounded notes of victory, causing the rebel cavalry to flee in panic from the field. This description is largely confirmed by Arredondo's battle-field report although the general wrote that it was the insurgents whose energies flagged, not those of his soldiers. He reported that the enemy had been completely routed, and so he "ordered the music to start up and my drummer to beat the reveille" in order to animate his troops.[43] The similarity of the two descriptions affirms Navarro's account and supports the credibility of his sources.

Arredondo's artillery and infantry pounded the Republican Army of the North for hours until its ranks broke. Navarro gave a stirring account of the desperate flight that followed, describing how the insurgents ran for their lives with the Spanish cavalry in hot pursuit. Over a distance of several miles, with slashing sabers and lances in hand, the Spanish troopers killed most of the insurgents. When Toledo marched to the Medina, his force consisted of 800 to 900 Tejanos and other Mexicans, 300 to 400 Anglos, about 100 Lipan Apache, and a small number of other Indians. On the royalist side, Arredondo reported that he had 635 infantry and 1,195 cavalry. After Arredondo won the day, he compiled a report at the battleground. He found "a body count of six hundred plus one hundred prisoners who are being executed," not including those who were pursued and killed during the aftermath. The Republican Army of the North was obliterated; fewer than one hundred of them escaped alive.[44]

Although the Battle of Medina lasted well into the afternoon of August 18, Indian allies of the insurgents saw the writing on the wall early and were the first to bring news of the defeat to Béxar. Father J. M. Rodríguez saw warriors galloping through the town shouting "gachupino mucho, melicano nara" (Spaniards much; Americano [Mexicano?] nothing)."[45] Pandemonium ruled as Bexareños with family members who had participated in the insurgency prepared to leave as quickly as possible. Pushing, shoving, and cursing all in their path, survivors rushed into town to retrieve what possessions they could take with them and fled to the northeast, hoping to reach Louisiana. Among those fleeing was eighteen-year-old José Antonio Navarro. Just why he went into exile is puzzling. If he were a noncombatant, it would seem that his brother José Ángel, a royalist in good standing with Arredondo, would have protected him. Perhaps, despite his disability, he had taken part in the battle in some way, even if only indirectly.

The Spanish cavalry under Elizondo pursued the desperate refugees. José Antonio had a head start that enabled him to cross the Trinity River ahead of his pursuers, but he was well aware that others were not so fortunate. He later recorded that, after the Battle of Medina, Elizondo left Béxar with 500 men in pursuit of the Bexareño fugitives, who were on the road to the United States. At the Trinity River on the old road from San Antonio to Nacogdoches he overtook a body of men and families, and there shot 105 people. José Antonio and his party probably narrowly escaped this fate. In his "Autobiographical Notes" he included an account of his family's flight to Louisiana:

> [The] Battle of Medina was lost, and with it the last hope of the Mexican Patriots, and the Internal Provinces of Mexico. My Mother, then alone, with the minor Children left Béxar, my oldest Brother Angel, absent from Béxar fleeing in the interior of Mexico from the persecutions of Arredondo, my Uncle Ruiz, my Brother-in-Law, the husband of my sister Maria Josefa Veramendi, and myself may have been wandering in the State of Louisiana—behold here a family scattered and persecute[d by] so many disasters.

He added bitterly: "For this reason my younger [brothers] and myself have lost the Years of flowe[r of] our youth, waisting [sic] years with out impr[oving our]selves, but in participating in the affliction [of] our forefathers."[46]

Navarro's account of the insurgent exodus is enhanced by details from the firsthand account of an anonymous woman who also fled Béxar in August 1813. She later dictated the story of her experience, which corroborates Navarro's and provides graphic details about the desperate efforts of those, like José Antonio and others, who did their utmost to escape the wrath of Arredondo. "La Béxarena" said that her father had supported the insurgent side. After the loss of the battle of August 18, her family abandoned all their possessions in order to flee their enemies. She, her mother, an uncle, and three cousins spent twelve days in difficult travel, crossing many rivers and streams, before they came to the Trinity River. Here, Elizondo's troops overtook the straggling band of about 150 refugees. Berating them as traitors and insurgents, the soldiers lanced one of La Béxareña's cousins and prepared to shoot him. Her mother begged the soldiers to allow him to confess first; they replied that he could confess to the devils in Hell. According to her, more than 100 men were executed at that place. The soldiers escorted the remainder of the party back to Béxar, where the women were put to work in *La Quinta*—the women's prison where Arredondo forced those from insurgent families to work grinding corn and making tortillas for his troops.[47]

Among General Arredondo's officers was a nineteen-year-old lieutenant named Antonio López de Santa Anna. Sometime after the Battle of Medina, Santa Anna is said to have met members of the Navarro family. Reportedly, he was so enchanted by José Antonio Navarro's sixteen-year-old sister, María Antonia, that he wanted to marry her. The family objected to such a proposal because of Santa Anna's bad reputation, which included accusations that he had stolen money from military funds.[48]

Governor Benito de Armiñán sent spies into Louisiana to bring back information about Tejano exiles and obtained information by questioning pardoned rebels who later returned from Louisiana. As a result, in 1814, authorities learned that Ruiz was living at Bayou Pierre near Natchitoches, maintaining himself doing "work of the country." More importantly, he had not been observed collaborating with revolutionaries. José Antonio Navarro probably lived nearby in similar conditions. While some have concluded that he spent his exile in New Orleans, available evidence does not support that assumption. Because of their close relationship, it is likely that where Ruiz could be found, José Antonio would be found also. Spanish authorities were concerned about the large number of Tejanos exiled in Louisiana, where they could be plotting attacks against Texas, and several pardons were offered to induce them to return. Francisco Martínez, of the Spanish consulate in New Orleans, proclaimed a royal pardon in Natchitoches for exiled insurgents on October 15, 1815. This amnesty was even more comprehensive and forgiving than a previous offer made by Arredondo. To qualify for the consulate pardon, exiles had to do no more than write to King Ferdinand VII saying that they truthfully repented all the excesses they had committed, and that they would live quietly and obey his laws faithfully. This appears to be the pardon that José Antonio accepted, which enabled him to return home. Thus by the end of the year, Navarro, with pardon in hand, probably joined other Tejanos on the road back to Béxar.[49]

In Béxar, the Navarro and Veramendi families were free of charges of having been revolutionaries. While much of their personal property had been lost in the chaos of August 1813, ownership of their homes was secure. Juan Martín Veramendi had regained possession of his confiscated house in 1815 and cleared his name of accusations of disloyalty.[50] Adding an extra measure of security was the fact that José Ángel

Navarro served on the city council during 1815 and 1816. Thus, unlike many other Bexareños, José Antonio Navarro had the great fortune to come home to a family whose estate was largely intact, and whose members were not mostly dead, impoverished, or banished. Only one family member was missing to make this reunion complete: Ruiz, who for some reason clearly trusted no Spanish pardon. A likely reason is that he may have been complicit in the killing of Salcedo and Herrera, for which no pardon would be sufficient. He steadfastly remained in Louisiana until 1821, when Mexican independence was won.

José Antonio Navarro turned 21 in 1816, the year he returned to Béxar from exile. He had lost years of his youth, and the ominous clouds of revolution that still hung over colonial Mexico. With a little luck and much hard work, José Antonio could capitalize on his own intellect and education to rebuild the damaged family fortune and to achieve his own version of the American Dream that his father had come to Texas to pursue.

CHAPTER TWO

Emerging Leader, 1816–22

JOSÉ ANTONIO NAVARRO returned to Béxar after more than two years in exile. Devastation caused by the royalist occupation confronted him in every direction. Many prominent citizens lived in dire circumstances, while others remained in exile. Indians were quick to exploit Béxar's weakness. Soon after Navarro's arrival, the city council sent a heartfelt plea to Military Governor Mariano Varela detailing the severity of the problems and asking for assistance. The council declared, "Indian attacks [had] left the people groaning" and prevented farmers from sowing crops.[1]

Residents had another complaint against the government: the commandeering of resources without compensation. In the best of times, the Texas economy was fragile. Chronic underpopulation hindered economic growth; the non-Indian population of the province never exceeded 4,000 under Spanish rule.[2] Geographic isolation from the population centers of New Spain made trade to the south difficult, expensive, and dangerous. Most Bexareños derived little more than a marginal existence. General Joaquín de Arredondo overwhelmed this vulnerable economy when he occupied Béxar with a hungry army of some 1,800 men after the defeat of the insurgents in 1813. His troops decimated the wild livestock on which Bexareños depended. The military provided little security to the Bexareños, yet burdened them with satisfying the soldiers' needs. Navarro and his compatriots thus faced the challenge of making a living in an insecure and impoverished environment on Mexico's northern frontier during the country's fitful struggle for independence.

After Navarro and Juan Martín de Veramendi returned, the extended family was almost fully reunited. The only missing member of the family circle was José Francisco Ruiz, who remained in Louisiana exile. He had good reason to be suspicious of the many pardons offered him, for the government still considered him a dangerous rebel. The family circle must have been alarmed by events in late September. Acting on a di-

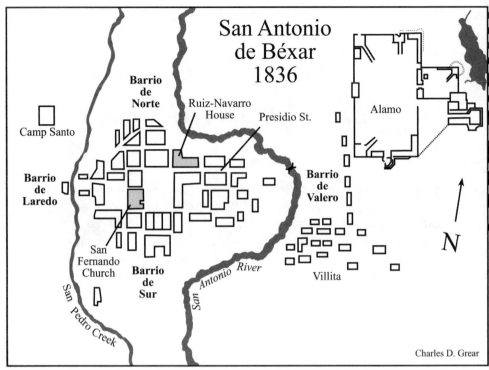

San Antonio de Béxar as it appeared in 1836. The map shows the location of the Ruiz-Navarro House and the four barrios Navarro likely strolled through after returning from his Louisiana exile in 1816.

rect order from Commandant General Arredondo, soldiers barged into the Ruiz household, and pushing aside his wife and children, searched for correspondence with rebels. They clearly came up empty-handed, as a few days later the commandant general was informed that nothing of interest had been found.[3] Nevertheless, the violation of a family member's home must have worried Navarro and Veramendi that the finger of suspicion might soon point at them, given their family connection to Ruiz and their prior insurgent associations. Both were, in effect, on probation as a condition of the pardons they had received.

Soon after his return, though, Navarro may have explored the streets and alleys of his hometown to see conditions for himself. It is easy to imagine that he inspected each of the four *barrios*, or neighborhoods, into which it was divided—Valero, Laredo, Norte, and Sur. To the east, Navarro would have passed through the *potrero* (the fields and pasturage inside the big bend in the San Antonio River) and crossed the bridge into the Barrio de Valero to stand before the high walls of the Alamo, a landmark that dominated and defined the barrio. Founded as the Spanish mission San Antonio de Valero, it had become a fortress for the soldiers of Arredondo's occupying army. Reminiscing, Navarro recalled as a boy seeing the troops, transferred there from Alamo de Parras, converting it into a makeshift fort and nostalgically calling it "the Alamo."[4] In addition to the troops, about fifty families lived in the Barrio de Valero.

Returning to Main Plaza and walking through the Barrio del Sur, past the confiscated house of Erasmo Seguín, Navarro would have come to La Quinta, the building in which Arredondo forced women of Béxar to prepare tortillas for his troops. From that gloomy monument, he might have walked west and crossed San Pedro Creek, the boundary for the Barrio de Laredo. Commonly known as Laredito, it took its name from the Camino Real to Laredo that originated there. At this junction, he could have seen the house of María Loreto de Castañeda, a widow with three children. Her lot was more than an acre and would later become Navarro's homesite. To the north lay the Campo Santo where he most likely would have visited his father's grave. Although the senior Navarro had been the first one buried there, during José Antonio's exile in Louisiana the population of the cemetery had increased to more than 500.[5] A large number of the deaths had resulted from revolutionary conflicts, Indian attacks, epidemics such as cholera, and a high infant mortality rate, all of which made the Campo Santo a stark reminder of the fragile reality of life in the barrios of Béxar. In the course of his exploration Navarro would have found the people of Béxar to be a racially diverse community, as they had been at the time of his birth. He could have greeted heads of households variously designated as *español, mestizo, mulato, indio,* and *coyote.* Moreover, he might have been familiar with two free Negro families.[6]

Crossing back over San Pedro Creek and walking east along Presidio Street (present-day Commerce Street), he would have passed the San Antonio de Béxar presidio, occupied by more royalist troops—not a place for a recently pardoned rebel to linger. Returning to his home in the Barrio del Norte, along Real Street, he very likely would have stopped to chat with a pretty young woman named Margarita de la Garza, whose family lived a short distance north of the Navarro residence. Not long after José Antonio's return, a spark of mutual attraction was struck and he and Margarita began a courtship that would result in a lifelong commitment. At the head of Margarita's family was her mother, Xaviera Flores. The two other household members were Margarita's younger brother, Francisco de la Garza, and José Francisco Gallardo, godson of Xaviera's half-sister, Margila Chirino.[7] (Appendix One discusses Margarita de la Garza's background in more detail.)

Although the properties of the Navarro and Flores properties lay within a few blocks of each other, family and material circumstances put the two households in distinctly different social classes. The Navarros lived in a substantial limestone house in a prominent area of town. Located near the presidio and San Fernando Church, it came to be known as "Navarro Corner." In contrast, the Flores' home stood on a narrow strip of land to the north, along a lane that led to the cemetery. Years later, Margarita described the house where her mother lived for more than sixty years as being constructed of *palos y cascara* (posts and tree bark).[8] The Navarros were a prominent family that had intermarried with other prominent families. The Flores family, by all available evidence, lived in poverty, supported by manual labor that yielded little income.

Social class evidently meant little to José Antonio because did not choose a wife from one of Béxar's principal families. Descriptions given in later years suggest that he was a good-looking young man in 1816, and a family member described him as being of medium height.[9] Friends mention his ruddy complexion, and judging by photographs taken when he was older, he must have been considered a handsome man. Moreover, he was a man of energy, intelligence, and ambition. However, his injured leg and resulting limp may have had reduced his appeal to women from his own social class. Even so, death and exile surely had so reduced the number of marriageable men that Navarro should have been a "good catch." But in the end, no convincing explanation clarifies his choice. Perhaps the mysterious workings of the heart that can overcome social and familial barriers were responsible. In any case, José Antonio Navarro and Margarita de la Garza brought their first child, a daughter named María Casimira del Cármen, into the world in the spring of 1817.[10]

Evidently no marriage ceremony preceded the birth of María Casimira del Cármen. Public records provide convincing evidence that José Antonio Navarro and Margarita de Garza were not married in the Catholic Church, at least not before 1833. This conclusion rests on two sets of official documents: San Antonio de Béxar census listings and San Fernando Church baptismal records. Taken together they provide strong evidence that José Antonio and Margarita did not marry. Seven Béxar censuses that list residents' marital state were conducted from 1817 to 1832. Each census shows José Antonio and Margarita as single and living in separate households—Margarita with her mother, Xaviera; José

Antonio in the household of his mother, Josefa Ruiz.[11] Further evidence is provided by the baptismal records in the archives of San Fernando Church. They recorded the date, the age of the child at the time of baptism, and the names of parents. The names of paternal and maternal grandparents were usually listed along with those of godparents and the officiating priest. In addition, a notation was made as to whether the child was "natural" or "legitimate." The latter designation applied only when the parents had been married in the Catholic Church, and the distinction had a legal basis. A child born to a couple who were free to marry but chose not to—the case with José Antonio and Margarita— was called a natural child (*hijo natural*). The possibility remained in those cases, however, for subsequent legal recognition or acknowledgement, or even a legitimization by the father.[12] San Fernando Church documents record the baptisms of five of Navarro's seven children. Each notes that the baptism was of a natural child rather than a legitimate child, supporting the conclusion that between 1817 and 1833 José Antonio and Margarita were not married in the church.[13]

Natural children were common in New Spain and other parts of colonial Latin America, both in large cities and frontier villages like Béxar. A survey of San Fernando Church records from 1816 through 1819—during which time José Antonio and Margarita had their first two children—shows that San Fernando Church priests performed 243 baptisms, 34 percent of which were of natural children. Several prominent Bexareños had children out of wedlock during the years after 1816, including José Antonio's brother José Ángel.[14] Unlike his brother, José Antonio made a lifelong commitment to his children and their mother. He and Margarita formed a lasting bond in which they represented each other as man and wife and were accepted as such by family, friends, and the public at large.[15]

Once José Antonio had family responsibilities, the challenge of making a living in an impoverished and unstable environment was more pressing. The future looked bleak, and his academic skills did little at first to help him adjust to changed times. He had experience in the mercantile business, but during his exile the family store ceased operations after revolutionary conflict disrupted and reduced the importation of goods. Many Tejanos, including Navarro, found an alternative way to support themselves, at least partially: contraband. This illegal yet profitable trade became one of the few ways to make money and provide for civilian needs in those desperate times.

To start anew, José Antonio needed political as well as economic connections. His older brother, José Ángel, would have been a good resource in the municipal government because he had served as a member of the city council in 1815, and he had military associations. As a family member close to the power structure, José Ángel would have been able to discretely advise and inform his brother about political matters. In addition, the Navarros' astute brother-in-law, Juan Martín de Veramendi, could also provide insights and ideas concerning future mercantile opportunities.

The families' prospects were bolstered by a welcome change in the political environment of Texas in the spring of 1817, when Antonio Martínez became governor. As an advocate for the people in his jurisdiction, his laissez-faire attitude and relaxed enforcement of contraband laws helped them cope with severe shortages. At the same time, the governor defended soldiers when they were caught with illegal goods. He admitted in a report to Viceroy Juan Ruiz Apodaca that, "Even I took for my use, having no other supply, some plates, cups, crockery, pens, ink, sealing wax, and other such items." Further justifying soldiers' trades, the governor argued that the goods they brought into Texas were in effect compensation for expenses incurred during a long and arduous trip for which he had no funds to pay them. Word about the new governor's attitude quickly spread, and José Antonio Navarro expanded his trading operations. It mattered little that Martínez was denounced when a patrol he sent to the Louisiana frontier returned in December 1817 with a large quantity of merchandise for which they had traded horses. He tried to minimize the issue by declaring that the goods brought from Louisiana were for the soldiers' personal use, and he emphasized the great need for such items in his province. But the list of contraband filled seven pages and included 900 pounds of tobacco, a particularly flagrant violation because the sale of tobacco was a royal monopoly.[16] Despite Martínez's troubles, eager traders like Navarro saw that the door to trade with Louisiana had opened a crack. They would soon push that door wide open by driving herds of horses and mules through it.

The next year electrifying news swept through Béxar and galvanized everyone's attention. Governor Martínez required the city council to provide an estimate from each family of the damages incurred as a result of the 1813 Gutiérrez-Magee expedition.[17] The Spanish crown probably wanted the declarations as a bargaining chip to use in its negotiations with the United States to establish the boundary between Texas and Louisiana. Nevertheless, the records generated provide a valuable perspective on the wealth that Bexareños possessed in 1818.

José Antonio Navarro worked side by side with Alcalde Baron de Bastrop, witnessing his certification of the declarations of losses. Navarro

Memoria que manifiesta D.ª M.ª Josefa Ruiz de las pér-
didas que se le han ocasionado desde la entrada de los Anglo-
americanos a estas Provincias es á saber.

Pesos R.ˢ

Por Ochocientos palos de buena madera q.
me quemaron de mi Jardin, quando se apode-
raron de mi Casa, á 4 p.ˢ el ciento — — — — — "032"0"

Por el Rancho que abandoné de S. Antonio
de Leon, á causa de la entrada de ellos, con
los bienes sig.ᵗᵉˢ

Como 260 Reses de fierro arriba que se pas-
toreaban en el ditto sin ygualar lo mediano; ⎱1820"0"
á precio de 7 p.ˢ — — — — — — — — — ⎰

Por 27 caballos mansos q.ᵉ tambien se me dis-
persaron; á 10 pesos — — — — — — — "270"0"

Por una Yegua mansa — — — — — — — "04"0"

Todo lo cual — Total — # 2.126"0"

Prudencialm.ᵗᵉ calculado, es lo que conozco haber perdi-
do, dexando salvo alguna pequeña cantidad que
se me haya pasado, de mas, ó menos, en la que no
pude anotar acertadam.ᵗᵉ; y lo Firmó á mi mandado
mi hijo José Antonio, hoy en Bexar á 11 de No-
viembre de 1818.

Por mi Sra. Madre.

Josef Ant.º Navarro

En el mismo dia siendo pres.ᵗᵉ el Ynteresado á
nombre de su Sra. Madre; D.ª M.ª Josefa Ruiz,
se le recibió Juram.ᵗᵒ que hizo por Dios N.ᵗᵒ S.ᵒʳ y
por una Señal de Sta. cruz, so cuyo cargo prome-
tió y promete, haber ditto verdad en todo quanto tie

José Antonio Navarro wrote this declaration on behalf his mother, describing the
property the family lost during the revolutions of 1813. This is the earliest known example
of José Antonio Navarro's writing. Bexar Archives, di_05762, the Dolph Briscoe Center
for American History, the University of Texas at Austin.

prepared his own mother's statement to be certified, creating his first written document to survive for future historians.[18] He also prepared the Veramendi declaration, since Juan Martín was away on a military expedition at the time. The Veramendi claim totaled 21,666.5 pesos, the second largest in Béxar. It is interesting to note that this is one of the declarations that demonstrates the existence of debt peonage in Béxar because Veramendi's application refers to six peons who left while owing him a total of 555 pesos.[19]

Navarro's work with Bastrop lasted only about two months and he probably received little pay, if any. Now a grown man of twenty-three and the father of a child, Navarro addressed the problem of obtaining daily necessities as best he could. By 1818, he found opportunities to engage in trade that took place between Béxar and La Bahía (present-day Goliad). He previously had received permission from Governor Martínez to travel between these towns, and it was thus that he began to establish himself as an independent merchant.[20] More important than the small profits he realized from these trips were the connections he made with various individuals in La Bahía. With these associations would come new opportunities for greater, albeit illegal, profits. At the beginning of 1819, Margarita was pregnant with their second child. The need to provide for his growing family and to prove himself as a capable person, despite his physical disability, was about to drive Navarro to risk a dangerous journey in pursuit of contraband.

By early 1819, José Antonio had managed to acquire a load of shirts.[21] These were valuable items on the frontier, where good cloth and clothing were difficult to obtain. Martínez had reported to Arredondo that the soldiers of both Béxar and La Bahía complained about being dressed in rags. Some "had nothing to wear but sheepskins, and others could not leave their quarters because they were naked."[22] Navarro decided to take his shirts to La Bahía, where he hoped to sell them at a better price than he could obtain in Béxar. He must have known that Arredondo had recently appointed Juan Manuel Zambrano, the subdeacon of San Fernando Church and one of his favorite Bexareño royalists, as commander of the presidio at La Bahía. He probably also knew that the ambitious Zambrano was using his position to operate an extensive contraband operation, revealing again his "special talent for total disorder," as Navarro later described it.[23]

During February or early March 1819, Navarro requested permission from the governor for himself and his servant, Damián Rodríguez, to travel to La Bahía. It was a routine request, like others he had made, and Martínez approved it without question.[24] When Navarro and Damián arrived in La Bahía around the first of April, they found the residents trembling with fear and seething with anger. Immediately after taking charge of the presidio, Zambrano had begun to intimidate and bully both soldiers and civilians. Less than a month after Zambrano's arrival, an officer wrote to the governor begging him "to liberate him from the ruinous caprices of this lion."[25] For the flimsiest of reasons, or no reason at all, Zambrano humiliated people by publicly berating and beating them. He had a husband and wife locked into stocks. Others he ordered tied to a cannon and beaten. By the spring of 1819, he had the populace thoroughly cowed, and such was his authority and oppression that no one openly opposed him.[26] Such a man was not likely disposed to wait for a broken colonial supply system, shut down by revolutionary chaos, to provide for the needs of himself and his men. Vested with the authority of both the church and the army, Zambrano's arrogant personality led him to believe he was not subject to mere laws and regulations, and he made his own trade arrangements.

Navarro's arrival at La Bahía coincided with that of a contraband expedition sent by Zambrano to exchange livestock for goods, so Navarro saw firsthand how the system worked. While he could have sold his shirts for a nominal profit, he saw an opportunity to make even greater earnings. He could invest the proceeds of the shirts in horses and mules, drive the stock to Carcasiu in Louisiana, and then trade them. Upon his return he would have a stock of merchandise worth much more than the price of the shirts in La Bahía. Moreover, this opportunity offered Navarro the possibility of yet another benefit. Such a venture would be comparable to an expedition to Galveston that José Ángel Navarro and Juan Martín de Veramendi had embarked on the previous year.[27] Perhaps he might even meet his relatives along the trail and surprise them with his courageous enterprise. A trip to Carcasiu would demonstrate his capability and competence to his family and himself.

At this time, a contagious disease was killing horses in Texas. Governor Martínez reported, "horses are suffering from a sickness of the mouth that quickly [disables] them . . . the same happened in La Bahía, where the commandant reports that more than seventy animals have died."[28] This epidemic justified the importation of horses from the towns along the Rio Grande, a key step to continuing trade with Louisiana. Zambrano ordered another expedition to Carcasiu and offered its leadership to José Antonio Navarro, who did not hesitate to accept. Zambrano assigned La Bahía militiamen Nicolas and Manuel Carvajal to accompany Navarro, who also brought his servant, Damián. To raise money to invest in the trading operation, Navarro sold his lot of shirts to Zambrano for 140 pesos and purchased horses and mules that Zambrano had brought from the Rio Grande.[29]

On Saturday, April 10, Navarro and his three companions left La Bahía. They carried passports issued by Zambrano authorizing them to go to Camargo on the Rio Grande. If Zambrano's records of passports were checked, it would appear that Navarro's party was going south to acquire horses and mules or for other legitimate trading purposes. Upon leaving La Bahía, however, Navarro rode north to Louisiana. His party herded about forty-five horses and mules, of which José Antonio owned ten mules, six mares, and one stallion. Additional members joined the group the next day, Easter Sunday. Norato de Luna, a blacksmith from Aguascalientes who had lived in La Bahía for six years, knew about Navarro's expedition and was desperate to relieve the poverty of his family, left town without bothering to get a passport. Two more men joined the group at about the same time: Miguel de Arredondo, a soldier from the presidio at La Bahía, and Ermenegildo de la Cruz, known as "the invalid." Arredondo and Cruz brought eight to ten animals, increasing the total number of animals to about fifty-five.[30] As the group traveled north, Navarro must have felt a sense of exaltation. Along the wilderness trail to Carcasiu, he was a man among men of the rough outdoors. He was risking his life and the capital he had accumulated by embarking on a difficult, dangerous journey, as he later said, to help relieve the misery of his family and that of his companions.

Documents establish that Navarro's party returned to La Bahía by June 19. That night presidio officials arrested Navarro and charged him with the crime of having gone into the interior without a license. Four of his comrades were also arrested: Manuel and Nicolas Carvajal, Damián Rodríguez, and Norato de Luna. Although the accused were not directly charged with contraband activities, alleged illegal trade was a central part of the investigation that followed. Navarro and the others had passports authorizing them to go to the Villas del Norte (Northern Towns)—the settlements along the Rio Grande such as Camargo—not into the interior. Had Navarro's party actually gone there, officials on the Rio Grande would have made notations on their passports—and there were none.[31]

During the investigation in La Bahía, five of the six defendants gave testimony that was consistent, in fact almost identical, with the others. But there was a sixth member of Navarro's party who was a loose cannon. Pablo Ramírez, a youth from Reynosa, Tamaulipas, had joined Navarro at Carcasiu for the return trip to La Bahía. He provided authorities with an account of activities that completely contradicted his fellow defendants. While Navarro claimed that Indians stole their stock before they arrived at Carcasiu, and they were only able to obtain a few supplies for the return trip, Ramírez testified that Navarro's party arrived with many mules and horses that they traded for merchandise. The question of who was telling the truth became the focus of an inquiry lasting sixty days. Investigators questioned Ramírez first and clearly found him to be credible. That he was not charged with a crime nor confined, while the other five defendants were locked in the guardhouse, indicates his status as a trusted witness for the prosecution.

When prosecutor Joaquín Sáenz initiated the investigation on June 21, he learned that Ramírez had been employed by Pedro Villarreal of Refugio as a *vaquero* (cowboy). In January 1819, Villarreal had sent him with a teamster to get salt at La Sal del Rey. While carrying out this task, two men took him captive and forced him to help drive some horses to Carcasiu. After arriving, no longer needing his services, the two men freed Ramírez, leaving him stranded. The youth waited, hoping to encounter someone to travel with for a safe journey home. He saw Navarro's party "bring a herd of mules" to a "Frenchman who lived near Carcasiu," and he testified that they exchanged the mules for merchandise. He did not recall the exact number of animals, "but there were plenty." He also said that Rodríguez and the Carvajals sold some mules to Antonio Curbelo, who had been a prominent fugitive from Béxar since 1813. According to Ramírez, the amount of merchandise obtained by Navarro's party must have been considerable. He described pack animals loaded with goods. Two loads belonged to Navarro, one to Rodríguez, and the remaining two to the Carvajals. Luna seems to have made the long, arduous, journey for nothing more than a small hatchet.[32]

While the trading was going on at Carcasiu, major changes had taken place in La Bahía. Due to many complaints, Governor Martínez, by order of Arredondo, relieved Zambrano of his command and ordered his arrest; soldiers took him to Béxar on May 9. Prior to Navarro's return, Lieutenant Francisco García conducted a thorough investigation into Zambrano's activities and found evidence of the expedition. He denounced Navarro and his party, charged them with taking 200 horses to Louisiana, and suggested how the group could be caught in the act upon its return. When Navarro's party arrived near La Bahía in June, they must have learned about Zambrano's arrest and García's investigation and realized that they were in danger of being jailed for trading in contraband. Ramírez testified that on June 18 Navarro had left him behind at an oak grove on Manahuilla Creek. The next day, at noon, Manuel Carvajal returned and told Ramírez to present himself at the presidio, which he did that evening. Thus, when Sáenz asked Ramirez what happened to the loads of contraband merchandise, he could not say. The youth did tell Sáenz that the defendants had made a pact that when they went into town to present themselves, they would say that they had come from the Rio Grande, as authorized by their passports. If by chance it was discovered that they had gone into the interior, they would claim that what they had brought was nothing more than some *sobornales* (small items). When Navarro and his comrades walked into La Bahía late on June 19, they were immediately arrested.[33]

After Sáenz finished interrogating Ramírez, he promptly interrogated Navarro and his four associates. (Only Navarro's testimony will be examined in detail here because the testimony of the others was nearly identical to his.) About eight o'clock on the morning of June 22, Sáenz ordered Navarro to be brought from the guardhouse. In response to preliminary questions, Navarro said he was a native of San Antonio de Béxar, a resident of La Bahía, and a merchant by occupation. He admitted that the passports provided by Zambrano had authorized him and his associates to go to the Rio Grande, but this was a pretext to travel to the Louisiana border. Navarro said that poverty obligated them to commit this "act of weakness." He declared that his only purpose was to merchandise some goods to remedy the increasing destitution of his mother and family. Because of his lameness, he added, he could not labor for his subsistence. Consequently, he had gone on the trip, taking his own herd of ten mules, six mares, and a horse. These animals, with the other stock, had made a herd of about fifty-five head.[34]

Sáenz asked Navarro to what destination they were taking their horses and mules. In reply, Navarro told his version of the events of the expedition, contradicting Ramírez. He said his party's destination was Carcasiu and that while en route, they had the bad luck to be attacked along the San Jacinto River by Tahuacano Indians under the cover of night. The Indians took their entire herd, leaving them only their personal mounts, which had been tethered. When Navarro's group reached Carcasiu, their only desire was to obtain a small amount of supplies for their return trip. Sáenz challenged Navarro, demanding to know how could he say that the Tahuacano Indians took their horse herd when it had been established by Ramírez that the group arrived at Carcasiu with some of the mules and horses. Navarro said this was not true, and he denied the claim that he had delivered all of the horses to the Frenchman and Curbelo. Sáenz then took a different tack, asking how Navarro could deny the charge when it was certain that, in exchange for livestock, he and his associates purchased contraband goods, loaded them on two mules and three horses, and brought them back to La Bahía. He pressed Navarro to tell the truth because of the responsibility he had before God in view of the oath he had sworn. Navarro again denied the charges and repeated what he had already said.[35]

Sáenz then questioned Navarro about Ramírez's statement that he had been left at Monahuilla Creek for a time. This was a critical issue because it raised the possibility that merchandise had been hidden. Sáenz asked Navarro what purpose they had, after leaving Ramírez, to sneak into La Bahía the night before they presented themselves at the presidio. Navarro replied, according to the notary, that "the question is without basis"; after his departure from Carcasiu, he did not for one moment separate from any of his associates before his arrival at La Bahía—much less would he have done so when they were on guard against the enemy Indians. Navarro said that all members of his party returned with him except Ermenegildo de la Cruz and Miguel de Arredondo, who traveled by boat to Matagorda. With this, Navarro concluded and signed his testimony, affirming its truth by the oath he had taken.[36] Thus the first stage of the investigation, the taking of statements, ended with Navarro and his codefendants denying under oath every incriminating part of Ramírez's testimony.

The second stage of the investigation began immediately after Navarro's testimony, at ten o'clock in the morning on June 22. It involved a procedure called the *careo*, a confrontation where defendants stood face-to-face with their accusers and responded to their accusations. As Sáenz had done with the taking of the testimonies, he began the careo with Navarro's codefendants. Each one again denied Ramírez's claims, this time to his face. Sáenz brought Navarro and Ramírez together and had them sworn, and each described what they knew of the other. The confrontation was brief. Navarro stated that he had read Ramírez's testimony and disagreed with it because it was false. Sáenz asked Ramírez if he understood that Navarro had denied his testimony. Ramírez again affirmed that the particulars of what he had said were true. Since the confrontation was deadlocked, Sáenz concluded the investigation. He, notary José Galán, and Navarro signed a document detailing what had transpired at the careo. Ramírez, as an illiterate, marked it with an "X."[37]

Sáenz clearly believed Ramírez's testimony over that of Navarro and his associates. It is difficult to disagree with the prosecutor because Ramírez made a credible witness. Having no stake in the alleged contraband, Ramírez had no reason to lie about it. Moreover, as a youth he was unlikely to have been experienced in lying before the intimidating presence of formidable authorities. In addition, Ramírez had no reason to make false accusations against Navarro's party; they had befriended the shanghaied youth by giving him safe passage to La Bahía and sharing their provisions with him along the way. However, as a reward for his cooperation, Ramírez would soon be on the road home to Reynosa, where he disappeared from the pages of history, while Navarro would be on the road to Béxar, where he would be jailed. Ironically, if Navarro and his party did acquire a large quantity of merchandise, as Ramírez testified, the goods were never found. After the interrogations, Sáenz wrote, "regarding the five loads of contraband declared by Pablo Ramírez—the most energetic efforts, the searching of their houses and the houses of other suspects, have failed to uncover them."[38]

Local authorities such as Sáenz conducted the interrogation phase in criminal cases, but judgments of guilt or innocence and choices of punishment were made by higher authorities. Thus, at the conclusion of the interrogation, the file that held Navarro's fate was sent to Béxar. Governor Martínez then sent the material to Arredondo in Monterrey. In a cover letter, Martínez explained that "he awaited superior disposition about this case, and until such resolution he was keeping the subjects in jail." On July 15, the Navarro documents arrived in Monterrey, at the office of Assessor-Auditor of War Rafael Llanos, where Arredondo initialed them.[39] Llanos had the responsibility of recommending a decision in Navarro's case to Arredondo, but it would be a long time before a determination was made. Meanwhile, Navarro looked out on a narrow view of the world from behind prison bars. In his "Autobiographical Notes" he wrote that he lost the years of the flower of his youth exiled in Louisiana from 1813 to 1816.[40] Now he would spend more years mired in the Spanish judicial process.

Navarro, Luna, Rodríguez, and the Carvajals were marched to Béxar under guard. On their arrival they found the town in a state of utter devastation unlike anything ever seen before. On July 5, 1819, between six and seven o'clock in the morning, heavy rains brought a torrent of flood waters rushing down the San Antonio River. The swift rising waters had surged out of the riverbanks, destroying wooden houses, corrals, the new bridge connecting to the Alamo, and everything else that was not substantial and secure.[41] It was the greatest natural catastrophe ever experienced in the community. Flood damage to the royal facilities on Main Plaza forced Governor Martínez to order Navarro and his fellow prisoners locked up temporarily at Mission San Juan ten miles away. A few days later, they were moved to the jail in town. Navarro formally asked local officials to commute his arrest and that of Rodríguez, but this was denied because the case had already been sent to Arredondo.[42]

The transfer into town, though, was an enormous boon for Navarro because he then had family members only two blocks away. This allowed easier visitation, and the delivery of food and other things he needed.

With his imprisonment at Béxar in July 1819, Navarro began an eighteen-month period of limbo. In Monterrey, Llano and Arredondo ignored his case, placing it low on their list of priorities. Navarro's only consolation in the midst of his misfortune was the satisfaction of having courageously risked life, liberty, and property in an effort to benefit his family. From this point of view, his contraband expedition may have been a success. The merchandise that Ramírez said Navarro acquired in Carcasiu was never found, perhaps because he succeeded in conveying these goods to his family by coordinating their secret removal from La Bahía to Béxar.

Navarro suffered from the uncertainty surrounding the charges against him, and he fought for his freedom with pen and paper. The literacy he had painstakingly developed became of paramount importance. During 1820, he wrote four petitions. On May 1, he wrote to Arredondo that he was ruined because he was not able to engage in trade. He explained: "One can obviously see that I am incapable of taking up farming. By taking away from the work of trips in the province, I am left with no means to sustain myself, for I have not inch of farm land and have never learned this work."[43] Navarro's wording implies that he was no longer behind bars, but was restricted from traveling outside of Béxar. This is confirmed by his attendance at meetings of the city council. A month and a half passed with no response from Arredondo, so on June 18, Navarro wrote a brief follow-up petition. He admitted his guilt, saying that he had "inadvertently committed a fault," and he appealed for mercy and compassion from Arredondo. As "a good citizen . . . who had stumbled inadvertently [and was now] perishing under [the] hard weight of cauterizing punishment," he requested to "be set free so that I may procure some means to make a living." When Navarro's petition came to Arredondo's desk, he noted in the margin for Martínez to be informed of the conditions of Navarro's imprisonment.[44] Navarro's hopes must have soared on June 21 when he read a proclamation from King Ferdinand VII that extended pardons to certain prisoners, including contrabandists. He addressed his third petition to Martínez, asking him to send it to Arredondo, "so that in view of the exalted determination of the sovereign, he will decree my liberty from the prison I have suffered for one year and twenty-three days to this date."[45]

While Navarro waited for a response from Arredondo, dramatic political shifts occurred. At a meeting of the *ayuntamiento* (town council) of Béxar on July 26, 1820, the members opened a packet from the governor that contained a proclamation ordering the recently approved constitution of the Spanish monarchy be made public and allegiance sworn to it, which was done that same day.[46] In January 1820, soldiers had mutinied at Cádiz and began a rebellion that forced King Ferdinand VII to accept the liberal Constitution of 1812, which he had previously quashed. All officials were required to swear allegiance to the new constitution. In Béxar, some must have been mystified at pledging loyalty to a document they had never seen. The council immediately wrote to Arredondo asking for a copy, and they held no regular sessions for the next month while they waited for it. Navarro, however, must have been heartened by the news, for it revealed a crack in the absolutist authority of Spanish rule that could only improve his chances of winning freedom.

Implementation of the Constitution of 1812 led to Navarro's first participation in government. Arredondo sent instructions to the ayuntamiento to elect a new city council according to the Constitution, which required the popular election of electors whose votes in turn would select the alcalde and council members. Parishioners met on July 23, 1820, to select a junta of nine electors, one of whom was Navarro.[47] The junta in turn chose an alcalde, Erasmo Seguín; three councilmen, José Flores, Father José Darío Zambrano, and Juan Martín de Veramendi; and Vicente Gortari to be *síndico procurador* (city attorney).[48] The council thus became a mix of royalists and ex-insurgents, which seemed to indicate that a healing process was helping to soothe past animosities. More important for Navarro, when the Bexareños selected him as an elector they demonstrated confidence and respect for their long-suffering countryman. Despite the lingering charges against him, at this point he was free to go wherever he wished, as long as he did not leave Béxar.[49]

Navarro's case languished in Llano's office for nearly two years. It might have been resolved sooner had it not been for the charges against Juan Manuel Zambrano. The two cases were apparently linked as a result of both being charged with contraband activity at La Bahía. Higher authorities most likely wanted Zambrano's case to be resolved first and it was complicated by his Catholic Church affiliation. Any resolution of the charges against him had to be coordinated between military and church authorities. Ecclesiastical law required Zambrano to go to Monterrey for trial, but he used one excuse after another to avoid being sent out of Béxar. Governor Martínez became annoyed with the troublesome subdeacon and longed to see him stand trial in Monterrey. He denounced Zambrano's defiant temperament, advising Arredondo that the subdeacon's "arrogant character can only bring many problems to this government if he remains in this province." Navarro likely had no way to know how the delayed action in Zambrano's case affected him. He repeatedly complained about the uncertainty of his sentence to Arredondo and Martínez, but he received no reply to his first three petitions. Then in December 1820 he wrote a fourth petition to the governor that cut the Gordian knot. Navarro posed the reasonable question of whether the "eighteen months and nine days" confinement that he had suffered was appropriate for his offense. He reminded Governor Martínez that he had requested clemency based on a royal pardon proclaimed in Béxar on June 21, and added, "Upon this pardon I base my absolute right to liberty. At the end of Article 2 it says: 'this mercy is extended to contrabandists who introduced or removed prohibited items.'" [50]

Navarro asked Martínez to send his fourth petition to Arredondo for a decision. The missive landed on Arredondo's desk on January 30, 1821, when he initialed it, thus finally concluding Navarro's case. Officials based their decision on three factors: the petitions Navarro sent; the failure to ever locate the five loads of contraband; and the royal pardon that certainly covered Navarro and his fellow prisoners. Accordingly, Arredondo's order to Martínez reached Béxar by March 3, when the long-suffering Navarro was liberated from legal restraints and travel restrictions and restored to his full rights as a Spanish citizen. [51]

What Navarro did with his newfound freedom can only be guessed. Perhaps he worked with Veramendi's mercantile operation. In any case, he must have been very interested in, and possibly involved with, the important political events that unfolded as the year progressed and Mexico won its independence. From the vantage point of his family circle, Navarro enjoyed an invaluable opportunity to learn all sides of the issues the ayuntamiento considered. While rules prohibited council members from discussing their proceedings with nonmembers, there can be little doubt that José Ángel Navarro and Veramendi would have confided in José Antonio Navarro to some extent. As an insider, José Antonio could easily follow the conflicts and tensions between the governor and the council as each side endeavored to impose on the other its interpretations of constitutional provisions and decrees. The transformation of the ayuntamiento during the five years since his return from exile would have been evident. The council had evolved from a body subservient to the governor into a form of democratic government that acted boldly to achieve its goals. The understanding of how a constitutionally based government worked would provide a foundation for his political future. His in-depth knowledge of public affairs impressed his fellow Bexareños, and they would soon choose him for more important offices.

The Navarro family was well represented in the Béxar ayuntamiento of 1821. The council, with José Angel as the alcalde and Veramendi as a member, began to assert and even expand its authority. One bone of contention, both symbolic and substantive, was the issue of the ayuntamiento hall, previously confiscated by royal authorities. Immediately after taking their oaths of office, the members petitioned for the return of the facility that had been the council chambers since 1792. The structure was attached to the Casas Reales on the east side of Main Plaza.[52] Governor Manuel Salcedo had confiscated this property in 1812, evidently in retaliation for the council's support of the rebellion against him. In 1821, Arredondo approved the council's petition for the return of the hall and ordered Governor Martínez to comply with his decision. Navarro thus saw the ayuntamiento win a major victory at the expense of the governor, who was dismayed. Martínez considered the council to be encroaching on his personal domain since the disputed rooms were attached to the Casas Reales, which included not only the governor's office, but also his residence. Referring to Arredondo's indifference, a bitter Martínez declared that his superior officer would not care that if instead of residing in a governor's palace, "I and my family were put out on the street where I would be forced to present myself to His Majesty from a jacal."[53] The ayuntamiento's repossession of its chambers represented a victory, but the facility required extensive repairs, which José Antonio Navarro supervised on behalf of the council.[54]

Greater events soon occupied the Béxar council. In February 1821, Agustín Iturbide successfully led rebel forces against the Spanish crown's army. Apprised of royalist reversals, Bexareños waited to see what events might follow, perhaps doubting that any significant change would occur. Months passed. Then in July, José Ángel Navarro, as alcalde, received a mysterious message from Governor Martínez: "It is in the best service of the nation that tomorrow, the 17th, at eight o'clock in the morning that the ayuntamiento meet in this house of the governor to hold a consultation." The obvious urgency in Martínez's note did not seem to permit even one day's delay, so Navarro quickly notified the other council members, alerted military officers, and summoned parish priest Refugio de la Garza. When all had assembled in the council's chambers, Martínez opened and read a communication from Arredondo. It contained his direct order to proceed immediately to swear independence from Spain publicly and with pleasure, in accordance with Iturbide's proclamations. Arredondo reported that all Monterrey officials—military, civil, and ecclesiastical—had declared for independence from Spain at his headquarters. This astonishing news must have shaken the assembly of Bexareño leaders. A long discussion followed as the group considered this "grave and delicate" matter. All resolved to conform and comply with Arredondo's order, though José Ángel Navarro emphasized his support for Martínez. He explained that he would "only obey the governor's dispositions" because "he recognized the governor as the only legitimate authority in the province."[55]

Two days later, in the cool early hours of that July morning, the oath of allegiance took place. José Antonio Navarro and the residents of Béxar gathered in front of the Casas Reales to witness the dramatic ceremony. An image of Jesus Christ stood upon a table in front of the group, with a copy of the New Testament beside it. Initiating the ceremony, Father de la Garza, "publicly in the view of all," swore allegiance to the Kingdom of Mexico. Then, Father de la Garza administered the oath of independence as prescribed by Arredondo to all in order of rank, beginning with Governor Martínez, then fellow priest José Darío Zambrano, the ayuntamiento members, and the troops. The ceremony concluded with the singing of the Te Deum, followed by a salute of booming cannons and ringing church bells. With these actions, Bexareños cut their ties to Spain and brought Texas under the rule of the Mexican Empire. Within days of the ceremony, word arrived of the changing of the guard in Monterrey. Arredondo had resigned as commandant general of the eastern provinces and had been replaced with General Gaspar López.[56] Bexareños responded to this watershed event with great rejoicing.

The news of Mexican independence must have been riveting for José Antonio Navarro. As a close observer of the ayuntamiento, he saw how the momentous changes undermined the authority and weighed down the spirits of Governor Martínez, leaving him with a doubtful future. Though the governor endured criticism from an increasingly ungrateful citizenry, he nonetheless carried out his responsibilities with dignity, working toward an orderly transition from Spanish to Mexican rule. By September, he faced an aggressive council and found it difficult to govern. After five years at the helm of Texas, Martínez, tired and worn out, wrote to López that he had "no ambition to command."[57]

Among the problems an independent Mexico faced was underpopulation along its northern frontier, especially in Texas where the non-Indian population had never exceeded 4,000. Mexican liberals, aware of the expansion of the United States, argued in favor of foreign immigration that would bring in skilled, industrious settlers. Just prior to Mexican independence, Spain had tried to recruit foreigners; now

Mexico would follow suit.[58] About the same time that Navarro received his pardon and the Béxar council won the return of its hall, intriguing news had arrived from the Provincial Deputation in Monterrey. On behalf of Arredondo, who had not yet resigned, the deputation informed the Béxar council that it had approved Moses Austin's petition to bring 300 families to Texas. In addition to the permission given Austin, the deputation added that it had approved the establishment of the port of La Bahía de San Bernardo, as previously authorized by a royal decree.[59] Bexareños must have celebrated this news, for the establishment of such a port would advance their long sought goal of free trade. They believed that a port combined with the arrival of Anglo colonists would do much to improve Texas's economy. Tejano leaders would come to see these settlers as a "vested interest."[60] Texas appeared to be on the brink of dynamic advancements brought about by political reform, the establishment of a port, and the imminent arrival of Anglo colonists.

The next step in this chain of events was for Governor Martínez to send Erasmo Seguín to Natchitoches to tell Austin that his colonization petition had been approved. On his travels Seguín observed the area between Nacogdoches and Natchitoches, where a neutrality agreement signed in 1806 had created a legal no man's land. His critical eye was deeply troubled by the disorder he saw among the settlers there. Clearly alarmed, he reported to Martínez that events were moving forward at a pace that was too fast and "I would say scandalous."[61] No procedures for receiving immigrants existed, so there was no orderly way of settling them, designating lands, and securing titles. Leadership was lacking, Mexican authority was weak or nonexistent, and matters were rapidly spinning out of control. To complicate the situation further, Moses Austin died, and so, despite earlier misgivings, Stephen F. Austin decided to carry out his father's colonization dream. From Natchitoches he traveled to Béxar to survey Texas lands, to meet with Spanish officials, and to determine a location for his colony's headquarters.

The younger Austin was already thinking about bringing more colonists than the 300 that his father had requested. On July 1, 1821, he wrote a letter calculated to gain extensive publication in the United States that offered a tantalizing invitation to prospective colonists.[62] José Antonio Navarro and other leaders of Béxar had supported the original petition to bring 300 Anglo families to Texas, but they did not anticipate a tsunami of immigrants. In the United States, because of the economic problems brought about by the Panic of 1819, many sought to rebuild their lives by emigrating to Texas. Austin offered hope and opportunity to landless, debt-ridden North Americans at a time of great need; with

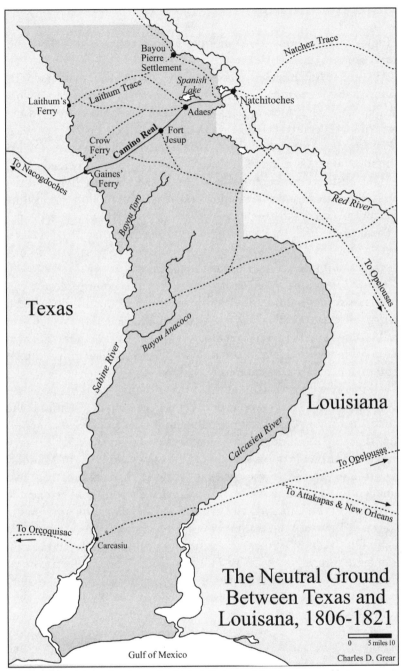

The Neutral Ground
Between Texas and
Louisana, 1806-1821

0   5 miles 10

Charles D. Grear

After the Louisiana Purchase, the United States and Spain were unable to agree on
a boundary between Louisiana and Texas. To avert a military clash, the two powers
agreed to establish a neutral ground free of settlement in 1806 (the two governments
were compelled to send joint military expeditions to the area in 1810 and 1812 to
expel settlers, however). While in exile, José Antonio Navarro lived just to the east
of Neutral Ground in Natchitoches, and in 1819 he participated in a contraband
expedition to Carcasiu (now Calcasieu Pass) on the eastern bank of the Sabine River.

a single letter he threw open a door to Texas through which thousands would soon pour.

Austin left Natchitoches accompanied by several Tejanos, including Seguín, and rode to meet with Martínez to confirm plans for his colony. On the way Austin took copious notes about the land, water, and timber. His party camped within a few miles of Béxar on August 12. In the morning, as they prepared to leave, jubilant Tejanos greeted them, bringing the news of independence.[63] The Bexareños provided Austin with the best accommodations they had. Because few of them had ever seen an American, José Antonio Navarro and the entire community probably turned out to see the son of Moses, upon whom the leadership of Béxar pinned high hopes for the betterment of Texas. Austin stayed in Béxar for ten days, taking time to outline his proposal and become acquainted with the citizens of the capital city.

Austin knew little Spanish at this time, but he communicated with Bexareños through Baron de Bastrop. Bastrop and Austin conversed in French and Bastrop translated into Spanish. In discussions with Governor Martínez and the ayuntamiento, Austin explored the possibilities of Anglo colonization. He also certainly mingled socially with prominent families and began to develop important relationships.

Navarro likely met Austin at this time, although no record exists of any introduction. Theirs would have been a meeting of like minds that was the beginning of a lasting relationship marked by personal friendship, shared political ideals, and material ambition. Austin wanted to rebuild his family fortune, lost through business failures in Missouri; Navarro also wanted to increase his family's interests that had been damaged during the previous revolutionary decade. Both would rise above mere fortune making and come to see that their true mission was to develop Texas economically and represent the interests of its people. Austin left Béxar on August 20 and traveled to La Bahía, continuing to familiarize himself with Texas and its people. From La Bahía, he returned to Natchitoches in October. By that time he was convinced of the wisdom of his father's dream of planting a colony in Texas.

At the same time Austin was making his plans, ships had begun sailing for the Texas coast. As soon as news of Mexican independence reached New Orleans in 1821, vessels had set out for Matagorda Bay loaded with merchandise for which there were no import procedures in place. The need for a system to collect import duties was immediate. A report from La Bahía to Governor Martínez revealed, for example, that one ship had brought silk taffeta from Barcelona, French handkerchiefs, hatchets, barrels of brandy, gin, clocks, Irish cloth, necklaces, combs, thread, cinnamon, crockery, and 130 pounds of tobacco. [64]

Navarro's mercantilist fervor must have been excited by this news, and he would have been overjoyed to learn that the ayuntamiento had chosen his brother-in-law, Veramendi, to be the first customs agent.[65] The position was not only a step up the political ladder for Veramendi, it meant that the Navarro-Ruiz-Veramendi family was ideally placed to profit from this flow of merchandise. Veramendi could not only collect taxes on it, he could buy choice items himself and provide access to mercantile opportunities for his relatives.

The value of merchandise passing through the port of La Bahía increased rapidly and became a major source of government revenue, far surpassing all other municipal tax sources combined. But the Béxar ayuntamiento received little of this bonanza: accounts for 1821 show no record of it. The council did receive 302 pesos early in the following year, but in February, General Gaspar López ordered that the ayuntamiento would receive no more of the customs income. Instead, the funds were to be used to support his troops. This created an unexpected crisis for the council, as alcalde José Ángel Navarro revealed in an accounting of the municipal government's income and payments for 1821. The council received 161 pesos and expended 136, leaving a balance of 25 pesos for 1822.[66] Without the customs revenue, the ayuntamiento had to rely on taxes levied on roundups of *mesteños* (wild horses and cattle) and fines collected.

It was in this dire situation that José Antonio Navarro took an active role in the government of Béxar under the Mexican Empire. In December 1821, Governor Martínez held an election for the first ayuntamiento to serve after independence. Following the same procedure employed in the previous election under the 1812 Spanish Constitution, electors selected by parish members gathered on December 24 at the council chambers to cast their ballots. For first and second alcalde, they picked José María de Jesús Salinas and Juan José Flores, respectively. They also elected José Antonio Navarro to be the *regidor* (first-ranking councilman) of the eight elected.[67] Although Navarro thus occupied an influential position, council minutes reveal only a few of his opinions and actions. One was his response to the lax attitude of some members toward their duties. Early in 1822, Navarro also urged the importance of secrecy about council meetings, which was ironic in light of his own access to earlier council deliberations through his family connections. He said that details of the ayuntamiento's resolutions in regular and special meetings had been revealed, for he had heard them discussed in public conversations. When another member remarked that the council was plagued by member absences, the ayuntamiento resolved that a twenty-five-peso fine would be levied against anyone who revealed the council's secrets, and it approved a five peso fine for unexcused absences.[68] During the year, Navarro presided over the council as an acting alcalde, and he served as an arbitrator, a judge in water management disputes, robberies, and cattle poaching.

The new ayuntamiento, having taken its oath on December 24, immediately took up where the previous one left off—challenging the governor, who did his best to retain control. The Béxar council met in either a *cabildo ordinario* or a *cabildo extraordinario* (regular or special session), and the first alcalde or the ranking member present usually presided. However, the governor could preside over any meeting if he chose to, and Martínez chose to direct all the new council sessions but one through January 1822. Nonetheless, he received no respite. The council's opening salvo was to request the removal of Governor Martínez, accusing him of bad government management and causing damage to the citizenry. In addition, the council took up the cause of persons whose property had been confiscated in 1813. Its view was that the confiscations were illegal under the provisions of the 1812 Spanish Constitution, and that a September 1820 decree from the Spanish Cortes providing for the return of confiscated property should be enforced.[69]

Another top priority for Navarro and his fellow council members was the matter of selecting two delegates to represent Texas in the Constituent Congress at Mexico City. This body would write a suitable constitution and select an emperor for the new Mexican Empire. Once again, Navarro participated in the selection process. As with the election of municipal officers, electors chose the congressional representatives. The ayuntamientos of Béxar and La Bahía would choose electors, who together with the Béxar council would select the delegates. The ayuntamiento chose José Antonio Navarro to be Béxar's district elector, noting that he "esteemed independence [and] demonstrated good conduct and integrity." After deliberating, Navarro, the other electors, and the ayuntamiento chose Father Refugio de la Garza as their congressional representative: Erasmo Seguín was made the alternate in case De la Garza could not serve. The council members wrote detailed instructions for their delegate. They also compiled a long list of requests that outlined their primary concerns: 4,000 troops with mounts and supplies, free trade by land and sea, assignment of the lands of the Valero and Concepcion missions to the ayuntamiento for its support, separation of civil government from the military, distribution of land to residents and immigrants at reasonable prices, return of property taken in 1813, and reimbursement of residents for previous voluntary and forced loans. On February 2, the council gave De la Garza some money for travel expenses, taken from import duties. He left for Mexico City the next day, but Seguín did not go.[70]

The need for an elementary school occupied the attention of the council during 1822. A year earlier, the ayuntamiento had optimistically expected a school to be opened that would replace "informal teaching sessions in the streets and plazas." Navarro and his colleagues worked toward this goal. During two of its January meetings, the council agreed to open an elementary school with Domingo Bustillos as schoolmaster. Bustillos agreed to serve as the children's teacher, "insofar as my knowledge and funds permit." Veramendi collected some donations for the school, and Navarro, "despite his illness," was charged with making up for the months not covered by the donations. In March, the council agreed to pay a schoolmaster from the *mesteño* funds.[70] Despite these resolutions supporting education, the problems of raising adequate funds and keeping a competent teacher seemed insoluble. In October, the school issue again came before the council but, as before, discussion of the problem was deferred until the next meeting. Given the lack of funding, it was practically impossible for the community to maintain a school, and the issue did not appear again on the council's agenda for the remainder of the year.

On March 21, 1822, second alcalde José Flores left the ayuntamiento and did not return until the following August. As first councilman, Navarro filled the vacant post. The following week, the council led by Navarro pointed out to the governor the problem of squatters settling illegally between the Sabine and Red rivers. They demanded to know how Martínez would "inform the foreigners of their obligation to present themselves to the government to adjudicate the lands on which they wished to settle." In fact, the ayuntamiento was using this issue as a means to pressure Martínez to leave office. The members must have known that the governor did not have the military means to control illegal immigration across the Sabine. Indeed earlier in March the commandant at La Bahía informed Martínez that his soldiers were lacking muskets and pistols, and Béxar troops could not have been any better armed.[71]

One of Navarro's responsibilities as acting alcalde was to preside over the legal process of conciliation, which was designed to resolve civil cases and minor disputes. The system, established by the Laws of the Indies in 1772, called for *hombres buenos* (prominent citizens) to serve as arbitrators. The process was evidently not utilized in Béxar until the reestablishment of the Spanish Constitution of 1812, which contained provisions for the second alcalde to serve as the conciliatory judge. When someone brought a dispute before the judge, normally he would appoint two leading citizens—one to hear the complainant and the other to hear the accused. Both would discuss the case and reach a recommendation that the judge would use to render a decision. Many cases resulted in a compromise rather that a clear verdict in favor of one party or the other. Compromise had been an essential part of frontier justice during the Spanish colonial period, and records show that it continued to be an important means of settling civil disputes.[72]

In the first conciliatory case for which Navarro served as the judge, Juana Francisca de los Santos Coy demanded 415 pesos from Miguel Martínez. She claimed he owed this to her because he had taken this amount from her husband, Geronimo Treviño, after he died on his way to Louisiana. To hear both sides of the dispute, Navarro named, as hombres buenos Gaspar Flores to represent Francisca and Erasmo Seguín to speak for Martínez. Navarro read their opinions and declared that it was not proved that 415 pesos were actually taken. In the discussions with the hombres buenos, however, Martínez's wife had admitted that she received 100 pesos from the deceased's funds. Consequently, Navarro decreed that the accused pay that amount to the complainant. Both parties agreed to abide by the court's decision and promised not to continue the dispute.[73]

Conciliation cases included a wide variety of complaints. In addition to disputes over money, there were conflicts over debts, unauthorized use of draft animals, personal injury, and insults. Interestingly, Navarro sat in judgment of his mother-in-law, Xaviera Flores, without recusing himself. Leonarda Vásquez demanded that Flores return a horse that she said she bought from a Lipan Apache. She refused to surrender the horse and requested a judicial determination by means of hombres buenos. Navarro named José Dario Zambrano to represent Vásquez and Seguín for Flores, then ruled against his mother-in-law after listening to their opinions. He determined that no Indian had stolen the horse and it was to be returned to Vásquez. In addition, he instructed Xaviera Flores not to buy branded horses that had not been acquired in an honest sale. As a consolation, perhaps to keep peace in the family, he awarded her two pesos.[74]

Navarro's term ended in August with the return of second alcalde Flores to the ayuntamiento; however, Navarro later experienced other aspects of the conciliation system. On many occasions he served as an hombre bueno, and once he was the complainant in a dispute over the services of a servant. Navarro, it seems, had temporarily sold the services of one José Rocque Charles to Josefa de la Garza, but Charles left the employ of De la Garza before completing the term of his service. Judge Baron de Bastrop, based on the findings of the hombres buenos, determined that Charles was to make up the time that he owed on Navarro's behalf, amounting to a value of thirty-eight pesos, within three months. But if he ran away, Navarro would be responsible for paying De la Garza one-half of the thirty-eight pesos. Navarro demanded that De la Garza acknowledge that the original debt was now paid in full. In response, Bastrop appended a note that Charles had fulfilled his obligation.[75] This incident demonstrates that servants were often debt peons rather than free, hired persons. The distinction would be important in another dispute over a servant involving Navarro.

While he was acting second alcalde, another of Navarro's duties had been to act as liaison between the ayuntamiento and Governor Martínez. In this capacity, Navarro immediately seized the initiative to assert council power at the expense of the Governor's authority. He wrote to Martínez on March 29 about thefts by soldiers, informing him that the ayuntamiento was taking action to prevent such robberies and putting pressure on him to support its action. In one instance someone reported that Antonia Cantú had fresh meat in her house, which aroused suspicion because cows were few in number. Navarro went to Cantú's house, questioned her, and determined that Enrique Guerrero, son of a Béxar veteran soldier, had given her the meat. Exercising council authority, Navarro directed Guerrero to appear before him. Guerrero said that his son, Patricio, and Seferino Aguero had killed an unbranded cow. Navarro told Martinez that he would "proceed against the two men involved in the crime with all the rigor of justice," which would "serve as an example to others of similar conduct." Navarro added that he hoped the governor would "carry out the consequences that I judged appropriate for the soldier Enríquez, who had dared to allow his son and the other person to rob." He pointedly added that this incident was proof that soldiers, as well as civilians, were harming the community and that thefts deserved severe punishment. This forceful letter shocked Martínez, who quickly replied that he doubted the extent of Navarro's authority. Navarro responded that the departure of Flores had elevated him to the office of second alcalde, and as such he would now "be in charge of the administration of justice."[76]

Having established his readiness to confront the governor, most of Navarro's subsequent communications with Martínez were more perfunctory. For example, he provided the governor with quarterly lists of birth, deaths, and marriages. In turn, the governor relayed to Navarro numerous decrees received from the congress in Mexico City, and Navarro replied to acknowledge receipt of the decrees and convey the council's views on them. On June 18, 1822, news arrived that the Mexican Empire now had an emperor. The ayuntamiento met in a special session with Navarro serving as first alcalde in the absence of José Salinas, who would soon return and have the unpleasant duty of writing to the governor about Navarro's accusations of robbery against soldiers of the Alamo Company. But on this day, Navarro read a letter from Martínez with an enclosed decree saying that congress had proclaimed Agustín de Iturbide as emperor. The long-suffering Martínez got his wish a few months later when Iturbide relieved the governor of his command and approved the nomination of José Felix Trespalacios in his place. Trespalacios arrived by mid-August, and the final curtain fell on the Spanish colonial period in Béxar as Martínez, the last Spanish governor of Texas, rode out of town toward Mexico City.[77]

Although Navarro had reestablished his merchant enterprise before Veramendi became the tax collector at La Bahía, the end of his term as alcalde and the departure of Martínez apparently created a good opportunity to take advantage of his brother-in-law's position. On September 5, 1822 he obtained permission from the Foreigners Administration, that is, from Veramendi, to take goods wherever he wished in Coahuila. Navarro was absent from ayuntamiento meetings from September through November, suggesting that his trading venture lasted almost three months. He was again in attendance at council meetings in late November, near the end of his term of office and just in time to enjoy the annual festivities surrounding the feast day of Our Lady of Guadalupe, celebrated throughout Mexico on December 12.[78] Each year Bexareños organized solemn and joyous events, to celebrate the occasion, which was both a profoundly religious and a high-spirited time. Navarro, enjoying his political and economic success, must have looked forward to what resembled a carnival. Bullfights were a main feature and to create an arena, Bexareños formed a circle around the plaza, perhaps with thrills and excitement similar to the running of the bulls in Pamplona, Spain. Vendors had booths for games and to sell food. Games of chance were permitted including card games, *tabla, boliche* (a bowling game), and other diversions. Perhaps slack rope walkers entertained with acrobatics and risqué comedy, as Zebulon Pike had seen in Presidio Rio Grande in 1807.[79]

Despite the impending Guadalupe festival, a cloud of apprehension about events in Mexico City must have troubled the ayuntamiento. On December 5, Navarro and the other members read a decree from Iturbide saying that he had dissolved the congress to which all Bexareños had solemnly sworn allegiance earlier in the year. The consequences of the emperor's astonishing action could only be guessed at. The Béxar council anxiously awaited a report from Refugio de la Garza, their representative in the now defunct congress. De la Garza had arrived in Mexico City at the end of March, and in April he had written an enthusiastic report to the Béxar ayuntamiento. In it, he noted that "25,000 permanent veteran troops are destined for the ports and frontiers . . . of these 5,300 will be for Texas—as soon as funds can be found."[80] Funds were not found, however, and the troops never arrived. As a member of the Constituent Congress, De la Garza participated in crowning Iturbide emperor on July 21, 1822. Sadly, the new regime proved unable to solve Mexico's problems; it remained isolated, bankrupt, and stymied by the monumental problem of molding a nation from peninsular Spaniards, Creoles, persons of mixed race, and unassimilated Indian groups.

Whatever the political maneuvering taking place in Mexico City might be, life for the moment went on as usual in Béxar. On December 12, Navarro and the other council members met briefly and then attended the festival of Our Lady of Guadalupe. Navarro's term as a councilman ended on December 24, when popularly selected electors chose the ayuntamiento for 1823, with Ignacio Pérez and Baron de Bastrop as the first and second alcaldes, respectively. Again the Navarro family circle was represented, with José Ángel Navarro and Veramendi joining the council. Five days later José Antonio Navarro and Margarita welcomed a second daughter, María Gertrudis Josefa Navarro, to their family. She was baptized on January 1, 1823, in a happy event that heralded the start of an even brighter phase of her father's life.[81]

CHAPTER THREE

The Making of a Legislator, 1822–28

A T THE END OF José Antonio Navarro's term as a councilman
in late 1822, disturbing news began arriving from Mexico City. At
its first meeting on January 2, 1823, the new ayuntamiento read denunciations from imperial officials of "the traitor Santa Anna."[1] General
Antonio López de Santa Anna had initiated a military insurrection at
Veracruz and proclaimed a republic in early December. His efforts, combined with those of other leaders, such as Guadalupe Victoria and José
Antonio de Echávarri, forced Iturbide from the imperial throne. Then
the Plan de Casa Mata, a manifesto that abolished the Mexican Empire
and opened the way for the creation of a new, liberal government was
issued.[2] How Navarro reacted to these events is not known directly, but
there seems little doubt that he would have shared the sentiments of
his fellow Bexareños, and their response was clear. Military and civilian
leaders at first refused to conform to the model of decentralized government promoted by the Plan de Casa Mata. The dramatic actions that
followed in Béxar have not been well reported in Texas historiography,
so they will be examined here in detail. The events are critical because,
although his role must often be presumed, it was through them that
José Antonio Navarro became actively involved in reshaping Texas.

Perhaps Bexareños hesitated to support the Plan de Casa Mata immediately because they were uncertain about the political outcome of
the revolution in Mexico City. They must have been reluctant to yet
again renounce vows of allegiance. During 1822 the people of Béxar
had sworn solemn oaths of allegiance to independence, to the Mexican
Empire, to the Constituent Congress, and to various juntas. Bexareños likely were hearing rumors and receiving many conflicting reports
about the political changes in the national capital, reports that understandably would have made them even more cautious. In the midst of
uncertainty, the ayuntamiento, as the municipal government of Béxar,

provided an anchor of stability for its citizens. Its loyalty, however, was about to be challenged.[3]

At the end of March, General Santa Anna sent a proclamation to the inhabitants of the Interior Provinces denouncing Iturbide and threatening them with military action if they did not accept his plan for a liberal, federal government.[4] Preparing to back up his words, he moved his military forces north to San Luís Potosí. In the Eastern Interior Provinces, which included Texas, Commandant Gaspar López, an Iturbide loyalist, resigned his position. Felipe de la Garza, brother of the Béxar priest, Refugio de la Garza, replaced López in April. Reports that leaders in Saltillo and Monterrey had accepted Santa Anna's federal plan did not impress the Bexareños. They took their oaths to the empire seriously and balked at renouncing them. This attitude was undoubtedly influenced by Governor José Félix Trespalacios, an Iturbide appointee. On March 21, he wrote to López enclosing a petition demonstrating that the Bexareños unanimously remained loyal to Iturbide. The Texas governor made his position clear: "The ayuntamiento of this capital, the officers, troops, the respectable clerics, and all the citizens signed below . . . with an oath they have taken in the face of the empire that they will obey no other orders than those of the Emperor Agustín I."[5] This list of citizens has never been found, but there can be little doubt that it included the signature of José Antonio Navarro.

The next day the Béxar ayuntamiento wrote to the Provincial Governing Council of Monterrey in reply to its memo of March 10 reporting that it had accepted the Plan de Casa Mata. The Bexareños said, "we have no reluctance in manifesting to you that for no reason can we support the same sentiments as yours because of the solemn oaths and votes with which this ayuntamiento is anchored to the government and legitimate authorities of this emperor." In La Bahía, the ayuntamiento, military officers, the priest, and several prominent citizens met at the house of presidio commander Francisco García and signed a statement swearing undying loyalty to Iturbide "to the last drop of blood."[6] Mexican republicans to the south saw the Tejano leaders' act of principled resolution as a betrayal, and it would take the next three months to resolve their differences. Communication was made especially difficult by the great distances that meant letters were always a week or two behind events.

Soon after their heartfelt assurances of loyalty to the empire, Bexareño leaders realized that they had made a significant mistake and had isolated themselves from the rest of the nation. Trespalacios understood the situation, knew his position as Texas governor was untenable, and prepared to leave. Upset ayuntamiento members were forced to provide substantial explanations to Béxar residents to justify their a reversal in accepting the Plan de Casa Mata. Anticipating Trespalacios's departure, Béxar leaders organized a *junta gubernativa* (governing council) of their own. The members were the Baron de Bastrop, Erasmo Seguín, José Francisco Ruiz, Juan de Castañeda, Francisco Roxo, and Juan Manuel Zambrano. On April 15 the junta formally accepted the Plan de Casa Mata, but not without fiery opposition from Zambrano. Outraged that his colleagues had violated their oaths by accepting the Plan de Casa Mata, he lambasted them with torrents of verbal abuse and angry accusations. Four days later he resigned from the junta.[7]

The Béxar junta at its organization invited La Bahía to send a representative. On April 21, the alcalde of the ayuntamiento in La Bahía, José Miguel Alderete, sent a terse note to Trespalacios. He acknowledged receiving the Bexareño acceptance of the Plan de Casa Mata, but he declared that his "ayuntamiento has no idea what is in the plan" and asked that a copy be sent. Four days later, La Bahía's council asked Francisco García to represent them on the Béxar junta and to determine the current state of affairs. This was the same García who previously spoke of dying with guns blazing against liberal constitutionalists. Later, he sensibly took a less dramatic approach to maintaining his royalist honor and simply refused the request. La Bahíans then chose well-known merchant José Antonio Navarro to replace García. Revealing their uncertainty, they instructed Navarro to "learn what is the present state of affairs of the State and report them immediately" and also to "investigate by whatever means possible what the general will of the nation is regarding the proposed system of government."[8]

By late April 1823, leaders in Béxar had come to terms with the political reality that the empire had been overthrown. On April 15, after the junta declared its acceptance of the Plan de Casa Mata, other civil, military, and ecclesiastical functionaries at Béxar did likewise. When the news arrived at Monterrey that Texas was no longer in rebellion, people "celebrated with great relief and to the sound of ringing bells." Trespalacios left Béxar on May 3, promising disingenuously that he would "energetically represent the needs of Texas in Monterrey." It was well that he did leave, for Santa Anna wrote him a threatening letter from San Luís Potosí: "Will your province refuse to yield to the general will [of the nation]? You well know the weakness of your province . . . and there is no possibility for you to resist the troops I will speedily bring against you."[9]

The departure of Trespalacios did not bring peace in Béxar, where the junta tried to settle conflicts fomented by Zambrano. Never one to bury the hatchet, he appeared before the ayuntamiento on June 6, 1823, asking that the junta be dissolved.[10] Of course the members ignored Zambrano because the junta performed the functions of the governor and could not responsibly relinquish that role until the vacancy was filled. Adding to the political turmoil, there would be no elected executive of Mexico for the junta to address until Guadalupe Victoria took office as president in October 1824. Thus, the junta would have to cope with national leaders, such as Santa Anna, who had threatened military action against their province. Because the junta in Béxar was the only governing body in Texas that had proclaimed in favor of the Plan de Casa Mata, it was not tainted by pledges of loyalty to the defunct Mexican Empire. Its future course was made clear when Refugio de la Garza wrote to the Béxar ayuntamiento from Mexico City in May 1823 that the Congress had decided the national government would be a federal republic.[11] The Béxar junta could demonstrate that Texas was a member in good standing of the new Republic of Mexico and thus lead the way in mending fences.

On June 11, junta members Baron de Bastrop, Juan de Castañeda, Erasmo Seguín, and José Antonio Navarro, utilizing their combined skills of political expression, finished drafting two memos explaining the loyalist statements made by the Béxar ayuntamiento in March. They directed a blunt communication to Santa Anna explaining their actions and accusing him of overreacting, especially with the letter he sent to Trespalacios on May 6 threatening military action. Justifying their signed statements of loyalty to Iturbide on March 21, the junta members explained that a lack of necessary information obliged them to take this mistaken first step, and that they quickly took "the glorious second step, on April 15, when they accepted the Plan formulated at Casa Mata." They concluded by asserting that Santa Anna had rushed to judgment by threatening the Tejanos without determining whether their actions were criminal.[12]

The junta's second memo was addressed to José Ignacio García Illueca, the secretary of state for the interim government, and it presented a most careful and reasoned argument for the political rehabilitation of Texas. On April 28, 1823, Illueca had sent a scathing denouncement of Trespalacios to representatives of Nuevo León. He said that the governor had betrayed his country and that an overwhelming military force was being assembled so that "the rebellious ex-governor to Texas will be pursued and routed in every quarter." Navarro and the other junta members responded to Illueca's denunciation with a lengthy, detailed explanation of their province's "strong commitment to the liberal political system for independence," beginning in 1810. They expressed their "astonishment and sadness to be treated along with the governor as a traitor" because of their declarations of loyalty to Iturbide in March. The junta never intended to separate itself from the rest of Mexico, or to recognize a foreign power, and it affirmed its continuous fidelity, which Santa Anna had questioned and then imperiously demanded in terms that were "horribly described in Government periodicals and public papers." The Tejanos feared anarchy and only acted out of caution when the true situation was not yet known, so none of them deserved "the dishonorable epithet of traitor."[13] Having explained themselves to both Santa Anna and Illueca, the Béxar junta also sent memos expressing their contrition to the neighboring authorities, including Commandant General Felipe de la Garza and the councils of Monterrey, Monclova, and Nuevo León.[14]

Leaving the governor's authority in the hands of a junta—a citizens' council—in the best of times was a stressful, extraordinary measure, and even more so when the citizens were suspected rebels. The junta members probably felt some relief when orders arrived from Mexico City that dissolved Béxar's junta and named Lieutenant Colonel Luciano García as the interim Texas governor. By July 8, García had arrived in Béxar to assume the governorship of Texas, and on that day Juan Martín de Veramendi wrote to him saying that the junta had now ceased to exist.[15] After a six-month period of political upheaval, the Béxar government finally returned to its previous state, with the ayuntamiento as the local governing body responsible to the governor.

García's tenure as governor was brief, for his position was abolished in September, but during it he made several important decisions that greatly affected Texas and José Antonio Navarro. At about the same time García arrived to take office, Stephen F. Austin returned to Béxar, where he was reunited with his brother, James E. B. Austin, who had lived for a year with the Seguíns. More importantly, Stephen spent most of the month of July conferring with supporters of his colony. No doubt many hours were spent hours with the Baron de Bastrop, who was appointed by García on July 17 as the first commissioner to issue land titles for Austin's colony. Austin must also have found time to pursue his relations with Ruiz, Veramendi, and the Navarros, especially the rising political star of Béxar, José Antonio Navarro.[16]

In September, García informed the ayuntamiento that he had received orders from the supreme executive power that the civil and military governments were to be separated in all the provinces. Thus, he was transferring his authority on an interim basis to the first alcalde of Béxar, Manuel Iturri Castillo.[17] The ensuing year was the start of a new era for Mexico. In October 1824, congressional delegates finished their tremendous task, and the Constitution of the Republic of Mexico was proclaimed. Under it, Texas was combined with Coahuila to make a single state with its governor headquartered in Saltillo, the capital. As 1824 came to an end, it was also the close of an era in Béxar, marked by the death of Zambrano, who was the embodiment of unreconstructed royalist sentiment.[18] With the passing of Zambrano a turbulent life ended, much of which had been spent in conflict with fellow Tejanos. Many who had suffered the tongue-lashings he was quick to unleash, as well as lawsuits and physical attacks, may not have been sad to see him go. Certainly Navarro was among them.

During 1824, Navarro had conducted his activities in the private sector, although he was in close touch with ayuntamiento affairs as demonstrated by his signature on various pieces of council correspondence. He exercised his ability as an advocate by representing Peter Longueville (who was allegedly an associate of filibuster Philip Nolan, an American mustanger and filibuster in Texas in the 1790s) in a land dispute. Similarly, he continued representing José Ángel Navarro in a request filed in November 1823 on his behalf for concessions of land and irrigation water that were being distributed from the extinguished Mission San José. At the same time, both Navarro and Veramendi, as agents for Ruiz, made a request for land and water from the same mission. That request was approved in 1825. While evidence of Navarro's role in Texas commerce is lacking for 1824, he probably worked with his family members, including his brother Eugenio and Veramendi, in what must have been a cooperative mercantile operation. Between the years 1823 and 1825, as a lieutenant in the Flying Company of the Internal Provinces, Eugenio received permits to transport goods from Béxar to Coahuila. Most likely these goods were introduced into Texas from Louisiana and needed to clear customs at La Bahía through Veramendi as administrator.[19]

Between 1825 and 1827, information about Navarro is limited to three subjects: an abortive attempt to approve him as the Béxar council secretary, his mercantile efforts, and a brief part he played in the Fredonian Rebellion. The ayuntamiento in 1825 named him secretary, but the appointment ran into complications. Navarro could count on strong family support in the ayuntamiento, since electors in the December 1824 election chose Veramendi to be first alcalde and Luciano Navarro, José Antonio's brother, as a councilman.[20] Trouble arose because during the previous year the ayuntamiento had no secretary. Hilario de la

Peña had served as the scribe, providing a modest service at a salary of fifteen pesos per month, but the council clearly preferred to have Navarro's superior writing skills and political expertise. On February 3, the ayuntamiento met and agreed to name a more capable secretary. But when the appointment of Navarro, at a monthly salary of twenty-five pesos, was reported to Governor Rafael González, he responded with a strong reprimand. First, he demanded that the council observe the chain of command by communicating with him through the political chief that had been appointed for the district of Béxar. Next, he wanted to know if the previous secretary had been removed from his position and what salary he had earned. Citing an 1813 Spanish law, he said a secretary could not be removed without permission from the superior government, and that a twenty-five-peso salary would not be allowed if it exceeded what had been paid the previous year.[21]

Informed of the governor's decision, Navarro resigned from the position. No doubt he objected to the alternative of working as a mere "scribe" at half the salary he had expected. He received no support from Béxar political chief José Antonio Saucedo, who sided with the governor. Saucedo himself had worked as ayuntamiento secretary in 1821 for about eight pesos per month. He told the governor that the services provided by Peña were adequate and that, moreover, the poverty-stricken council had been hard pressed to pay his salary of fifteen pesos per month. Memos continued to pass between the governor and the ayuntamiento encouraging Navarro to accept the title of secretary, not scribe, but for fifteen pesos per month. Navarro refused each appeal, the last of which occurred in June 1825, four months after he was first appointed.[22]

Records show that even before Navarro resigned his position as secretary he had made a living by importing and selling merchandise. Close cooperation between Navarro and Veramendi family members is evident. Veramendi sent copies of accounts for the months of June, July, and August 1825 that included the activities of the Navarro brothers—José Ángel, José Antonio, and Eugenio.[23] Their interwoven mercantile networks are manifest in these financial records. José Antonio's mingling of trade and political alliances would soon extend beyond his family circle to include Stephen F. Austin, who became a trusted associate with whom he shared common interests.

The greatest concerns of Béxar leaders in 1825–26 involved immigration from the United States under the national and state colonization laws enacted in 1824 and 1825. These laws worked together and allowed foreigners other than Austin to become empresarios (land agents or contractors) and governed their actions. One of the most notable of these empresarios was Haden Edwards, whose pugnacious attitude and aggressive actions precipitated a colonization dispute known as the Fredonian Rebellion. Like all empresarios, he was to uphold land grants certified by the Spanish and Mexican governments, provide an organization for the protection of all colonists in the area, and receive a land commissioner appointed by the Mexican government. He arrived in Nacogdoches on September 25, 1825, and informed all landowners that they would have to present evidence of their claims or their land would be forfeited. This naturally offended the older settlers. Edwards would only benefit from the arrival of new settlers because he received five leagues of land for every one hundred families after settlement, thus he had an interest in dispossessing the existing land owners. This he did by requiring all landowners to show evidence of their titles or forfeit their land. The long-time residents in the area around Nacogdoches where he was authorized to settle people were mainly Tejano and unable to meet his demands and thus lost their lands. In this way Edwards was instrumental in pitting the long-time residents of Nacogdoches against the newcomers.

His actions caused alarm in Austin's colony, Béxar, Saltillo, and even Mexico City. The situation deteriorated when Saucedo overturned the election of Edwards' handpicked alcalde. Edwards refused to accept this decision, so Saucedo sent troops to Nacogdoches under the command of Lieutenant Colonel Mateo Ahumada, José Antonio Navarro's brother-in-law. About ten days after Ahumada left Béxar, the Edwards faction responded with a Declaration of Independence signed on December 21, 1826, proclaiming the Republic of Fredonia.[24]

Navarro used his influence to calm fears inflamed by Edwards's agitation and by Ahumada's troops. At the request of Saucedo, he addressed a letter to the residents of Nacogdoches. Austin wrote similar notes at the same time to discourage the Fredonian rebels and their sympathizers, urging restraint and moderation since he feared that the Nacogdoches rebellion would reflect badly on his own colonists. That Navarro joined Austin in this important assignment showed his ascending political influence; he was a man to whom the troubled people of Nacogdoches would listen. The tone of his letter was conciliatory: "Friends, this is not the time to be preoccupied and ignorant of the agitation of four malevolent adventurers who have tried to compromise good men and peaceful citizens. It is those who have come to the attention of the government, which is why troops are on the march to that place as of today, December 13, to maintain order." He added, "If some malefactors want to exaggerate and discredit the troops, saying they are going to fight and rob and otherwise do wrong to the residents—Anglo Americans as well as Mexicans—tell them that they are lying, that the Mexican troops have no need to rob or do any harm to maintain themselves." Furthermore, Saucedo was going to Nacogdoches "with no other purpose than, like a father, to listen to your complaints." Navarro closed by saying that he was a "compatriot who knows you, esteems you, and will never deceive you."[25] At the end of January 1827, Ahumada and his troops arrived in Nacogdoches, and the revolution ended with the rebels fleeing into Louisiana.

Navarro and Austin had also been communicating about commercial matters as they worked to end the Fredonian Rebellion. Navarro often prevailed upon Austin to act as a purchasing agent for goods from New Orleans. On February 27, 1827, shortly after the rebellion was put down, Austin wrote to Navarro from San Felipe to acknowledge receipt of $130 and an order sent for seventy-five pounds of coffee. He continued, "The rest of the money that I have . . . I kept to pay for merchandise from Orleans and I will pay what is lacking or short." Austin also reported the price he thought an acquaintance would accept for corn so that Navarro could bargain effectively for it. Although burdened with the demands of his colony, Austin obviously wanted to curry favor with Navarro by assisting his mercantile operation. He added, "If a good assortment of clothing arrives I shall advise you and you can command me frankly and with liberty as a sincere friend in anything that is of use and I shall at all times take great pleasure in executing your orders, if you stand on ceremony I shall be very sorry."[26] It is evident that the two men had forged an economic as well as political relationship by 1827. When Austin called Navarro "a sincere friend," he obviously considered Navarro to be both a personal ally and a valued supporter of his colonization enterprise. This would prove critically important for both men as Texas continued to develop.

A divisive issue emerged in Texas as Anglos from the southern United States settled in Austin's colony and elsewhere. The Mexican Constitution of 1824 stated only general principles pertaining to immigration and land distribution, leaving the details to state governments. It did not address the issue of slavery. *Coahuiltexanos* approved a constitution for Coahuila and Texas by 1827 as well as the 1825 state colonization law. A looming influence during these proceedings was Austin, who tirelessly promoted the importation of slaves into Texas from the United States. He contended that the South's prosperous cotton economy should extend beyond the immigrant colonies of Texas into Coahuila. Important

*Stephen F. Austin. José Antonio Navarro was a friend and supporter of the famed
empresario. Prints and Photographs Collection, di_05641, the Dolph Briscoe Center for
American History, the University of Texas at Austin.*

leaders embraced this proposal, and so Tejanos such as Navarro supported economic development in various ways, including tax exemptions for colonists and keeping the border open to slavery.[27] Slaves were
seen as essential for the labor-intensive cotton industry. The equation
was simple: no slaves, no cotton.

Elected as the representative from Béxar to the legislature at Saltillo,
the capital of Coahuila and Texas, the Baron de Bastrop, in cooperation
with Austin, did his best to shape the colonization law and constitu-

tion, but he achieved only limited success with regard to the issue of importing slaves. Even though most Tejanos did not own slaves, many saw their prosperity linked with the success of Anglo American colonization in the state. As historian Andrés Tijerina has written, "their protective attitude toward Anglo Americans led Tejanos into direct conflict with the more conservative centralists of Mexico and eventually alienated them from the growing centralist government in Mexico City."[28] But when the representatives in Saltillo turned their attention to writing a state constitution, the hopes of Austin and his Tejano allies for legal slave importation received a crippling setback. Article 13 of the new charter declared no one could be born a slave in Coahuila and Texas, and importing slaves was forbidden. In Béxar, Saucedo wrote to Austin about the "mortal blow Texas received with the constitutional article prohibiting slavery." He urged Austin to tell all Texas citizens and municipalities to write to the Baron de Bastrop about their opposition to the article, "otherwise all will be lost." Saucedo promised to do what he could, but without communication by Texans with the government in Saltillo, "I fear that little or nothing will be gained."[29]

Austin's attitude toward slavery was conflicted. He clearly saw slavery as a curse on civilized man and an affront to liberal ideals, yet he also recognized that to develop economically, "Texas *must* be a slave country."[30] José Antonio Navarro's attitude toward slavery, like that of other Tejano leaders and Austin, was essentially pragmatic. But Navarro's attitude was also shaped by a cultural tradition in which the distinctions between enslaved and free persons were blurred. At the time of his birth in 1795, three slaves lived in the Navarro household: Ignacio López, his wife, María Zapata, and their seven-day-old daughter, María Claudia, who was baptized on February 27, the same day that José Antonio Navarro was born.[31] It is important to note that Ignacio and María were united in a marriage recognized as valid by the Catholic Church and civil authorities, as is demonstrated by the notation of their daughter as "legitimate." Ángel Navarro, and other slave owners of Béxar, followed the Catholic tradition established in Spanish America that recognized the legal marriage and baptism of slaves, who were seen as equal in the eyes of God. This tradition created a perception of more humane treatment. Louisiana slaves saw Spanish Texas as a refuge where they would receive better treatment under Spanish law and tradition. One runaway, Richar(d), said he, his wife, and children fled Louisiana seeking aid in Spanish Texas because they believed the laws of the Catholic King were kinder and more pious. Another fugitive was described as saying that "he understood the Spanish laws to be more lenient than those of his America."[32] After slaveholders settled in Texas in large numbers, this reputation persisted. It just moved south across the Rio Grande into Mexico, which was thought by slaves to be a "'Paradise for happiness."[33]

As a result of the racial tolerance found in the Catholic Church, intermarriage of Europeans, Indians, and Africans in Spanish America produced a variety of ethnic combinations with a multitude of terms used to designate them. This was especially true in the frontier regions, where much smaller resident populations led to more frequent alliances and marriages across racial lines. For example, there are seventy baptisms recorded for San Fernando Church in 1795, including José Antonio Navarro's. Descriptions of these children include *español, mestizo, mulato, indio, coyote, lobo,* and *tresalvo.*[34] As historian Jesús F. de la Teja has noted, these *castas,* or racial designations, were not necessarily fixed and could change over time, depending on circumstances.[35] Some labels were not what they appeared to be: Spanish (*español* or *española*) did not mean someone from Spain. It was a racial designation that essentially meant "white" and indicated a claim to be a descendant of Spaniards. True peninsular Spaniards were usually designated by the province or city in Spain of their birth. Thus the frontier community of Béxar, which shaped the values of José Antonio, was a socially and racially dynamic mixture of people that sharply contrasted with the relatively inflexible social structure of the American South with regard to racial relations and slavery. While Navarro would later own slaves, his political arguments and actions revealed a less rigid conceptualization of race and law.

Navarro's political beliefs, including his opinions on slavery, would be tested at a new level in 1827. In the spring, after ratifying the constitution for Coahuila and Texas, the three state jurisdictions elected twelve *diputados* (deputies) to represent their districts in the first state legislature, set to begin in July 1827.[36] In Béxar, the election was held on May 27, and the electors selected José Antonio Navarro and José Miguel de Arciniega to serve as deputies. Juan Martín de Veramendi was chosen as a supplementary deputy. José Antonio was absent at this time, in New Orleans on a business trip, but Arciniega quickly prepared to leave for Saltillo. Travel money was scarce; only one hundred pesos could be found along with a quantity of paper money left over from Trespalacios's ill-conceived Bank of Texas, established during the Mexican Empire. Somehow additional funds were raised, and Arciniega left Béxar with a military escort and rode south, passing through Laredo. The legislature began its sessions on June 28, ahead of schedule, but Arciniega finally arrived on July 10 and presented his credentials. He was duly sworn and seated that same day.[37]

Navarro, unlike his fellow delegate, did not hurry to Saltillo. He returned from New Orleans during the first days of July on Captain Celestin Forrestal's ship, the *Rover*. He arranged for carts to haul his merchandise to Goliad to be taxed, arrived there on July 7, and did not reach Béxar until the night of July 11. Two days later he wrote to Saucedo, expressing his appreciation for the great honor of being chosen to represent Texas. He explained, however, that he had just arrived from New Orleans, that his leg was inflamed, and that consequently he needed time to recuperate before starting his journey to Saltillo. It would be a month and a half before he could leave. Navarro needed time not only to recover, but also to make arrangements for the sale of his goods. He also had another reason to delay leaving for Saltillo: Austin was coming to Béxar and the two men would travel together. The empresario was on his way to Saltillo to present a long list of concerns to the state government.[38] Navarro no doubt looked forward to meeting with Austin to discuss the actions he and Arciniega would take in the legislature to advance the development of Texas. By this time, Austin's colonists and other Anglo immigrants outnumbered the Tejanos by a ratio of at least eight to one, so their needs could not be ignored—nor did Navarro wish to do so, for he represented them as well as his fellow Tejanos.

Austin arrived in Béxar by August 9, 1827. The state constitution directed that deputies' travel expenses be paid with state funds. Saucedo had no money for Navarro's travel expenses, so he requested one hundred eighty pesos from ayuntamiento funds in the form of a loan to be repaid by the state. In cooperation with Ahumada, his brother-in-law, Navarro arranged a military escort of fifteen men to travel with him and Austin. The two men reportedly left Béxar for Saltillo on September 1. During their journey Navarro had the opportunity to renew his friendship with Austin and to plan a strategy for legislation regarding the slaves that Austin thought were crucial for the success of his colony. Following the same route as Arciniega, Navarro arrived in Laredo on September 10. In the company of another escort of four men, riding by way of Lampazos, Navarro and Austin reached Saltillo on September 22. That same day Navarro sent a note to the governor, saying that he had arrived and would report to the legislature as soon as his baggage arrived.[39]

Two days later Navarro went to the municipal building in the center of Saltillo, the Casas Consistoriales, where the legislature met. He waited at the chamber entrance while the members debated his credentials. He must have noticed the abrasive attitude of some of his future colleagues.[40] Legislative President Ramón García Rojas said that because Navarro's papers had been examined at the time of Miguel Arciniega's arrival, further review was unnecessary, and to save time, Navarro should be administered the oath of office forthwith. José Francisco Madero, a representative from the Monclova district, objected. Madero, whom Navarro would later describe as "one of my antagonists," insisted that the joint credentials should first be sent to the *comisión de poderes* (commission of powers) for its recommendation. The other members disagreed and voted to allow Navarro to enter the legislative chamber, where he was duly sworn and took his seat. At that time, the sounds of a boisterous celebration from the plaza invaded the chamber—a result of the week-long festival commemorating independence. Either because of the noisy interference, or perhaps out of a desire to join the festivities, the president adjourned the session until the next morning.[41]

Navarro may have welcomed the opportunity to spend another day exploring Saltillo, a city of about eighteen thousand persons nestled in a cradle of mountains about one mile above sea level. Then, as today, its dry cool climate provided a welcome relief from the oppressive humidity of Béxar. Evidently this was his first return to Saltillo since his boyhood, when he continued his education in the city for a brief time. Excitement was in the air not only because of the independence celebration, but also from the annual trade fair and the offerings of merchandise, commodities, livestock, and zestful entertainment that accompanied such an event. Because Navarro had acquired a substantial shipment of goods in New Orleans, it is more than likely that he brought a selection of merchandise to sell, thus gaining the bonus of a business trip combined with his expense-paid journey to Saltillo. It is hard to imagine that a sharp trader like Navarro would neglect picking such a ripe plum of opportunity.

As he had when he was a young student, Navarro in 1827 probably lodged with his aunt, Petra de la Peña, and Refugita, her beautiful Comanche servant—as Navarro described her. During his stay in Saltillo, Austin enjoyed the hospitality of Aunt Petra on several occasions when he came to confer with Navarro. Using his considerable personal charm, Austin captured the admiration of Doña Petra and promised to write to her. Months later she expressed disappointment at not having received any letters. Navarro chided Austin for his social negligence and firmly instructed him to write to Aunt Petra, saying only half-jokingly that otherwise "I will not pardon you for this, neither will I be the lawyer to [help you] escape justice for behavior that [to our way of thinking] is foreign in you."[42]

Prior to his arrival in Saltillo, José Antonio Navarro missed nearly three months of the first legislative sessions. During his absence, Manuel Arciniega ably represented the Department of Texas and proposed two pieces of legislation. The first concerned regulating the *corridas de mesteños*, the roundups of wild livestock, which had been one of the principal natural resources of Texas since the earliest days. The current regulations had been in force since the 1778 visit of Teodoro de Croix, who claimed all wild stock for the king, so Arciniega was mindful that the new state of Coahuila and Texas needed a similar law with important amendments. The mesteños—cattle and horses—represented a cash crop for export, an important food supply, and valuable leather byproducts. During the chaotic years after 1813 the wild stock had been severely depleted by indiscriminant capture and slaughter. Arciniega proposed a measure that would maintain and increase this important resource by limiting the time within which the mesteños could be legally chased and captured. He recommended a "hunting season" that would last from the beginning of September to the end of February. His proposal met with approval, even by the irascible Madero, who suggested the season be decreased by one month.[43]

Arciniega's second proposal was not successful. In it, he requested "the removal of all obstacles preventing the State (from) reimbursing 8,608 pesos that he said the government owed the Béxar ayuntamiento and various individuals from what Governor Felix Trespalacios had spent in paper money (from the Bank of Texas)." After its first reading, the proposal was sent to the Hacienda Committee for review.[44] It evidently died there, because the subject did not reappear for the rest of the term. Understandably the legislature, which was strapped for cash to pay its constitutional obligations, had little interest in undoing fiscal damage wrought by the schemes of a past governor who had been an appointee of the vanquished monarchy.

Navarro, once settled in his legislative seat, wasted little time in joining his fellow Tejano in proposing reforms. On October 15, he and Arciniega jointly proposed that the state government provide 800 pesos to repair the council hall, the jail, and other government buildings in Béxar. The proposal was sent to the Second Hacienda Committee for review.[45] In the discussions that followed, the 800 peso figure was reduced to 600 pesos. In the end, probably no funds were actually approved because of the dire shortage of state revenues. Their proposal does indicate, however, that Bexareños had been unable to complete the restoration of these public buildings, begun in 1822, and that they hoped the state government would assist them.

By early October, urgent business required Arciniega to return to Texas. He obtained a permit on October 6 to temporarily leave the legislature. He reported sick on the 18th and left Saltillo, being absent with leave for three months—the remainder of the first part of the legislative session.[46] No explanation has been found for his departure; he probably responded to some crisis of a personal nature. At the time Arciniega left Saltillo, Navarro had been on the job for little more than one relatively uneventful month. Left alone to represent Texas, he struggled as the legislature focused on more controversial issues, particularly the expulsion of peninsular Spaniards from the republic, funding the state government, and the sensitive issue of slavery.

Anti-Spanish sentiment among the Mexican masses became intense, and the angry cry of "Down with the Gachupines!" was heard constantly. Following a Spanish attack on Veracruz, Congress decreed their expulsion. The issue of expelling Spaniards became a subject of hot debate in all the Mexican state legislatures during 1827. Following the lead of Congress, the legislature of Coahuila and Texas authorized Decree No. 38, which required all Spaniards "accused by public authority" to leave the state within thirty days of the decree's publication, November 27, 1827. Navarro abstained from voting because he disagreed with the terms upon which the proposal was founded. This decree notwithstanding, Coahuila and Texas was not a hotbed of anti-Spanish sentiment. Following the proclamation, the legislature considered numerous appeals from Spaniards living in the state, and the members voted to grant exemptions in most cases. In fact, few peninsular Spaniards immigrated to Texas during the colonial period or afterwards, and their presence was not considered threatening. The most prominent Spaniard in Béxar in 1827 was the highly respected Miguel Iturri Castillo, who successfully fought expulsion and regained his confiscated property. For Tejanos, the expulsion of Spaniards was not as important an issue as it was in central Mexico, where Spaniards were seen as oppressors possessing ill-gotten wealth. Charts compiled by historian Harold Sims show that of fifty-seven Spaniards ordered deported from Coahuila and Texas, fifty-three were granted exceptions. In contrast, the Federal District, which included Mexico City, ordered 1,033 Spaniards expelled, but granted only 114 exceptions.[47]

A main function of the legislature was to establish procedures and regulations for governmental functions called for by the state constitution. This included the creation of a treasury. Final discussions for this took place on November 7, a day when Navarro served as the interim president (in the absence of José Francisco Madero). The minutes were read for twenty-seven articles to establish the treasury, to be promulgated as Decree No. 30. Navarro proposed a final article to dress the treasurer with a stylistic flourish for formal occasions: "The treasurer on ceremonial days will dress in black and use a red sash flecked with gold, but without tassels or braids, fastened over the jacket. In public ceremonies he will be seated with the ayuntamiento." The addition was discussed, only slightly amended, and approved.[48] Later, Decree No. 30, establishing the treasury, would become the object of a serious conflict that would pit Navarro and Arciniega against each other.

The issue that generated the most controversy, longest speeches, and most heated discussions was the pressing problem of generating income to pay state salaries and other costs of government. The legislature began addressing the problem at its first session. It worked feverishly to initiate numerous measures that provided little return in revenue. Auctions were organized for bids for the right to hold cockfights. They increased fees on billiard parlors. Raffles were licensed. A decree passed to levy a tax of 2 percent on money entering or leaving the state, and a 3 percent tax on silver. As noted above, a tax was fixed on captured wild livestock. Additional stations were set up to collect a sales tax. The state monopoly in the sale of tobacco was reinforced and severe fines set for contraband violations. In addition, the legislature passed decrees designed to protect the wine industry at Parras in northern Coahuila by restricting the import of wine.[49] The increase of state funds brought in by these feeble measures cannot have amounted to much. Additional revenue came from the sale of land to colonists and import duties. It turned out, however, that these measures were insufficient to pay the salaries of the state officers prescribed by the constitution. These insufficiencies would lead to another rift between Navarro and Arciniega that reflected a split in the legislature as a whole.

From the time of Navarro's arrival in September until the legislature recessed in November, its members passed twenty-one decrees. The second legislative session began on January 1, 1828. Arciniega returned in February from whatever pressing business had occupied him for the previous three months. The first ten decrees adopted by the legislators were of a routine nature and passed without incident, but soon after Arciniega's return, discussions of measures to reduce state expenditures erupted into a major crisis. He and four other representatives (not including Navarro) jointly submitted a proposal on March 22 that had the effect of a bombshell. Because the revenues for the state were insufficient to pay the costs of all the officials that the constitution had designated, Arciniega's group argued that substantial staff cuts had to be made until such time as the state could afford to pay salaries. They recommended that the vice governor be paid only when he substituted for the governor; that the governor's council be suspended; that except in Texas, alcaldes would temporarily replace political chiefs in municipalities and district capitals; and that Decree No. 30 creating the office of treasurer would be suspended.[50]

When the legislators discussed these proposed cost-cutting measures on March 26, resistance was immediate and vociferous. Madero emerged as the main opponent of the proposal. He expressed outrage, taking the illogical position that what the constitution dictated could not be questioned but only carried out, regardless of the funds available. "The constitution created the [governor's] council," he thundered, citing Article 121 in support of his position and ridiculing the suggestion that the permanent council could substitute as the governor's counselors. He critiqued every detail of the proposal from Arciniega and his allies in a lengthy, verbose argument. When the legislators voted on whether or not the measure should receive further consideration, Arciniega, Navarro, and others defeated Madero and his supporters.[51] The sessions devoted to austerity proposals continued for nearly a month. Little conciliatory discussion took place; instead, most of the legislators devoted their time to long, impassioned speeches.

Navarro's address about the proposed austerity measures was longer by far than any other pronouncement he made at this legislature. He agreed in principle with his "antagonist," Madero, that the action was unconstitutional. But the conflict between constitutionality and revenue could not be resolved by increasing the state's income: evidently amending the constitution was not considered an option. So Navarro at first voted in favor of Arciniega's proposal and then, persuaded of the unconstitutionality of suspending government offices, voted with Madero. Lengthy and heated discussions followed day after day until April 17, when the efforts of Madero, Navarro, and others failed and Arciniega's Decree No. 50 became law by a vote of eight to four. However, this austerity measure was not laid to rest. Two days later Decree No. 52 noted that a "proper decision" regarding Decree No. 50 was being delayed in order to attend to other matters.[52]

During the next two weeks, the legislators approved routine decrees pertaining to procedural matters of the municipalities. During that interval, Navarro introduced a proposal that would advance his highest legislative priority: the circumvention of Article 13, which proclaimed that "From and after the promulgation of the constitution in the capital of each district no one shall be born a slave in the state and after six months the introduction of slaves under any pretext shall not be permitted."[53] The highest priority for Navarro was to secure the passage of a decree to evade the restrictions of Article 13 on behalf of the Anglo American colonists and the leaders of Coahuila and Texas who wanted to develop a cotton industry. He undoubtedly had discussed this subject with Austin at length and planned strategies before the empresario left Saltillo for Texas in December 1827. Austin insisted then and later that "Texas can not progress under the restriction of Article 13," in other words, without the introduction of more slave laborers. Because officials such as Navarro in Texas and northern Mexico considered the Anglo colonists to be a "vested interest," toleration of slavery became an essential part of their support.[54]

By the end of April 1828, Navarro was prepared to make his move to circumvent Article 13. He had established his status as a legislator among his peers, and expressed opinions concerning a variety of legislative proposals. He maintained a modest profile by speaking out decisively on matters of interest to Texas, and also matters of principle, but he avoided expressing opinions in the gratuitous, verbose manner of some of his fellow representatives. As a member of the Colonization Committee, he also held a strategic position from which to influence legislation pertaining to the broader subject of immigration.

By this time the legislature had already passed two measures regarding slavery, only one of which Navarro endorsed. He actually arrived in Saltillo after the first, Decree No. 18, had passed. It provided for slave censuses and reports of slave deaths, and it put teeth into Article 13 by defining penalties for the importation of slaves. Following a rule that had been in effect since Spanish times, the decree empowered slaves to change owners if a buyer could be found to pay the latter his original cost. Circumstances under which a slave could be freed were also established. Navarro signed Decree No. 35, which was a brief amendment to No. 18. It added the qualification that in cases where owners were killed by unknown persons or died in any irregular circumstances, their slaves would not be freed.[55]

These two decrees, added to Article 13, represented the laws in effect in Coahuila and Texas that pertained to slavery. The federal colonization law did not address slavery, delegating the management of immigration to the states while ignoring previous decrees that restricted the import, sale, and even ownership of slaves. The state colonization law of 1825 was vague about slavery to the point of being meaningless, which is how Juan Antonio Padilla described it in response to a query from Austin. The only real barrier to slavery was Article 13 of the state constitution.[56] Therefore,

Navarro focused on that article in fashioning a law that would greatly influence the fate of Austin's colony and bolster the dream of a cotton empire held by Mexican leaders of Coahuila and Texas.

The idea for circumventing Article 13 evidently originated with Peter Ellis Bean, who had learned earlier, through the grapevine in Mexico City, that conservatives in the legislature in Saltillo intended to outlaw slavery, which they did by means of Article 13. In July 1826, Bean informed Austin of his concern and suggested a solution: slaves could purchase their value, by contract, at the border and be brought into Texas as indentured servants, owing to their "former masters" a debt so large that it could never be repaid with their labor. With Austin's assistance, Navarro shaped this idea into a proposed decree in Colonization Committee meetings. It is not known who the other members were besides Navarro, but it clear that he introduced the idea at Austin's instigation and persuaded the other members to support it. On April 30, the Colonization Committee gave the first reading of a proposed decree that concluded with the following proposition: "that all contracts made outside of the state of Coahuila and Texas between immigrants and their servants prior to settlement in the state will be guaranteed as valid." At San Felipe, the capital of Austin's colony, the Anglo ayuntamiento had already passed an initiative using wording that closely matched the draft presented in Saltillo, revealing the influence of Austin on what became known as the Law of Contracts.[57]

The language of Navarro's decree was subtle, but straightforward on the surface. Unlike most other legislative proposals, it credited no committee member as the author, nor was slavery mentioned, so the attention of the legislators turned immediately to other issues, as was usual with the first reading of a proposal. On May 3, the proposed Law of Contracts appeared on the legislative calendar. It was the last item considered that day, after deliberations on a number of more mundane considerations. While the legislators discussed the recommendation of the Colonization Committee, Navarro no doubt spoke for the measure, describing it as a law that guaranteed contracts originating in foreign countries. He explained the basis for the measure, probably downplaying (or not mentioning) how it could be applied to slaves; after all, the proposal only referred to servants whom the colonists might introduce. The members discussed the Committee's proposal for the rest of the day and then approved it.[58]

On May 5, the Law of Contracts was read and approved, and so it became the law of the land as Decree No. 56, which read as follows:

The Congress of the State of Coahuila and Texas, attending to the deficiency of working men to give activity to agriculture and the other arts, and desiring to facilitate their introduction into the State, as well as the growth and prosperity of the said branches, has thought proper to decree:

All contracts, not in opposition to the laws of the State, that have been entered into in foreign countries, between emigrants who come to settle in this State, or between the inhabitants thereof, and the servants and day laborers or working men whom they introduce, are hereby guaranteed to be valid in the said State.

For its fulfillment, the Governor of the State shall cause it to be printed, published, and circulated.

Given at the city of Leóna Vicario [Saltillo] on the 5th of May, 1828.[59]

Navarro immediately reported the decree's passage to Béxar. On May 15, Political Chief Ramón Músquiz relayed the news to Austin, informing him of the legislature's approval of "a law that guarantees foreign contracts made between Coahuiltecan citizens and workers who want to come to serve them." Two days later Navarro wrote to Austin, replying to Austin's letter of May 7. "I had the good fortune to win the game and achieve the law that sanctions and authorizes contracts made in foreign countries that you desired, and I have the pleasure to inform you that it will go out in today's mail." After referring to Decree No. 50, and the lengthy, noisy dispute about it, Navarro added the following mysterious passage: "You will appreciate this law as a gift that I make to you in payment for the courage you have shown me by keeping your silence—about which you have proposed that I write nothing but nothing. But as I have already said, I am a friend . . . and I have forgotten about these grievances."[60] Perhaps Navarro meant by Austin's "keeping your silence," that the legislation could not have passed had it became generally known that it would in effect permit the introduction of slaves, which Austin had openly supported.

Arciniega also wrote to Austin the same day regarding the passage of the Law of Contracts. He declared that good luck was responsible for the passage of Decree No. 56; that it passed while the other legislators' attention was focused on a controversy over the cost-cutting measures of Decree No. 50.[61] Indeed, Arciniega claimed that it would have been defeated had it not been for the excitement generated by that controversial decree, which is a puzzling statement, because it is not true. The conspicuous inconsistency in what the two legislators told Austin is recorded in the legislative minutes. Both Navarro and Arciniega in their May 17 letters indicated that luck was responsible for the passage of Decree No. 56, and that it passed during the controversy over the cost-cutting measures of Decree No. 50. But Arciniega reported that the Law of Contracts would have been defeated had it not been for the turmoil attending Decree No. 50. In fact, that measure was approved on April 17. An interval of nearly three weeks passed before Navarro first proposed the Law of Contracts on May 3, during which time numerous matters had been considered.

A closer study of the legislative record further undermines Navarro and Arciniega in their claims that Decree No. 50 was the subject of controversy around May 3 and that Navarro took advantage of this confusion to "slip the measure through without discussion" while the other members were distracted.[62] While it is true that Governor José María Viesca subsequently did return Decree No. 50 to the legislature for further discussion because of concerns about its constitutionality, there was a pronounced lull marked by routine measures during which Decree No. 56 passed. Moreover, while it did not pass "without discussion," the proposed bill passed through the same procedures of review, discussion, and voting as had other proposals. Navarro introduced the measure for its first reading on May 3. At the next session, on May 5, the decree was read and received final approval and was sent to Viesca, who signed it.

Navarro, Arciniega, and Padilla had worried that the proposed law might be defeated, as Padilla expressed in his letter to Austin, and so they were entitled to some self-congratulation, and even exaggeration, in letters to Austin reporting their success. But it is also clear that Navarro and Arciniega coordinated their messages to Austin, crediting good luck for their victory rather than their legislative skill. Possibly this was to conceal a deal Navarro might have made with Madero: that he would vote with him on Decree 50 if Madero would not oppose the passage of Decree 56. In any case, passage of the Law of Contracts marked the high point of Navarro's participation in the first state legislature of Coahuila and Texas. The second term concluded on May 15, 1828, and the legislature did not reconvene again until August.

Whether by luck or skill, the passage of Decree No. 56 certainly was Navarro's primary achievement during his first term as a state legislator, but because his purpose was to evade a constitutional provision in order to allow slaves to be brought into Texas from the United States, it was not his finest hour by contemporary standards. However, Navarro clearly took a pragmatic attitude toward slavery, as did other Tejano leaders, and did not necessarily sanction the institution on moral grounds. Permission of slavery was crucial in facilitating immigration from the United States, which many Tejano leaders thought was the key to Texas's future prosperity. After years of grinding poverty, the belief that Austin's colonists would stimulate the economic development of Texas was a powerful end that justified the means of importing slaves. Saucedo expressed proslavery sentiments on behalf of Austin, as did other Tejano leaders. Veramendi, Padilla, and José María Balmaceda, who succeeded Saucedo as a land commissioner in Texas, had similar views, which they made known to the authorities. Francisco Ruiz expressed his concern for the ill effects of Article 13 in a letter to Austin, as did the governor of Coahuila and Texas, who wrote to Austin that "the progress of Coahuila depends on the progress of Texas," an implied endorsement of slavery.[63]

The legislature began its next session on August 28, 1828, but Navarro arrived and was sworn in on September 1.[64] The legislators focused their attention on presidential politics, a matter of vital importance, as the winners would be the Republic of Mexico's second president and vice president. The four-year term of President Guadalupe Victoria was ending, and the federal constitution of 1824 called for each state legislature to elect its candidate. The president would then be chosen by a majority of the legislatures. There were no popular elections. Navarro and his colleagues nominated generals Vicente Guerrero and Manuel Gómez Pedraza, and then chose Guerrero as their winner by an absolute majority. They elected General Anastacio Bustamante to be vice president.[65] Following these elections, the legislators elected Juan Vicente Campos, an associate of Navarro, as their federal senator.

Guerrero, Victoria's war minister and a hero of the independence movement, was well known in Coahuila and Texas because he had served since 1821 as the captain general of the Eastern Interior Provinces. He eventually won the presidency, but not in the way the Saltillo legislators expected. This time the selection of a president was determined not by ballots, but by mob violence. When the votes of the state legislatures were counted in Mexico City, Gómez Pedraza had won by a small margin, but this decision did not stand. Moderates who thought the revolution had gone far enough favored Pedraza, but those who wanted more reforms and coercive actions against the Spaniards supported Guerrero. The latter challenged the election results, and Santa Anna almost immediately announced his support for Guerrero, igniting a bloody struggle for political dominance. In a propaganda initiative, Governor Lorenzo de Zavala of the state of Mexico incited the urban lower classes in a spiral of animosity of incendiary proportions. Riots ensued, mobs sacked the national palace in Mexico City, and President-elect Gómez Pedraza and his cabinet fled for their lives. Victoria, as the incumbent, then nominated Guerrero to be president and the Congress declared him elected, with Bustamante as his vice president.[66]

Meanwhile in Saltillo, Navarro and his colleagues continued their work as the first legislature neared its end. They did not receive reliable reports of the events in Mexico City until February 1829. Instead, they turned their attention to local matters, among which were two items of particular importance. The first concerned the location of the capital of Coahuila and Texas. The state constitution did not specify a site and left the selection of a location to the legislature. The first capital chosen was Saltillo, which historically was the capital of the Spanish province of Nueva Vizcaya. Monclova had been the capital of Coahuila since the seventeenth century, and legislators proposed that it again serve as the capital. After discussions the measure was put to a vote and the result was Decree No. 64, which declared Monclova to be the capital of Coahuila and Texas. It passed by a vote was six to four, with Navarro and Arciniega voting for the measure.[67] Their vote represented the opinion of most Tejanos, who had chafed under the distant government in Saltillo, which appeared to have little concern for Texas interests and problems. Although representatives from Monclova were ready to act immediately—the next day Monclova's ayuntamiento and residents offered to pay the costs of transferring the state government to their city—relocating the capital had to wait five years until political conditions were favorable and Veramendi of Béxar was governor.

Another item of local interest has resulted in a persistent rumor about Navarro that lacks foundation as it contends that he was the "father of the Texas homestead law."[68] Decree No. 70, often referred to as a homestead law, protected Austin's settlers from foreclosure for a period of twelve years because of debts incurred outside of Mexico prior to their acquisition of lands. This measure was another pro-immigration bill promoted by Austin, and undoubtedly Navarro would have actively supported such legislation. However, the actual proposal that became Decree No. 70 was introduced and passed during the second legislature, four months after Navarro had left Saltillo. Debt protection was high on the legislative agenda, for it had been the first law passed by the new legislature (on January 13, 1829). The effects of this legislation were long lasting and significant. It was the first of its kind in Texas, and it can be considered a distinctive Texan contribution to jurisprudence. Subsequent legislators incorporated its principal idea into Texas laws to protect homes from foreclosure, beginning with the first Texas Homestead Law of 1839 and continuing to the present day. But if anyone can be described as the "father of the Texas homestead law," it would have to be Austin, because he was the prime mover behind Decree No. 70. Evidently he found an obscure fifteenth-century Spanish precedent, which he dusted off to justify his argument.[69]

Regarding Navarro's true role in the first legislature of Coahuila and Texas, one close associate wrote, "if it were possible to collect the reports of the debates of the legislature . . . they would show Navarro's efforts to save Texas from marked legislative persecution."[70] Fortunately such records exist: the *Actas del Primer Congreso Constitucional del Estado Libre de Coahuila y Tejas* (*Acts of the First Constitutional Congress of the Free State of Coahuila and Texas*). These are not a mere compilation of legislative decrees, but rather constitute a daily journal that preserved verbatim the speeches, lively debates, procedural issues, and other interesting details that show how the decrees were shaped. These records permit an evaluation of Navarro's legislative efforts that is needed to correct a widely quoted assertion about how Navarro's fellow legislators treated him. Jacob De Cordova wrote that Navarro met with "suspicion" and "blind opposition" from his colleagues in the legislature. They opposed him on measures favorable to Texas, dubbing him the "Americanized Texan."[71] In fact, the records show no such animosity. Navarro was clearly accepted as a full-fledged member of the state legislature and was appreciated by his fellows—some of whom opposed him on certain issues and supported him on others and vice versa. In reviewing the historical record at Saltillo, the depiction of Navarro as a legislative pariah is without foundation.

As the end of his second legislative session neared, Navarro began the process of acquiring the land to which he was entitled as a Mexican citizen. On September 13, he asked Governor Viesca to grant him four leagues at the Capote Spring.[72] This property fronted the Guadalupe River on its west bank where the Capote Hills are located, about twelve miles southeast of present-day Seguin. The governor forwarded Navarro's petition to the Béxar ayuntamiento for its review and report. The legislature closed on September 30, 1828, and Navarro left for Béxar soon afterwards.

Twentieth-century historians have severely criticized the first state legislature of Coahuila and Texas. Vito Alessio Robles wrote, "there was seen in this government and legislature a fever of legislation, almost always out of touch with reality . . . with laws and decrees promulgated one day that were reformed or abrogated soon after." He adds that many useless decrees were passed and others, done with the best of intentions, had no effect beyond the paper upon which they were written.[73] This critique is too severe when all the evidence is considered. The initial attempt to form a state government had to be done virtually from scratch, and the poverty of the state provided a meager tax base to fund any government. Moreover, attempting to shape into one state the divergent interests of the former provinces of Texas and Coahuila was a daunting task, with the added complication of the introduction into Texas of thousands of Anglo colonists. In fairness, the efforts of Navarro and his colleagues must be seen as good faith attempts to work in accord with a new, untested constitution and with leaders who lacked experience in government. They indeed encountered many difficult obstacles in finances, interpretation of laws, and clashes of egos, but they did pass sixty-nine decrees, and their successes would provide a basis for subsequent, better legislative efforts. Certainly Navarro, who applied the lessons of cautious pragmatism learned in revolutionary Béxar, had played a prominent role in decisions that would deeply affect the future of Texas.

CHAPTER FOUR

Businessman, Land Commissioner, and Politician, 1828–35

AFTER HIS SINGLE TERM in the Coahuila and Texas legislature, Navarro perhaps anticipated a quiet career focused on his business operations. Instead, he found himself struggling like a juggler trying to keep three balls in the air as he managed his tasks as a businessman, a land commissioner, and a politician. He also had a growing family to care for. Despite all of these concerns, it was during this period that Navarro may have realized that he was living the American Dream his father had sought. He acquired property, including two country residences, and became a rancher as well as a merchant. He faltered in his first effort as a land commissioner, but he was given another appointment and did as well as anyone could expect. Political matters overshadowed everything else, however, and as Texas moved toward revolution, Navarro, like many other Bexareños who had endured decades of political turmoil, found himself moving from cautious conservatism to support of positions and leaders that Mexico City's central government considered rebellious.

While Navarro was traveling back to Béxar from Saltillo after the legislature adjourned in late 1828, government couriers raced ahead of him. Among the material they carried was Navarro's petition for land forwarded by Governor José María Viesca in the form of an *amparo* (a grant approved for an unspecified location). The political chief and ayuntamiento were the authorities that would evaluate the claim to ensure that property boundaries did not overlap, and then return them for the governor's final approval. The Béxar council considered Navarro's petition in October and found a contradiction with the location he had requested. When Navarro finally returned to Béxar on November 9, worn out from his arduous journey, he met with the unpleasant news that his request for the Capote Springs tract had been rejected. José La Baum had petitioned for the Capote land in 1826; the council had granted his

Texas Land Measure

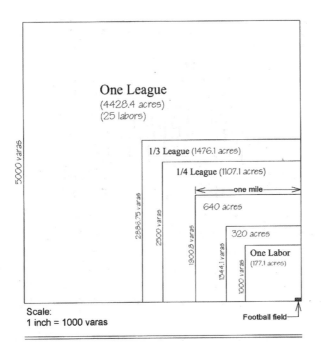

One League
(4428.4 acres)
(25 labors)

1/3 League (1476.1 acres)

1/4 League (1107.1 acres)

one mile

640 acres

320 acres

One Labor
(177.1 acres)

5000 varas

2836.75 varas

2500 varas

1900.8 varas

1344.1 varas

1000 varas

Scale:
1 inch = 1000 varas

Football field

One Vara = 33 1/3 inches
One Chain (Gunter) = 66 feet
One Cordel = 50 varas
One Acre = 208.71 feet square
One Marine League = 3 nautical miles (3.45 statute miles)
One Nautical Mile = 6080 feet
One Statute Mile = 5280 feet

To convert varas to feet: Divide varas by .36
To convert feet to varas: Multiply feet by .36

Archives and Records Division, Texas General Land Office

Chart showing a comparison of the Spanish and English land measures used in nineteenth-century Texas. Courtesy of the Texas General Land Office, Austin.

request, and Viesca subsequently approved it. Navarro would have to find another site for his four leagues.[1]

While trying to locate his four leagues, Navarro still had to feed his family. A few days after his return, he was rested and ready to resume his career as a trader. He wrote to Austin on November 27, saying (with evident relief) that he was "no longer a legislator but a merchant," and that he needed Austin's help to obtain supplies for the winter. Navarro asked if there was any coffee and gunpowder at San Felipe. "If so," he directed, "get for me by your hand three hundred pounds of the former (at no more than two *reales* [25 cents] per pound) and eight *arrobas* [200 pounds] of powder of the best quality or the regular [sort] that is in New Orleans for seven pesos per *arroba*." If these items were not available, he asked Austin to order them on Navarro's account. He would pay the cost of the goods plus shipping when he came to retrieve the merchandise or sent for it. Navarro also informed Austin that he had at least six mules and two or three horses for sale because he had lost his pastureland. Again he directed Austin to "Tell me if I should send them to you—if they would sell at some good price." "Above all," Navarro urged, "attend to my shipment of coffee and powder," because such items were in short supply. He added that corn was also needed. Navarro concluded, "If you would like to continue our friendly correspondence, it will bring much pleasure to your friend who, for now, limits himself to [requesting] these shipments."[2]

Correspondence between Navarro and Austin shows that the business relationship between the two had grown stronger, and Navarro felt comfortable asking for Austin's help in obtaining merchandise. He also confided in Austin about national politics. For example, in a January 1829 letter, Navarro discussed, "the suffering of his spirit regarding the affairs in Mexico" brought about by Vicente Guerrero and Lorenzo de Zavala. He held both of these leaders in high regard, but Navarro told Austin he regretted their disregard of the federal constitution through which they had come to power—meaning Guerrero's military overthrow of the duly elected president, Manuel Gómez Pedraza. Business, however, was almost always included in Navarro's correspondence with the empresario. In the same letter, he ordered thirty *fanegas* (fifty bushels), of corn admitting that he was "an importuning man." He continued to regard Austin as a reliable agent for obtaining goods to bring to Béxar.[3]

Austin also wrote to Navarro on a variety of topics. He had compiled information for a map of Texas, and in 1828 he arranged for it to be printed in Philadelphia by Henry S. Tanner. The next year he sent copies of it to local, state, and federal officials, dedicating it to President

Vicente Guerrero. Austin alerted Navarro that the map would be coming to the Béxar ayuntamiento and asked him to promote its benefits. He wanted Bexareño leaders to recommend that his map be published. Slavery also resurfaced in their correspondence. Although Navarro's Decree No. 56 had passed, providing a legal maneuver for bringing slaves into Texas, Austin was not satisfied. He continued to urge that Article 13 in the state constitution for Coahuila and Texas, which prohibited slavery, ought to be suspended for ten years, and he told Navarro that its repeal was the best way to do this. Austin at the same time wrote to José Francisco Ruiz in Béxar on this subject. Ruiz, loath to commit himself, replied that he knew little about political matters and had not heard anything about "the article regarding slavery."[4]

Navarro and Austin's correspondence in 1829 also reveals that a personal bond had developed between the two men. For example, Austin's letter to Navarro on October 19 includes an outpouring of grief over the death of his brother, James E. B. Austin, who had died of yellow fever in New Orleans. Austin, who himself had been seriously ill, wrote, "I have just returned . . . from the brink of the grave and I have received a terrible blow in the death of my only brother who has been my companion in so many travails we have endured together in these desolate lands." Austin said that he regarded Navarro as a "true friend and Texan," and he wanted to ask his advice on plans to advance the interests of Texas. Austin wrote that he and Samuel May Williams were translating Mexican laws into English, explaining that "The work is very essential and there is nothing more necessary and important for the welfare of Texas for the reason that most of the inhabitants do not understand a word of Spanish and it is entirely impossible to govern a people with laws whose existence the masses absolutely ignore."[5] To reinforce his point, he declared that regulating land claims was one of the most important concerns for the people of Texas.

Navarro replied to Austin ten days later, expressing heartfelt sympathy for the loss of his brother, cut down in the prime of life. But he also urged him not to give in to despair, pointing out that men cannot escape the inevitable actions of nature and offering the metaphorical aphorism that one had to "avoid equipping death with spurs by feeding our sorrow." On political matters, Navarro reported that Tejanos had expressed strong opposition to Guerrero's "astonishing law" of September 15 abolishing slavery. He was referring to the president's declaration that slavery was outlawed in almost all of Mexico. Navarro reported that not only had a petition been sent to Governor Viesca about it, but that Ramón Músquiz as the political chief at Béxar had suspended local publication of Guerrero's decree until an appeal for exemption could be ruled on. He assured Austin that the proclamation would probably not be implemented in Texas (and it was not).[6]

At the end of 1829, Navarro likely anticipated dedicating the coming year to improving his finances. During the fourteen years since his return from Louisiana, he had worked steadily to build his mercantile operation and find a place for himself in the political establishment at the local and state level. In 1830 he expected to increase his trade activities and take possession of the land granted to him by the state government. Despite these intentions, he was called upon to continue public service. When Béxar municipal electors convened as usual in December and elected the ayuntamiento for the next year, Navarro was chosen as síndico procurador (city attorney). The duties of síndico procurador varied from place to place since formal instructions for the position were not defined, and tradition often determined the responsibilities of the office. He was also elected treasurer.[7] With his prior service on the council and having recently finished a term in the legislature, it did not appear that the coming year would offer much challenge for a man with Navarro's experience; however, his talents would be severely tested in the upcoming months.

Following Navarro's appointment as síndico procurador, Political Chief Músquiz handed him a difficult assignment. The commandant general of Texas, Antonio Elozúa, had decided to expand his military facilities into private lands in the Barrio de Valero. It fell to Navarro to inform land owners that their property was to be taken, to explain the necessity of this action, and to assure them they would receive just compensation for their property's value. He was to employ his persuasive skills to avoid any prolonged delays. Fifteen owners were listed for Navarro to contact, including the ayuntamiento and prominent Bexareños such as Vicente Gortari, José Dario Zambrano, and Political Chief Músquiz.[8] Records do not show how or if Navarro accomplished this assignment. Other issues before the council, such as cleaning the *acequias* (irrigation canals), securing locations for corrals, collecting taxes on livestock, and gathering income from raffles and dances were less controversial and Navarro appears to have handled them easily.

Navarro did not let his city council responsibilities or land negotiations interfere with his other business operations. In the October 1829 letter in which Austin had reported the death of his brother, he had urged Navarro to take advantage of the state law that enabled native-born Mexican citizens to acquire eleven leagues of land. They could get four leagues by grant as a *poblador*, or settler, paying only the surveying and procedural costs; seven additional leagues could be purchased. Unaware that Navarro had already applied for four leagues, Austin offered to acquire the eleven leagues (48,708 acres) for Navarro and locate it in his colony. In exchange for half of the land, Austin would select a tract, pay the surveying and procedural expenses, and assist in getting families to perform the cultivation required by law. In addition, he would insure the land was not occupied by squatters and that the timber had not been destroyed. Navarro would be responsible for paying the cost of seven leagues to the government. Thus Austin offered, in return for half of eleven leagues of prime land, to take care of procedures, and to prevent squatter claims. Navarro's only responsibility was to pay certain costs.[9]

Navarro studied Austin's proposal and decided that it was unacceptable. He wrote that he hesitated to buy the eleven leagues because he was not in a position to take on a large debt. He preferred to buy eleven leagues in his own name and keep only four for himself. He would sell the remaining seven leagues to Austin or one of his friends, remarking that he thought the land would sell immediately. Navarro dismissed Austin's offer to pay the surveying and procedural costs, noting that this was of little consequence. His counterproposal also stated that Austin or his friends would pay all of the expenses, including any fees, to the government. By this method, Navarro would gain title to four leagues of land at no cost to himself. On January 16, 1830, he wrote to Governor Viesca, saying the four leagues already granted him as a settler were insufficient for the ranch he wished to establish. He requested that eleven more leagues be conceded to him.[10]

Austin wasted little time in finding a buyer for Navarro's land. By February 1830, Richard R. Royall arrived in Béxar, met with Navarro, and agreed to buy eleven leagues on the terms Navarro wanted. A few days later, however, Navarro received a reply from Viesca denying his request. The governor informed him that the law limited citizens to owning eleven leagues. Because Navarro had already been awarded four leagues in late 1828, he could only obtain seven more by purchase, which Viesca approved. Navarro immediately reported to Austin:

> I contracted, as per your recommendation, to sell to Richard Royall land that the government conceded to me as a legitimate sale. Richard agreed to pay me six hundred pesos in good money for the total costs stipulated by law, the documentation, measurements, et cet. including my profit. The concession arrived today, but the government sold me seven leagues, not the eleven I requested, for the reason that I had already received four as a settler.

Navarro insisted that he would sell the seven leagues to Royall, but only for the 600 pesos. Taking a hard line, he added that if Royall wanted to change the contract, "I will rescind the offer and not sell anything."[11]

Royall accepted the revised contract, but Navarro would pay a heavy price in frustration and aggravation for his first and only foray into land speculation. He would be occupied with this transaction for more than two years before the deal was finally closed. But at the time it seemed to him that he was on his way to making a quick profit, which he could invest in merchandise. In the same letter in which he delivered the ultimatum for Royall, Navarro asked Austin to send him a small bottle of tobacco seed, which he "badly needed." Probably he had a medicinal use in mind for the seed, or, because spring would soon begin, he may have wanted to grow the plant; tobacco was always in demand since virtually everyone was addicted to it. In late March, Austin wrote Navarro that no tobacco seed was available but that he would keep looking. Austin was becoming more preoccupied with politics, worrying that officials in Mexico City would dictate measures "ruinous to Texas." He confided to Navarro that "my hope is in the State government."[12] Meanwhile, Navarro focused on business. He sent José María Cárdenas to pick up the three *arrobas* (75 pounds) of coffee Austin had obtained for him, and he also sent a herd of stock to be sold for his account, including "four excellent mules."[13] There was always a market for horses, mules, and cows in Austin's Colony, but merchandise provided higher profits. Austin assisted Navarro at San Felipe, but because of the empresario's political duties, his effectiveness as an intermediary purchaser for Navarro became limited.

By the spring of 1830, Navarro had accumulated sufficient capital to travel to the mercantile capital of the American South, New Orleans, to personally select the goods he wanted. On April 1, he asked the Béxar council to grant him leave to go to the Crescent City. This was done, and they named as interim treasurer Francisco Xavier Bustillos, to whom Navarro turned over forty-two pesos in taxes collected during March. A week later he boarded a ship at Matagorda and sailed to New Orleans. At about the time that Navarro began his trip, the Mexican Congress approved a dramatic measure that undermined its relationship with the Texan colonists. The Law of April 6, 1830, officially closed Texas to North American immigration. Anglo American immigrants vastly outnumbered native Tejanos, which alarmed authorities in Mexico City. They saw this as a grave threat to the continuance of Texas as a part of Mexico. The most damaging part of the new law, from Austin's point of view, was Article 11, which declared incomplete empresario contracts to be null and void. Strict enforcement of this article would strike a blow to Austin's colonization plan for Texas, because of the four empresario contracts he had, only one had the required number of families. In addition, plans for other colonies would be quashed by the rule of Article 11. The Law of April 6, 1830, marked a turning point, after which relations between Mexico and Texas deteriorated, spiraling downward into violence.[14]

Navarro probably first heard about the Law of April 6, 1830, while he was in New Orleans, but there was nothing to be done about it—he had cargo to ship. Around the first of June he arrived at the Texas coast on the *Sun* and disembarked with his goods at Aransas Pass. A few days later he transported his cargo to Goliad (formerly La Bahía).[15] Ten years had passed since his arrest there for contraband trade. He had come a long way since that unfortunate beginning, and Tejanos now recognized him as a man of influence and a prosperous merchant, one who could afford to go to New Orleans and personally select goods from the city's international markets. At Goliad, on June 10, he made an inventory of the items. Included were fabrics from fine silk to ordinary cloth, 754 pounds of coffee, 661 pounds of rice, 5 barrels of sweet wine from Málaga, 435 pounds of white sugar, 50 pounds of black pepper, and 2 barrels of gin, noodles, almonds, cinnamon, and cheeses from Flanders.[16] The large quantities suggest a thriving operation with sales from Béxar to Saltillo.

Having made arrangements for the transportation and disposition of his goods from Goliad, Navarro returned to Béxar in mid-June. Sorting through his accumulated mail, he probably first opened a letter from Governor Viesca. Inside he found a decree, made in response to a request from Benjamin R. Milam, naming him as commissioner to distribute lands for the recently approved Wavell colony. Milam was the agent selected by Arthur G. Wavell to establish his colony along the northern area of Texas on the Red River. This included a settlement called Pecan Point, by which name the colony would be best known. By accepting this appointment, Navarro began a new direction, one that over the next two years would present new and sometimes exasperating challenges.[17]

Austin learned of the appointment before Navarro returned from New Orleans. On May 31, writing from Béxar, the empresario congratulated him, saying he thought it would be "of much advantage to you." Austin had to leave before Navarro's return, so he apologized for congratulating him through the "mute medium of paper and ink" rather than in person. Austin was not a disinterested observer; he likely hoped that development of Wavell's colony would strengthen his own position regarding his unfulfilled contracts threatened by the Law of April 6, 1830. Austin said nothing to Navarro about possible complications that could result from the provisions of that legislation. Instead, he urged Navarro to act quickly, telling him that a surveyor must be named as soon as possible. Austin recommended José María Jesús de Carvajal for the job, confessing, however, that he needed additional training. He offered to provide this to Carvajal in his own home at San Felipe, adding "he is young with very notable advancements in the sciences and has a good English education" and so would be "very useful to you in many ways." Evidently Austin did not realize that Carvajal was Navarro's kinsman, as José Antonio's brother Luciano had married José María's sister Teodora.[18]

Austin's upbeat letter encouraged Navarro, who was ready for a new challenge, especially one that would offer a profit. He wrote Austin toward the end of June that he was energetically making preparations for his commission. He gave Austin instructions to be sent to Nacogdoches for preparatory work to be done before his arrival, and he spoke of hiring another surveyor in addition to Carvajal. Regarding the need for additional training for Carvajal he wrote, "Tell José María Carvajal to apply himself in learning the measurements in Spanish, because otherwise I will be hampered by a man who is not useful and makes double work for me." Despite his show of confidence, Navarro felt insecure about his commission. He had no significant experience in land distribution or dealing with rough frontiersmen in a wilderness where it would be his job to lay out towns and establish ayuntamientos, as his instructions required. Understandably he felt concern about these responsibilities, and he said as much when he told Austin he hoped to visit with him "for you to enlighten me regarding this commission of which I know little."[19]

At the same time Navarro was considering accepting the Pecan Point commission, he again turned his attention to his four-league claim that had languished for a year and a half. On July 16, 1830, he wrote to Músquiz "solemnly and firmly" claiming land from the Gachupin Trail to be located on the Atascosa River and to include the Agua Negra Spring. He asked Músquiz to forward his request to the Béxar city council for its approval and for an *amparo* to protect his claim. The ayuntamiento read Navarro's petition and again found that a prior claim to the land existed. Having lost the Capote land and now having his choice on the Atascosa denied, Navarro must have been infuriated. Músquiz came to his rescue, ruling that because of the superior authority of the state government, Navarro could have his leagues after all.[20] But procedural matters would grind on for another year before Navarro received title to the land and the boundaries were defined by a survey.

Meanwhile, he continued to mull over the offer to serve as the Pecan Point land commissioner. No doubt he prudently conferred with Juan Martín de Veramendi and Erasmo Seguín, who had firsthand knowledge of the troublesome character of Pecan Point settlers and could realistically advise him about problems he might encounter there. Finally, Navarro wrote to Viesca on July 19 and accepted the appointment. He made sure the governor understood the problems that could accompany an attempt to bring order to such an isolated area, occupied by obstreperous frontiersmen, where the boundaries were not formally defined and there was a long tradition of lawlessness. He explained to Viesca that he would need flexibility in applying the colonization laws "because of the inveterate vices of these colonies, isolated for many years."[21] Experience would later cause him to support a stricter interpretation of colonization laws.

Navarro's appointment was an important and powerful position, because only land commissioners—not empresarios—could issue titles to land in Mexican Texas. Much of Navarro's time for the next two years would be spent on these activities, first in the Pecan Point Colony of Arthur G. Wavell, but primarily in the colony of Green DeWitt—for Pecan Point would soon become a casualty of the Law of April 6, 1830.

Wavell was an ambitious English soldier of fortune. He convinced the Mexican government that he could introduce hundreds of English and Irish colonists who would block illicit North American immigration into the border region, where Anglo settlement was prohibited. Wavell's contract, which he secured with the assistance of Austin, was dated March 9, 1826, and his lands were south of the Red River near the area known as Pecan Point, occupied by Anglos since 1806. It had served as an Indian trading post and a refuge where no government had been established. Wavell never set foot in his colony. He shuttled between Mexico City and England, where he attempted to organize prospective colonists, and delegated preparations in Texas to his agent, Benjamin R. Milam.[22]

In Béxar, Carvajal wrote to Austin at the beginning of September 1830 about the upcoming departure of "my dear cousin" (as he styled Navarro) on his trip to Pecan Point. Carvajal admitted that he had been dragging his feet, perhaps a confession that he had not taken advantage of Austin's offer to help him master surveying techniques. Navarro had also not been moving very quickly. During September, he settled his personal affairs and municipal duties, and he made final preparations for his journey. Bexareños celebrated Mexican independence on September 16, which required his attendance. As directed by the ayuntamiento in his capacity as síndico procurador, he prepared recommendations for the appointment of a new political chief, as required by state law. Three candidates had to be submitted to Governor Viesca for approval. On September 22, he completed a draft of his opinion: his first choice was to retain Músquiz, his second choice was Veramendi, and his third choice was Antonio Saucedo. When he presented his recommendation to the council for a vote, the members approved it after considerable discussion. During this meeting Navarro informed the council he was leaving soon for Pecan Point, about which they had been told in July, and he asked that a replacement be named. This was done immediately, and José María Cárdenas was sworn in as síndico procurador.[23]

One last obligation remained: to pay Donaciano Ruiz for repairs to San Fernando Church. On November 1, Navarro compiled an itemized list of Ruiz's expenses and noted that his brother José Ángel had offered to make this payment. A short time later, probably a month behind schedule on November 3, 1830, José Antonio Navarro and his entourage departed Béxar on their 350-mile trip to Nacogdoches via San Felipe. They arrived by the 13th at San Felipe, where Austin was preparing to leave for Saltillo to serve in the third state legislature. He gave Navarro a letter for Michel B. Menard, whom Austin wanted to serve as his agent in Nacogdoches during his absence. Navarro's party finally arrived in Nacogdoches toward the end of November and he delivered Austin's letter to Menard.[24]

Upon arrival in Nacogdoches Navarro must have been enraged to discover that his commission for Pecan Point had been canceled before it even began. Wavell, despite his best efforts, had failed to bring settlers from England and Ireland, and the fact that most of the settlers in his colony came from the United States violated the Law of April 6, 1830. Furthermore, there was no well-defined boundary for the Pecan Point area, and the governor of Arkansas Territory argued that much of it was under his authority. General Manuel de Mier y Terán, commandant general of the Interior Provinces, denied the Arkansas claim but nonetheless ordered a suspension of titles being issued to settlers in Pecan Point.[25] To find that no titles would be issued after months of preparations, expenditures for equipment and supplies, and a dangerous, month-long trip must have left Navarro shaking with helpless anger. But there was nothing he could do except to express his disgust with the situation, which he did in a letter to Músquiz:

I began my journey with heavy expenses. I brought a writer, a surveyor, working men, besides other expenses I had as you have seen.
Now, it is impossible for me to continue with my commission, due
to a contradictory order I have just received from His Excellency, the
Governor, which was issued on October the thirtieth, and the one
you have just sent me from His Excellency, the Commandant General
(Terán) . . . I am planning to return to Béxar within four days, before
my interests are ruined. I expect to receive just compensation for my
troubles and losses . . . . I had no other alternative than obey as a good
citizen the order of the commission which I least expected, which was
imposed on me at a time when I was most peacefully conducting my
business.[26]

Shortly after the new year began, Jose de las Piedras, commander of the
Nacogdoches garrison, reported that he had met with Navarro, but the
latter had quit his commission and left for Béxar.[27]

Piedras was sympathetic to Navarro's plight and also that of Wavell's
colonists. He wrote to Austin that Navarro was in agreement with his
way of thinking in regard to allowing more immigrants in and protecting them from exclusion. After receiving the news of the suspension
of the Pecan Point colony, Músquiz sent to Governor Viesca all of the
original letters of Piedras and Navarro relative to the matter, along with
a report of the financial damages Navarro may have incurred. Músquiz
also forwarded to Navarro a copy of a letter Piedras had written on December 2, urging that Navarro be given some reimbursement for his
expenses on the trip to Nacogdoches. A few days later, Piedras affirmed
that Navarro "had derived nothing, and has been compelled to appeal to
the generosity of friends in order to return."[28]

Navarro arrived in Béxar around February 1, 1831, evidently traveling
the direct route along the Camino Real because he had no need to return by way of San Felipe. On February 3, he wrote to Samuel May Williams expressing concern about his reputation and the pending land sale
to Royall. He was also irritated that Williams had not forwarded some
stamped official letterhead (for which Navarro was responsible) that was
sent from Nacogdoches. Navarro was quick to forgive, however, saying,
"I am fortunate to know how to forget everything." He urged Williams to
remember his seven-league sale, and to be careful in assisting Royall in
selecting the land in Navarro's name in Austin's colony, "for the matters
of colonization are delicate." Still depressed regarding the Pecan Point
fiasco, Navarro signed off on a self-disparaging note, referring to "the
uselessness of your most secure and sincere friend."[29]

Within a few days Navarro's optimism returned. He wrote to Williams again on February 17 with good news. "Our always appreciable Músquiz" had been approved as political chief, while he was pleased to report that a law had passed making Nacogdoches a separate district governed by a *jefe de partido* (party chief)—"a project I left pending at the time I was in the legislature." Most important, Navarro reported, "Today I have received a letter from the governor of the state . . . naming me the commissioner for the colony of Green DeWitt in Gonzales. I am accepting it because, although it is small, I see little chance otherwise that I can [regain] my losses." Navarro could not help but add that while he did not intend to formally complain about Viesca's part in the Pecan Point disaster, "it was the Governor's mistake and that is hard for me, because of the esteem I have for Señor Viesca." Navarro's prospects had improved when Veramendi was elected vice governor of Coahuila and Texas in January. This bolstered his relationship with the state government. Navarro also mentioned to Williams that Austin and Carvajal had written an article favorable to him about the Pecan Point misadventure, to appear in the *Texas Gazette* at San Felipe. Wanting to do everything possible to salvage his reputation and reassure the settlers of Gonzales, his new charges, he asked Williams to "promptly print an additional article in the *Gazette*, saying that 'the government had on this date named me commissioner for Gonzales in just repayment for my setbacks.'"[30]

On March 14, Navarro wrote two letters to the governor. In the first he formally accepted the DeWitt land commission; in the second, he began what would be a tedious effort to acquire and locate this seven leagues of land in accordance with his responsibilities as the DeWitt commissioner. Already foreseeing problems, he explained to Viesca that since he was planning to select the land in DeWitt's colony during the empresario's absence, "I will not be able to confer possession of the lands and titles upon myself." He offered an easy solution to the dilemma: "I ask Your Excellency to order, through the political chief, the authority for the alcalde of the colony to put me in possession of the land and titles when I am ready to request them."[31] At the same time, Navarro continued to develop closer relationships with Williams, whom Austin had left in charge at San Felipe when he left for Saltillo to serve in the third legislature, and with his friend Miguel Arciniega, who now served as the land commissioner for Austin's colony.

By the end of March, Navarro must have been preparing to leave for Gonzales to begin his work as commissioner, but he had a multitude of loose ends to tie up. Above all, he worried about the matter of his land sale. In February, he had told the Governor that he wanted to locate his leagues in DeWitt's colony; now, a month later, he wrote to Williams that he wanted them in Austin's colony—probably to avoid the appearance of a conflict of interest, about which he had previously written to Viesca. Navarro explained, "You and Mr. Stephen [would] do me a great favor then if you could take the seven leagues of land in that colony which I have bought from the government. Because of the delicate business of colonization I do not wish to get them in any other colony." He had seen copies of the *Texas Gazette* with an article about his DeWitt commission, thanked Williams for that favor, and asked him for another. He told Williams that he was ordering eight boxes of tobacco and eight barrels of gunpowder. Navarro asked Williams to delegate the matter to a person of confidence and pledged that he would send payment for the materials and shipping charges. He also asked Williams to remember to send a shipment of playing cards to his brother Eugenio at Goliad. Apologizing for not writing sooner, he explained, "I found myself in the middle of a wedding, that is my brother José Ángel's to Miss Juana Ramírez. He sends his regards to you with regard to his new [marital] state."[32]

Navarro hurried during the first days of April to complete preparations for his trip to Gonzales. DeWitt's colony bordered on that of Martín De León, so Political Chief Músquiz sent Navarro copies of contracts from the De León colony to help prevent or settle disputed land claims. On April 4, Músquiz also appointed Navarro as a special commissioner to award land to Margila Chirino, the widow of José Francisco Salinas and the half-sister of Navarro's wife.[33] Having apparently resolved that matter, Navarro left Béxar and arrived in Gonzales by the 10th. On April 14, Byrd Lockhart appeared before him and qualified to serve as his principal surveyor. That same day James Bowie arrived with a letter from Williams to Navarro. Bowie was traveling to Béxar, where he would marry Navarro's niece, Ursula de Veramendi, on April 25 and thus become a member of the Navarro-Ruiz-Veramendi family. Navarro thanked Williams for having endorsed Bowie as a friend, saying, "I presented my respects to Señor Bowie although there was nothing I could do for him because he needed nothing from me and much less since he was traveling to Béxar at the time."[34]

Navarro had just begun issuing titles in Gonzales when the time allotted for the completion of DeWitt's colony expired. DeWitt had requested an extension, which was denied in Saltillo, and Músquiz instructed Antonio Elozúa as the commander of troops in Texas to prevent the introduction of families into DeWitt's colony. Elozúa responded immediately by sending orders to garrisons and detachments throughout Texas. Anticipating such a default, Músquiz had previously asked

Navarro to report the number of families in his colony and how many more were scheduled to come. Navarro replied to Músquiz that DeWitt had told him he still needed 317 families to complete his contract. He added that the settlers already in place were discouraged by the lack of security and other conditions, while DeWitt worried that he would never receive his premium lands as an empresario. Navarro of course protested against the order to block settlers from DeWitt's colony, but he confessed to Austin that he had only issued eighty titles and 190 more were needed to complete the colony. Navarro must have realized there was no way that DeWitt could fulfill his contract, but the commander of the small military detachment at Gonzales was instructed to work "in consultation" with him on all such matters.[35] In the end, Navarro's hard work enabled 82 more families to gain admission to the colony, for a total of 162.

Bringing new families to DeWitt's Colony was not the only problem that vexed Navarro. Conflicts over land claims between DeWitt and De León had begun in 1825. De León had established his colony in 1824, near present-day Victoria. DeWitt arrived in 1825 and saw families from De León's colony settling in what he believed to be a part of his grant. Hostility resulted from overlapping claims until the dispute was resolved by Músquiz in favor of DeWitt, clearing the way for Navarro to continue issuing titles. By August 1831, Navarro explained to Músquiz that he was unable to comply with an order concerning frontage of surveys on watercourses because most surveys in DeWitt's colony had been made prior to his arrival as commissioner. Shortly thereafter, Músquiz announced his intention to travel to DeWitt's colony to resolve a conflict resulting from José María Salinas's desire to locate his four-league grant in an area where other settlers had claims. A few days later, Músquiz sent Navarro an inquiry from the new governor, José María Letona, that suggested moving scattered settlers to DeWitt's colony and asked Navarro for a report on the matter. Navarro did not neglect his personal interests while he was engaged in selling land for others. While waiting to take possession of his grant on the Atascosa River, he wrote to Letona about the seven leagues he had asked to buy from the government. He wanted to locate it in DeWitt's colony, and since the empresario was absent he repeated his suggestion that the Gonzales alcalde be authorized to provide him with deeds. Letona replied on April 15, just ten days after taking office as governor, complying with Navarro's request.[36]

During the spring and summer of 1831 Navarro wrote frequently to Samuel May Williams, filling his letters with personal comments as well as business concerns. With Austin in the legislature at Saltillo, Williams was his main friend and associate who had expertise in colonization. Some letters reveal Navarro's sense of humor. Williams had married a Tejana and converted to Catholicism. Navarro jokingly told him that he hoped he would not become an "orthodox fanatic." On a serious note, Navarro expressed irritation with his commission. The colonists, he said, were more concerned with money and cows than land titles. Mocking their broken Spanish he said: *"mi no güante toma titulo: mi se bá pa Santo Antonio"* ("I don't want to take land title, I am going to San Antonio"). He also wanted to get back to San Antonio, as Béxar was becoming known, and said only half-jokingly: "that is my song [too] and by God I am really going to do it." He asked about Royall and the seven leagues, and emphasized that it would be "an absolute conflict of interest" for him to issue titles to himself in DeWitt's colony. Worse, he had learned that Royall wanted to transfer title to John Caldwell, a stranger who might not even be a legal settler. This would violate the state's colonization law and "damage my reputation." Navarro was "starting to feel regret about the wretched contract" with Royall, though he assured Williams that he "was a slave to my word and to my honor, and . . . shall carry it out as I have said." In closing, Navarro lamented that he had gotten no mail from below the Rio Grande lately: "It seems that excepting you all my friends have closed their books on me. I am so angry, that if I weren't like the [porcupine?] whose anger is used up after it loses its bristles, I would be worse than [José Francisco] Madero!" Lest Williams take Navarro's reference to his old legislative opponent too seriously, Navarro added that he was "in the mood for joking around."[37]

Perhaps feeling lonely at Gonzales, Navarro sent another chatty letter to Williams the next day. He admitted that he had no real reason to do so, "since my business, anger, and devilishness were vented in my last letter to you." Navarro discussed his "old companion and friend" Arciniega and the "Colorados," meaning the colonists living on the Colorado River in Austin's colony. Navarro said they had an "I-don't-know-what interest, although sometimes they anger me by the temerity with which they advance their affairs." This, it seems, was a reference to the ignorance or indifference of these people to the Mexican laws under which they lived. He asked how Austin and Williams judged the quality of lands in their colony, as he wished to apply the same criteria to DeWitt's lands.[38]

Near the end of May, Navarro dispatched two more letters to Williams. He again apologized for pestering Williams so much but declared his intention to keep doing it: "As you know, the best lover is the most jealous, and this happens to me to the point of intolerance towards my friends." He wanted Williams to hurry Royall in buying his seven leagues. In a jocular mood he said he looked forward to visiting with Arciniega, setting him down on the bare floor, and giving him a "stern lecture." He did convey some good news: that the state legislature had decided to pay him 424 pesos "for the unfortunate trip I made for my Pecan Point Commission." It would be applied to what Navarro owed the state for the seven purchased leagues, meaning that a half or a third of the debt was already paid, "which has encouraged me greatly." Perhaps as a final joke, though one with a clear message, he asked Williams to give a passport, in English, to the "boys" carrying his letter so that they would not be confused with "bandoleros."[39]

By June, Navarro was becoming even more apprehensive about the propriety of selling his seven leagues. He contacted Williams, asking him to help "rid me of a moral annoyance with respect to the conduct observed by the gentleman Royal [sic] who [sells] lands he does not yet own." which was not the agreement Navarro had made. He proposed that Williams, as his agent, locate the property in Austin's colony and issue proper titles. Royall would pay Williams for his services, and Navarro would examine the paperwork before it went to the government. He called his contract with Royall "this messy affair which I deplore more than the famous pains of purgatory" and styled it an "ugly business, although legal." One month later, he begged Austin, as a friend, to "get rid of a nuisance for me." He wanted Austin to locate the seven leagues in his colony, issue a title at once, and "let the Mustafa of Persia settle them if he wishes." Navarro was so disgusted with the business with Royall that all he wanted was the money owed him, regardless of who took possession of the land. He made this clear to Austin: "By God, I implore of you to expedite titles for me! So that they be settled in my name at once by the Colorados."[40]

When Austin wrote a letter expressing similar concerns, it was Navarro's turn to be supportive: "You have reason to be disgusted with the demands of colonization, but it appears that you have not given a thought to anything more judicious. To prolong the days of your life you need to separate yourself from these matters that because of your rectitude have weighed you down." Trying to get Austin to relax, he recalled the old folk saying: "Give in to desire and you will come out smelling of flowers (date a deceo y olerás a poleó [sic])." Navarro had to admit that he did not take his own advice, for "I always have a bad aroma because I never leave anything undone for the next day." Still, he was not as bad as Austin, because "I, my friend, care little for what they call fame. What do I care if I am considered to be a Socrates after I am dead? A long life is precious for all and with a regular esteem of my contemporaries is all I desire." Rather than have Austin take offense, though, Navarro concluded, "I approve of your resolute determination."[41]

Navarro's land tangles were not his only business concerns. A statement by José Ángel Navarro at Goliad in June 1831 shows that the family was still in the mercantile business, importing crockery, cloth, tools, and coffee to sell. At the same time that he was offering folksy advice to Austin, José Antonio reported that someone had stolen three hundred pesos and some cows from him. He believed the thief would go to Natchitoches and asked that Austin send letters to friends there, hoping the scoundrel could be caught and his money recovered. As for the cattle, if found they were to be delivered to Jared Groce. One month later, Navarro wrote Williams about the stolen money and cows, plus a lost branding iron. As for his duties as a land commissioner, Navarro said he had not worked in eleven days and confessed that he was bored, but he was expecting Bowie, who would bring many titles to be processed.[42]

Navarro had returned to Béxar from Gonzales by September 1831 to finalize his grant for four leagues of land on the Atascosa River. On October 2 he wrote to the Béxar alcalde, giving him more precise landmarks to delineate the land, emphasizing that it was to include the Agua Negra Spring, and asking for a "scientific surveyor" to measure and record the bounds. Two days later, José María Jesús de Carvajal, his kinsman who had served as surveyor for the failed Pecan Point colony, completed the survey for Navarro. He officially reported the claim as having four arable *labores de temporal* (representing 177 acres each), with the rest classified as pasture. Thus Navarro had 708 arable acres and 17,004 of pasture. For this huge tract, Navarro owed 125.25 pesos to the state government—115.25 for the pasture and 10 for the *labores*. A major part of Navarro's personal land concerns was resolved when he gained title to the land on the Atascosa on October 6, 1831, three years after he had filed for the tract.[43] José María Salinas, as the alcalde of Béxar and land commissioner for the Béxar district, signed the final document.

As soon as he obtained title to the Atascosa grant, Navarro returned to Gonzales to resume his responsibilities as a land commissioner. In addition to his regular tasks, he had to make time to serve as a special commissioner for Veramendi, who in September 1831 had requested that someone be appointed to put him in possession of five leagues of land granted to him. Political Chief Músquiz notified Navarro that he was to assist his brother-in-law. Veramendi had found promising sites to the north of Béxar. He asked for two leagues on the Comal Springs, site of present-day New Braunfels, and two at the San Marcos Springs, site of present-day San Marcos. The remaining league was to be on springs near the Guadalupe River. In November, Veramendi met with Navarro in Gonzales to begin the final process of securing a title and on November 10, Navarro awarded him possession and title to the land and springs as requested.[44]

Navarro left Gonzales and returned to Béxar by the beginning of 1832 to finish paperwork concerning his duties as a land commissioner and attend to personal affairs, which included buying more town property. On January 11 he bought a lot from María Josefa Rodríguez north of town near the point where the irrigation ditch called Acequia Madre de Valero began at San Pedro Springs. On April 16 he bought the lot on Laredo Street where he would later build a home. He paid María Loreto de Castañeda, widow of Pedro Morales, 100 pesos for the 1.2-acre tract fronting on San Pedro Creek to the east, Laredo Street on the west, and Nueva Street on the south.[45] On the lot stood a *chamacuero*, a shelter made of vertical posts and leather, that had evidently served as Castañeda's residence.

Navarro's work to locate a two-league grant for Margila Chirino is of particular interest because he would buy the land from her and use it as ranch and residence for eight years. Chirino had, with Navarro's assistance, completed the procedures to secure her late husband's grant, but now she needed to choose a location. During March 1832, she wrote to Navarro, as the DeWitt commissioner, asking him to locate her two leagues on San Geronimo Creek, a tributary of the Guadalupe. Three months later, he forwarded her request to DeWitt for verification that the requested land was within the boundaries of his colony, which it was. Navarro completed the required documentation, the land was surveyed, and on July 1 Chirino received possession of and title to her property.[46] While attending to his personal interests, Navarro also finished the DeWitt paperwork. By the end of the January he submitted six dossiers to Músquiz, including the work had done as special commissioner for Chirino and Veramendi.[47]

Navarro's land deal with Royall was still pending. Indeed, he had not yet even gained title to the seven-league grant. He wrote to Williams that he was concerned that Royall, and his buyer, Caldwell, wanted to locate the tract outside of Austin's colony. Changing his position, he said that if Caldwell would take the land in DeWitt's colony, he could promptly obtain the title for him. But if Caldwell wanted a site in the defunct Wavell colony that could also be done—if he waited until the government formally declared those lands vacant. Exasperated, Navarro said he had already spent 424 pesos, and that if he had to wait ten years for his buyers to act, then how had he benefited?[48] Austin wrote to Williams about the situation. He noted that Navarro had a "thousand anxieties" about the land contracted for sale to Royall; that at first he wanted it located in Austin's colony, and then he wanted it in DeWitt's colony. Finally, "He now says that he cannot request the Govr. to appoint a new Comr. to put him in possession on the west of the Colorado, for it will make him appear ridiculous in the eyes of the govt. to be changing about so often." Austin advised Royall and Caldwell to locate the land in DeWitt's colony and finish the business at once. He explained to Williams, "They must understand that this purchase is in the eyes of the law totally void and of no effect until they are in a situation to hold land by purchase legally in their own names, and until the possession is legally given, and a transfer from Navarro [is recorded] . . . for this reason they run the risk of losing all by delay and by being too particular." Austin also reminded Williams that a proposal was before the legislature to reform the colonization law so that titles could be issued more quickly.[49]

On April 12, Navarro again wrote to Williams with two main concerns. First was the status of his seven-league sale. Saying he planned to return to Gonzales by the end of the month, he asked Williams to tell Caldwell to visit him there. He had heard that Caldwell's brother-in-law proposed to give him twenty-five cows with calves as partial payment, to which Navarro was agreeable. Navarro's second concern was that, having taking a stand against an infraction of the colonization law, disgruntled colonists were critical of him. He had nullified an attempted land sale by W. Moreland, a DeWitt colonist who left Texas, and thus clashed with Thomas Jefferson Chambers, who supported Moreland's clandestine efforts. Navarro assured Williams, and asked him to assure colonists that he supported colonization, but he was not willing to ignore a blatant infringement of the law. Navarro explained, "You and other North American friends are aware of my liberalism; that I am not a political fanatic; that I have always been—and still remain—enthusiastic about colonization because of the intimate knowledge that only thus will Texas be made to bloom." But "No other interpretation . . . is possible," he said, "even if you were to combine the [wisdom of the] Sorbonne of France and the University of Salamanca." Navarro insisted that no animosity to foreigners could be attributed to him because his actions had proven otherwise. But "in matters of law, of justice and of reason, Dear God! . . . I lose my self-control to the point that I would confront my own mother!" Less dramatically, Navarro added, "We cannot fool ourselves. We all know the sad theater for speculators that Texas has been converted to with respect to land. Nevertheless, we cannot stand by while misdeeds are committed publicly, as Moreland did right in our face."[50]

In the spring of 1832, Royall and Caldwell were finally ready to buy Navarro's seven leagues. They did not want the property to be in Austin's or DeWitt's colonies and were willing to wait until the defunct Wavell colony lands were declared vacant. They probably wanted to locate the leagues there in coordination with Austin's plan to take possession of land on both banks of the upper Colorado River in the vicinity of Onion Creek, where he planned to establish a utopian community centered upon an academy. On May 13, abiding by the wishes of Royall and Caldwell, Navarro wrote Political Chief Músquiz saying he no longer wanted the land located in DeWitt's colony but rather in land that had been assigned to Milam, an area just declared vacant. He told Músquiz that he had decided to take the lands on the south bank of the Colorado River at a point about five to six and one-half leagues above the Béxar Road (better known as the *Camino Real*). The land was a short distance southeast of the future site of Austin, the capital of Texas. Navarro asked that Arciniega, as Austin's land commissioner, be instructed to give him possession of the land and issue a title. Orders to this effect came in June, and Royall performed the survey. At last on July 10, 1832, Navarro received the long-sought seven leagues. Arciniega issued the title to 30,996 acres on the south bank of the Colorado River, as Navarro had requested at the behest of Royall and Caldwell. The fee Navarro owed for the land was 752 pesos, from which 424 pesos were deducted, evidently for what was owed him for his work for the Pecan Point colony, leaving a balance due of 328 pesos.[51]

Ten more months passed before Navarro finally completed the land sale and rid himself of a seven-league, three-year affliction. In Béxar, on April 2, 1833, he sold the claim to John Caldwell, "a naturalized colonist of Austin's enterprise," for a purchase price of 1,302 pesos in common money (*dinero común*). Deducting the 328 pesos Navarro owed the state, his gross profit was 974 pesos.[52] It is unlikely that Navarro, after enduring "a thousand anxieties" over the course of three years, thought the outcome was worth the effort. This distressing experience ended his speculation in land under Mexican rule, though he did continue to acquire land by purchasing from individuals.

While Navarro was struggling with his land sale and responsibilities to colonists at Gonzales, José Francisco Madero tried to pile more work on him. Madero, the land commissioner for a colony on the lower Trinity River known as Liberty (*La Villa de la Santísima Trinidad de la Libertad*), had encountered unpleasant complications. While issuing titles to settlers at Liberty, Madero became embroiled in a dispute with Juan Davis Bradburn, the commandant at Anahuac. Settlers rebelled against Bradburn during the summer of 1832, but also drove Madero out of Texas. In a letter to Williams, Madero said he was delegating his commission to Navarro, as authorized by the state government, and he was sending Navarro the colony paperwork. Navarro evidently considered taking on this responsibility, for notes in his handwriting indicate he was reviewing colonization laws, economic regulations for towns, and various decrees. In the end, however, he did not accept this appointment. Perhaps he was dissuaded by the fact that Bradburn jailed Madero and his surveyor, Carvajal, because of turmoil among the settlers, and he wisely chose not to become involved in disputes far from home that might become violent.[53]

Navarro had struggled through a minefield of legal and moral complexities to acquire extensive lands. Besides the aggravating problem with the seven leagues, he was responsible for finishing the paperwork on DeWitt's colony. He accomplished this during early November 1832 and submitted the entire file to Political Chief Músquiz. Included was a list of 162 Anglo colonists to whom he had granted land titles, a list of the native and naturalized Mexican citizens to whom he had issued titles, a list of grantees given land in 1831 and 1832, and associated paperwork. These grantees fell far short of the 300 families DeWitt had contracted to introduce. With his report, Navarro sent a map, saying he had "completely finished his work." No other commissioner completed his work as comprehensively as Navarro did. To resolve the problems of DeWitt's incomplete colony, Veramendi, who succeeded Letona as governor when the latter died in September 1832, placed its administration under the authority of De León, whose son Fernando subsequently served as the land commissioner. In December 1832 Political Chief Músquiz informed Veramendi that Navarro had completed distributing all lands in DeWitt's colony, despite the problems that had occurred.[54]

With this responsibility behind him, Navarro directed his full attention to continuing his mercantile business and beginning a ranching operation. The goal of rebuilding his family's wealth, toward which he had worked since 1816, was within reach. He had already bought two town lots earlier in 1832. Within a year of acquiring Atascosa Ranch, considerable numbers of livestock appear in Navarro's possession. The 1832 Béxar census shows that he had fifty-five cows, forty-one bulls, ten oxen, seven horses, two mares, and four mules.[55] Almost certainly these animals became seed herds for Atascosa Ranch. The oxen and mules had a dual purpose. They could pull wagons loaded with merchandise

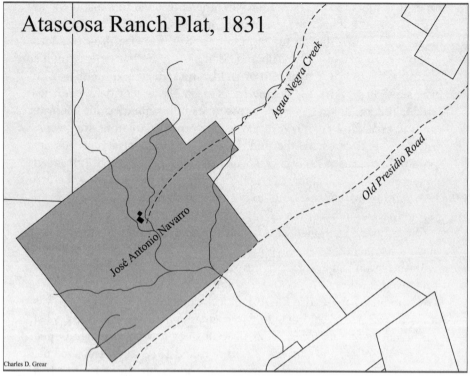

José Antonio Navarro's four-league Atascosa Ranch, so called because it straddled the Atacosa River. It was located about thirty miles south of San Antonio and became his primary residence after 1855.

and goods to and from the ports, and they could pull plows to culti-vate land for the crops that enabled a ranch to be largely self-sufficient. In addition, with Navarro's "political brother" Veramendi seated in the governor's office, the future looked bright for José Antonio Navarro as he advanced toward the American Dream. Once more, however, politics intervened and diverted his attention from his personal eco-nomic concerns.

At the national level, 1832 was a year of conflict between the sup-porters of two generals: Anastacio Bustamante and Antonio López de Santa Anna. Bustamante's centralist government, which took power after a coup in 1829, was harsh and repressive. Santa Anna, promoting the federalist cause and the 1824 Constitution, challenged Bustamante during 1832 and entered Mexico City on January 3, 1833, at the head of a triumphant procession. In March he was chosen president, again proclaiming liberalism and federalism. The Santa Anna party enjoyed widespread support among the Texas colonists, who thought his support of federalism favored their interests. His liberal façade, however, soon dissolved; he asserted that Mexico was not ready for democracy and in 1834 established a centralist government as repressive as the one it replaced.

Meanwhile, Austin and Anglo American colonists were encouraged by the 1832 revolt led by Santa Anna and hoped that conditions favored a separation of Texas and Coahuila. In October, their representatives met at San Felipe and wrote a petition listing the problems of the union of Coahuila and Texas and justifying its division into separate states. No Tejanos attended the convention. Speaking for the Bexareños, Political Chief Músquiz informed the San Felipe representatives that, while he sympathized with their concerns, their meeting, done without permission, was illegal. Knowing that his petition would require the approval of Tejano leaders, Austin traveled to Béxar in December to make his case for separation. In an unofficial meeting on December 5, he lobbied the Navarros and other leaders for five hours, urging them to adopt an aggressive stance in support of statehood. Clearly he expected that his friend Navarro and other Bexareños would agree with him, and he was right. "They were unanimous," he wrote to Williams, "and I have full confidence that what was agreed upon will be carried into effect."[56]

Having agreed with Austin, the Béxar ayuntamiento named a committee on December 6 to write a draft document. Two council members were selected: José Ángel Navarro and José Cassiano, along with four individuals not on the council: José Antonio Navarro, Refugio de la Garza, José María Balmaceda, and Erasmo Seguín. Austin hoped they would produce a statement favoring a separation of Texas and Coahuila. Showing his manipulative side, he said, "Then, they will be so compromised that there will be no backing out, even if they wished to do so, which they will not." On December 19, the ayuntamiento and forty-two other Bexareños met in a public session to discuss the draft petition drawn up by the Navarros and the other committee members. The petition criticized the existing state government and suggested fourteen measures as remedies for the problems that disturbed the Texans. The document clearly reflected Austin's influence—except that it did not call for the separation of Texas from Coahuila. Forty-nine Bexareños, including the ayuntamiento, approved the petition with their signatures.[57]

The Béxar petition is an extraordinary document because it represents the only public statement from Tejano leaders about the problems they confronted in Texas and their suggested solutions. At the same time, Austin's growing impatience was clear. To force the issue of statehood, he had overreached himself and unwisely urged the Béxar council to give an ultimatum to the government demanding that if full resolution of grievances was not accomplished by March 1, Texans would "proceed immediately to organize a local government." The Bexareños had listened politely to Austin's entreaties, agreed with him in principle, and incorporated some of his suggestions in their petition. When Austin left Béxar, he was certain that he had convinced them to follow his directions and that the political chief was firmly on his side. "Músquiz, after all," he wrote to Williams, "is one of the best friends to Texas and the truest that lives in this place." Determined to have statehood, Austin totally misread the Bexareño leaders' conviction that it was premature to push for separation. In his thinking, a "Friend of Texas" meant someone who unquestionably shared his vision for Texas, which Músquiz and the Navarros, apparently did not. Indeed, the former had become convinced of the need to sustain the union of Texas and Coahuila to prevent its separation from Mexico.[58]

Soon after Austin left Béxar, the ayuntamiento wrote to Governor Veramendi, expressing in blunt terms their negative attitude toward the San Felipe convention and Austin's attempt to mediate with Bexareño leaders. Much to Músquiz's satisfaction, the ayuntamiento declared its resolute opposition to separate statehood and rejected support for the Plan de Veracruz (in favor of Santa Anna over Bustamante), which Austin had endorsed. Santa Anna had not yet won, and Bexareños were doubtful about his chances. Only Seguín thought he would succeed. With notable foresight about the situation, the Béxar council asked Veramendi for reforms that would prevent a revolution. Unfortunately for him, and for them, any reform efforts were hampered by the acceleration of a conflict between Monclova and Saltillo over which city would be the capital of Coahuila and Texas. This tale of two cities began as a clash between local leaders and culminated in a dispute that, with other elements, precipitated Mexico's loss of Texas.[59]

Veramendi's assumption of power as governor in Saltillo, after the sudden death of his predecessor, must have greatly cheered his fellow Bexareños and all of Texas. After years of limited input into state government, they were now represented by one of their own. Moreover, Veramendi came into office with a legislature that was decidedly favorable to Texas. On March 2, 1833, the legislators considered petitions from Béxar, Goliad, and Parras to move the capital from Saltillo to Monclova, and they approved the measure a few days later. After an efficient transition of only twenty days, the legislature opened its first session in Monclova on April 1. But the matter was not settled, as was made evident by the success of the Saltillo deputies in adding the words "for now" to the article that transferred the capital to Monclova. The tension would build between Saltillo and Monclova until it exploded two years later.[60]

Navarro was able to help his brother-in-law with one small aspect of the regional conflict. About the time Veramendi became governor, troops from Monclova were transferred to Béxar. These soldiers were near the point of mutiny because of a lack of pay and supplies. Commandant Elozúa at Béxar wrote to Veramendi, "I have absolutely no provisions for them." He suggested that Navarro could loan enough goods to supply the detachment for a month and a half; otherwise, the Monclova troops at Béxar would have to be removed or disbanded. Navarro fortunately was in a position to do this. He had accumulated considerable cash reserves by means of merchandising and his position as a land commissioner. He had already made a small loan to the destitute soldiers in January 1833, and in March he made the additional, larger loan for the same purpose, for which he was repaid in April. Perhaps in gratitude for this assistance, Veramendi in April informed Navarro that he had been elected a "supplementary deputy" to Congress by the electoral junta of the state.[61] Although this was a role that did not require him to attend congressional sessions, it was nonetheless an honor and evidence of the continued ascent of Navarro's political star.

In late April and May, Navarro met for the last time with his old friend Austin, who arrived in Béxar on his way to Mexico City. Exasperated by the political instability, Austin had decided to go to the federal capital to advocate for Texas statehood and a repeal of the Law of April 6, 1830. While in Béxar from April 28 through May 10, he made another attempt to gain support for an assembly similar to the second convention that had just concluded in San Felipe. Such meetings were clearly illegal under Mexican law, since only state legislatures could petition Congress. After three days of long and emotional discussions, only Seguín endorsed this idea, but he refused to go with Austin to Mexico City, citing personal reasons. In reality, Austin had already passed the point of no return. If statehood was denied, he had said before coming to Béxar, "I am ready for war or anything." Although no record has been found, Navarro and Austin must have met and discussed political affairs. No doubt Navarro would have been aware of Austin's agitated state of mind and would have counseled him, just as he had done nearly two years before when he told Austin that he was too involved in matters of colonization and advised him to relax in order to prolong the days of his life.[62] Austin did not follow Navarro's advice and rode out of Béxar for the last time on May 10. Navarro never saw his friend again.

At the time of Austin's visit, Navarro must have been feeling quite content about his lot in life. He had made a profit of 974 pesos from his sale of seven leagues and full repayment on his loan to support the Monclova troops in Béxar. His family was also increasing. While he and his wife, Margarita de la Garza, continued to live apart, they had another son, José Ángel III, in 1827, and yet another, Celso Cornelio, in 1830. Navarro lived with his mother, grandmother, and siblings; Margarita and the children stayed with her mother. On March 9, 1833, Refugio de la Garza baptized the eight-day-old Wenseslao Eusebio Navarro at San Fernando Church. The child was evidently named after Saint Wenceslaus, the patron saint of the modern Czech Republic. The name, however, did not take, and the sixth Navarro child was always known as "Sixto." At the end of June, Navarro received in Goliad ten carts of supplies to sell. Included were more than 1,000 pounds each of rice, sugar, coffee, and soap. Other items included flour, 124 pounds of iron, more than 100 dozen pieces of white crockery, candles, [olive] oil, wine, whisky, and Chinese tea.[63] As the year passed, Navarro's personal affairs seemed likely to continue toward greater well-being and prosperity, the American Dream his father had pursued. However, few could foresee the catastrophic events that would rock Texas just over the horizon.

Some hint of the trouble to come emerged again at the garrison in Béxar. The stubborn problem of paying and supplying the troops from Monclova reached crisis proportions in the summer of 1833. The supplies Navarro had provided earlier that year were exhausted, and Captain Alejandro Treviño reported in July to Commandant Elozúa that the Monclova soldiers refused to serve. A corporal spoke for the troops, saying that they had neither been paid nor given supplies. Elozúa managed to keep them in service for another month, in part because Navarro again provided food and merchandise to the garrison. Several Mexican military and civil officials at this time sent bleak reports on Texas to their superiors, and Elozúa was no different. Months before his retirement in September, he wrote, "There remain in Texas no more than the presidial companies of Béxar, Alamo, Monclova, and Bahía del Espíritu Santo; these troops represent little force and could be considered null . . . for their needs are such that most of them have had to neglect their service in order to work to provide for themselves."[64]

Personal tragedy wracked Navarro's extended family in the late summer of 1833. Barely eight months after beginning his term as governor, Veramendi died in a cholera epidemic. Ironically, he had taken action to halt the spread of the disease. Believing that cholera was spread by human contact, like smallpox, he had sent an order on August 13 to the political chief of Saltillo to quarantine persons who developed symptoms. If the jail was full, the official was to expropriate "individual houses in which to place and contain the sickened persons." When the disease quickly spread to Monclova, killing four people, the legislature adjourned on September 3. But it was too late. Cholera, a water-borne bacterium had entered the upper reaches of the acequia that provided much of Monclova's water supply. According to burial records, the epidemic ravaged Monclova for thirty-one days, through September 30. During that month a total of 458 deaths from cholera were recorded. Among the dead was the entire Veramendi family. The first casualty, on the 6th, was Veramendi's wife, María Josefa, the sister of José Antonio Navarro. The governor died at six o'clock the next morning. On the 10th, Ursula, who had married James Bowie, died; and on the 13th, an adopted Veramendi child also died. The Veramendis were buried in the *Panteón del Hospital* cemetery at Monclova. They were hastily interred, probably in mass graves, along with the hundreds of others who died so quickly during the time of the *colera grande*.[65] With these untimely deaths, one-third of the Navarro extended family circle came to a sudden, tragic end.

Worried about the epidemic, but unaware of the Veramendis' deaths, Navarro wrote to Williams on September 11, urgently requesting a supply of medicines: camphor, calomel, *purga de Jalapa* (a laxative), and laudanum. He explained: "I assure you my head is very occupied in thinking how to liberate us if it [attacks] us. I am completely unconcerned about business and think of nothing but to assure you that this is the first letter I have written in the last three months." News of the deaths of the Veramendis arrived on the 26th and Navarro immediately relayed it to Williams:

> My Dear Friend . . . When I spoke to you about the brutal cholera, I felt an inexplicable uneasiness and sad premonition; in effect, what should I expect but misfortune? My brother Veramendi, my sister Josefa, and Urzulita de Bowie have died in an horrifying manner in Monclova . . . .I have lost a special brother-in-law in Veramendi, and Texas a good son, a loyal and good friend. The Government of the State of Texas has suffered a political loss.[66]

Navarro asked Williams to notify Bowie, who was in Natchez, that his wife, Ursula, was dead. That same day, Navarro's mother, Josefa Ruiz, informed the alcalde that, because Veramendi died without a will, she, as the grandmother, would have custody of the "eight orphans . . . and that these minors being natives of (Béxar) must necessarily come to the bosom of the surviving family." No baptismal records were found for any children of Bowie and Ursula.[67]

Three days after receiving the tragic news from Monclova, Navarro made radical changes in his life. He sold his interest in his childhood home, the Ruiz-Navarro house at the corner of Presidio and Flores Street, where he had lived with his family for more than twenty-five years. This seems less a business transaction than a closing of one period of his life and the beginning of another. Shunning stilted legal phrases, Navarro wrote an informal statement on September 29, when he sold to his brother José Luciano for one hundred pesos in cash "that part of my paternal inheritance in the house on Flores Street that is next to the house of my brother, José Angel." Revealing the personal nature of the transaction, he added that although the value of his share of the house might be worth more, this arrangement was a family matter in which all the heirs had participated. In fact, his brothers and sisters had sold their interest in the property to Luciano in 1827.[68]

By cutting the ties to his childhood home, Navarro took an important step toward personal independence. His family was close, and he was not the only child who stayed at home with his mother and grandmother into adulthood; his brother, José Ángel, did the same. But because he had been disabled as a youth, José Antonio's ties to his family may have been particularly strong. It is easy to imagine that they pampered him, and even perhaps underestimated him. In 1833, however, he was thirty-eight years old and had a wife and six children. It was time to be on his own.

When Navarro left his childhood home, he clearly intended to develop his ranch on the Atascosa River, since he registered a brand in November 1833. Navarro's personal brand merged the initials *J*, *A*, and *N°*—a standard abbreviation. He hired Ramón Rubio as a cowboy and overseer.[69] Perhaps Navarro's oldest son, José Antonio George, now fourteen years of age, was eager to go out to the ranch to help his father and learn the skills of a *vaquero*. Within a short time they built a simple ranch house, and Navarro began the practice he followed for the rest of his life of alternating his residence between a ranch house and a town house.

While Navarro was starting his ranch, Austin's efforts to gain statehood for Texas were going nowhere. He had lobbied Mexican officials, including Vice President Valentín Gómez Farías and President Santa Anna, for months, but to no avail. Despairing of his efforts to obtain separate statehood, his judgment frayed by exhaustion and depression, he wrote an ill-advised letter from Mexico City to the Béxar ayuntamiento on October 2, 1833, urging them to organize a government independent of Coahuila and to ask other ayuntamientos to do the same. Alarmed at the obvious illegality of what Austin proposed, and to protect itself, the Béxar ayuntamiento sent the incriminating document to officials in Monclova, and from there it went to Saltillo, where Austin arrived on January 2, 1834. The next day he was stunned when officials he knew personally placed him under arrest.[70] Soldiers escorted Austin back to Mexico City, where he was imprisoned.

News of Austin's arrest quickly reached Texas. On January 17, interim political chief Juan N. Seguín, knowing Navarro had contacts in Mexico, wrote to him demanding to know the circumstances and reliability of the reports of Austin's arrest. That same day, Austin wrote to the Béxar ayuntamiento from Monterrey to explain matters and express hope that no disturbances among his colonists would result from his arrest. Realizing that his leadership in Texas was probably at an end or severely compromised, he added reflectively, "I am reaching the end of my years, my strength and health." In February, Navarro sent Williams his appraisal of Austin's folly: "I told [him] about many things in order for him to avoid these misfortunes. I talked to him, in the way one should talk to friends, but he did not listen to me." Navarro concluded that "This predicament brought on by his impatience—albeit with the greatest truth and justice—led him to a puerile naiveté that caused him to be caught like a surprised child, overconfident that his presence in Mexico could save everything."[71]

Cholera, or a similar disease, reached Béxar by the spring of 1834, when it took the life of Navarro's grandmother and then his mother. The Navarro and Ruiz families gathered to bury Manuela de la Peña, Navarro's maternal grandmother, on May 18. The Campo Santo burial records do not list his mother, Josefa Ruiz de Navarro. Perhaps in the confusion of the epidemic her name was accidentally omitted, or maybe she died at his Atascosa Ranch and was buried there. Navarro returned to the ranch and stayed from July 1 to September 8 to escape the illness that killed so many people.[72] While waiting for the epidemic to run its course, he had the opportunity to build facilities, accumulate some livestock (upon which to use his brand), and break new ground for raising corn and other crops.

Tragedy and political turmoil did not deter Navarro from continuing to expand his business operations. He bought the land from Margila Chirino that he had awarded her when he was DeWitt's land commissioner. This was a transaction within his extended family, because Chirino was his wife's half-sister. Her two leagues included prime farm land and were located about five miles north of present-day Seguin. Known as the San Geronimo Ranch, the property eventually became the primary country home for Navarro and his family from 1840 until the end of 1853. Navarro also worked in the merchant trade in cooperation with Ignacio Herrera. In December, they jointly received permission to transport fourteen chests of goods to the Presidio Rio Grande (present-day Guerrero, Coahuila). Included were a large variety of cloth, crockery, knives, shaving razors, and harnesses.[73]

Another of Navarro's transactions during 1834 that deserves particular attention concerns his *criada* (servant), a black woman named Meralla. In November he signed a receipt saying that John W. Smith had paid him a total of twenty-four pesos for her services from April 28 through October 28.[74] Perhaps Navarro owned Meralla outright, just as slaves were bought and sold by Anglo Americans. There was, however, another labor arrangement familiar to Tejanos: voluntary servitude by contract, as was the case with José Rocque Charles and Navarro in 1822. This may have been the nature of his relationship with Meralla as well. In both situations, Navarro had contracted with others for the services of a person bound to him as a servant in a manner very similar to that which he had successfully introduced into the laws of Coahuila and Texas to evade the state constitution's prohibition on slavery.

Navarro and other ranchers also obtained the services of convicts to work on their ranches. Thirty-four convicts were sent to Béxar, where Political Chief Seguín and the ayuntamiento had the responsibility of finding them work to discharge their sentences, which ranged from one to five years. One was kept at the Béxar jail and twelve went to Goliad and a place referred to as "Guadalupe." The remaining twenty-one were assigned to nine ranchers, who were required to provide them with work, food, and clothing. The Béxar ayuntamiento ordered two to work for Navarro: Geronimo Moreno, a *jornalero* (laborer), and Pascual Angiano, a *labrador y vaquero* (farmer and cowboy). The sentence of both men was two years of forced labor. Navarro probably put them under the supervision of Rámon Rubio, his overseer at the Atascosa ranch. Apparently Moreno was more trouble than he was worth. After he tried to escape in June 1834, Navarro brought him before an ayuntamiento official to ask that he be reassigned.[75]

Navarro may have wished to avoid involvement in political issues in order to focus on his personal affairs, but it would have been impossible to ignore the continuous arrival of extraordinary reports and rumors from Mexico City, Saltillo, and Monclova. He must have heard reports that when Santa Anna resumed the presidency in April 1834,

Vice President Farías had fled the capital. Rumors also circulated that Santa Anna, as the "Protector of the Nation," was being hailed as the only authority in Mexico. This turned out to be true, for Santa Anna performed a political about-face after reassuming the presidency that stood Mexican politics on its head. He had come to power supporting liberals, federalists, and anticlerics. Then in the spring of 1834 he proclaimed himself a centralist under the conservative slogan *Religión y Fueros*, which promoted religious and military privileges. Supported by religious and military leaders, Santa Anna dissolved Congress, dismissed state legislatures and governors, and completely overthrew the Constitution of 1824. Besides inciting the rage of federalists, his abrupt political metamorphosis sowed seeds of unrest and uncertainty in every corner of Mexico.[76]

In Coahuila and Texas, Santa Anna's actions created chaos. The leaders of Saltillo saw an opportunity to return the state capital to their city, and they endorsed Santa Anna. In Monclova, officials reacted to the news with fury and the legislature angrily denounced Santa Anna's centralist government. Unfazed, the Saltillo centralists elected their own governor, declared the Monclova government unconstitutional, and annulled all decrees passed there since 1833. Saltillo's deputies resigned from the Monclova government and returned home, while their supporters prepared to take up arms. Navarro must have been mortified at these events. He was a sensitive man, with deep family roots in Saltillo, but he also endorsed the federalist sympathies expressed in Monclova. It is easy to imagine the sadness he must have felt to see the two principal towns of Coahuila divided against each other and preparing for civil war. Historical events seemed to present Tejanos with two unpleasant alternatives: domination by the Anglos, who had become the majority in Texas, or by the conservative centralists, who seemed poised to take control of Mexico.[77]

By October, Navarro and a majority of other Bexareño leaders had made up their minds as to where they stood on Mexico's political struggle. Not surprisingly, they came down firmly on the side of the federalists and opposed Santa Anna's centralist regime. On October 7, 1834, Bexareños met publicly to discuss the conflict between Saltillo and Monclova. They signed a petition that began by declaring, "Mexico and the Federal System is Our Motto." They condemned the insular attitude of Saltillo leaders: "[T]he spirit of localism guides our brothers and sisters of Saltillo . . . [causing them to ignore the needs of Texas such that they] felt obliged to disavow the constitutional government and congress of the state and arbitrarily establish one in that city and to annul all the decrees given since January 1, 1833."[78] The signers pointed out that conflicts resulting in fatal consequences could follow because many towns remained loyal to the legitimate (Monclova) government, while Saltillo could count on national military forces to coerce recognition of its government. The Bexareños affirmed that order prevailed in Texas, but in a thinly veiled warning they asserted that they would take action to suppress anarchy or to secure their lives and interests. They called for all ayuntamientos in Texas to send representatives to meet in Béxar and decide how best to protect themselves. Forty-nine Bexareños signed this manifesto, including José Antonio and Luciano Navarro, Juan N. and Erasmo Seguín, and José Francisco Ruiz—a virtual "who's who" of the Bexareño leadership. Conspicuously missing was José Ángel Navarro. Perhaps he was out of town. It is also possible that he understood the vulnerability of Béxar to any military forces and did not wish to compromise himself by signing an anti-Santa Anna document.

The proposed convention did not materialize, perhaps due to apprehension about contentious reactions from Anglo colonists, or perhaps concern for how it might affect Austin's chances for a release from prison. Nevertheless, the petition demonstrates the Bexareños' unity in support of the Monclova government and against Santa Anna. In addressing the threat of possible anarchy, the Bexareños made it clear that they would defend themselves and their interests. Navarro shared this view but was not optimistic about the Monclova government. He communicated to Williams, in strong language, his stark assessment of the available options. He criticized the legislature in Monclova as "inept and always tilting toward misfortune." The confusion and disorder throughout the state left leaders without any sure path to take. Correctly foreseeing the shape of future events, he declared:

> I am writing this letter long before the mail arrives, so I am unaware of any news. I believe, however, none of it will be good but will only tell of militarism and death of our sacrosanct liberties; we will soon see how these things turn out. I believe that Texas, absolutely all Texas, should first be reduced to ashes [rather than] to live in slavery under a despotic government. [The] time is approaching and the moments are becoming precious and momentous.

To Navarro, the circumstances represented "the most miserable condition of the Mexican states since their independence."[79]

As 1835 began, Texas edged closer to armed insurrection. At the beginning of the year, Seguín stepped down as political chief in Béxar. José Ángel Navarro assumed this office on an interim basis, while at

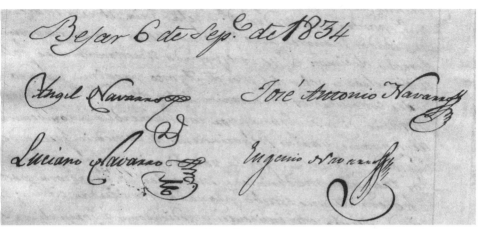

Signatures of the four Navarro brothers, Ángel, José Antonio, Luciano, and Eugenio, from a document dated September 6, 1834. Bexar Archives, di_06760, the Dolph Briscoe Center for American History, the University of Texas at Austin.

the same time keeping his office as alcalde. Seguín turned his attention to military matters and in effect began organizing an insurgency. As the year wore on, his efforts resulted in the formation of a company of Tejano warriors that would fight in the Siege of Béxar and the Battle of San Jacinto. On the other hand, José Ángel Navarro did nothing to burn bridges with Santa Anna's regime. He became an intermediary between colonists and Mexican army officers: first, with Colonel Domingo de Ugartechea (Antonio Elozúa's replacement), who commanded the Béxar garrison, and then with General Martín Perfecto de Cos, who arrived later in the year with the purpose of putting down rebellion in Texas. Meanwhile, Bexareños continued their good faith effort to participate in the Monclova state government by sending José María Jesús de Carvajal, Navarro's erstwhile surveyor, as Béxar's deputy to the legislature there.[80]

Navarro continued to tend to his business amid increasing political tensions. In March he traveled to Goliad to take possession of another shipment of goods. Besides candles and various plates, the parcels contained mostly food, including boxes of raisins and figs, barrels of flour, a sack of coffee and boxes of white sugar. In addition, there was the unhappy task, begun the previous year, of inventorying and assessing the Veramendi estate. This enormous obligation required the close attention of José Antonio and his three brothers. Preliminary work was completed in February, when Luciano paid taxes on the estate. Later that year, he moved into the Veramendi residence in Béxar, which probably was done to prevent Bowie from getting it. It does not appear that Bowie received anything from the estate, and indeed, the Navarros may have maneuvered to exclude him entirely. The Veramendi estate inventories listed extensive ranch lands, grazing rights, town properties, and lands at San José Mission, as well as land and money owed to the estate. The holdings totaled at least twenty leagues (88,560 acres) and included the San Marcos Springs and Comal Springs at present-day San Marcos and New Braunfels.[81]

At Monclova, the final legislature of Coahuila and Texas began in an atmosphere of crisis. Samuel May Williams, representing the Brazos district, understood Monclova's isolation and its vulnerability to central-ist attacks, and he was not one to let a serious crisis go to waste. In the company of several friends, he offered a solution to the legislators. He proposed to bring to Monclova 1,000 armed, mounted men to defend the government. In exchange he would receive a 400-league grant of Texas lands—nearly eighteen million acres. The deal never happened, and raising such a force was a fantasy far beyond anything Williams could deliver. But there were consequences to his proposal, which provoked indignation in all directions and must have dismayed his old friend, Navarro. With this brazen, cynical effort, Williams betrayed Austin and compromised his reputation by entangling him in rumors that he was a party to Williams's folly. He earned the scorn of the Texas colonists who had worked for years to secure their land and avoid suspicion. In addition, Williams and six other men were charged with being revolu-tionaries and had to flee to Béxar. In sum, the proposal did not provide the support Monclova needed, but instead brought about a controversy that was a factor in bringing Santa Anna's army into Texas.[82]

Just as Williams began touting his proposal of 1,000 militiamen in exchange for 400 leagues of land, the legislators tried to pull Navarro into national politics. On March 4, they chose him and Victor Blanco as senators to represent Coahuila and Texas in the Mexican Congress. Interestingly, in a letter to Williams from Mexico City, where he was still confined, Austin correctly predicted the elections of both men. What was not certain was whether Navarro would take the job. Reports of the political chaos at Monclova must have made him think twice about com-mitting himself to Monclova's cause in Mexico City, where he would expose himself to definite risks. He declined the offer on April 6, plead-ing "illness" and explaining that the current session of congress was near its end.[83] Deputies James Grant and Carvajal responded on April 29, urging him, on behalf of the legislature, to leave for Mexico City in spite of his illness, saying that his presence was needed to defend the republican ideals then under attack. Navarro, wisely sensing that events were spinning out of control, again declined the nomination.

José Francisco Ruiz urged Navarro to understand the situation in clear terms, reminding him of José Antonio's father's motto "Bread is Bead and Wine is Wine." He told his nephew that he has lost all hope that Mexico could govern itself. "The die is cast," he said, "and in a few months will begin the revolution that will forever separate Texas from the Republic of Mexico. Ruiz concluded with the advice "Do not go to the Senate in Mexico, for you will only assist in quenching the dying embers of Mexican liberty."[84] Considering that Santa Anna had consolidated his powers and was poised to crush federalist rebels in Zacatecas, this was good counsel. Also, by April 7, 1835, the Monclova government was itself in rebellion against the centralists.

Navarro continued to support the financially strapped Monclova government, as he and several other merchants had done since 1833. On May 11, 1835, just a few days before the fall of the Monclova government, Governor Agustín Viesca sent an order to Béxar for the tax collector to make payments to Navarro, his brother Eugenio, and José María Balmaceda for money they had loaned the state government in Monclova. Gaspar Flores, as tax collector, authorized payment to José Antonio Navarro the following day, but the disbursement was not made until November 11, when Navarro signed a receipt. About the time that he ordered Navarro's payment, Governor Viesca began a frantic effort to raise another 1,000 pesos. The Texas ayuntamientos evidently regarded the Monclova government as a lost cause, for nothing came of it. From Béxar, José Ángel Navarro as political chief wrote, "not a single peso was to be found in the tax collector's funds." Only loyal individual creditors responded positively. José Antonio Navarro, Eugenio Navarro, and Balmaceda said they would furnish whatever additional funds were needed to make up the 1,000 pesos, if they would be repaid within six to eight months.[85] This last loan probably did not take place because time was running out for the Viesca government, as centralist military troops marched toward Monclova. By the time Navarro was paid in November, Viesca was a refugee in Texas.

On May 21, 1835, Viesca signed the last decree of the Monclova legislature. To say the legislators "recessed" was a considerable understatement. In reality, the approach of General Cos and his troops with arrest warrants compelled the legislators to leave town in a hurry to avoid capture. Viesca did not move fast enough and was taken prisoner by Cos. Williams escaped from Monclova, but when he arrived in Béxar on June

6, soldiers under the command of Ugartechea promptly arrested him and several associates. Navarro plotted to help Williams escape. That same day he bought a horse for forty-five pesos — triple the usual price. Two days later, observing legal niceties, Navarro conveyed ownership of the horse to Williams with a signed receipt. A week later an embarrassed Ugartechea reported that Williams and other foreigners had escaped the previous night. Officials at Béxar who reported the escape blamed it on the local militia, many of whom were probably sympathetic to Williams, if not also complicit in his escape. A few weeks later, Navarro collected 892 pesos from four Bexareños for seven leagues of land sold to them "on the account of Samuel M. Williams." He evidently brokered these transactions to help Williams raise some cash that he no doubt needed after the fiasco at Monclova.[86]

Even as political events declined into military campaigns and arrests, Navarro and his family tended to business. Williams's gratitude to Navarro for providing a horse and selling his land was made evident in the terms for the latter: Navarro's brother Luciano bought three of the leagues for eighty pesos, a price substantially lower than the other sales. The Navarro brothers continued to cooperate in efforts to import goods to sell. Eugenio Navarro devoted more of his time to this enterprise after he left military service in 1831. A large shipment of merchandise arrived at Goliad during June 1833 with his initials, *EN*, marked in the margins of the invoice. Evidently the shipment was his, but he was unable to go to Goliad receive the goods. José Antonio Navarro received the shipment for him, paid the duties, and obtained a permit to take the goods to Béxar.[87]

Like the Navarros, other Tejanos in Béxar tried to live normal lives even with the signs of war all around. At the beginning of 1835, Bexareños displayed their positive energy and cultural interest by establishing a society for theatrical presentations, in addition to the customary dances. Juan N. Seguín, as the society president, arranged for a tragedy at the theater. The performance, scheduled for Sunday, January 13, was to include between-the-acts entertainment and a dance. On September 7, José Ángel Navarro and Ugartechea provided funds for the annual *Diez and Seis* celebration of Mexican independence. The money paid for refreshments, coffee, and two dances.[88] Clearly, as alcalde, José Ángel Navarro actively worked to keep a positive relationship between Ugartechea and the Bexareños.

Tax records show that dances were sometimes held in the Casa de la Quinta. This was almost certainly the same structure General Arredondo converted into a chamber of horrors in 1813, where women of Béxar endured pain, indignities, and humiliation, and worked long hours to make tortillas for royalist soldiers. Now, eleven years later the hall would reverberate with the spirited sounds of guitar, violin, *gritos* (shouts), swirling skirts, and scuffling boots. It must have been heartening to see people enjoying themselves even in the shadow of misery, scarcities, and an uncertain future.[89]

CHAPTER FIVE

Mexican-Texan, 1835–40

REVOLUTION RETURNED TO BÉXAR, and Texas, in the fall of 1835. The Navarros again suffered grievous losses, and two of the four brothers died before the end of the decade. José Antonio Navarro also lost his beloved uncle and mentor José Francisco Ruiz. Despite these setbacks, José Antonio again emerged as a leader among the Tejanos, representing his fellow Bexareños in both the Constitutional Convention of 1836 and the third Congress of the Republic of Texas. Navarro expanded his property and built a new home, while his eldest son married and another left Texas to secure an advanced education. Navarro lived the American Dream that his father had sought by coming to Texas, but it came with great responsibilities, which he shouldered without complaint.

Concerned about the growing tensions at Béxar, Commandant Domingo de Ugartechea tried to defuse the situation, or at least disarm those who might cause trouble. Informed that a cannon had been loaned to the Green DeWitt colony several years earlier, he ordered Political Chief José Ángel Navarro to write a letter to the alcalde of Gonzales requiring its immediate return. Ugartechea then sent Captain Francisco Castañeda with a squadron of soldiers to retrieve the cannon, by force if necessary. Castañeda arrived at Gonzales on September 29 and was met by rebellious colonists who refused to cooperate, saying he was a "centralist and they were federalists." Armed conflict began when shots were exchanged and defiant colonists waved a cloth with the challenge "Come and Take it" sewn onto it. With one soldier killed and another wounded, Castañeda was forced to return to Béxar without the cannon.[1] The confrontation at Gonzales pushed the conflict between Mexican centralists and Anglo colonists to the point where it could only be settled by force of arms—the Texas Revolution was underway.

José Antonio expected violence to follow in the wake of the fight at Gonzales. Informed that colonists were advancing on Béxar, packed up his family and left town, as did other Tejano families. He went to his

Atascosa ranch with his wife, Margarita, and their five children, aged two to eighteen. Early in October, General Martín Perfecto de Cos and several hundred troops passed near the ranch on their way to Béxar to put down the rebellion. Cos did not see Navarro, but he later testified that, while it was common knowledge that Navarro's sympathy lay with the colonists, he knew that Navarro remained at his ranch during the Siege of Bexar and did not take an active part in the hostilities nor support the insurrection in any way. Days later, Bexareños watched as Cos arrived in their community with 400 soldiers. Captain Castañeda returned about this time and reported the Gonzales uprising. In response, Governor Rafael Eca y Músquiz told José Ángel Navarro to assist Ugartechea and Cos with their military objectives.[2] These circumstances put José Angel in a difficult position because he could not forget that many of his fellow Tejanos, including his relatives, held federalist sympathies. They understood his predicament, however, and, as subsequent events show, did not regard him as a traitor because of his cooperation with the occupying centralist forces.

While Cos settled his troops in Béxar, several hundred colonists were on the march from Gonzales, intent on continuing the hostilities. Other colonists, aligned with either the Peace Party or the War Party, gathered at San Felipe for a consultation. The result was a "Declaration of the People of Texas . . . that they had taken up arms against General Antonio López de Santa Anna's centralist government and established a provisional government." The Consultation declared that the social compact that bound Texas to Mexico was dissolved. Threatened by despots, they had taken up arms in defense of their rights and liberties and "the Republican Principles of the Federal Constitution of Mexico of eighteen hundred and twenty-four." Meanwhile, insurgents arrived at the outskirts of Béxar. Inspired by Benjamin R. Milam, they surrounded General Cos's army and began a siege. When the colonists attacked on December 7, 1835, they forced their way into the "house of José Antonio Navarro" by late evening. Rebels under Milam's command also occupied the nearby Veramendi House, where Luciano Navarro and his family lived. He later recalled that the rebels "took and used several articles of clothing, the provisions, and destroyed many articles of value." Coincidentally, the only Anglo to die in the fight for Béxar was Milam, who was killed at the Veramendi House. Cos, who retreated into the Alamo, realized that his position was hopeless. Cut off from supplies or reinforcements, he raised a white flag on December 9 and the next day accepted the terms of surrender offered to him. On the 13th, he marched his troops out of Béxar toward Saltillo.[3]

Unlike some Tejano families who were divided in their opinions, the Navarros were united in their desire for a federalist government based upon popular sovereignty, a constitution, and elected officials. It has been said that José Ángel and Eugenio Navarro backed the centralists, while José Antonio and Luciano supported the revolutionaries. This was not the case. Circumstances forced José Ángel to obey the orders of Ugarte-chea and Cos. Luciano's position became clear as soon as Anglo victors occupied the Alamo and appealed for sustenance to the citizens of Béxar. Texas Colonel James C. Neill wrote General Sam Houston that Luciano Navarro and Gaspar Flores had offered all their goods, groceries, and cattle to the army. The question of Eugenio's loyalty is more compli-cated. Navarro family tradition, as explained by José Antonio's grandson, places Eugenio as a soldier with Cos at Béxar. Credible evidence contra-dicts this account. Eugenio had left the military in 1831. Furthermore, Neill wrote in January 1836, that "Eugene" Navarro had sent a courier from San Luís Potosí to his brother (probably José Antonio) with the news that Santa Anna was raising troops to march on Texas. He gave numbers and locations of troops, along with the information that Santa Anna intended to "reduce [Texas] to the state it originally was in 1820."[4] From this, it is clear that Eugenio's sympathies lay with the federalist rebels in Texas and that he actively assisted their cause.

Texas leaders were aware that only a battle had been won at Béxar, not the war. Few doubted that Santa Anna would be on the march to retake Texas by force, just as he had done the previous spring at Zacatecas, where his troops killed several thousand Mexican federalists who op-posed him. Amid the confusion, the provisional government appointed Sam Houston to create and command a military force for defense. Pro-visional Governor Henry Smith issued a proclamation on December 13, 1835, that called for the election of delegates in each Texas settlement. These delegates would convene at the town of Washington-on-the-Bra-zos to write a constitution for a permanent government. José Antonio Navarro returned to Béxar from his ranch just as local leaders prepared to elect their delegates. On February 1, Tejanos gathered in the Alamo. Judging by the records, more than eighty voted. While the procedures are not entirely understandable, the outcome is clear. The final vote was divided between four candidates: José Antonio Navarro, sixty-five votes; José Francisco Ruiz, sixty-one; Erasmo Seguín, sixty; and Gaspar Flores, fifty-nine. Juan N. Seguín formally notified Ruiz and Navarro of their election to represent Béxar at the convention. Anglo volunteers at the Alamo demanded representation as well, and they elected Samuel Maverick and Jesse Badgett.[5]

Navarro and his uncle Ruiz left Béxar together for Washington-on-the-Brazos on February 20, 1836. Colonel William B. Travis ordered that they be escorted by four soldiers: Blas Herrera, Francisco Gómez, Eusebio Farías, and Antonio Coe. Maverick and Badgett traveled separately from this group. Navarro and Ruiz rode along the Camino Real, braving the icy winds and drizzle of a blue norther as they approached their destination.[6] Navarro and Ruiz reached Washington-on-the Brazos on the last day of February and found the temporary capital surrounded by the tents and other rude shelters of delegates and interested observers. They were initially obliged to use the same because the tiny town's accommodations consisted of only a single inn and a few simple log cabins. While Washington-on-the-Brazos functioned as a distribution point for goods brought up the Brazos River, it had a population of only about one hundred. The sole building large enough to serve as a meeting hall for the convention was unfinished. Most conspicuously it lacked windows—which were covered with cloth in an attempt to shield the delegates and their papers from the cold, wind, and rain.

William Fairfax Gray recorded many interesting personal observations in his diary about Navarro, Ruiz, and other delegates. Gray, who was from Virginia, was not a delegate and attended the meetings as an observer. About the same time Navarro and Ruiz arrived, Gray noted there was intense commotion caused by the receipt of the "I shall never surrender or retreat" letter from Travis. News of the siege of the Alamo and the plight of its defenders prompted feverish talk of riding to their defense. The arrival of Lorenzo de Zavala contributed to the excitement. The next day Houston arrived, and Gray wrote in his diary, "he created more sensation than that of any other man."[7]

The emotional fever crested the next day, March 1, when the convention's first session convened. At two o'clock in the afternoon the delegates got down to business with an ad hoc committee examining credentials. Forty-four delegates were present, representing twenty Texas towns, and more arrived over the next several days. The delegates elected Richard Ellis, representing Pecan Point, as president, and he chose a committee of five delegates to write a declaration of independence, with George C. Childress as chair. Meanwhile, Navarro and Ruiz realized they had a communication problem because convention proceedings were in English, a language neither of them understood well. At least three delegates were bilingual and probably helped the two Bexareños during the sessions. James Power, a delegate from Refugio, was married to a Mexican woman and spoke Spanish, while Lorenzo de Zavala and John McMullen were bilingual.[8]

The next day, after long and tedious procedural considerations, Childress produced a draft of the Texas Declaration of Independence and read it to the convention. Like that of the United States, the Texas declaration contained a statement on the nature of government, a list of grievances, and a final pronouncement of independence. Separation from Mexico was justified by a brief philosophical argument. As submitted, the declaration charged that the government of Mexico had ceased to protect the lives, liberty, and property of the people; that it had been changed from a federal republic to a despotic, centralist, military rule; and that the people of Texas had protested the misdeeds of the government without obtaining satisfaction. Another ad hoc committee reviewed the document and recommended its approval. Put to a vote, it was unanimously approved and adopted without any further questions or changes. However, when Childress later submitted a written copy, it was so full of errors that it was "returned to the committee for corrections and to make enlarged copies."[9] It was probably that evening when Navarro and Ruiz had a chance to review the declaration with the aid of one of the bilingual attendees.

The next day, March 3, all members present signed the five enlarged copies of the declaration, which were sent to Béxar, Goliad, Nacogdoches, Brazoria, and San Felipe—where one thousand copies were to be printed. Navarro's state of mind and composure at this time have been variously interpreted. Three writers claim he was reluctant to sign the declaration. Jacob De Cordova's 1858 sketch describes Navarro's quandary as follows: "Navarro . . . had an ardent desire to establish a free government for Texas; and yet he trembled at the thought of having to sanction with his signature the eternal separation of Texas from the mother-country." De Cordova added that when Navarro saw the only choice was between liberty or despotism, he signed the declaration, and from that day forward was one of the most ardent defenders of Texas liberty. The 1876 account of Navarro's life, written by an "Old Texan" (probably Narciso Leal) and other friends who knew him, provided some details as told by Navarro himself:

> [Navarro] often related to us that he was one of the last in the Convention to agree to the final separation of Texas [from Mexico], and he felt a pride that it was so, as a man loyal to his first country, until he was persuaded that there was no other course possible under the circumstances. Navarro was finally convinced that the only alternative between liberty and an ignominious death was to act promptly, and he subscribed with a firm hand his signature to the Declaration.

Reuben M. Potter, who served as Navarro's legislative translator in 1845, enlarged the above accounts in his version of the story published in 1878. He has Navarro quaking in his boots when the fateful moment came, but his mentor and uncle, Ruiz, who had just signed the document, "took him by the arm and led him to the desk where the instrument awaited his signature." Having signed it, Navarro "felt that the first plunge which puts an end to all shrinking was over. From that moment on he never swerved from the obligation he then incurred."[10]

Despite the solid appearance of these three sources, their accounts of Navarro's hesitancy have a quality of exaggeration about them, which is often the case when a story is told, retold, and embellished over time. Two facts do not support the idea that Navarro was a hesitant signer. First, the contemporary observations in William Fairfax Gray's diary do not record any reluctance on Navarro's part to sign the Declaration. Gray did remark on two other delegates who were reluctant: "[John S.] Roberts and [Charles S.] Taylor from Nacogdoches at first expressed some difficulty about signing, but finally yielded and added their names."[11] Second, although the "Old Texan" quoted Navarro as saying that he was among the last to sign, the placement of Navarro's signature on the declaration contradicts this statement. He was not among the last to sign; in fact, his signature is near the top, six or seven names down. Undoubtedly Navarro did feel strong emotions at this symbolic act breaking all bonds with Mexico. But the idea that he was overwrought to the point of helpless inaction and needed Ruiz to lead him to the table and put the pen in his hand is not credible and should not be taken literally. Thus, descriptions of the "hesitant Navarro" indecisively waiting until the end to sign are not consistent with observations of an eyewitness or with the sequence of the signatures on the declaration itself. Moreover, Navarro certainly understood that the die had been cast for independence months before.

After signing the declaration, the convention adjourned for a few days. Ruiz, Navarro, Gray, Zavala, and Badgett obtained shelter with a roof by renting a carpenter's shop. Navarro and Ruiz became better acquainted with Gray, who had been making an effort to learn Spanish. They did manage to communicate about practical matters. Gray regarded Zavala as the most interesting of his roommates, describing him as obliging, kind, and very polite. But "So are Ruis [sic] and Navarro. They seem much gratified at my efforts to learn Spanish; they and the servants all help me, correct my mistakes, and praise my diligence. They, however, do not speak English as Zavala does. They are a kind people, but indolent. My industry in writing and studying amazes them."[12] Both

Navarro and Ruiz were excellent writers. If they were amazed at Gray's diligent effort in writing, it was probably because, other than Stephen F. Austin and Samuel May Williams, most Anglo colonists they had seen were semi-illiterate frontiersmen.

Gray had come to Texas to buy land as an agent representing Thomas J. Green and Albert T. Burnley; thus it did not take him long to talk with his roommates about his primary interest. On March 10, 1835, he wrote, "Navarro today showed me a deed for five leagues of land below the San Antonio road, and on the head waters of the_____ [sic], which he offers for $1,500 per league. It is an old Mexican title which he bought." Ruiz and Zavala also had land in Texas that they wanted to sell. Navarro evidently took Gray to be a gullible novice, since $1,500 per league was an exorbitant price—nearly ten times what he had paid for the San Geronimo Ranch less than two years earlier. Deals such as the one he offered to Gray, and many others on a much grander scale, became the focus of angry debates in the convention, whose members would pay special attention to the huge land claims of speculators who had far greater ambitions than Navarro. In the end, the issue of Mexican land grants hung over the convention like thunderclouds.[13]

On the first day of the Convention, Ellis had appointed twenty-one delegates as a committee, which included Navarro and Zavala, to write a constitution for the Republic of Texas. They began their work on Monday, March 7, choosing Martin Parmer as their chairman. Around noon, Robert Potter dropped a bomb such that if Navarro had been dozing it made him sit up straight in his chair. Potter, representing anti-speculator interests, proposed a draconian solution that not only would have invalidated the large Monclova grants, but also eleven-league grants such as Navarro's. He recommended inserting into the proposed constitution a requirement that "no claim of eleven leagues of land or more shall be valid; and all titles . . . for more than one League and one Labor of Land (Empresarios excepted) shall be null and void and of no effect." The journal of the convention does not record what must have been a very spirited debate, during which Navarro would certainly have objected loudly to Potter's proposal. Setting aside the issue of Monclova grants, which would later be invalidated, the convention affirmed that claims to eleven leagues of land would remain valid.[14] Although records of the votes on this issue (and most others) were not preserved, there can be little doubt that Navarro voted against Potter. Because public opposition to eleven-league grants was widespread, support for a ban would persist, and Navarro would remain an outspoken advocate for preserving the validity of the eleven-league grants. After all, some of these had been subdivided and resold in many parcels going back almost ten years. To invalidate them would be to undercut the validity of a very large number of land titles.

While the eleven-league grants issued under the government of Coahuila and Texas were maintained as valid, the constitution committee had no sympathy for the big land speculators. It declared null and void grants of 1,100 leagues of land made during 1834 and 1835 by the desperate Monclova government, whose existence had been threatened by centralist forces. Despite their attention to land matters, a sense of urgency prevailed among the committee members, spurred by desperate letters from the Alamo warning of the danger of being overrun by a contingent of Santa Anna's army. After only two days of deliberations, Martin Parmer, as chair, presented a draft constitution to the convention. His committee members had not reinvented the wheel; their work was largely based on the United States Constitution, with portions borrowed from several state constitutions. The draft also provided continuity from Mexican rule to the new government by stating that all existing laws, not inconsistent with the constitution, would remain in force until specifically changed.[15]

As was the case with the Texas Declaration of Independence, the first draft of the new constitution was close in wording and structure to the document that was finally approved. There were three areas that reflected original thinking. They addressed slavery in unambiguous terms, declaring that persons of color who were slaves before the Texas Revolution would remain slaves. Invalidating the Law of April 6, 1830, Congress could not ban the import of slaves into the Republic. In addition, no one could free slaves without the consent of Congress and no free person of African descent, "either in whole or in part, [would] be permitted to reside permanently in the Republic without the consent of Congress." To penalize those who refused to support Texas in the coming fight, the committee added: "All persons who shall leave the country for the purpose of evading participations in the present struggle, or shall refuse to participate in it, or shall give aid or assistance to the present enemy, shall forfeit all rights of citizenship, and such lands as they may hold in the republic." Thinking that Santa Anna still besieged the Alamo, the committee understandably felt the new republic was in grave danger.[16] Years later Navarro contended forcefully that this forfeiture provision had been drafted hastily and under duress, consequently it should not be used as a basis for canceling land titles long after the danger had passed.

The delegates finally adopted the Constitution of the Republic of

Texas at midnight on March 16, 1836, but their session continued into the early morning hours. Until popular elections could be held, they chose David G. Burnet to serve as president and Zavala to be vice president. Secretaries of state, treasury, war, and navy were also elected, along with other officers; and a hasty contract for a $1,000,000 loan was authorized. The officials were sworn in at four o'clock in the morning, the convention ended, and the Republic of Texas began. Gray's diary described the agitated conditions that prevailed at the end of the convention as a whirlwind of confusion and irregularity. Navarro wrote that some members left "before the ink had dried from the signatures" and that some did not sign at all.[17]

The journals of the convention and Gray's diary allow an evaluation of Navarro's role with respect to the Declaration of Independence and Constitution. He is sometimes credited with being an author of the former. In fact, his contribution was minimal or nonexistent, which was true of almost all of the delegates. The writing of the declaration was assigned to George C. Childress, who presented a draft that seems to have been written before the convention. Independence was a foregone conclusion, and no heated debates were needed as long as a competent document was presented, which is what happened. Navarro's signature was his contribution to the Texas Declaration of Independence. On the other hand, Navarro had an opportunity to contribute to the Constitution. He sat next to William Menefee on the first day of the constitutional deliberations and took part in the discussions. Menefee recalled that Navarro "made numerous suggestions regarding phraseology, demonstrating his familiarity with Republican institutions." The journal of the convention does not indicate that Navarro was prominent in daily events, unlike the bilingual Zavala, but this record is so limited that it is not possible to determine much about the contributions of many members.[18] Thus it is not possible to know the extent of Navarro's contributions or his votes on the issues, but it can be reasonably assumed that he would have opposed any invalidation of the eleven-league grants because of his subsequent public defense of them. Since much of the Constitution was adopted from existing sources, neither he nor the other members contributed much on executive, legislative, and judicial matters.

After the Constitution was approved, few were able to sleep because of rising panic and the urgent need to get out of range of Santa Anna's cavalry, which they knew must be approaching. Patrols had been ordered out, and numerous false alarms sounded during the night. Navarro, Ruiz, and Zavala, being native Mexicans whom Santa Anna would consider the worst traitors, must have felt a particular urgency to get out of harm's way. On the night of March 17, Gray wrote, "My Mexican friends are packing up, with the intention of crossing the Brazos to-night." A report that Mexican forces were near the town of Bastrop added to the urgency. At about ten o'clock Zavala, Ruiz, and Navarro left with their attendants, horses, and pack mules. They traveled down the Brazos River for two days to Jared E. Groce's plantation. Here the group learned the details of the final attack on the Alamo from one of the survivors, William B. Travis's young slave, Joe. Gray watched the black man's interrogation and was impressed with his modesty, apparent candor, and powerful memory. Navarro and Ruiz left the next morning for San Felipe, while Gray and Zavala, accompanied by other republic officials, departed for Harrisburg.[19]

According to Gray, when Navarro and Ruiz left Groce's plantation, they intended to make their way to Brazoria or Velasco, where they could take a ship to New Orleans. On the way, they found that Houston's army had abandoned San Felipe on March 29 in the face of Santa Anna's rapid advance. Years later, testifying at his trial for treason in Mexico City, Navarro said he traveled to Natchitoches from Washington-on-the-Brazos. Navarro and Ruiz probably returned to Groce's plantation with Houston's retreating army and there joined individuals who were going to Nacogdoches, as others had done.[20] From Nacogdoches, the two Bexareños probably hurried east to Natchitoches, where they had friends. Ruiz remained there, but Navarro continued on to New Orleans.

About the time that Navarro arrived in Natchitoches, the forces of Houston and Santa Anna were converging in a corner formed by the San Jacinto River and Buffalo Bayou. Houston had done nothing but retreat in the face of Santa Anna's advance, and the Mexican general had dismissed Houston's army as no serious threat. Perhaps this contemptuous attitude stemmed in part from his experience in Texas in 1813, at the Battle of Medina, where Mexican professionals demolished a poorly trained, ragtag army of Tejano revolutionaries, American adventurers, and Indians. In 1836, Santa Anna faced another ragged army of irregulars, and he confidently expected the same crushing result. On the morning of April 21, General Cos with more than 500 men rejoined Santa Anna, making a total of some 1,200 soldiers. Houston's forces numbered just slightly more than 900, including Juan N. Seguín and his company of Tejano cavalrymen. By late afternoon, not expecting action, Santa Anna ordered his troops to stand down to rest. In the well-known battle of San Jacinto, which ensued shortly thereafter, Houston's men routed the Mexican forces in a twenty-minute battle.[21] Although Navarro was not present at the battle, Santa Anna would later take a measure of revenge upon him rather than Houston, who had taken advantage of the Mexican general's pride and overconfidence to win an overwhelming victory—and Texas independence.

Mexican troops stationed in Béxar left soon after Santa Anna's defeat. José Ángel Navarro and other Bexareños rejoiced when the last of the soldiers who occupied their town were gone. Joseph H. Barnard, a Goliad prisoner who had been spared so he could tend wounded Mexican troops in Béxar (where he lived with José Ángel Navarro), described Bexareños' expressions of delight in his journal:

> Some of them broke out into transports of joy that made them act quite ludicrously. The grave and dignified person of mine host, [José Ángel] Navarro, who is at least forty-five years old and far gone with hydrothorax, was seen capering about the streets like a boy in a perfect ecstasy of glee. He said that now he should recover his health; that nothing but the impure air occasioned by the residence of the Mexican troops made him sick. Alas! his confidence availed him nothing; he died about two weeks after the troops left.

Barnard also noted that Navarro family members had remained in Béxar during the siege of the Alamo and were not molested, even though José Antonio Navarro was at the Texas Convention and his brother Luciano had fled the city. Unable to think of a better reason, Barnard speculated that money might have secured the Navarro family's "good treatment."[22]

Although the Mexican troops left San Antonio, Juan N. Seguín, who returned with his company soon afterward, worried about a counterattack. Having only twenty-two poorly provisioned men, he judged Béxar was indefensible with these forces and decided to retreat east, closer to Houston's force. As a consequence, on June 21, he ordered the citizens to also evacuate Béxar and to "carry off the cattle to where the enemy can not make use of them." Barnard does not mention this, and the evacuation evidently did not occur. In the meantime, José Antonio Navarro remained in New Orleans, where he was joined by Erasmo Seguín and they met with Gray. On May 12, Gray noted that the two Tejanos were staying at the "Hotel des Habitans et Strangers." When Gray called on them, he was introduced to a "Mr. Flores of Béjar." This was probably Gaspar Flores, another Tejano who sought refuge in New Orleans. Gray saw the two Bexareño refugees again at Lake Borgne: "At the Lake House met my Mexican friends, Navarro and Seguín, who had been on a trip to the lake and returned to town with me." Upon returning to the city, they saw Sam Houston (who had sought medical treatment in New Orleans for the wound he suffered at San Jacinto) and his staff.[23]

Navarro had left New Orleans and returned to Texas by October 1836. Because of his extensive purchases in previous years, he probably had good credit in New Orleans and likely took advantage of it to bring a load of merchandise back with him. He also brought goods from New Orleans for Juana Ramírez, his sister-in-law. He arrived at Béxar with renewed interest in joining his brothers Eugenio and Luciano in the mercantile business. Disruptions of trade during the Texas Revolution had led to scarcities of goods that provided fertile opportunities for merchants such as the Navarros to distribute goods in both Texas and Mexico. They wasted little time in advancing their reputation as successful merchants. Soon, news of the Navarro brothers' imports had spread to San Fernando (later renamed Zaragoza) in Coahuila, where Captain Juan José Galván noted that Luciano and his brother "The Cripple" had disembarked at Goliad. Eugenio Navarro was traveling to Béxar with a pass, bringing merchandise that he and the others had bought. Galván wanted to form a partnership with Eugenio in the purchase of these goods and have them pass inspection at San Fernando, which he said he could easily do. Galván instructed his associate, Jesús de la Garza, to "arrange the deals as best you can and tell me what we are to do to make a little money."[24]

The first Congress of the Republic of Texas met at Columbia in October 1836, about the time José Antonio Navarro returned from New Orleans. The people of Béxar elected Ruiz as their senator and Thomas J. Green to the House of Representatives. At the first Senate session, on October 3, credentials were examined and Ruiz was quickly admitted. He took part in all of the sessions except those held during the first week of December. The two most important actions taken by the Senate pertained to land grants and the boundaries of the Republic. Prior to the Texas Convention, the sale of public land and issuance of titles had been suspended pending the establishment of an orderly system of recording land titles. This measure was also intended to prevent the exploitation of the enormous grants given to speculators by the Monclova government. The Constitution guaranteed that land titles granted under Spain and Mexico would be honored, but this rule applied only to "perfected" titles. The Senate decided that any applications for land begun under Mexican colonization laws but not completed would revert to the public domain. At the same time, the Senate greatly expanded Texas by approving boundaries "beginning at the mouth of the Sabine, west along the Gulf of Mexico . . . to the mouth of the Rio Grande, then up the principal stream to its source."[25] This amounted to an audacious claim of a vast area that included the eastern half of the Mexican state of New Mexico, eastern Chihuahua, and northern portions of Tamaulipas and Coahuila. The Republic would try to effect this claim by military force, which would prove to be far beyond its abilities. This fact would become painfully clear during the disastrous Santa Fe Expedition of 1841, for which Navarro served as a commissioner.

Stephen F. Austin lived his final days at Columbia while Congress was meeting. When he first returned from imprisonment in Mexico City, he resumed his leadership in Texas affairs, but failing health and enemies who spread malicious rumors prevented him from taking a prominent role. In the election for president he came in a distant third, as voters chose Sam Houston by an overwhelming margin. At Columbia, he lived in a shed owned by a friend. Ruiz probably visited him and provided news of his old friend Navarro. Congress adjourned on December 22, just as another blue norther swept through Columbia. Austin, who was already in poor health, caught a severe cold, and the infection spread to his lungs and turned into pneumonia. Various treatments were tried, but to no avail, and he died at age forty-three on the morning of December 27. Just five years earlier, Navarro had warned Austin about the danger of exhausting himself because he understood Austin's tendency to take on excessive work and responsibility. Navarro had advised him that "You must be well irritated with worries of colonization, but it seems to me it would be wiser—and thus to prolong the days of your life—to separate yourself from some affairs that because of your own virtue have gravitated your way."[26] Sadly, Austin did not heed Navarro's advice.

Navarro focused on affairs in Béxar, while his uncle Ruiz worked in Columbia. José Antonio found his community again stripped of most of its resources as a result of the siege the previous December and the subsequent occupation by Santa Anna's army. His older brother, José Ángel, had passed away in June, so José Antonio and his younger brother Eugenio worked together to settle the estate and divide it among José Ángel's children.[27] The somber mood at Béxar was resolved at the end of February 1837, with a ceremony that Juan N. Seguín organized for the burial of the burnt remains of the Alamo defenders. The ashes had been found in three piles, so the two smaller piles were placed in a black coffin and brought to San Fernando Church for a ceremony. Then the coffin was returned to the site of the pyres in a solemn procession. Three volleys were discharged at each of the first two ash sites, and at the third, the coffin was interred along with the ashes that remained.

After the volleys, in a ringing speech, Seguín told the audience, which no doubt included the Navarros:

> Companions in Arms! These remains which we have the honor of carrying on our shoulders are those of the valiant heroes who . . . preferred to die a thousand times than submit themselves to the tyrant's yoke. With the venerable remains of our worthy companions as witnesses, I invite you to declare to the entire world, "Texas shall be free and independent, or we shall perish in glorious combat."[28]

With these proud words, the ceremony concluded and Bexareños and newly arrived Anglos returned to the task of rebuilding their community.

The reality remained that Seguín by that time (1837) commanded a military force at Béxar of just 110 men, and they were desperate for supplies. Many of his soldiers lacked horses and even shoes. Nevertheless, it was Seguín's duty to guard San Antonio, for rumors circulated of possible Mexican attacks. Navarro again advanced funds for the defense of Béxar. He provided Seguín with a loan from the contents of his store valued at 1, 690 pesos, but this was not enough. Seguín's men, about one-fourth Tejanos and the remainder Anglos, confiscated livestock and corn from Béxar civilians for their use. Bexareños, who had survived the siege of Béxar and the depredations of Santa Anna's army, were again exposed to the ravages of military men who commandeered whatever resources they wanted by force. Seed for planting was taken, as were draft animals for plowing. Foragers stripped the land of trees and brush for miles in every direction. Bexareños who made long trips to gather firewood often had it confiscated by the Republic of Texas army. Seguín's men burned fence posts and even doors for cooking and warmth.[29]

After José Antonio and Eugenio finished their work on their brother's estate, they decided to meet personally with President Houston to seek relief for the suffering people of Béxar. José Antonio also wanted to present his claim to the auditor for repayment of nearly $2,000 owed him by the Republic of Texas. The two Navarro brothers traveled east to Columbia, the temporary capital, where they arrived by March 23. On that date, José Antonio wrote a long letter to Houston detailing the problems at Béxar. He began by reminding the president that he had supported Texas independence with the hope of obtaining a just government. While such a government "is now fortunately presiding over our country's destiny," Navarro declared that enlightened justice did not exist in Béxar, where the Republic of Texas army was trampling the rights of citizens. Navarro continued, saying, "This is an attack on the basic principles of a system of Liberty we proclaim, contradicting it by act and manifestation." He recounted the outrages that had occurred, including property losses, unfair imprisonment of citizens, and insults in demeanor and language. Navarro explained the obvious, that when borrowed horses and carts were not returned, people were reluctant to lend their remaining horses and carts to the army and hid them. Then the soldiers responded by sending armed parties at night to confiscate all horses found. "These and other forms of extortion," he wrote, "are generally preceded by improper language and insulting threats." Among the prominent citizens detained without cause was "Mr. Miguel Arciniega, formerly a Judge of Béxar until last February, an honorable man, head of a large family, who because of his shy and humble spirit was unable to take part in things revolutionary." As a result of "military tyranny," residents lived in fear of losing their remaining possessions or being taken to jail. He concluded by asking Houston to intervene directly in the situation.[30]

Documents indicate that Navarro succeeded in meeting with Houston to discuss his claim for goods given to Juan Seguín and 1,690 pesos, which was approved. Undoubtedly, he took the opportunity to again emphasize the predicament of Bexareños that he had detailed in his letter. Navarro's plea for Béxar produced positive results. Houston immediately wrote to Henry W. Karnes, who was in charge at Béxar during Seguín's absence, telling him, "For God's sake have the persons and property of Béxar protected." Houston understood the urgent need for horses, but he directed Karnes to look elsewhere, authorizing him "to take any horses or mules belonging to the public which you can find between the Colorado and the San Antonio, unless they are in public service."[31]

José Antonio Navarro returned from Columbia just in time to be included in the first Bexar County government. The previous year Congress had appointed Joseph Baker as the chief justice at Béxar. On May 1, 1837, Baker presided over an installation of new county officers, each of whom pledged a $5,000 bond to the president of the Republic of Texas.[32] John W. Smith became the county clerk and Samuel Kinney was named sheriff. The court appointed a sixteen-member grand jury whose proceedings were to be conducted in Spanish and English. Navarro served as an associate justice, and his responsibilities also included overseeing the admission of wills, serving as a probate judge, and certifying sales of land claims known as headright grants.[33] In addition he recorded loyalty statements from Tejanos, required as a condition for receiving headright grants.[34] While the county government was being formed in

Béxar under the Republic of Texas, so was the city government. The Navarro family was well represented on the new council; among the first members elected were Eugenio Navarro as city treasurer and Francisco Antonio Ruiz, José Francisco's son, as a councilman.[35] To pay the costs of government, Congress in June 1837 authorized counties to levy a property tax. By the end of the year, Assessor John W. Smith had compiled a listing of 278 Bexareños, Anglo and Tejano, who possessed property—rural land, town lots, livestock, stores, and other items—to be taxed at the rate of a half percent of the assessed value.[36]

While serving as an associate justice, Navarro continued to petition the Republic for reimbursement. In addition to the claim noted above, he asked for his salary and travel expenses for his participation at the convention at Washington-on-the-Brazos. He certified that he was owed for seventeen days salary, at $5.00 per day, and 350 miles at $5.00 per each 25 miles, for a total of $155.00. He also submitted several smaller claims for cash and various goods—including skillets, Dutch ovens, and other cooking equipment—that he had provided. He also negotiated with three fellow Tejanos to purchase their claims to land guaranteed by the Republic. The constitution promised these headright grants to heads of households and single men who were living in Texas as of March 4, 1836, and met other requirements.[37] The Republic of Texas headright claim consisted of a league (4,428 acres) and one labor (177 acres) of land. There was a distinction between a headright claim and a headright certificate, although the difference was often blurred. The former was a contract, or sale, between a buyer and a person entitled to claim headright land, which was recorded in the county deed records. The latter was a certificate from the county board of land commissioners, which entitled the holder to select and have surveyed land in the public domain and to continue the process to eventually obtain a patent (title) No legal mechanism was in place, however, to locate, survey, and grant titles because the first congress mandated that all public land matters were to be processed by a yet-to-be-established general land office. Nonetheless, the law allowed headright claims to be bought and sold, which meant that those, like Navarro, who could not claim a headright because they had already obtained public land under Mexican rule, gained a new opportunity to acquire more real estate.

To many Bexareños in 1837 and 1838, the promise of land must have appeared doubtful and made them more willing to sell their headrights in return for immediate cash. As a result many Tejanos sold their rights for much less than what the land would eventually be worth. Good reasons for the immediate sale of headrights can be deduced from conditions at the time. First, headright land was not free. Official fees, depending upon the quality of the land, could total seventy-five dollars—an expense far beyond the resources of many. Second, a successful Mexican counterattack could abolish claims to headright land overnight. Reports from spies and rumors reinforced this fear. Sam Houston wrote to Juan N. Seguín reporting a rumor that 4,000 to 5,000 Mexican troops were ready to march into Texas.[38] Finally, the administration of land laws had been suspended until the required land office opened, which would not happen until October 1837. These uncertainties bred fear and anxiety among many Tejanos and triggered a rush to sell their headrights. There was no shortage of buyers with cash to offer anyone willing to sell. All in all, the headright sales in Béxar appear to have been essentially contracts between willing buyers and sellers. Speculators, however, who had the capital to spend and were willing to gamble on the prospect that Texas would remain independent, may well have used the climate of fear to convince Bexareños to sell their land rights.

Navarro's nephew José Luís Carvajal was the first to buy a headright claim on April 6, 1837—4,605 acres from Francisco Leal, for which he paid $1,000. The next day prospective sellers began lining up to sell their rights to various individuals. During 1837, Béxar officials recorded sales of over 1.5 million acres in 404 contracts, even though there was no land law in effect for the Republic. In 1838 there were 216 contracts for sales of almost 800,000 acres. This marked the height of headright sales in Béxar since half of these contracts were quickly resold by buyers, whereas only twenty of the earlier contracts from 1837 were resold. After these two peak years, there were only fifty-five such purchases between 1839 and 1842, an average of only twenty per year. By that time the supply of Tejanos willing to sell their land rights had been exhausted at Béxar. The prices paid for each allotment of 4,605 ranged from $500 to $5,000.[39] Since headrights represented a claim to public land, not to specific property, this disparity in cost implies that competition among the speculators may have driven up headright prices.

Payment for headrights could pose an interesting challenge for buyers. Money in gold or silver coins was scarce, no banks existed in Texas, and the Republic did not issue its first currency (interest-bearing promissory notes called "Red Backs") until the fall of 1837. The primary medium of exchange was notes from chartered banks of southern U.S. states such as Louisiana, Alabama, and Tennessee. For example, the 1838 inventory of Eugenio Navarro's estate listed $185 in silver, along with $500 in "New Orleans Bank paper," $40 in "Alabama Bank paper," and $217 in "[Republic of] Texas paper."[40] The money supply directly affected the participation of Tejanos, including the Navarros, in the buying and selling of headrights. José Antonio Navarro purchased only three claims: a league and labor from Leonardo Gil for $70; one-third league from Francisco Flores for $75; and a league and labor from Francisco de la Garza (his brother-in-law) for $800 in "current money of the Republic."[41] The extreme difference in prices paid for Bexareño headrights, such as that of Navarro's payments to Gil and Flores compared to that of De la Garza, is puzzling, ranging from less than $100 to $5,000. Only the right to claim land in the public domain was being sold, not land itself. Therefore one headright claim should have been no more valuable than another. Time would become a factor, since the best land would be claimed first, even though a land office through which land could be surveyed and titles issued did not exist until the next year. Navarro probably paid Gil and Flores in specie, while De la Garza may have received discounted notes, or perhaps some claims of doubtful value against the Republic. Gold and silver were the preferred medium of exchange. As Edward Dwyer noted in 1836, "Bank notes will not do to purchase land from Mexicans."[42]

The steps for obtaining title for headright claims were complicated and little published information about them is available.[43] Thus the procedure that José Antonio Navarro followed from the time he purchased Gil's headright until he actually obtained title to land offers a model worth examining. All claimants had to file an affidavit of entitlement to headright land with the county government, affirming that he or she (many women qualified as heads of households) met the requirements set forth in the Constitution. Then the claimant could sell or assign the right to a buyer for an agreed upon price. In the case of Gil, as a married man he was entitled to claim 4,605 acres, a league and labor, the right to which he sold to Navarro on May 18, 1837. Gil then signed an oath that he was a married man, head of a household, lived in Texas at the time of the signing of the Declaration of Independence, and had not avoided military service or fought against Texas in the Revolution.[44] Chief Justice Baker recorded Gil's statement on May 19, 1837. At this point, Navarro's transaction had proceeded as far as was possible until the formation of the General Land Office.

The second step in the process had to wait until the next year, when the General Land Office was established with county land boards authorized to issue certificates for headrights. Navarro appeared before the Bexar County Board of Land Commissioners on March 2, 1838, presented the contract signed by Gil the previous year, and was awarded headright certificate Number 292.[45] With this certificate in hand, Navarro could proceed with the next steps: locate unclaimed land in the public domain, have it surveyed, and pay the fees based upon the classification of the land as determined by the surveyor. The procedure was suspended at this point because of his participation in the Santa Fe Expedition (discussed in the next chapter). Upon his return, he resumed the procedure by locating the league and labor in separate locations, the former on the Pedernales River and the latter on the Frio. He completed the process and obtained title to these properties in 1846, nine years after his initial purchase.

Since his return from exile in 1816 through 1837, Navarro had come far in his pursuit of the American Dream. His wealth had grown immensely despite the damage in and around Béxar resulting from the revolutions of 1821 and 1836. The 1837 tax assessment shows that his rural land holdings totaled 30,996 acres. Of these, 17,712 acres were on the Atascosa River and 8,856 acres were on San Geronimo Creek. He also held two 8,856-acre tracts that he had acquired after 1834, not including his headright claims. The value of all Bexar County rural land was assessed at fifty cents per acre, with only two exceptions. Navarro's land on the San Geronimo was one of those exceptions; it was assessed at one dollar per acre due to its high quality. In addition to rural land, Navarro's other listed property included 3 horses, 4 mules, 234 cattle, 5 lots in town, and miscellaneous property valued at $15,700. He was credited with two stores, which were not taxed, but were assessed $50 each for annual licenses. Navarro's assessment of $15,700 for miscellaneous property was much greater than any other taxpayer, the next largest being $3,114. Most of his assessment probably represented the merchandise in his two stores. If so, he must have had by far the most extensive supply of goods in San Antonio at that time, which is not surprising because there were only eight other stores that bought licenses. His inventory would have included goods he had imported, along with merchandise he inherited the previous year from his brother José Ángel. José Antonio Navarro was quite prosperous, and he paid more than 6 percent of the total taxes levied in Bexar County for 1837.[46]

José Antonio Navarro was also a successful rancher despite the disruptions of the Texas Revolution. His reported herd of 234 head of cattle (valued at $1,200) was larger than that of any other Bexareño. The limited number of stock reported on the tax roll reflects the damage done to the herds during the Texas Revolution. Only fourteen Tejanos reported more than fifty head. José Antonio and Eugenio Navarro referred to such losses while compiling the inventory of their older brother's estate: "Due to the revolution, the [José Ángel Navarro] ranch has been abandoned; thus, making it impossible to know the number of cattle which exist, for they are all scattered."[47] According to José Ángel's records, there should have been 173 head of cattle in January of 1836. Only ninety-nine head from his herd were eventually located.

Other Navarro family members also had extensive property holdings. Luciano Navarro was assessed taxes for 15,498 acres of land in Béxar and Victoria, 25 town lots, and various livestock. He had $1,900 worth of miscellaneous property. In addition, he was listed as the guardian of Marcos "Berry" [Veramendi], who was assessed for 22,140 acres of land and $450 worth of miscellaneous property. The taxable property listed for José Eugenio Navarro is incomplete. He was credited with 4,428 acres and 2 horses, but the remainder of his property and tax paid appears to have been omitted accidentally; an inventory of his estate made after his death in 1838 shows he was a wealthy man. José Antonio's uncle, José Francisco Ruiz, was also one of the largest landowners, having a total of 39,852 acres.[48]

While he continued to expand his business interests in the wake of the Texas Revolution, Navarro experienced change in his immediate family. He and Margarita de la Garza had their seventh and last child, Josefa Elena. Although no baptismal record for her has been found, census records indicate that she was born between 1835 and 1837, at the same time the older children were leaving the nest. José Antonio George Navarro was coming into his own as a young man, while the Navarro's oldest daughter, María Casimira, married Robert Patton.[49]

In early 1838 José Antonio Navarro became embroiled in a dispute about a servant that erupted into an embarrassing public incident. Cornelius P. Van Ness, a Vermont native and lawyer who had arrived in San Antonio a year ealier. Evidently an abolitionist, he questioned Navarro's his right to the services of a female servant. Navarro's defense to the newcomer's challenge included a comprehensive explanation of the situation. First, the tradition of indentured servitude at Béxar was not affected by the 1836 Constitution or the laws of the Republic. Second, Navarro noted that because of an illness he was bedridden and, because his numerous family members depended on him for support, he needed a household servant. Finally, he declared that the servant had left him without fulfilling her obligations: "She is a woman in whose presence I paid a quantity of gold and silver and she was obliged by the previous laws, still in effect, to serve me as a cook or to repay me the money if she no longer wishes to serve."[50]

Navarro's dispute with Van Ness reveals the complexity of the growing conflict over the issue of servitude, including indentured servitude and slavery. Navarro stressed the legality of indentures under established laws, customs, and uninterrupted practice. He explained that his was not an isolated case and suggested to Van Ness that he "notice in the county the numerous servants that exist under the same conditions." This was not the first dispute Navarro had had involving an indentured servant. Rocque Charles, whose services Navarro sold to Josefa de la Garza, ran away before completing the time he owed. The woman discussed by Navarro and Van Ness was also not a slave, and that conclusion is supported by the 1837 Bexar County tax assessment, which lists no slaves for Navarro.[51]

Continuing his explanation to Van Ness, Navarro wrote, "I have since learned that she has entered the service of Mr. [Edward] Dwyer. I sent for her, or for what is owed to me, but have received no satisfactory explanation for this assault on my property except that the Constitution orders it so." Navarro knew the Texas Constitution well, having participated in its creation, and he lectured Van Ness: "You have seen the Constitution: it does not deserve to be given such an appalling interpretation of its articles." To Navarro, it was clear that document did not alter the laws for indentures. Navarro conceded that the sad condition of this class of servants was repugnant to liberty, but "the love of liberty and generous impulse are not sufficient for the invalidation of the condition of those who have voluntarily made themselves servants." He expressed outrage at being labeled an enemy of liberty and freedom by adding: "I profoundly do feel [aggrieved] that under the sacred mantle of liberty a man such as I could be attacked. I am faithful to the laws, reason, and friendship and I will be the first to procure the individual liberty of these poor servants on the day the Congress provides a general [legislative] measure for it."[52]

Navarro conferred with Mayor Henry Daingerfield, hoping for the quiet return of his servant without difficulties after he found that she had left Dwyer and was living with a young man in what Navarro called a den of ruffians. When he sent for her again, the "ruffians" she lived with came to his house and shouted insults. Apparently the tumult of the Texas Revolution had made angry vagabonds of men whose livelihoods had been interrupted.

Navarro predicted to Van Ness, "You will see a whirlwind of these idlers who are rising up to [challenge] us in the name of liberty and I meanwhile remain with the unspeakable feeling of having been the first victim in the midst of my friends." The city council had discussed the problem months earlier, expressing alarm about the number of vagabonds at San Antonio—some of whom were former soldiers from

Santa Anna's army. The council approved a measure to the effect that "those who had created debts by contract to pay with their labor [indentures] could remain [while] those not employed in 'decent and useful'" work were to be expelled. Navarro's problem with his indentured servant thus included not only questions of law but also threats of mob retaliation. He wisely decided to back down from trying to recover the servant rather than have ruffians inflict further insults or harm upon him or his family.[53] He gave her a written account of the money she owed him, but there is no record of payment.

A few weeks later Navarro lost his youngest brother, Eugenio, to the violence infesting their community. Eugenio died in a violent confrontation with a man named Tinsley.[54] At the beginning of 1838, Eugenio operated a store stocked with a large inventory of practical and luxury items. At the age of thirty-five, he was wealthy and in the prime of his life. His house and storeroom were in a prominent location, sometimes referred to as "the Navarro Corner," near the northeast corner of Plaza de Armas fronting on Flores Street.[55] His prospects for building upon his accomplishments and enjoying a long, successful life were excellent, but such was not to be.

An eyewitness provided a detailed account of Eugenio's death, albeit many years later. Speaking to a reporter in 1891, Rafael Aldrete recalled the events he had seen fifty-three years earlier, when he was a young man of twenty-four. He said that he was an employee of a store located across the street from Eugenio's operation. Early on the morning of May 6, 1838, he witnessed part of the deadly encounter between Eugenio and Tinsley, whom Aldrete described as a thug and a gambler. Tinsley had angrily confronted a female neighbor and not being able to attack a woman, he looked for another target upon which to vent his rage. Tinsley then chose Eugenio because he thought he was both prominent and timid.[56]

While waiting for his employer's store to open, Aldrete said he saw Tinsley put a paper on Eugenio's door. José Antonio Navarro then walked around the corner, taking a morning stroll. He read it and asked Aldrete who had placed it there, then tore it down and walked away. He probably intended to tell his brother about Tinsley's note, but tragically he did not find him in time. Minutes later Eugenio opened his store. While he was measuring coffee to sell to a German carpenter, Tinsley strode into the store brandishing a cowhide quirt. Aldrete, realizing a bloody conflict might be imminent, walked over for a closer look. He saw Tinsley pull a derringer from his pocket, reach across the store counter, strike Eugenio in the face with the cowhide, and fire a ball into his chest. The shot hit Eugenio's diamond pin, which lodged in his heart. Although mortally wounded, Eugenio attacked Tinsley by plunging a knife into his chest. Within minutes, both lay dead.[57]

The outpouring of sympathy for the Navarro family after the murder resulted in a signal honor for Eugenio. On May 7, 1838, he was buried inside San Fernando Church, at a time when such burials had been forbidden by church officials. Beneath the cupola on the north side a plaque was placed that read: "Here lies Eugenio Navarro, a native of this city of Béxar, dead on May 6, 1838 at the age of 34 years, 5 months, and 21 days. He died an innocent victim of a pistol shot by a vengeful adversary, who also succumbed from a knife thrust by [Eugenio Navarro], defender of his honor and person."[58] His heirs divided his property, rather than dividing the proceeds of its sale. José Antonio Navarro was awarded Eugenio's home and a silversmith shop adjacent to it, a certificate for 295 acres of land, and debts owed to the estate totaling 1,485 pesos. The merchandise he received, valued at about 1,600 pesos, included a reference map of the United States and four books: *Nature Explained, English Grammar Mastered in 22 Lessons, How to be Happy,* and *The Sacred Heart of Jesus.*[59] Evidently it was from Eugenio Navarro's estate that José Antonio acquired what would be called the Navarro House on Flores Street.

A few days after the settlement of Eugenio's estate, José Antonio Navarro was nominated to serve in the House of Representatives of the Third Congress of the Republic of Texas. County officials also prepared to elect the third president and vice president of the Republic. Election records show that citizens in Bexar County cast their votes on September 3, 1838, in three polling places: the courthouse, La Villita, and the ranch home of María Calvillo. Mirabeau B. Lamar, hero of the Battle of San Jacinto and vice president under President Sam Houston, received an overwhelming majority of votes for president. The contest for state representative was more competitive and controversial. José Antonio Navarro and five other candidates received votes. At the first district, the courthouse, Navarro came in third behind Van Ness and William E. Howth. When the total vote was counted, including ballots from La Villita and the Calvillo ranch, Navarro narrowly defeated Howth, and Van Ness received the most votes. Thus voters selected Navarro and Van Ness as the two state representatives for San Antonio, as Béxar had been officially designated that year.[60]

Howth received reports of voting irregularities at La Villita and the Calvillo ranch that left him fuming. A week after the election he prepared to contest the returns at these two polling places by taking depositions to document electoral misdeeds. He then wrote to Navarro, in-

Capitol building of the Republic of Texas in Houston, 1837–39, where Navarro served as a congressman. Institute of Texan Cultures, #075-0557, University of Texas at San Antonio. Source: D. W. C. Baker, A Texas Scrapbook *(New York: A. S. Barnes & Co., 1875).*

forming him of his intention to challenge his election before the House of Representatives and enclosed a seven-point declaration of irregularities at the Calvillo ranch. His accusations included charges that election judges engaged in electioneering, kept the polls open when they should have been closed, destroyed ballots not to their liking, kept the polls open an extra day, admitted illegal votes for Navarro, and rejected legal votes for Howth. Regarding La Villita, Howth said that the entire vote there should be set aside because the election judges had not taken the oath required by law. Howth concluded that "[I]n consequence of the above facts herein above set forth I contend that setting aside the two polls the one held at the ranch of Madame Calvillo and the other at the La Villita that you have not received a majority of the legal votes in the county of Béxar." Navarro had to go to the office of Chief Justice Erasmo Seguín

on September 12, when Howth took depositions from several individuals (Navarro had the opportunity to question them if he chose).[61] Howth
would present these along with his challenge to Navarro's election to the
House of Representatives at Houston later that year.

Despite Howth's impending challenge, County Clerk John W. Smith
certified the election result on October 23, counting as valid the votes
from La Villita and the Calvillo ranch.[62] As soon as his election was
certified, Navarro left San Antonio and traveled to Houston, stopping
in Gonzales to meet with James W. Robinson, who was serving as the
judge of the fourth judicial district. Robinson sent a letter in Navarro's
care about the need for defense against Indian and Mexican attacks to
president-elect Lamar. Navarro arrived in Houston, which was not a
pretty sight, around the first of November. The town of about 4,000
people had existed for only two years and it teemed with boisterous
crowds that included residents, legislative entourages, lobbyists, and
various hangers-on. They were crammed into about 600 buildings,
many of which were squalid shacks and huts, and the town was well
supplied with saloons.[63]

Navarro presented his credentials in the Hall of Representatives and
took the oath of office. The first roll call for congressional members was
held on November 5, 1838, and James Dill (also referred to as "Dilmore") was assigned to be Navarro's interpreter. The next day Navarro was
named to the Naval Affairs Committee. Howth challenged Navarro's
election, as he had threatened in September, but after considering the
case the Committee on Privileges and Elections decided in favor of Navarro. He and Juan Seguín, a senator from the Bexar District, were the
only Tejanos in the Third Congress, whose sessions continued until
January 24, 1839. The two of them took their seats in the aftermath of
a rebellion that had broken out at Nacogdoches the previous summer
instigated by Vicente Cordova and other disaffected Tejanos. Although
quickly quashed, this revolt left doubts about the loyalties of Tejanos.
The trial of the ringleaders was still going on when the congressional
session began.[64] There was little sympathy for issues that would specifically benefit native Mexicans.

The acts and resolutions of the Third Congress show that defense of
Texas from the Mexican army and Indian attacks were among the main
legislative concerns, but there were many other issues considered by the
Béxar representatives and their colleagues. Six acts and resolutions specifically aimed at frontier defense were signed into law. Other priorities
included ways to raise revenue, incorporation of new towns, relief for
various persons who had supported the revolution, and establishment

of a general land office and a post office. While it is difficult to determine exactly which issues Navarro supported, he would certainly have focused on maintaining the validity of eleven-league grants. Animosity toward these and other grants issued by the government of Coahuila and Texas reappeared. George W. Hill, who chaired a select committee on this matter, reported that "many extensive and fertile portions of our country are held under grants obtained under the Federal Republic of Mexico, and from the state government of Coahuila and Texas, and from the great quantity of land thus accumulated, or claimed by a few individuals, some of whom are not citizens of our Republic, such lands remain in a waste, and uncultivated condition." He said that his committee was convinced that many of the grants had been obtained by fraud, had been illegally located, and were surveyed by unauthorized persons. Hill also referred to wrongful headright procedures. He asked for legislation to make grants obtained by fraud available to honest farmers.[65] This initiative did not pass, but it is an example of the animosity toward eleven-league grants and the attempts to invalidate them that Navarro consistently opposed.

Of the other issues considered, Navarro surely supported a proposal to translate the laws of the Republic into Spanish. Perhaps he supported the act that was an early version of the homestead law that protected each head of household by securing for them fifty acres of land, tools, and household property. As a member of the Naval Committee, he no doubt helped finalize the purchase of a steamship, the *Charleston*, for $120,000. His old friend Samuel May Williams acted as the owner's agent. The *Charleston* was a stout side-wheeler that could serve as a passenger ship, a towing vessel, or a warship. Navarro's role as a representative of his Tejano constituents is manifested in a dramatic speech he addressed to the Speaker of the House, John M. Hansford, in support of an act to protect Tejano land rights.[66] The terrible reality that threatened many Tejanos was the law mandating that all land claims based on incomplete, pending, or non-existent titles revert to the public domain. Such land could be claimed by anyone who possessed a headright certificate.

While greed was certainly one motivation for trying to take Tejano land, another can be deduced. Taking Tejanos' premium land located near San Antonio was easy compared to incurring the expenses and trouble of going out into the rapidly shrinking public domain. Land of less value was to be found to the west, in the dangerous *Comanchería*. In addition, many Tejanos' land holdings were extensive, and sometimes they were unaware of encroachment on their property. Once headright settlers established themselves, it became difficult to dislodge them, requiring lawsuits and expensive lawyers, and leaving one open to the vagaries of judges and the courts. Navarro and Seguín proposed legislation to protect Tejanos from legalistic attacks on their land, which had often been held by their families for generations.

Charges of Anglo American aggression against Bexareño landowners were common, while documented examples are rare. But one such case occurred in Bexar County while Navarro was serving in the Third Congress, and he used it to demonstrate the need for legislation to protect Tejanos who lacked a deed to long-held family lands. In 1838 the descendants of Joaquín Leal, led by José de la Garza and his wife, Consolación Leal, were at the point of being dispossessed of their land. John W. Smith and several other Anglos had initiated proceedings to classify the land owned by the Leals as in the public domain. Smith, as the Béxar county clerk, and his allies, had examined Tejano land documentation to look for vulnerable titles. The Leal property was their first target. The land in question, granted to Leal in 1778, fronted on the east bank of the San Antonio River, extending east between Seco and Calaveras creeks. The Leal family said that as a result of the turbulence of revolutions beginning in 1813, Spanish records and subsequent confirmations of the grant had been lost. This made their claim vulnerable and attracted the attention of Smith and others.[67]

The Leal family named several individuals as defendants in their case, including Smith, Ephraim Bollinger, William McCraven, John Neill, William Richardson, John S. Simpson, and Robert C. Trimble. Trimble was the county surveyor, while Neill was an immediate threat because he had physically occupied part of their property, had began plowing it, had moved cattle to it, and was chopping down trees, evidently to build a residence. The Leal family employed Henry Daingerfield, who had just ended his term as San Antonio's mayor, as their attorney. They petitioned the Fourth District Court, asking for the immediate eviction of Neill and a prohibition on further surveys or issuance of titles. Finally, they asked for a reasonable time to obtain their titles, which they believed to be in the archives of Mexico; these would provide a basis for a permanent injunction against any further proceedings. The verdict of Judge James Robinson was swift and decisive in favor of the complainants. He ordered John Borden, commissioner of the General Land Office, not to issue any patent or title from the Leal land to any of the defendants.[68]

While the Leal family was seeking legal action to protect their land, they must have written to their representatives in the Third Congress asking for assistance. Navarro and Seguín prepared a bill authorizing the General Land Office to issue titles to Tejanos who had incomplete land titles. It went from the Senate to the House of Representatives, where it was read at the end of the legislative session. Navarro and Van Ness defended the bill against an objection from a representative from Nacogdoches. In an impassioned speech, addressed to Speaker Hansford, Navarro used arguments from the Leal-De La Garza petition for the benefit of many other Tejanos. He began by trying to minimize the impact that passage of the bill would have so as not to alarm his fellow legislators. He noted that in Bexar County, there were families, "few indeed in number," who possessed small tracts of land granted by the Spanish government. Navarro explained that "these persons have continued undisturbed to hold and to cultivate the lands thus obtained and so ancient. So well-known and unquestionable have been their possession rights that the property has been inherited from the father to the sons, and to the grand-children of the original holders."[69]

Law and common practice, then, had secured the Tejanos' right of ownership, but Navarro expanded upon the issue of legality. He described two classes of owners whose property was threatened. The first included those who had once possessed written titles that were lost, stolen, or disappeared in the damage and destruction to the public records in the Béxar archives. The second class of owners was made up of those who had been unable to obtain titles because of war. He argued that Spanish laws, subsequently adopted by Mexico, provided that an individual in peaceable possession of any portion of public land not appropriated to municipal or national purposes for ten years thereby acquired a right to obtain a title. In Spanish, it was called *buena fé* (good faith), which provided the right to demand and receive a title to such land upon paying the proper fees. He added:

> I ask, Sir, will this government be so rigorous—will our laws be so unjust as to deprive such persons of their property, because through unforeseen and unavoidable accidents, they are not provided with documentary proof of title to their lands? No Sir—law and equity have everywhere provided a remedy for such accidents; and the bill sent by the Senate appears to me of this character. The individuals named in that bill, possess their lands by long prescription, and the provision to issue to them titles to their land, would seem to me as just, as their rights to such title is indisputable."[70]

Although the Leal family was able to successfully defend their land ownership in court, Navarro spoke out for those who could not do so and needed the protection of reasonable laws.

Appealing to the fair-mindedness of his legislative colleagues, Navarro declared that there were many unscrupulous men who, counting on the ignorance of the people, would survey their land and claim it as their own. Again he explained that

> [T]he unfortunate people alluded to, cannot come forward with their titles. They know nothing of the forms necessary to their defense; nor even anything of the very language in which they are called on to defend themselves. Encouraged by such circumstances, there are not lacking men, who, hungry for land, and calculating on their skill in the chicanery of the existing laws, as well as on the helpless ignorance of the innocent settlers have surveyed the property of these simple people; and in some instances, have even effected a forcible intrusion upon the disputed land.[71]

Navarro repeated that approval of the bill would in no way interfere with any particular law. He challenged the Texas representatives to say what part of the Constitution or laws would be infringed upon if Congress were to provide that the individuals in question would have their titles ratified and confirmed. He anticipated that some opponents would say that Tejanos could use the courts to defend their property rights, just as the Leals had done. He dismissed this idea by pointing out that prohibitive cost, legal intimidation, and judicial complexity made the courts inaccessible to most Tejanos.

The efforts of Navarro and Seguín were noble, but they were ultimately defeated. Lacking the services of his translator, Navarro delivered his lengthy speech to the House of Representatives in Spanish, a language most of them did not understand. His fellow representatives did not have access to an English version of the speech until the Houston *Telegraph and Texas Register* published it in an English translation on January 29, 1839, after the Third Congress had adjourned. Despite the best efforts of Navarro, Seguín, and Van Ness, no bill protecting Tejano legacy land rights was ever signed into law.[72]

It may not have helped their case that Navarro severely criticized President Mirabeau B. Lamar. Navarro expressed outrage that Lamar had replaced Sam Houston's cabinet with appointees of his own and thus, in Navarro's opinion, deprived the Republic of the services of many well-qualified, experienced men. He denounced Lamar's "adherence" to "that odious and injurious system, generally termed that of 'rotation in office.'"[73] He also predicted gloom and misfortune for the administration of Lamar who, he sarcastically implied, had been elected only because he was a veteran of the Battle of San Jacinto. Here Navarro trod dangerously close to attacking the Texian Holy of Holies. His imprudent statements unnecessarily created animosity in the new administration and must have aroused anger and resentment among Anglos. The consequence of his criticisms could only have been to reduce what goodwill there was in and around the capital toward Tejanos. Ironically, two years later Navarro would disregard his own dire prediction and unwisely commit himself to Lamar's grandest blunder: the Santa Fe Expedition.

Another issue of concern to the Bexareño legislators and their Tejano constituents was the Catholic faith in Texas. Early in January 1839, before Congress adjourned, Navarro and Seguín met with Father John Timon to discuss ways to promote Catholicism in Texas. Prior to the Revolution, Texas had been under the ecclesiastical jurisdiction of the Bishop of Monterrey, whose authority ended in 1836. Moreover, as Navarro and Seguín knew, the Catholic churches of Texas were destitute and lacked devoted priests. To address these problems, and to fill the void left by the separation of Texas from the Diocese of Monterrey, the Bishop of New Orleans, Anthony Blanc, sent Timon to Texas to report on the state of the Catholic Church and to make recommendations to revitalize the faith. Timon of course went to Houston where, contrary to the reputed anti-Catholicism of Anglos, he received a warm welcome. He preached several sermons during his stay, including one to Navarro and his fellow congressmen in the Hall of Representatives, and many, including Baptist ministers, attended and listened respectfully.[74]

Unable to inspect all of Texas or even to go to San Antonio, Timon relied upon informants such as Navarro and Seguín for information. The two were unsparing in their criticism of Refugio de la Garza and José Antonio Valdés, parish priests at San Antonio and Goliad respectively. Hoping for some assistance from Blanc, they described in somewhat exaggerated detail the dismal depths to which the Catholic faith had sunk in Texas. Navarro and Seguín's criticism convinced Timon. He condemned the two priests and gained their summary dismissal. On a more positive note, Navarro and Seguín were optimistic that they could obtain a grant for four leagues of public land to establish a college at San Antonio if Timon would agree for his Vincentian Order to supervise it. Red River County had obtained such a grant to endow DeKalb College, and San Augustine University had been established with a four-league grant. But, lacking support in Congress, Navarro and

Seguín's efforts came to nothing. Perhaps Navarro then regretted his intemperate remarks about President Lamar and the Battle of San Jacinto. Over the next few years, five more colleges and universities were built with four-league grants, but none in San Antonio.[75]

Navarro was elected to a second term in the House of Representatives but did not serve, reportedly because of illness. Nathaniel Lewis replaced him. Navarro, regardless of his health, was probably not eager to serve another term. At the beginning of 1839, he had many reasons to return to San Antonio. He was planning to or had already begun to move his primary residence to the San Geronimo Ranch. He possessed three headright certificates for which he needed to select lands from the diminishing public domain. He would have wanted to attend the wedding of his oldest son José Antonio George to Juana Chávez, scheduled for May 1839. It is also easy to suppose that Navarro did not relish the contentious rounds of legislative debate that were quite difficult to follow even with a translator, and one was not always available. In 1828 he had been glad to leave the legislature of Coahuila and Texas, whose sessions were conducted in his native language.[76] His sentiments were probably much the same in January 1839, when the Third Congress of the Republic of Texas ended and he headed home.

Navarro returned to San Antonio around the end of February 1839. He must have been pleased to find that his brother Luciano and cousin Francisco Antonio Ruiz had been elected to the city council in January. Voters had elected an Anglo, Samuel Maverick as mayor, but Tejanos remained a majority on the council, holding six of the eight places.[77] Thus the local government was characterized by a working relationship between Tejanos and Anglos, and Navarro did his part to bridge political gaps. That summer, though he had publicly denounced Lamar, Navarro expressed his concerns as a private citizen to public officials by asking for aid in fighting Indians, Mexican robbers, and city crime. Lamar's reputation for his aggressive anti-Indian policy was well known and appreciated in San Antonio, which had been subjected to devastating attacks since the Spanish era. This was the first of Navarro's letters to Lamar's administration warning of dangers from the south and soliciting help, and it would not be his last. For example, at the end of January 1840, he wrote another letter warning of the immediate threat of Mexican troops gathered at Matamoros. He reported that while they apparently did not have sufficient numbers to retake Texas, they might launch a raid.[78]

Turning his attention to personal affairs, Navarro began immediately to locate lands and build a home. On April 14, he completed the sur-

San Geronimo Plat

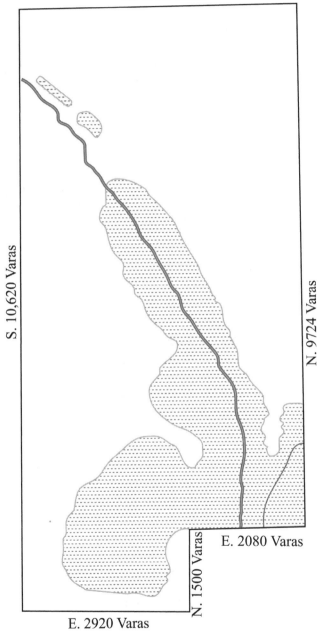

W. 4990 Varas

S. 10,620 Varas

N. 9724 Varas

E. 2080 Varas

N. 1500 Varas

E. 2920 Varas

In 1834, José Antonio Navarro purchased this two-league ranch for $250, known as the San Geronimo Ranch because San Geronimo Creek ran through it. Located about seven miles north of Seguin, Texas, it was the Navarro family residence from the 1840s until 1853, when he sold it for $16,000.

vey for the league and labor that he had obtained from Francisco de la Garza. Navarro managed to pick land in an advantageous location. The Atascosa River sliced through the tract, which adjoined a league that belonged to his brother Luciano. It was also located close to his Atascosa Ranch. He paid a $35 fee for three labors classified as arable and the remainder as pasture.[79] By early 1840, Navarro completed his house on the San Geronimo Ranch. Its manager was probably Ramón Rubio, who had served as his overseer at the Atascosa Ranch since 1832. Some members of the Navarro family were certainly living at the San Geronimo Ranch in the spring of 1840 when a desperate young man arrived at their door. Captured by Comanche Indians, Joseph Powell had managed to escape and fled to the "house of José Antonio Navarro on the Guadalupe River." The Navarros cared for him and eventually returned him to his family. The new ranch produced income from its livestock. Later that year, Navarro sold ten cows to the Republic of Texas Army. Colonel William Cazneau gave him a promissory note for $850 that was paid the next month.[80]

Expanding the operations at San Geronimo Ranch had become necessary because Indian attacks had left the Atascosa Ranch in ruins, with crosses marking graves where workers were buried.[81] Perhaps these concerns led Navarro, who now had a homesite on the San Geronimo, to maintain his residence in San Antonio until he left on the Santa Fe Expedition in 1841. Too, he had business to conduct in town, and his presence in San Antonio was also needed because he was elected as a city councilman in January 1840. Navarro served on the city council from January to August, then in September served as a commissioner to examine land titles under the 1840 "Act for the detection of fraudulent land certificates."[82] Such an assignment would have been very important to him, for obvious reasons. From that time forward he divided his time between his residence in San Antonio and his ranches.

The year 1840 also brought changes in Navarro's family relationships. In January he lost his beloved uncle, José Francisco Ruiz. Parish priest Refugio de la Garza recorded the burial on January 20, 1840, writing that Ruiz was a widower, aged 61, and had died of hydropsy (edema). Navarro must have felt Ruiz's death deeply. The fatherly figure to whom he had always looked for advice and guidance was now gone, and José Antonio stood alone as the senior member of the extended family.[83] Later in 1840, Navarro said goodbye to his son Ángel as he sent him to Cape Girardeau, Missouri, to continue his education at St. Vincent's College. Years later a classmate recalled that Father John Odin had escorted Ángel and the other boys as they traveled from Houston

José Francisco Ruiz, uncle and mentor of José Antonio Navarro. Alamo Collection,
Gift of Mrs. Ruby Hermes and Mrs. Marie O. Gomez to the Daughters of the
Republic of Texas.

on the steamship *Savanna* to New Orleans and then up the Mississippi River to Missouri. The school's congregation records show that "Angel Navarro, son of A. Navarro, from Texas," was a student from May 1, 1841 to October 29, 1847.[84] In 1848, again with the support of his father, Ángel traveled to Cambridge, Massachusetts, and enrolled at Harvard College, whence he graduated with a bachelor's degree in law the following year.

The enrollment of Ángel Navarro at St. Vincent's and later Harvard made clear just how much progress his father had made in living the American Dream sought by Ángel's namesake grandfather. José Antonio Navarro not only had property and enough money to send his son away to school, but he also had the respect of his community for his work in representing them in various legislative forums. During his lifetime, the Tejano settlement of Béxar had become the increasingly Anglo-dominated town of San Antonio, but he had weathered the changes and the revolutions that accompanied them. As he passed middle age, José Antonio may have begun to contemplate a quiet retirement in which to enjoy the fruits of his labors. But such was not to be, as he would once more be called upon to assume a leadership role for the troubled Republic of Texas.

CHAPTER SIX

Statesman and Prisoner, 1840–45

DURING 1840 AND 1841 two presidents with bold ideas lobbied José Antonio Navarro for his services. They were Jesús de Cárdenas, provisional president of the nascent Republic of the Rio Grande, and Mirabeau B. Lamar, president of the Republic of Texas. Navarro did not succumb to the blandishments of Cárdenas, but Lamar played upon his devotion to Texas and reputation as a mediator. Navarro thus made the greatest mistake of his life by agreeing to serve as a commissioner for the ill-fated Santa Fe Expedition. The expedition—a joint political, military, and commercial enterprise—was intended by Lamar to open trade between Texas and New Mexico and establish Texan control of the Santa Fe area. When Navarro and his fellow expedition volunteers surrendered in New Mexico, Navarro became a prisoner of General Antonio López de Santa Anna, who reveled in the capture of a Tejano who had signed the Texas Declaration of Independence. With one wrong decision, Navarro's American Dream became a nightmare.

Cárdenas—and other leaders in the border states of Nuevo León, Tamaulipas, and Coahuila—opposed the centralist government in distant Mexico City. These states had considerable economic independence and their leaders hoped to secede from Mexico and establish the Republic of the Rio Grande, based on the Constitution of 1824. Aware of José Antonio Navarro's political influence, they attempted to enlist his support for their cause. During May 1840 letters from Navarro, Cárdenas, and George Fisher arguing the pros and cons of the proposed republic appeared in the *Austin City Gazette*. One from Cárdenas to Navarro candidly asked Navarro to serve as an "agent" to further political and commercial ties with Texas. Aware of the delicate negotiations with Mexico to recognize Texas's independence, Navarro declined. He first gave the excuse that his responsibilities as a member of the Bexar County Land Commission prevented such a commitment. Then he spoke plainly to Cárdenas about the main reason for his decline: the proposal was contrary to Republic of Texas policy. He explained that the government of

Texas, guided by public opinion, would not interfere officially with the domestic quarrels of the Mexicans because of its own difficulties with Mexico, which directly affected Texas's future.[1]

Canales also met with President Lamar, who likewise wanted nothing to do with the Republic of the Rio Grande. Since he was negotiating with Mexico for recognition of Texas's independence, he saw no benefit in communicating with leaders of a rebellion. At the same time, newspapers that supported Lamar's political opponent, Sam Houston, opposed providing aid to Cárdenas and his associates.[2] Prominent Texans, including Navarro, felt a great sympathy to the federalist cause, seeing it as comparable to the Texas Revolution, but their hopes for Mexico's recognition of Texas prevented their support for Cárdenas.

Having wisely refused the pleas of Cárdenas on behalf of the ill-fated Republic of the Rio Grande, the next year José Antonio Navarro made the worst mistake of his life. At the importuning of President Lamar, he reluctantly agreed to participate in, and thus lend his prestige to, an aggressive venture into New Mexico: the Santa Fe Expedition. That decision cost him more than three years of agonizing captivity, seriously damaged his health, and nearly cost him his life. The complete failure of the Santa Fe Expedition resulted in legal charges that focused on Navarro alone, even though his fellow campaigners numbered more than 300.

Navarro's attitude toward requests to participate in the expedition seems to have evolved from outright refusal to reluctant acceptance. The reasons for the march to Santa Fe should be fully understood to explain Navarro's participation. The idea of an expansionist Texas began during the euphoric days after independence. Some impassioned merchants predicted that opening trade with Santa Fe would pave the way for Texas to expand to the west and consolidate all the lands from New Mexico to Alta California under the Lone Star Flag. Expansionist hopes soon faded in the face of reality. The Republic of Texas was overwhelmed by debt and on the verge of a financial crisis.[3] Its fiscal problems were aggravated by the Panic of 1837, the adverse effects of which virtually coincided with the duration of the Republic. Lamar was especially frustrated as the depression hampered his plans for the republic to provide education, defense, and other government services.

Lamar's election had revived expansionist ambitions. In his inaugural address he emphasized that the region east of the Rio Grande belonged to Texas by virtue of a resolution passed in the First Congress of the Republic. Acquisition of the part of New Mexico that lay east of the Rio Grande, including the capital, Santa Fe, became the centerpiece of his foreign policy. Through direct efforts and diplomatic overtures to Mexico by the United States and Great Britain, Lamar attempted to gain recognition of Texas's independence with a Rio Grande boundary, and he even tried to buy the disputed territory for $5 million. Nothing came of these initiatives. Lamar then tried to rally legislative support for an expedition to establish trade with Santa Fe and thus bolster Texas's claim to land in New Mexico. He predicted not only profit for merchants from his proposed expedition, but also customs and tax revenue that would increase the Republic's income. Again he met with resistance. At the beginning of Mexican independence in 1821, New Mexicans had welcomed Missouri traders into Santa Fe, but by 1840, viewed expansion-minded Texans as a threat. Many Texans also opposed expansion. The Texas Congress, led by Sam Houston, twice refused to approve an expedition to Santa Fe.[4]

Lamar looked for a way to circumvent the obstinate legislators. Escalating his determination was news he received from Americans living in Santa Fe that convinced him the people of that region would welcome the opportunity to come under Texas's control. William J. Jones and William G. Dryden provided him with glowing reports that were wildly optimistic. Jones assured Lamar that Mexican rule could be overthrown easily, and he claimed, "The revolutionary spirit is warm in New Mexico." Lamar conceived a plan for an expedition to instigate a revolt, to be funded by a combination of government and private resources. Historian Stanley Siegel has noted that despite congressional opposition, Lamar asserted that "as commander in chief, he could employ the military of the Republic upon any mission he chose." He obtained funds by forcing the republic's Treasurer, John C. Chalmers, to authorize $100,000 for a plan to achieve two objectives: establish trade and, if possible, take possession of Santa Fe.[5] Success would greatly expand the territory of Texas and pave the way for Texas merchants to establish a lucrative trade to Santa Fe.

Lamar moved his dream of trade and conquest forward by sending a letter, which would later be used against Navarro, inviting the citizens of Santa Fe to join Texas. He extolled the "glorious revolution" that freed Texas and pointed to Mexico's lack of civil harmony and frequent political convulsions. Coming to the point, he said:

> We tender to you a full participation in all our blessings. The great River of the North which you inhabit is the natural and convenient boundary of our territory, and we shall take great pleasure in hailing you as fellow-citizens, members of our young Republic, and

co-aspirants with us for all the glory of establishing a new, and happy, and free nation.

Lamar continued by assuring New Mexicans that Texas's liberal constitution conferred equal political rights to all, tolerated all religions, and guaranteed equality under the law. Showing amazing naiveté, he wrote that he trusted his letter would receive a sympathetic reception from New Mexican officials as well as citizens. In conclusion, he revealed that he was sending commissioners to explain fully the details of his proposal that "ought to perpetually cement the perfect union and identity of Santa Fe and Texas."[6]

By the summer of 1840 Lamar began politicking in San Antonio for an expedition to Santa Fe. Hugh McLeod, a prominent general in the Republic of Texas army, was likely the first to approach Navarro about supporting and perhaps joining the expedition. McLeod, who would lead it, met with Navarro and gained his support, but he met with opposition from the Seguíns. He wrote Lamar in August about the differences between these two prominent families, saying, "Seguine [sic] is my enemy . . . but the Navarro family can neutralize him, and I may count on the Beramendis [sic]." Evidently, while Navarro gave a positive response, he did not agree to go on the expedition at that time. He had responsibilities at home. He was on the city council and had posted a $5,000 bond to guarantee his proper performance of that responsibility.[7] Moreover, he wanted to continue developing his San Geronimo ranch and he had headright claims that needed attention.

In spring 1841 Navarro changed his mind about serving as a commissioner on the Santa Fe Expedition, but it still was not a straightforward decision. On April 28 William G. Cooke publicly announced the scheme in the *Austin City Gazette* and asked for volunteers to join it. Although Cooke wrote that he was "authorized to announce the names of Edward Burleson, Antonio Navarro, G[eorge] Van Ness and myself to represent our government with the people of Santa Fé," events show that Navarro and others had yet to make a final commitment to serve as commissioners.[8] Burleson subsequently declined, and Navarro could have done the same. He had obvious and compelling reasons to abandon any commitments he might have made to Lamar. He had a family of seven to support, had incurred the continuing expense of maintaining his son at school in Missouri, needed to locate and gain title to more than 5,000 acres of land for which he held claims, and had other business interests. Moreover, embarking on a long journey was dangerous because of the periodic illness he endured as a result of his injured leg.

That Navarro was wavering in his decision is supported by the fact that Lamar, accompanied by several principal officers of the planned expedition, traveled to San Antonio around the middle of May 1841. Certainly they intended to promote and inspire general support and enthusiasm for the Santa Fe enterprise, but their principal mission probably was to persuade Navarro to firmly commit to go, which he clearly had not yet done. Despite his differences with Lamar, Mayor Juan N. Seguín arranged for a twenty-one-gun salute for the president, and citizens were instructed to sweep the streets in front of their houses. Lamar arrived by May 15, when Seguín sent him a formal invitation to attend a ball.[9] Lamar was the first chief executive of the Republic to visit San Antonio; the residents were appreciative and received him warmly. No doubt they approved of his success in moving the capital from Houston to Austin. The move brought San Antonio closer to the seat of power, and Lamar was a firm supporter of frontier defense against Comanche attacks, a position that met with approval from the oft-raided community.

During his visit, Lamar met personally with Navarro, attempting without much success to gain a firm commitment. Navarro later recalled that when Lamar talked with him in San Antonio, "I openly refused . . . [because of] my large family and pecuniary interests." In addition, Navarro later claimed that he refused to go because he did not wish to witness the catastrophe that he foresaw. Although Navarro made this statement to Mexican authorities after being captured and it appears somewhat contrived, it was probably an accurate reflection of his disinclination to commit to the expedition at the time of Lamar's visit. In addition to asking for Navarro's help, Lamar asked to borrow his correspondence with Stephen F. Austin for the history of Texas that he planned to write. Lamar also requested that Navarro provide an autobiography. Navarro reluctantly gave Lamar the correspondence, and wrote an autobiographical sketch, but he still would not agree to serve as a commissioner for the Santa Fe Expedition. Having done his best to opportune and inveigle Navarro, Lamar returned to Austin.[10]

On May 18, 1841, Navarro wrote to Lamar regarding their meeting, apologizing for having to speak partly through an interpreter and with "my most miserable English." He did not mention the Santa Fe Expedition, but rather focused on the subject of Lamar's history of Texas. He emphasized the emotional value that his Austin letters had for him and made it clear that he wanted them returned—"to gratify the remainder of my life and so that, afterwards, my children may know that I was a friend of him who was a friend of liberty." Navarro later deplored the loss of the letters, which Lamar never returned. With the Austin letters and the autobiographical sketch, Navarro had also included notes about Joaquín de Arredondo's occupation of Béxar in 1813. He credited his uncle, José Francisco Ruiz, as a major influence on his life. In fact, had Ruiz been alive to council him, Navarro might have found the will to resist Lamar's entreaties. Navarro sent Lamar other notes with a vivid description of the abuses that women had suffered at Béxar in 1813 and how the Navarro, Ruiz, and Veramendi families experienced almost total ruin. There was some incorrect information, but it is clear that Navarro was developing an analysis of the revolutionary period of Béxar from 1811 to1813 that he would later put into his own historical publications, and that he wanted Lamar to appreciate the struggle Bexareños had endured to win their freedom from Spain.[11]

Despite Navarro's evident hesitation to join the Santa Fe Expedition, Lamar was persistent and persuasive. He needed a prominent Tejano as a commissioner to give his expedition credibility with New Mexicans. Since Seguín was considered an enemy of his scheme, Navarro was the only other prominent Tejano who could possibly convince New Mexicans that coming under Texan rule would benefit them. Moreover, Navarro's experience as a merchant would help establish the desired trade connection. As Navarro later admitted, he thought it unwise to continue opposing the president's wishes. Refusal to serve Texas on such an important mission would reflect badly on his loyalty at a time when Tejanos were held in low esteem by their Anglo countrymen. Moreover, Lamar played on Navarro's humanitarian sentiments, suggesting that violence could be avoided if Navarro would come and speak directly to Santa Fe's citizens. In addition, the job of commissioner paid well. By June 1, Navarro had made his final decision to accept Lamar's offer, and he walked into a store operated by Duncan C. Ogden and George T. Howard in San Antonio, where he collected an advance payment of $1,000 in cash and goods. The remaining $2,000 due him would be paid upon his return. A few days later, Reuben M. Potter wrote to Lamar that Navarro had "accepted the appointment as commissioner."[12]

Now that Navarro was part of the expedition, Lamar asked him to assist by translating documents. Potter reminded Lamar of his intention to write a longer proclamation to the citizens of Santa Fe and remarked, "you will be able to prepare your documents with his [Navarro's] assistance better than with mine, for though he is unacquainted with English, the aid of an ordinary interpreter will enable him to render them into Spanish." Little time remained before the expedition was to leave, and Potter suggested Navarro could translate the material as he traveled. The proclamation itself could be printed in Santa Fe. Using Potter's draft, Lamar produced a proclamation that was identical in content and tone to his letter to Santa Fe of April 14, 1840, but eight times longer. It was indeed translated into Spanish, probably with Navarro's assistance, and ironically was later presented as evidence at Navarro's trial in Mexico City. The English version of the proclamation read in part:

> The day is not far when you will see [Texas] become the richest, most powerful nation in America. It has been evident to you that everywhere a Texan sets foot, he transforms barrenness into fertility. Barbarians disappear, leaving the land to the skill of the farmer. . . . Commerce and industry flourish, as well as religion, non-corrupted by the abuses of rampant ecclesiastical power. As proof of the above it is sufficient to point out the many existing communities in Texas, founded peacefully in locations which had been heretofore inhabited by savages. Take a look at our Constitution and our laws, under which now live a large number of Mexican-Texans, who are your brothers, having blood, language and religion in common with you.

In conclusion, Lamar expressed what he obviously thought was a fallback in case the expedition failed to take over the government. Unrealistically, he hoped in that case the expedition's merchants could trade their goods and, having opened the door to subsequent trade, return peacefully to Texas.[13]

Lamar provided detailed instructions to his commissioners. They were to use peaceful means to obtain their objectives if possible, but military force if necessary. He wrote, "it is believed that forbearance, patience on the part of the Commissioners, and a gentleness of behavior, will conciliate at first their good will, and afterwards secure their confidence and esteem." The object of the expedition, however, was to take possession of governmental offices in Santa Fe and to establish a new administration using any cooperative local residents. Force was to be avoided if they were opposed by masses of people, but if there was local support or even indifference, military action could be used against the New Mexican troops.[14]

Navarro was not present when expedition members and well-wishers gathered in Austin on June 9, 1841, for a gala farewell celebration. They paraded before President Lamar and heard a stirring speech by Secretary of War Branch T. Archer. During the festivities a rousing song composed for the occasion was probably sung. Of its verses, the first expresses the exuberance of the expedition members and their supporters:

Forward comrades, firm and steady—
Hearts prepared and rifles ready.
From our mount-encircled valley,
Boldly forward let us sally—
Merrily, Texians march away!
To the hills of Santa Fé.

While others celebrated, Navarro prepared to leave San Antonio for Austin, where the members of the expedition gathered at several camps. More than 300 came, along with a large supply train. McLeod, as military commander of the expedition, organized the men into five companies—one of cavalry, one of artillery, and three of infantry. Observers noted twenty-two wagons pulled by oxen: ten of trade goods and the remainder filled with supplies. Four more merchandise wagons were added later, while seventy head of cattle provided meat.[15]

On June 18, José Antonio Navarro and the last of the volunteers arrived at an expedition camp north of Austin. Of about 320 members, records indicate only two were Latinos: José Antonio Navarro and Juan Carlos, a native of Taos, New Mexico, who was assigned to Company B. He would later offer his services as guide, with disastrous results. Navarro was ill and rode in a Jersey wagon (light carriage) along with George W. Kendall, who had sprained his ankle and could not walk. The condition of Navarro's leg was so bad that he also was unable to walk. If ever there was an occasion for Navarro to refuse a commitment because of illness, the summer of 1841 was the time. But his sense of duty overcame common sense and he chose to go. Having given his word, he was accustomed to respect it, as he would later say. On June 20, McLeod gave the order to depart.[16] The expedition members set out on what they thought would be a merry march to the "hills of Santa Fé." At that moment, if anyone harbored doubts about the outcome of the mission, it may have been Navarro. And indeed the participants would soon find themselves entangled in a nightmare of deprivation, disillusionment, and death in the trackless lands to the north.

As the expedition left Austin, it had the appearance of a parade, decorated as it was with fluttering banners. Captain Mathew "Old Paint" Caldwell, who had signed the Texas Declaration of Independence with Navarro, led the way with fifty solders, followed by a train of horsemen and wagons that stretched back at least a mile.[17] Behind this impressive façade were serious weaknesses. Their departure was nearly a month behind schedule, which reduced the prospects for sufficient grass along the way for the stock. McLeod arrived late and soon became ill, raising doubts about his ability to lead. The expedition brought no guides other than John Howland, who knew little about the country, and there was no map of the route to be traveled. Scouts determined the route the wagons were to follow from day-to-day.

The results of inadequate preparation became clear during the first days of the march. McLeod realized that overloaded wagons were going to break down often and require time-consuming repairs. On June 24, from Camp Navarro, near the Lampasas River, he sent a contingent to acquire more wagons and oxen and another to get more beeves. McLeod had difficulty maintaining order. Suffering from a fever, he left the expedition to seek treatment and did not return for sixteen days, prompting additional murmurs about his leadership. Ominously, on the 25th, one of the volunteers committed suicide.[18] Thus the problems of supply, leadership, and discipline encountered during the first week cast a shadow over the expedition's future.

On July 14, the expedition crossed the Brazos River and moved into uncharted territory. Here the expedition discovered that the designated guide, John Howland, had no knowledge of the country beyond. Other scouts were assigned to ride with him to find the route for the expedition to follow. One week later the expedition reached the heavily wooded region called the Cross Timbers. Travel became difficult and often required the use of axes and shovels to clear a path for the wagons, which were lightened when McLeod ordered all "useless baggage" to be abandoned, including a load of rancid dried beef. In the meantime, Navarro continued to ride in the Jersey wagon, pulled by two mules. After two weeks of hard traveling, Thomas Falconer, an Englishmen who had arrived in Austin just one month before the expedition departed, determined their approximate location by lunar observations. The news was not good: they had traveled about 300 miles almost due north from Austin and Santa Fe still lay more than four hundred miles to the northwest. The only good news for Navarro was that his leg had healed enough that he began riding horseback.[19] Continuing the march, scouts marked a route that turned more to the northwest, but problems mounted as the caravan lumbered on. Water became scarce, the men were at the point of mutiny, and discipline began to break down as some forged ahead looking for water.

The caravan passed through the western edge of the Cross Timbers and camped on Belknap Creek on July 30, 1841. The next day the group had its first encounter with Indians. The advance party had already made camp on the Little Wichita River, while the wagons, a mile behind, hurried to catch up. Archibald Fitzgerald drove the mules of the Jersey wagon, which brought up the rear and was just out of sight of the rest of the expedition. Inside, Navarro and Kendall held on tight as Fitzgerald drove the mules hard. Suddenly Navarro yelled "*Los Indios! Los Indios!*" and grabbed his rifle as three Comanches rode past them, chasing a buffalo. The Indians stopped at the edge of the camp, but the buffalo continued at a run, scattering men, pots, and pans, before a well-placed bullet brought it down. The next day, several half-starved dogs appeared that were presumed to have come from an Indian camp.[20] Fed with scraps, the dogs accompanied the group from that point and earned their keep as sentinels, barking at the stealthy approach of Indians.

The expedition never reached the Red River, the destination of the first leg of the journey to Santa Fe. Juan Carlos, the New Mexican, assured the group that he was familiar with the territory and in previous years had trapped up and down the Red River. He spoke so convincingly that he was transferred to the scouting company. On August 4, expedition members reached the Wichita River, a large stream that they misidentified as the long-sought Red River, which actually lay no more than thirty miles to the north. The expedition crossed and followed the Wichita west. Three days later, Carlos announced that he recognized their location and declared they were only about sixty leagues (150 miles) from the New Mexican town of San Miguel.[21] With renewed confidence, Navarro and his comrades continued west, unaware that geographical confusion, lack of provisions, and Indian attacks were forming a trap that would close around them.

On August 13, Caldwell returned from a scouting trip and reported the Brazos was only a few miles south of the camp. The members were stunned as they realized they were not on the Red River after all, which was confirmed by the diminishing flow of the stream they had followed. Despite this revelation, the next day the dispirited expedition continued west, camping in rough terrain by a spring saturated with gypsum, which was unpleasant to drink and caused diarrhea. The men muttered threats toward Carlos, and at dawn the next day he was nowhere to be found. Anxiety about their location grew and scouts were sent north in search of the Red River. Peter Gallagher, who accompanied the scouts, recorded that on August 18 they found the Red River about fifty miles to the north of the camp, and that its waters were as "salt [*sic*] as the Ocean." Their discovery was overshadowed by the reports of other groups that they had found what appeared to be promising routes. Captain Caldwell had located the South Pease River, which he said was the Red, further compounding the confusion. The caravan reached the South Pease and continued to the northwest past the Middle Pease to the North Pease. It was soon clear that this stream was not the Red, for it split into branches and the flow diminished. At least along this route lay prairie dog towns, which provided food for an expedition that was becoming more and more desperate. Had they pursued a northward route, they would have reached the true Red River and could have pursued their original plan to follow it west and then turn north to reach the Canadian River, western branches of which reached close to Santa Fe. Instead they marched deeper into rough terrain, to the steep walls of the Caprock escarpment that guarded the entrance to the treeless plains of the Llano Estacado.[22]

The expedition reached Quitaque Creek, a branch of the South Pease River, on August 28 and followed it into a welcome valley free of rocks and water free of gypsum. They made camp near the base of the Caprock. At this point the group had traveled more than 350 miles through harsh terrain, and endured scorching temperatures, torrential rains, Indian attacks, and internal dissent. No end to their trouble was in sight. Two days later, Kiowa Indians killed five expedition members, bringing the total number of men lost to about fifteen. McLeod named the place Camp Resolution, reflecting his dogged determination to proceed. At this point his men were fatigued and half-starved, completely lost, and lacked a guide or the knowledge needed to pass over the Llano Estacado. Despite Carlos's desertion, some still believed that New Mexican towns were nearby. To find them, McLeod selected ninety-nine of the healthiest, best mounted men under the command of Captains John Sutton and William G. Cooke. The Sutton party, which included Kendall, left camp on August 31, climbed the Caprock, and rode onto the plains. Along the way they met shepherds, who told Kendall that "the country was in arms against us." Near the town of Anton Chico, a teamster warned Kendall that Governor Armijo had spread the word that the Texans would "burn, slay and destroy as we went." They found nothing at Anton Chico to take back to those waiting at Camp Resolution, and the next day, Captain Dámaso Salazar and a contingent of soldiers from New Mexico captured Kendall's advance party as they rode north toward San Miguel.[23]

Meanwhile McLeod, Navarro, and others in the main party remained at Camp Resolution for twenty miserable days. Kiowa Indians harassed them and stole more than eighty horses, leaving seventy-six men to travel on foot. A blue norther swept through, bringing a numbing rain that added to the volunteers' misery. They butchered oxen for sustenance, consuming all parts of the animals but the horns and hooves. Finally news came when Cooke, who had avoided capture, hired three Mexican traders to take letters to those at Camp Resolution and guide them to San Miguel. The messengers arrived on September 15. After five days of preparation, McLeod's party climbed the Caprock and marched into the Llano Estacado, where "not a tree or bush, and hardly a weed could be seen in any direction." They managed to bring at least two wagons laden with merchandise and a cannon with them, but the lack of food was severe. After two days, the starving men killed the dogs that had followed them and slaughtered a broken-down ox. The next day some of the men tried to eat the hide after cooking it on coals and boiling it. For the first time, however, the expedition had competent guides—the three Mexican traders sent by Cooke. They crossed 150 miles of the Llano Estacado in eight days, losing only three men who left the main group and never returned. On September 29 the group made its descent down the western Caprock of New Mexico into Apache Canyon.[24]

The march continued with most of the men on foot. Scouts brought back ominous reports of mounted men, probably Mexican soldiers, seen in the distance. On October 4, at noon, McLeod's men arrived at a place called Laguna Colorada, where they camped. By this time the Mexican traders had prudently departed, fearful of the consequences of being caught with the Texans. That afternoon two Mexican soldiers rode into the camp and delivered letters from Colonel Juan Andrés Archuleta, who had a contingent of soldiers just over a hill. In a ploy to disarm the Texans, the letters said (according to a participant in the expedition), "If we came to trade in New Mexico we must deposit our arms there." McLeod responded by moving into a defensible position. That evening, he and Navarro went to Archuleta and discussed the situation. Archuleta attempted to lure Navarro to abandon the expedition, saying that by doing so, Armijo would be disposed to send a favorable report to the central government about Navarro's involvement in the expedition. Navarro replied that he would not dishonor himself by changing sides, even if his blood was to be shed. He thanked Archuleta for his offer, saying that he believed the colonel was truly trying to save his life, but added, "I doubt not that you will hold a surrendered prisoner of war in more respect than you would one who had saved his life by cowardice and infamy." Navarro reportedly concluded the interview with Colonel Archuleta by saying, "I have sworn to be a free Texan, and I will never foreswear."[25]

The Texans debated past midnight about what to do. McLeod wanted to fight, but his men were demoralized and suffered from malnutrition, scurvy, and exhaustion. He had less than seventy who were capable of resistance. Most of these were on foot, and their ammunition

San Miguel del Vado, New Mexico. Courtesy of the Palace of the Governors, (MNM/ DCA), #09777, Santa Fe.

was nearly gone. The alternative to fighting was Archuleta's appealing promise to treat the Texans fairly, feed them, and escort them to San Miguel, where they could begin negotiations about trade.[26] In his role as trade commissioner, Navarro was probably convinced, as were the expedition's merchants, of the virtue of surrender. For a time, McLeod resisted the humiliating reality of defeat, but the truth was that Archuleta had him checkmated. Resistance would be futile, and retreat was not an option.

McLeod agreed to surrender on the morning of October 5, 1841, and a formal capitulation was written and signed by officers on both sides. That same day, Archuleta wrote his report of the capture to Armijo. He said he had guaranteed that the lives of the officers and soldiers would be spared, not only by him "but also by disposition of General Armijo." The next day, at "the Vegas de las Gallianas [*sic*]," Armijo noted his approval of Archuleta's report. He affirmed, "it is understood [that the lives are guaranteed] of the entire number of the prisoner force, without exception of any person." Falconer later wrote that there was "a most distinct provision inserted for the protection of Señor Antonio Navarro."[27] However, this has never been found, nor did Navarro refer to it at his trial in Mexico City.

Colonel Archuleta sent José Antonio Navarro, McLeod, and other officers ahead of the main group. They arrived at San Miguel on October 9, 1841, and were placed under heavy guard in quarters fronting on the main plaza. Of the twenty-six wagons that had left Austin, two rolled into San Miguel. Physically sick, heartbroken, and uncertain about his fate, Navarro must have had little hope for the future. He, like Kendall, must have heard the sounds of the celebration on the main plaza outside their cells. Kendall recalled shouts of "Long live the Mexican Republic, Long live the brave General Armijo, long live the laws, and Death to the Texans." Celebrants fired muskets into the air; violins, mandolins, and trumpets played; church bells rang, and a Te Deum sounded from the nearby church.[28] These sounds of celebration surely added to the Texans' anxiety.

Worse than the festivities were the alarming rumors that Navarro and the others were to be marched to Mexico City. Navarro, fatigued, emaciated, sick, and dispirited, was sure he could not survive the rumored march. He managed to obtain paper and pen and wrote to Governor Armijo, pleading not to be taken out of New Mexico. Navarro explained his participation in the expedition, trying to minimize his role. He said that when Lamar came to San Antonio and solicited him to serve as a commissioner, he flatly refused. Navarro only relented, he wrote, when Lamar convinced him that, as a Spanish-speaking intermediary, he could prevent violence. The president "assured me in the most positive and convincing way that my function would be precisely to serve as a peaceful intermediary . . . by using my Spanish to explain it [the aspirations of Texas], and thereby prevent any commotion or use of weapons which in no case should be used." Having justified his presence in New Mexico, Navarro appealed to Armijo's compassion: "To remove me from here would be tantamount to killing me; therefore in this matter I appeal to the kindness of Your Excellency not to ignore the painful sufferings from a chronic illness like the one I bear." Navarro asked to meet with Armijo so the governor could see his wretched condition and exempt him from the journey to Mexico City.[29] He knew that, even if he survived the 1,600-mile march to the capital, his fate would then be in the hands of Santa Anna, who had recently regained power. The chances that he would ever see his family and friends in Texas again would be slim.

Armijo arrived in San Miguel the next day. Other members of the expedition also wrote to him. Kendall and Falconer emphasized that they were not citizens of Texas and asked for their freedom. Their efforts came to naught, and Armijo sent all papers related to the expedition to

General Manuel Armijo, Governor of New Mexico. Courtesy of the Palace of the Governors, (MNM/DCA), #050809, Santa Fe.

Minister of War José María Tornel. On the 16th, soldiers captured the last of the Sutton-Cooke party and brought them under heavy guard to the buildings around the main plaza. Now all members of the expedition were in custody. Looking northward, they had all seen the "Hills of Santa Fé," the subject of the merry song with which the expedition began, but San Miguel was as close as any of them would get to the New Mexican capital.[30]

Navarro, when he did not receive a reply from Armijo, wrote to a parish priest, José Leyva, asking him to intercede on his behalf to gain a meeting with the governor. He explained, "My heart was transfixed with a pain when I learned that The Most Excellent Commandant General has decided on my departure." "Evidently I am to be sacrificed down that long road," he added, and "I am certain that you will agree that His Excellency would decide to leave me if he would look upon me with his own eyes this evening and see the deplorable state of my ulcerated leg that is inflamed by the cold." Navarro again appealed to compassion asking, "For the love of humanity, will you and Don Juan Begil, intervene on my behalf with His Excellency? I am Mexican, and in my veins boils the same blood as in yours. Let me stay in Santa Fé, do not let me go in my present state in the hands of unknown troops." Anticipating his situation would not change, Navarro asked Leyva to get him some clothes from his trunk, along with some books and shoes. Peter Gallagher sadly noted that on the same day, "about two wagon-loads of goods" (much of which had belonged to Navarro) were hauled out to the plaza, where the governor supervised the distribution of the contents "amongst the Indians and Mexicans in the square." Navarro, dressed in dirty rags, watched while his clothing and other possessions were given away. Armijo also divided the small arms—pistols, muskets, and swords—among his militia and auxiliaries, and sent two captured flags to Mexico City. He kept in the plaza "as a trophy of the victory over the enemy, the excellent, well-mounted, eight-pound cannon and its munitions."[31]

Navarro was in the group of prisoners that left for Mexico City on October 16, under the command of Lieutenant Teodoro Quintana. Gallagher, McLeod, and other expedition officers accompanied Navarro. According to Falconer, they were "well treated on the road and had no cause for complaint. They were mounted [and] managed the journey without difficulty." After three days, Navarro's party reached the Rio Grande, where they began the part of their march called "Jornada del Muerto"—literally "Dead Man's Journey"—so called because rough terrain forced travelers to leave the Rio Grande and pass through a waterless ninety-mile route to where the road rejoined the river northwest of Paso del Norte (present-day Ciudad Juárez). Navarro's group arrived in Paso del Norte on November 1. Gallagher's diary makes no mention of any hardships encountered, probably because they had sufficient water, were mounted, and received humane treatment from Quintana.[32]

The prisoners in the other group were not so fortunate. They marched from San Miguel the day after Navarro's party left, under the command of Captain Dámaso Salazar. These men, who numbered about eighty-seven, traveled on foot, some barely able to walk. Salazar conducted a forced march that pushed them to exhaustion. Before arriving in Paso del Norte, he shot three who could not keep up, and two died of exposure.[33]

In Paso del Norte, Colonel José María Elias González, commander of the military department, took charge of the prisoners. Under his authority, conditions for the Texan captives improved enormously. Officers divided them into small groups and housed them with residents, who provided them with well-prepared meals of meat, eggs, bread, and wine. The prisoners rejoiced at "finding ourselves in the midst of plenty and treated as men." The day after their arrival González arranged a dinner and fandango, and Navarro and McLeod took all their meals with him. Kendall stayed at General González's house and wrote that he was a "gentlemanly officer, a well-bred, liberal, and a generous host." After a stay of nine days, the prisoners left for Chihuahua, 300 miles away. The entire populace of Paso del Norte turned out to see them off. González provided his personal carriage for Navarro, McLeod, Van Ness, and Kendall to use for the trip.[34] No doubt at his instruction, the guards treated the men well and provided sufficient food during the two-week journey.

As the group approached Chihuahua on November 22, some citizens came out to greet them. Kendall remembered that "They spoke to Mr. Navarro very kindly and said that himself and his friends could expect nothing but *hospitality* while in the city." About a mile from town, Governor García Conde and his entourage met them, shaking hands with Navarro, McLeod and several of the others. Military officers escorted the men through town, where multitudes gathered to see the spectacle of the ragged prisoners. "Mira! Mira! Los Tejanos, Los Tejanos" ("Look! Look! The Texans, The Texans") was on everyone's lips. The roofs of the cathedral, convent, and other buildings teemed with spectators. Officers led the prisoners to the Jesuits' Hospital and confined them in the *Salon de los Distinguidos*, which opened into the same courtyard where a firing squad had executed the father of the Mexican Revolution, Miguel Hidalgo.[35]

The prisoners had five days to recuperate and prepare for the next leg of their journey. Navarro had an influential friend in Chihuahua, María Gertrudis Valdez, the wife of James W. Magoffin, a prominent trader in the region. She was able to provide invaluable aid to Navarro and his fellow prisoners. "Navarro was acquainted with her, since she had lived at San Antonio de Béxar prior to the Texas Revolution," Kendall wrote, "and I believe he received permission to call upon her while we were in Chihuahua." Señora Magoffin treated Navarro to a sumptuous dinner. This angel of Chihuahua continued to feed and care for Navarro's fellow prisoners during their stay, evidently accepting drafts that Navarro and McLeod presented on behalf of the Texas government. Her kind efforts "materially improved" conditions for the prisoners. Navarro probably also obtained funds with the aid of the Magoffins. Cooke later confirmed this saying, "had it not been for the generosity of Mr. Navarro many more of the Texan prisoners would have perished than did." When drafts were ultimately presented to the Texas government for payment, an aghast President Houston complained to the House of Representatives that Navarro alone had signed a receipt for $1,000 in silver, while not a penny had been appropriated by the government to pay such expenses.[36]

Meanwhile, Governor Armijo had written to Governor Conde urging him to guard "with especial care" Navarro, McLeod, Cooke, Brenham, and Kendall "on account of their superior intelligence, standing, and influence." Navarro assuredly had all three. The care the Magoffins bestowed upon the prisoners shows that his influence ranged far to the west of San Antonio. Another instance of Navarro's influence is demonstrated by the aid provided by his brother-in-law, Colonel Mateo Ahumada, the former commander of the Department of Texas who had married Navarro's sister Antonia while serving at Béxar.[37] Ahumada furnished Navarro with a carriage and a pair of mules for the journey south to replace González's carriage, which had to be returned to Paso del Norte.

Soon after leaving Chihuahua, the prisoners began conspiring to escape. In desperation, they plotted to seize their guards, disarm them, and make a forced march back to the Rio Grande. Navarro opposed the scheme: "He was so lame that he could neither walk nor ride on horseback, and it was utterly impossible to escape in his carriage across the rough and broken mountains. His own destruction would have been inevitable, and this he told the men." Navarro's concern was in fact as much for his fellows as for himself. He assured his companions, with perspicacious foresight, that they would all be free within six months—

with the exception of him. Furthermore, he warned them that the safety of Cooke's party, which was traveling ahead, would be endangered by their escape attempt, whether successful or not. Kendall said that few believed Navarro, but "the old gentleman spoke with the spirit of prophecy" concerning his imprisonment.[38]

Some of the prisoners rejected Navarro's advice and persisted in their plotting. When Navarro realized that his arguments could not prevent an escape attempt, he told an officer of the guard about it. As a result, the guards increased their vigilance so that any attempt to escape had to be abandoned. Navarro's decision enraged the plotters, who denounced his betrayal. Francis R. Lubbock later wrote that Navarro was considered a traitor. Another conspirator later condemned Navarro for "blowing the plot," as he called it. But it took only a little persuasion to convince him that "the informer" had saved all their lives. He finally admitted that "after all, the old man acted right." It truly was a wildly impractical scheme: that nearly 300 Texans, without provisions, could walk across northern Mexico without attracting the attention of military forces or dying of exposure. Kendall later declared that had they carried out their escape plan, "hardly a man would have got through alive."[39]

Trouble awaited Navarro when his party arrived at Zacatecas near the end of December. Minister of War José María Tornel had sent a garbled order to the governor there, ordering him to keep Navarro and two others in close confinement and under strict guard. One of those whom Tornel named was "Colonel Milam," who had been killed at the Siege of Béxar in December 1835, and the other was "Robert Foster," who must have been Samuel Roberts, the secretary of state who issued Lamar's orders for the expedition. Roberts had not joined the campaign and was not a prisoner. Officials selected Thomas Falconer as a substitute and he was "accordingly placed in a small, close room with Mr. Navarro." As they continued their journey, an extra guard rode close by Navarro and Falconer, watching their every move.[40] Navarro's troubles with Tornel were just beginning. The minister of war was one of Santa Anna's most trusted officials, and they would focus their vindictive efforts on Navarro for the next three years, seeking to send him to the executioner's block.

During the last days of January 1842, the prisoners reached Tula, located about fifty miles northwest of Mexico City. After more than three months, the end of the 1,600-mile journey to the capital was in sight. Upon leaving Tula, soldiers separated Navarro from the group, placed him under a strong cavalry guard, and took him to the Acordada, a wretched facility which served as the national jail in Mexico City. Stephen F. Austin had been imprisoned there eight years earlier. As the iron gates clanged behind him, Navarro perhaps recalled ruefully what he had then written to Samuel May Williams about Austin's imprisonment, that "Austin was gullible and imprudent and was caught like a surprised child."[41] Sadly, Navarro had fallen into a similar trap when he joined the expedition to Santa Fe.

Kendall wrote that "no one could divine" the reason for Navarro's removal from the group. Many prisoners continued their march to the town of Perote, where they were confined in the San Carlos fortress; others, like Kendall, were confined in the San Lázaro leper colony, and then in the former convent of Santiago Tlatelolco.[42] In retrospect, it is clear that the reason for isolating Navarro was that Santa Anna realized his importance in Texas and Coahuila. At last he had within his grasp a man—Mexican-born no less—who had signed the treasonous Texas Declaration of Independence. As Navarro had predicted at the time of the escape plot, Santa Anna released all the expedition members by the end of the year except one, and he focused his wrath on that one prisoner: José Antonio Navarro.

Santa Anna's third and longest term as president had begun on October 5, 1841—the day Colonel Archuleta forced Navarro and the others to surrender at Laguna Colorada. Mexicans had not forgotten Santa Anna's debacle in Texas five years earlier, however, and the public reception for his return was conspicuously restrained. When he entered Mexico City as president, in a carriage drawn by four white horses, "not a solitary *viva* was heard." A few days later, as he had done in the past, he turned the responsibilities of the presidency over to his vice president, Nicolas Bravo, and left for his hacienda near Veracruz. But Santa Anna still dictated orders. Not only did he intend to retaliate against Navarro, but also against Texas, and he ordered retaliatory raids in response to the Santa Fe Expedition in March and September 1842, led by Generals Rafael Vásquez and Adrián Woll. These and other incursions demonstrated Santa Anna's anger toward Texas and Texans, as Navarro had anticipated and would soon experience firsthand.[43]

Even before Navarro reached the Acordada, Santa Anna ordered him to be tried for treason. The same day the Tejano limped into the Acordada, Minister of War Tornel notified the commandant general of Mexico's Federal District, Juan José Andrade, of the president's wishes concerning Navarro. Andrade was to immediately put Navarro on trial as a traitor before a military council. By Tornel's order the guard was to place Navarro in a secure cell in absolute isolation, but the prison did not have the resources to keep Navarro isolated from the other inmates. Tornel

Antonio López de Santa Anna. Courtesy of Texas State Library & Archives Commission.

sent Andrade seven expedition documents to be used as evidence. Included were Lamar's proclamation and Navarro's commission and instructions. Navarro's letter to Governor Armijo, which was identified as a confession, and a copy of the Constitution of Texas, apparently bearing Navarro's signature as a representative, were also included. Four days later Andrade issued the order for Navarro to be tried, and he sent the incriminating papers to General Mariano Morlet, who was instructed to prosecute Navarro as soon as possible. Andrade quoted Tornel to Morlet, saying Navarro was accused of treason because he "promoted and sustained a movement for the dismemberment of Texas and was one of the commissioners for the invasion of New Mexico."[44]

Prosecutor Morlet wasted no time. Throughout February, he gathered depositions to add to what was already known about Navarro's alleged crimes. On the 12th, he took the statements of Cooke and Richard F. Brenham at Santiago Tlatelolco, where they were imprisoned. Both admitted that they knew Navarro. They stated that the Santa Fe expedition had been Lamar's idea, not Navarro's, but that he had agreed to come along "in order to invite the authorities of New Mexico to join Texas." They confirmed that Navarro had served in the Texas Congress, but he had not joined any other hostile expeditions against Mexico "given that he has almost always been afflicted by the illness he suffers in one leg."[45] Morlet then deposed four military officers: General José Mariano Carrera de Manzanares, Colonels Carlos Ocampo and Fernando Urrua, and Battalion Commander Francisco Camacho. They provided testimony about Navarro's activities in Texas from 1827 to 1835. The prosecutor also included a report from Governor Armijo, who claimed that the Texans' surrender at Laguna Colorada was unconditional.

Armed with this array of documents and testimony, Prosecutor Morlet went to the Acordada on February 24, 1842, confronted Navarro, and took his testimony. Navarro began by stating that he was forty-four years old (he actually was forty-seven in 1842), a resident of San Antonio, a Roman Catholic, and a merchant. Asked if he knew why he was in prison, Navarro stated that it was because he had been made a prisoner of war in the Department of New Mexico. Referring to the Texas Revolution, he said he "joined the Texas adventurers" on March 2, 1836, because the *juntas populares* of Béxar had selected him as a delegate to the Convention. Rather than being enthusiastic about this duty, he said he "yielded to the energetic will of his fellow citizens" and thus found himself on March 2 "surrounded by a general conflagration of colonists who ardently demanded a declaration of independence."

About signing this document, Navarro said that he did so "seeking his own personal survival in that difficult situation." It seemed to him that no Mexican, not even the most patriotic, would have done anything else. He claimed that, prior to the Texan occupation of Béxar in December 1835, he had not even "the most minimal dealings with the colonists, either personally or by spoken or written word."[46] This, of course, was not true, unless he meant that he did not actively promote revolution.

Later in his testimony, Navarro described the services he had the rendered to Mexico. He emphasized his service in the legislature of Coahuila and Texas, having been named administrator in the customs house at Galveston, although this appointment did not take effect (because he declined), and the commissions he held to grant lands in the colonies of Pecan Point and Green DeWitt. He recalled his municipal offices, which he said gave him great "satisfaction because he believes that he performed these duties with loyalty, honor, and [personal] disinterest, as far as he knows, in favor of his Fatherland." Now, he said he had the misfortune of being unable to serve it and even, to some extent, had wronged it "due to a chain of imperious circumstances that he could not avoid." In other words, Navarro admitted that appearances made him look guilty of treason but maintained that he was actually the victim of events beyond his control. When asked why he had sided with the Texan rebels during the siege of Béxar, Navarro denied this had occurred. On the contrary, he said that General Martín Perfécto de Cos could confirm his neutrality, because while retreating from Béxar, Cos had stopped at neighboring ranches, where he obtained cattle to feed his men.[47]

Morlet then confronted Navarro with the most serious of the charges, one that would unquestionably justify a death penalty: that he had taken up arms against Mexico at the Battle of San Jacinto. In earlier testimony, Colonel Urrua claimed that Navarro had fought at San Jacinto with the company led by Juan N. Seguín. Because he was gravely wounded, Urrua was "unable to pay attention to everything that was happening and thus could not say assertively from whom he heard this, but [he] recalls very vividly that, generally, everyone said that Navarro was there with the expressed company." Navarro denied this damaging accusation vigorously, protesting that it was a "dreadful slander" and "false, absolutely false." He asserted that neither Cos nor Santa Anna could say that they had seen him with Seguín. In fact, by the time Navarro heard about the outcome of the battle, he was already in Natchitoches, and from there, "to evade the horrors of war," he went to New Orleans. The explanation for Urrua's confusion is that there was indeed a Navarro in Seguín's company at San Jacinto, but it was Nepomuceno Navarro, the son of José Ángel Navarro.[48]

Asked why he did not attempt to leave Texas while there was sufficient time and support to do so—especially while Santa Anna's troops had the Texans fleeing from his advance—Navarro replied that he was already in Washington-on-the-Brazos. Given that "his path was obstructed by the two lines of belligerent forces," returning to San Antonio was out of the question. And how could he be expected to leave Texas without his family and the possessions that he had secured "through sweat and hard work?" Goods, houses, and ranch lands would have been left unprotected. "Indeed," Navarro said, "there were precious few Mexicans citizens who were able to move out and carry a portion of their belongings under the protection of said troops." He also said the idea of abandoning his native country never entered his mind. Thus, when he left the Convention, he sought a temporary refuge in Natchitoches and New Orleans rather than attempt to go home.[49]

After questioning Navarro's conduct in the Texas Revolution, Morlet focused on the Santa Fe Expedition. He inquired how Navarro could excuse his participation in an effort to extend Texan authority over the Department of New Mexico. In his answers, Navarro shed some light on Lamar's visit to San Antonio and why he had felt obliged to accept the president's commission, but his statements must be taken with a grain of salt considering his status as a prisoner and the death sentence that he faced. He maintained that for six years he had been forced to represent himself outwardly as a Texan, unable to stand against a government that had established itself in that country through war. Because Mexico could not reassert control over Texas, Navarro said he had to rely on the other government. "While in this sad situation, the president of Texas came personally all the way to San Antonio to invite [him] to join the said commission, which he openly refused because he had neither the courage nor the health to travel to New Mexico." But Lamar insisted that his qualifications were appropriate, as the mission was neither hostile nor military but merely aimed at peaceful suasion. Navarro described how Lamar pressured him, insisting that if he considered himself a Texan he should join. He claimed the expedition was ready to leave, waiting only for Navarro's decision.[50]

Lamar did not directly force or threaten him, but Navarro argued that he had no option but to agree to his request. It was "not customary for any man in such a situation to daringly and haughtily oppose a government that currently had the law and the power in its hands." Navarro, despite apprehension about accepting the commission, did so because a refusal "would have provoked suspicions and prompted his inevitable ruin, that of his entire family, and that of the modest pecuniary interests with which he supports himself." Navarro asserted that no honest Mexican, when faced with a need for self-preservation of this sort, would have decided otherwise. Throughout all this testimony he continued to say that he had not borne arms against Mexico and was obliged to serve in offices of the Republic by popular vote and a duty to represent the best interests of the Tejano people.[51]

Navarro also described how he was made a prisoner on October 5, 1841, and the terms of surrender agreed upon that day. He said that Colonel Archuleta told General McLeod that while "He could not offer any other concession," Governor Armijo's orders allowed him "to guarantee the lives of all those who came with the Texan expedition." Archuleta gave McLeod a "written certificate of that promise," whereupon McLeod surrendered his command. Asked why Armijo's military report stated that the Texans surrendered unconditionally, Navarro said the governor must have made an error, and he repeated that "McLeod has in his possession an original document in which Señor Armijo allows Colonel Archuleta to pardon the lives of the prisoners if they gave themselves up with no other condition."[52]

At this point Morlet ended Navarro's interview. A document such as Navarro asserted was in McLeod's possession would impede the military court's right to impose a death sentence on any of the men captured in New Mexico. Morlet decided Navarro's assertion merited further investigation, and he sent a subordinate to the Perote Castle, where McLeod was imprisoned. McLeod was examined on March 6 and produced the disputed document, which was copied into the record. The letter from Armijo to Archuleta, dated October 5, 1841, included the key statement: "I have told Your Excellency, and repeat it here, that I have promised to pardon the lives of the enemy should it surrender, although it would not be allowed to carry any offensive weapon no matter how small it may be." McLeod was wise to have kept this document, as it proved pivotal to the fate of Navarro and the other prisoners. In addition, Navarro had said that General Cos could affirm that he peacefully stayed on his Atascosa Ranch and did not take sides during the Siege of Béxar, nor did he go with Seguín and take up arms at the battle of San Jacinto. Showing notable fairness to Navarro, Morlet located Cos at the town of Tuxpan, and sent him a questionnaire. On March 11, 1842, Cos confirmed that Navarro remained on his ranch. He recalled that while it was known that Navarro favored the Texan rebels, "neither at that time nor after . . .

[did] he take up arms to support them or help them in any way."[53] This testimony was crucial for refuting Urrua's damning accusation that Navarro had fought at San Jacinto.

Cos's deposition was the last one recorded by Morlet. Having assembled all the documentary evidence and testimony, Morlet called each of the witnesses and defendants separately and had the sworn deposition of each read aloud to allow them to approve or amend their statements. Next came the *careo* (face-to-face confrontation) of defendants with witnesses. Navarro agreed with the testimonies of Cooke, Brenham, and Carlos Ocampo, but he rejected the claims of Francisco Camacho and Fernando Urrua.[54] Cos's deposition supported Navarro's refutation of Camacho and Urrua.

During this first phase of the trial, Kendall, who had been released, managed to visit with Navarro in the Acordada. Kendall and others had been confined in the makeshift prison of Santiago Tlatelolco, a former convent. The day before his release, he participated in the improvised celebration of the sixth anniversary of "San Jacinto Day." The prisoners deceived their guards, saying that April 21 was the feast day of the patron saint of Texas. They even obtained red and white paint to paint a Texas flag on a wall. Authorities released Kendall on April 22. He planned to leave Mexico, but he was determined to visit Navarro before going. To gain entrance to the forbidding Acordada prison, Kendall obtained the assistance of "a young Englishman" who said he "could coax or bribe his way into the interior of the prison" and gain access to Navarro. The fellow was as good as his word. He and Kendall entered the prison and climbed the stairs to the second floor, passing crowds of ragged people who also hoped to visit friends or relatives. Guards led them through a labyrinth of passages filled with vile smells and prison noise to a heavy iron gate. It slowly swung open, and Navarro stood before them.[55]

Months of suffering had inflicted drastic changes on Navarro. Kendall wrote, "His unshaved face was pale and haggard, his hair long and uncombed, and his clothing were ragged and much soiled." Kendall also noted, "his fellow-prisoners, some of the most loathsome and abandoned wretches, had robbed him not only of his money but [also] his clothing." Lacking funds to pay for food, his only sustenance was a miserable allowance of beans and rice provided by the prison. Overcome with emotion, Navarro wept as he spoke of his wife and children in San Antonio, and of his son, Ángel, at college in Missouri. Kendall recalled, "[W]ith tearful eyes [he] begged me to convey to them information that he was still alive and not without hope of ultimate release." The guards allowed Kendall and Navarro only a few minutes. As they said their goodbyes, Kendall repeatedly shook hands with Navarro, at each grasp slipping a few dollars to him. Then the guards led Navarro away and the heavy iron doors closed with a horrendous clang. Kendall left the capital for Veracruz and returned to New Orleans by ship.[56] Navarro returned to the stinking, raucous Acordada, uncertain of his fate.

Santa Anna resumed the presidency from Vice President Nicolás Bravo at the beginning of May 1842. At that time prosecutor Morlet and defense attorney Francisco Linaste, a mere lieutenant, were preparing to present their cases before the military court. Santa Anna and his minister of war, Tornel, watched over this final phase of Navarro's trial for treason. The grand finale took place on May 18, when both Morlet and Linaste presented their final arguments. Morlet began by repeating that Navarro had committed treason "by promoting and supporting the dismemberment of the National Territory in connivance with the rebellious party from Texas." He then laid out five specific charges against Navarro: that he signed the Texas Constitution; that as a delegate to the 1836 Convention, he supported the withdrawal of Béxar's obedience from the Mexican government; that he voluntarily accepted a commission to foment revolt and dismember the Territory of New Mexico; that he intended to carry out this mission; and that he was captured in the act of invading the territory of Mexico, along with other traitors. Morlet hammered home his conclusion: "The truth of the above mentioned facts is so obvious that it does not require us to reinforce it with any evidence other than that shown in the proceedings . . . there is not even a single point of doubt about [his] crimes." He dismissed Navarro's claim that this had been forced on him by political events, noting that other Tejanos had found themselves in the same situation but had left for parts of the country still loyal to Mexico, even though they lost some of their property. After all, Morlet declared, "No sacrifice is too onerous in the name of the Fatherland."[57]

Morlet was a military authoritarian subservient to the desires of the higher powers who had appointed him. It is somewhat surprising, then, to observe that he demonstrated an even-handed dedication to the rule of law in Navarro's case. The prosecutor affirmed that the crimes to which Navarro had confessed demanded severe punishment. He found, however, two extenuating circumstances: first, that Navarro was a prisoner of war; and, second, that Governor Armijo had guaranteed the lives of all the members of the Texan forces and that they surrendered on that condition. As a result, Morlet said that capital punishment could not be applied to Navarro. "I conclude on behalf of the Nation," he said, "that, being unable to apply capital punishment to Don José Antonio Navarro, he should suffer the maximum punishment allowed by the law [i.e. life imprisonment]."[58] That statement was a damaging career decision for Morlet. Santa Anna and Tornel had followed Navarro's trial closely. Enraged at Morlet's stand against capital punishment, they replaced him later that same day with Colonel Manuel María Iturría.

Navarro's defense lawyer, Linaste, took the floor and confessed that he found himself "in a truly difficult and compromised position." As a zealous defender of his native land, he believed that preserving the integrity of its territory was a Mexican's most important duty. But because he had earned the confidence of Navarro, who had appointed him as his defense lawyer, it was his obligation to defend the accused as one who had fallen into misfortune and disgrace. Linaste addressed the two primary charges against Navarro: that he had attended the Texas Convention and signed the document by which that territory had seceded from Mexico, and that he joined the Santa Fe expedition with the goal of uniting New Mexico with Texas. Linaste based his main defense on Spanish jurist Félix José Reinoso's famous book of 1816, which defended citizens of Spain who were accused of collaborating with the French regime of Napoleon's brother, Joseph Bonaparte. Reinoso wrote that citizens no longer owed allegiance to a government that could not protect their rights. These rights included security and freedom, neither of which Bexareños enjoyed after the Texans took their town. In such a situation, citizens had to revert to "natural rights" and procure their security by all just and honest means. Linaste ignored the possibility that Navarro embraced the struggle against Santa Anna's despotism, and willingly went to the Convention to declare independence. Navarro, he said, had to "assert the right that is superior to all others," the right to preserve his life. "Such was the law of necessity," and the world recognized this right. Navarro and his neighbors in Béxar made choices that they otherwise would not have made. Abandoned by the Mexican government, Navarro was thus excused for conduct that would ensure his survival in an Anglo-ruled Texas.[59]

Linaste then addressed the second charge: that Navarro had willingly joined the Santa Fe expedition as a commissioner:

> As it has been shown in these Proceedings, the defendant was in his home, and a simple order from the so-called President of Texas was not enough to convince him to accept the commission for which he is accused; not only did [the President] go to Navarro's house, but had to spend days arguing before Navarro agreed to accept the appointment. He was left with no excuses; he pleaded excessively that he suffered

from a chronic illness in one leg, but this was not enough to dissuade the President, and so under these circumstances, what could a man do being under the unheard of orders of a figure who had in his hands that man's fate or, that of his family, and even his existence?

Having advanced these considerations and asking for mercy, Linaste said "I dare to ask that [the tribunal] declare that my defense shows that there is no crime and for that reason [the defendant] should be set absolutely free." Anticipating the denial of this request, the lawyer pleaded for Navarro's life. He begged the tribunal to honor Armijo's offer made in the name of the Supreme Government, to pardon their lives if they surrendered.[60]

Later that same day, May 18, 1842, the judges of the military court attended mass and then assembled in the Acordada. The seven justices were mid-level military officers. Colonel Antonio Barrios presided over the sentence hearing. Prior to having his sentence pronounced, Navarro was brought before the court and a summary of the proceedings was read to him. Assisted by his attorney, Navarro answered the judge's questions. He said he was not persuaded that he had committed the crime of which he was accused. He repeated that the charges against him arose, not as a result of his voluntary acts, but rather from circumstances in Texas at a time when there were no Mexican troops to rely on for support. Thus it had been necessary for him to "succumb to the Rulers of that Country." After his statement, guards escorted Navarro back to his cell.[61]

The judges pronounced Navarro guilty as charged. Disregarding prosecutor Morlet's opinion that Navarro should not be executed, all seven voted for the death penalty. Each wrote a brief justification, citing Title 10, Section 8, Article 45, of the General Bylaws of the Army. The new prosecutor, Iturría, immediately carried the records of the proceeding to General Andrade.[62] Navarro had reached one of the lowest points of his life. Living in misery and imprisoned with miscreants, perhaps he entertained the thought that being shot would be a mercy. Santa Anna and Tornel must have been pleased that, unlike Morlet, the judges knew what was expected of them and delivered it. No doubt they expected Andrade would promptly put Navarro in front of a firing squad.

Three days later, a hitch developed. *Auditor* (Legal Advisor) José Manuel Zozaya questioned Navarro's sentence in light of Morlet's opinion that capital punishment was not justified in his case. Zozaya wrote to Andrade, saying that he could disapprove the court's decision based on Morlet's interpretation of Governor Armijo's guarantee. He added the

"Prosecutor of the Proceedings did not dare to ask for the death sentence, and this alone is reason enough not to approve that tribunal's sentence; thus Your Excellency would be able to suspend approval of the sentence and notify the Military Supreme Court so that it is revised." Zozaya thus placed the decision squarely on Andrade's shoulders. According to military bylaws, commandant generals could overturn rulings by military courts if the legal advisor agreed, but Andrade would not go that far. On May 24, he did tell Tornel that he had sent Navarro's case to the Military Supreme Court for resolution.[63] Tornel must have flown into a rage at Andrade, but he did not immediately respond; instead he waited several months to see how the Military Supreme Court would rule. Meanwhile, Navarro languished in the Acordada, his fate depending on the will of the next court to challenge the authority of Santa Anna.

While the other Santa Fe Expedition members were released in June, Navarro's case lingered for weeks in the offices of the Military Supreme Court without resolution. Anxious about the court's progress, Tornel wrote to Andrade on August 24, inquiring about the status of the case. Andrade coolly replied the next day that, as he had previously informed Tornel, he had referred the case to the court and it had not been returned. Tornel immediately wrote to Melchor Álvarez, chief justice of the Military Supreme Court, recommending that Navarro's death sentence be upheld. Receiving only a noncommittal reply, Tornel noted that his recommendation should be sent again, "for since this is a crime of high treason a vindictive public demands his finish."[64]

On September 24, 1842, the court met and announced its decision. Chief Justice Álvarez and the other five judges ruled in favor of Navarro. They rejected the previous death sentence and confirmed the validity of Armijo's promise to spare the lives of all the expedition members. The six justices ordered that "Navarro remain a prisoner of war, according to his rank, under bond, in a healthy place in recognition of his broken health, and for the length of time that the supreme government sees fit."[65] Santa Anna believed the court's decision was a slap in his face and an insult to his authority. Seething, he and Tornel planned an aggressive response. Unaware that the highest officials of the nation were conspiring against him, the good news from the judges must have brought a small ray of hope to Navarro in the darkness of his cell in the Acordada. The court's reversal of the death sentence meant that his eventual release, although not likely, was not impossible.

Santa Anna and Tornel's offensive included using their influence with the press to inflame anti-Navarro sentiment. The *Mosquito Mexi-*

José María Tornel, Santa Anna's minister of war during Navarro's imprisonment in Mexico City. Courtesy of the Nettie Lee Benson Latin American Collection, University of Texas Libraries, the University of Texas at Austin.

cano, which had supported centralist views since 1835, printed an inflammatory editorial denouncing Navarro and the court's argument for revoking the death sentence. The writer proclaimed that Navarro confessed to "having betrayed the nation . . . by taking up arms on the side of those hordes who stole Texas." He argued that Governor Armijo's pledge to spare all of the prisoners had been fulfilled by the release of the others and that, because he had betrayed his country, an exception should be made in Navarro's case that would lead him to the gallows. The writer supposed that Navarro was to be set free on bond under conditions similar to house arrest. While the court's decision did provide for Navarro to post a bond and move to more comfortable quarters, authorities were not about to free Navarro on bond, and he remained behind the walls of the Acordada for the next year. [66]

A month after the second court's decision, Santa Anna's direct retribution began with a strike against the legal underlings who had dared to thwart his will. In an order to Andrade, Minister of War Tornel relayed Santa Anna's instructions to fire Zozaya, the legal advisor, and dismiss the Military Supreme Court. Tornel upbraided Andrade for accepting the opinion of the legal advisor and referring Navarro's case to the Military Supreme Court, and for the subsequent reversal of Navarro's conviction for the "heinous crime." Tornel said that it was with "surprise and disbelief" that Santa Anna received this news because he was confident that the government had granted Andrade jurisdiction to authorize Navarro's execution by invoking the seventh base of the Act of Tacubaya, which essentially put Santa Anna above the nation's laws in order "to do good and prevent evil." Tornel asserted that the legal advisor made a "pernicious mistake" by considering Navarro to be of the same status as the other Texans, "when in fact, the former, by virtue of being Mexican by birth, has committed the crime of treason."[67]

While Zozaya was technically only suspended from his duties for two months "for having delayed the prompt administration of justice which is so important in crimes of this magnitude," Santa Anna through Tornel was more vindictive toward the Military Supreme Court. He was infuriated that it "overstepped its boundaries by affirming that Navarro should be treated *according to his rank* . . . and acknowledging [him] as a true colonel." Santa Anna emphasized his point: to regard Navarro as a prisoner of war is the same as considering Texas to be a nation, because prisoners of war are taken in clashes between nations, which acknowledge rank and grant reciprocal privileges to each other's prisoners according to the laws of war. The president ordered the court's members to not only to be suspended from their functions but also to be put on trial themselves for the crime of having indirectly recognized Texas as an independent nation.[68] A new court was immediately appointed with General Melchor Músquiz as president.

Because it was Andrade who, by referring the case to the Military Supreme Court, made the decision that led to the reversal of the death sentence, it is odd that he was not sacked along with the others. Instead, Tornel ordered him to seek advice from other legal advisors concerning "what to do with regard to the many deviations committed in these proceedings, noting that the military court had not been declared incompetent to condemn José Antonio Navarro for his crime." Clearly, Santa Anna and Tornel hoped to restore the death sentence for Navarro by means of magistrates more compliant than Zozaya and the original Military Supreme Court. As instructed, Andrade forwarded Tornel's removal order to another legal advisor, José María de la Pesa. Aware of the delicate situation, Pesa took plenty of time to draft a lengthy, carefully reasoned response that reviewed the facts of the case, as well as military bylaws going back to 1769. In February 1843, he issued a decision that was a complete legal defeat for Santa Anna. He wrote, "the sentence issued by the Supreme Court of the Military is a sound execution of the law." Challenging Santa Anna directly, he added that under "no circumstance can it lead to the [dismissal of the] Ministers of the said Court."[69] The next day, Andrade forwarded the transcript of Navarro's case and Pesa's recommendation to Tornel, who did not pursue the matter further. In the end, the dedication of Morlet, Zozaya, Pesa, and Andrade to the rule of law saved Navarro from a firing squad or the gallows.

Santa Anna, however, had another trick up his sleeve to punish Navarro. He would see to it that the troublesome Tejano, contrary to the court's decision, would not be confined in a "healthy place"; instead, he had in mind a dungeon worse than the Acordada: San Juan de Ulúa. This heavily guarded fortress had been built in colonial times to protect the city of Veracruz and serve as a secure location for storing and transferring bullion to ships bound for Spain. After Mexican independence, it became a dreaded prison for political prisoners and incorrigibles. Navarro remained in the Acordada for another year after the revocation of his death sentence, while Santa Anna attended to affairs filled with pomp and circumstance. In September 1843, a grand celebration was being prepared in his honor as he prepared to turn the government over to Vice President Valentín Canalizo. On the 19th, Navarro gained access to pen and paper and wrote to Santa Anna, asking to be set free.[70] With customary thoroughness, he reviewed his entire case, but he ill-advisedly reminded Santa Anna about the military judges whom he had fired.

San Juan de Ulúa, the heavily guarded fortress where Navarro was imprisoned. Courtesy of the Nettie Lee Benson Latin American Collection, University of Texas Libraries, the University of Texas at Austin.

Navarro based his appeal on several considerations. He asked that the same amnesty given to the other expedition members be extended to him. He pleaded for sympathy on behalf of his family, who needed him, and the pain and suffering he had endured since his capture. Emphasizing his peaceful nature, he declared that he had not taken up arms against Mexico and explained in detail his participation in the March 1836 convention. Affirming his Mexican identity, Navarro said "The present generation and posterity will see me as a man [who was] always a Mexican." But it was precisely because he had been born a Mexican that Santa Anna considered him the worst kind of traitor, one deserving to be shot. Navarro's petition landed on Tornel's desk. After a brief review, already knowing Santa Anna's opinion of Navarro, Tornel added an order to the bottom of the page: "The one who petitions is not to be freed. Let corresponding orders be issued that, with the needed security, he must be marched to the castle of San Juan de Ulúa where he will remain in prison."[71]

Tornel immediately sent his decision to Canalizo, who the next day issued orders for Navarro's transportation to Veracruz. Guards informed Navarro of the frightening news of his imminent transfer to San Juan de Ulúa on September 26. Navarro at once wrote a second letter to Santa Anna. He emphasized the life-threatening condition of his leg, caused by a persistent, inflamed wound. The leg, he said had been "fractured in his childhood and that after thirty-five years the use of it had not returned." To avoid more excruciating pain, he asked to travel in a carriage. In desperation, Navarro appealed to the president's compassion, noting that they were both fathers and that if he were sent to San Juan de Ulúa, Navarro's children would likely become orphans. Explaining that he was unaccustomed to climates afflicted by yellow fever and "the black vomit, like Veracruz," he begged to be allowed to serve the remainder of his sentence at the Acordada or in the Perote prison near Puebla. Navarro's transfer to San Juan de Ulúa was postponed at the last minute for three weeks—not because of his anguished plea but because of the grand festival in Santa Anna's honor planned for the following day. On the September 27 occurred one of the most vainglorious exhibitions of Santa Anna's personality cult. The centerpiece was his amputated leg that he lost in 1838 during a battle with the French. Originally buried at his Jalapa estate, the leg was exhumed and carried in a parade to the Santa Paula Cemetery, where it was put in a crypt on a pedestal. An effusive eulogy and and bestowal of honors followed.[72]

Two weeks later on October 14 Acordada guards rousted Navarro out of bed during the early morning hours and placed him in the custody of *Alférez* (Second Lieutenant) Trinidad Velásquez. Escorted by a company of cavalry, they left the Acordada for Veracruz at six in the morning. The journey through mountainous terrain took ten days. In Veracruz, Velásquez delivered Navarro to General D. Benito Quijano, who informed Tornel that "the prisoner was immediately taken to the fortress of Ulúa where he will remain in prison in accord with what the provisional president had ordered." What Tornel had asked was that "the prisoner be held incommunicado in the most secure part of the Ulúa fortress."[73]

Navarro had escaped execution, but he now suffered the sentence of a living death. The court had sentenced him to confinement for as long as the supreme government deemed, and Navarro could be sure that, as long as Santa Anna remained president, he would never be released. Navarro feared abuse from his fellow inmates, but he also faced the possibility that his leg would become so infected that he would die a painful, lingering death, or that amputation would be required.

Although Navarro was ordered held incommunicado, within a few months this strict constraint was relaxed. George Van Ness visited Navarro on February 1, 1844, and found him afraid to leave his small "apartment" for fear that he would be sodomized by the depraved criminals among whom he was confined. His leg was infected, and had been numbed with cold on the trip to prison. Even though Navarro was not being held in solitary confinement, as Tornel had ordered, his fear of molestation made this status self-imposed. Even with death looming over him, Navarro did not surrender to despair and drew upon his sardonic wit to make an ironic gesture to Santa Anna. He wrote to him to propose that, in exchange for his freedom and return to Texas, he would "cooperate in the reincorporation of Texas into the Republic [of Mexico]." Navarro certainly agreed with what his uncle José Francisco Ruiz had declared in 1835: "only God could return Texas to the Mexican government."[74] To suggest the possibility of restoring Texas to Mexico nine years later was a ridiculous offer, one that cannot be taken seriously.

Navarro sent this absurd proposal to Quijano, asking him to forward it to Santa Anna. Incredibly, Quijano thought the offer had merit and added a recommendation: "In my humble opinion, the offer Navarro makes of cooperating in the restoration of Texas . . . by permitting him [to] return to [Texas] could produce good results." Quijano said he was persuaded that Navarro had influence in Texas and sincerely proposed to wash away his wrongs against the nation if trusted. Quijano's recommendation is puzzling. He evidently was unaware of the charges for which Navarro was convicted and Santa Anna's opinion of him. Quijano also showed himself to be gullible by endorsing Navarro's ludicrous offer. Santa Anna recognized Navarro's proposal for the insult it was. His angry reply came quickly: "José Antonio Navarro is an established traitor against his country and as such is unworthy of any consideration whatever." He scolded Quijano and recounted Navarro's crimes against Mexico as a signer of the Texas Declaration of Independence and a member of the Santa Fe Expedition. The president concluded by saying, "For these and other misdeeds, he was deserving of the gallows, but his destiny was to be liberated from it. But we must not be so charitable as to set him free on the basis of simple offers of reparation that, being a scoundrel, he would never fulfill."[75] Santa Anna confidently anticipated that if Navarro was not freed by someone as foolish as Quijano, San Juan de Ulúa would eliminate him as effectively as a firing squad or the gallows.

The reputation of San Juan de Ulúa was such that a sign could have been hung over the entrance with the inscription Dante saw as he entered Hell: "Abandon Hope All Ye Who Enter Here." Navarro endured his most rigorous imprisonment at the prison. Tornel gave emphatic orders to the officials at Veracruz that the prisoner be treated harshly. One of Navarro's descendants claims he was chained by the leg to a ring on the prison floor in one of the fortress's most dismal cells. After his return to Texas, this descendant said Navarro added a circle to his cattle brand to represent the ring to which he had been chained.[76]

Two accounts describe overtures Santa Anna allegedly made to Navarro while he was a prisoner in Mexico. One apparently came when Navarro was in the Acordada and the other at San Juan de Ulúa. After his return to Texas, Navarro claimed that Santa Anna sent two of his "confidential emissaries" to the Acordada with the purpose of persuading him "to abjure forever [his] home in Texas and bring [his] family to Mexico." The two allegedly said that "We are sure . . . that the generosity of GENERAL SANTA ANNA WILL NOT STOP with liberating you, but he will give you a lucrative position, either military or civil." Navarro reportedly responded with haughty words that would have insulted Santa Anna greatly if conveyed to him by his messengers:

> [This] unfortunate Texan authorizes you, gentlemen, to tell the President of the Republic that all the wealth of the mines of Zacatecas and Fresnillo cannot buy a heart, debilitated though it be by the foul atmosphere of these loathsome dungeons, and subsisting, as it is, only on the beans of the felons of Acordada. . . . Can General SANTA ANNA think that I will buy my liberty or life at the cost of vassalage and the contempt of my dear wife and children? Does he think that I could endure the humiliation of knowing that they were subjected to the degradation of suing for my pardon in those depraved and licentious halls, as, in truth, are the palaces of Mexico and Tacubaya? Does he think that there are no men of his race [who are] the exception to the rule of general infamy, which spreads like a pall over the land? If this audacious tyrant had a little respect for the honor of his fellow-countrymen, he would not treat me thus. . . . gentlemen, I see that Santa Anna is incapable of sentiment so elevated, but I believe that he is capable of erecting the pinnacle of his own glory and wealth on the ruin and demoralization of his fellow-citizens.

A short time later, Navarro was transferred to the San Juan de Ulúa dungeon, from which he did not expect to emerge alive, and is reported to have said, "I will die chained to this floor."[77]

Years later, Rueben M. Potter recounted a story that he probably heard from Navarro. He said that Navarro was held in Cell 51. An officer told Navarro that Santa Anna was in Veracruz and planned to visit the castle, and Navarro was told that his cell door would be left open so he would "have the opportunity to go forth and make a personal appeal to him [Santa Anna]." The evening came, and the door was left unlocked. Navarro sat in his cell listening for the approach of the military group. At length the measured step of a number of men was heard; among them, as Navarro described it, was the stumping of Santa Anna's accursed wooden leg. They paused at his cell and he heard Santa Anna say: "This is cell No. 51?" The reply was in the affirmative. He paused as if to make more inquiries, but finding that nothing came of it, he stumped onward. Navarro said that while he had no intention of humbling himself before the tyrant, the pause of his enemy at the cell door brought "an indescribable rush of memory, such as is said to come to a drowning man."[78]

Potter said that Navarro believed that Santa Anna had arranged this opportunity so that he might humble and degrade a prisoner "who had exasperated him by the indignant manner in which he [Navarro] had spurned his last advances." Potter reported that when the officer of the fortress noted that Navarro had not availed himself of his chance to beg Santa Anna for his freedom, Navarro replied, "No. Nothing was to be gained of that man by humiliation; and even if there had been, it was a price I was unwilling to pay." The records show that Navarro in fact directly asked only two things of Santa Anna during his long captivity in Mexico and offered nothing in return. The first was that he be given the same amnesty that the other Santa Fe Expedition prisoners received, which was denied. In the other, he asked not be sent to San Juan de Ulúa, but rather to remain a prisoner in the Acordada or in the Perote prison near Puebla, and this request was also denied.[79]

Navarro's fortunes seemed tied to Santa Anna's in an inverse relationship. At the end of 1843, as Navarro's health was declining at San Juan de Ulúa, Santa Anna's popularity was rising, despite a military defeat in Yucatán. As president-elect, he began the new year by presenting himself as a judicious dictator. Public adulation was showered upon him, and he enjoyed a series of dazzling but superficial triumphs. The Santa Anna Theater (later known as Bellas Artes) opened, and devotees erected an imposing bronze statue of the president gesturing toward the north, symbolizing that he would not yet concede Texas's independence. Cynical detractors noted that it also pointed toward the national mint. But Santa Anna levied unpopular taxes and imposed forced loans on the Catholic Church. A turning point in his presidency came during fall 1844 with the death of his wife, Doña Inéz García. She was enormously popular, and her death was accompanied by an outpouring of public grief. During this critical time, murmurs of revolt emerged among military officers who had helped bring him to the presidency only to be ignored. Then Santa Anna made an egregious mistake. In one of his most controversial and egocentric actions, he remarried barely a month after the death of Doña Inéz. His bride was Doña María Dolores de Tosta, a girl of fifteen. He did not even attend his own wedding; it was done by proxy in the Cathedral of Mexico.[80] Outrage resulted from this callous display of disrespect for the memory of Doña Inéz.

As Santa Anna lost power, Navarro managed to gain favors and a measure of freedom from his captors. His liberties came to the notice of the new minister of war, José Isidro Reyes, who replaced Tornel in August 1844. Quijano and the commander of the fortress, José Juan Clandero, received reprimands from Reyes after there were reports that the president's orders concerning Navarro were not being obeyed. Rather than being confined to a cell, Navarro apparently roamed the fort at will, lived among the officers, and complained about Santa Anna's harsh treatment of him. The two commanders were warned that severe steps would be taken if they did not correct the situation. Clandero replied to Reyes that the rumors about Navarro's lax treatment had some basis, but he denied responsibility. He also said he had not gotten reports from Navarro complaining about the president and his government. Nonetheless, Clandero wrote, "I have restricted his freedom, placing him in isolation in the pavilion next to the principal guardhouse—which provides the maximum security and where there will be no reason for his chronic illness to worsen."[81]

By this time, Santa Anna's presidency had become a house of cards. His unpopular remarriage, absolutist rule, disregard for fellow revolutionaries, ostentatious expenditures, and interference with Congress, all combined to provide the basis for a general rebellion against his government. On October 30, his former ally, General Mariano Paredes, charged Santa Anna with military and fiscal mismanagement. Other generals joined Paredes, and their combined armies marched on Mexico City. Congress denied Santa Anna funding, and his position became untenable. On November 28, he abandoned Mexico City and fled to Querétaro. With his departure, an outpouring of anger broke loose in the capital as outraged people imprisoned Vice President Canalizo, toppled many statues of Santa Anna, ransacked the Santa Anna theater, and removed his amputated leg from its crypt and dragged it through the streets. When Navarro heard the news, his hopes for release must have soared—and probably with no little satisfaction he learned that it was now Santa Anna who was accused of "high treason."[82]

Navarro wasted no time in renewing his initiatives. The one saving grace of San Juan de Ulúa was its proximity to Veracruz, where access to ships provided an avenue of escape. At the lowest point of his ordeal Navarro was sick, isolated, without resources, and virtually without hope. By late 1844, however, he had the crucial support of allies, who provided informal diplomatic assistance and some financial backing. At the end of 1843, Hugh McLeod had asked Charles Elliot, British chargé d'affaires to the Republic of Texas, to assist in obtaining Navarro's release. Three days later Elliot wrote to Foreign Secretary George Hamilton-Gordon, Earl of Aberdeen, about McLeod's request, asking him to instruct the British minister in Mexico to intercede in Navarro's favor: "His fate has always been the subject of great solicitude to the Government and people of Texas, and I am sure they would be grateful for the kind Offices of Her Majesty's Government." Perhaps it was with such aid that Navarro obtained the legal services of Luís María Aguilar, who wrote a detailed petition asking that Navarro be set free. He emphasized the abuses Navarro had suffered under the unjust administration of Santa Anna, in defiance of the directives of a military court. Aguilar repeated the specious offer Navarro had made—that he "had been an influential man in Texas who for a long time had impeded a proclamation of independence for that department and could do much to influence the recovery of it." He added that if Navarro were in Mexico City, he could provide valuable advice for a pacification of Texas.[83]

Despite the chaotic political climate, Navarro's freedom became a high-profile issue. Aguilar's petition soon gained the attention of the new president, José Joaquín de Herrera, and his council. The petition bounced back and forth among these authorities, each seeking advice and clarifying information. Navarro himself wrote to Herrera, on January 16, 1845, directing his attention to the many grievances he had suffered at the hands of Santa Anna and requesting his freedom. Recalling the military court's ruling that he was to be confined in a place "not unhealthy," he lamented: "But Oh the scandal of blind vengeance! The supreme government, or better said, Antonio López de Santa Anna, did not comply with the court's ruling, but instead imposed the reverse condition, confining [me] in the fortress of San Juan de Ulúa since October 24, 1843." On January 27, President Herrera ordered Navarro to be set free. But Ignacio de Mora, commander at Veracruz, reported that when he sent for the prisoner to inform him of the president's clemency, he discovered that Navarro "was absent from the plaza without permission and his whereabouts are unknown." Apparently an officer had allowed Navarro to wander about the town. Friends had helped Navarro flee before Herrera freed him. A ship took him from Veracruz to Havana in January. Ironically, while Navarro was finally traveling toward home, former President Santa Anna had left Querétaro and was fleeing for his life to Veracruz when soldiers caught him and put him in a jail in Jalapa, where he complained that his treatment was worse than when he was in the custody of the Texans.[84]

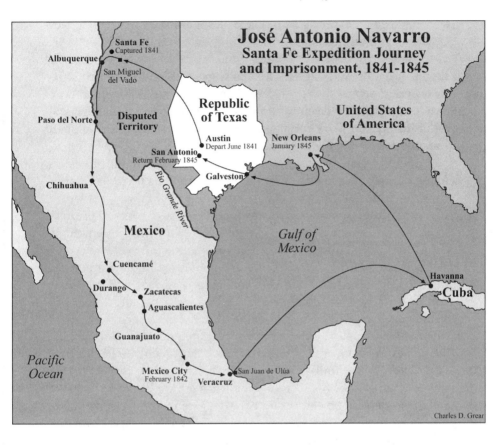

Navarro arrived in Havana just in time to board the ship *New York*, whose next port of call was New Orleans. He arrived there on January 18, "having left Vera Cruz with the clothes only which covered my body and the limited means furnished me by a good friend." He immediately wrote to William G. Cooke, his friend and companion from the Santa Fe Expedition, announcing, "With the most pleasing satisfaction, I communicate to you my arrival in this city on this day, two hours ago." Navarro claimed that he had important information for the Texas government, and he hinted that if funds and transportation were made available, he would travel to Washington on-the-Brazos and meet with officials there before going home. He enclosed a letter to his wife, Margarita, and asked Cooke to forward it to her. Soon after Navarro's arrival in New Orleans, his old friend George W. Kendall, provided lodging in the luxurious St. Charles Hotel.[85] No doubt Kendall made sure that Navarro received the best medical treatment the city had to offer, and he soon began recovering from his Mexican ordeal, remaining in New Orleans less than two weeks.

Navarro arrived in Galveston by January 29 and stepped onto the shores of his native land. His friends who wrote under the pen name "Old Texan" reported that "From his own lips he has frequently repeated to us that the day he again touched Texas soil . . . was the happiest of his life." Military companies welcomed him as a returning hero and escorted him to his hotel. He was praised as a "long oppressed but unyielding patriot," and such praise was repeated through the years. Along the way, people turned out to greet Navarro as he went home. A few miles from San Antonio, at Salado Creek, Mayor Edward Dwyer and a large group of prominent citizens met their native son and provided an escort, to the sounds of general rejoicing.[86] In town, he embraced his family for the first time in nearly four years.

No Texan, not even Stephen F. Austin, endured imprisonment and suffering on behalf of Texas comparable to Navarro's, either in duration or severity. That alone ranks him as a great patriot, a man who would not change his allegiance in the most hopeless of circumstances, whether at the Laguna Colorada or in Mexican dungeons. Having made the biggest mistake of his life, Navarro had hoped only to be delivered safely back to his family and friends in Texas. But the respect that he gained as a result of his suffering for Texas during his imprisonment, and the leadership he demonstrated, would result in his election to the 1845 Constitutional Convention within months of his release, and then to the Senate of the first and second legislatures of the state of Texas during the next few years. Navarro must have been greatly relieved to realize that his decision to join in the march to Santa Fe had not ruined the American Dream for him or his family.

CHAPTER SEVEN

Tejano Spokesman, 1845–53

U PON HIS RETURN TO TEXAS IN EARLY 1845, José Antonio Navarro found that division and animosity had deepened between Anglos and Tejanos. At the time of his departure for Santa Fe, Juan N. Seguín, a popular Tejano, had been the elected mayor of San Antonio. Memories were fresh of the Tejanos who fought in the Alamo and joined Sam Houston's army to defeat Santa Anna at San Jacinto. However, during 1842, two Mexican armies briefly occupied San Antonio and Anglo-Tejano relations had been severely damaged in the aftermath. Numerous casualties resulted from a handful of conflicts, including those killed in what became known as the Dawson Massacre. After the second raid in 1842, General Adrián Woll retreated into Mexico taking about fifty prominent Anglos as prisoners. The loyalty of Tejanos formerly known as friends of Texas had become suspect. In fact, Anglos viewed virtually all Tejanos with suspicion. Tejano livestock was stolen and the owners were powerless to recover it, and Indian depredations added to the ruin of their outlying ranches. Comanche Indians had killed Navarro's trusted overseer of thirteen years, Ramón Rubio, within a mile of San Geronimo Ranch.[1] These racially charged conditions continued unabated from 1842 through the time of Navarro's return.

The return of Navarro as a certified hero placed Anglos in an awkward position. How could they reconcile the prevailing negative view of Tejanos with Navarro's sterling example? The answer, published in the militant *Civilian and Galveston Gazette*, was to deny that Navarro was a Tejano:

> Although born and reared in the deserts surrounded [sic] city of San Antonio de Béxar, Col. Navarro is not of the abject race of Mexicans. His father was a Corsican of good birth, and, what is worthy of remark, born under the same roof with that [prodigy] of the human race, Napoleon Bonaparte.[2]

Navarro must have cringed to read this. He was no less Mexican because of his father's Corsican birth than was Juan Martín de Veramendi because of his father's birth in Spain. Throughout his life Navarro never tried to deny or diminish his Mexican origin. He felt deeply his Mexican identity, and his solidarity with Tejano countrymen was unwavering, as he would reveal at the 1845 Constitutional Convention.

It was a bittersweet return to Texas and home for Navarro in other ways as well. News of his delivery quickly reached Washington-on-the-Brazos, where the last Republic of Texas Congress was meeting. It expressed the widespread sentiment of appreciative Texans with a joint resolution requiring President Anson Jones to compensate Navarro for the losses he had suffered during his imprisonment. In addition, Bexar County tax records show no assessments on his property during the time of his incarceration. But when he called a family meeting at San Geronimo Ranch, he was dismayed to learn the education of his children had not progressed as he had hoped. They had no knowledge of the Latin and Greek classics and were still at only the most basic proficiency levels for reading, writing, and mathematics. Navarro's wife, Margarita, was of a somewhat more practical nature. She believed that book learning, though of great value, might be carried too far, and she suspected that her husband's serious troubles were due in part to his reading and thinking too much. When told that the names of Zavala, Ruiz, and Navarro would ring through the ages, she allegedly said:

> I am proud of my husband and his good name. I am proud of this thing called liberty; but the Spanish-speaking people of Texas are too few to survive in justice and prosperity among the Americans. We have given all to Texas and my children will have to survive below their blood and station in money, in education, and in society.

This attitude may represent how other Tejanas felt during the republican period. Her grandson, José Antonio Navarro III, also noted that, although his grandfather and others dedicated their lives and fortunes to the great cause of freedom for Texas, "We [Tejanos] have never yet recovered the fortunes; but we have a rich heritage in their lives."[3]

When Navarro returned to Texas in 1845, talk of annexation to the United States was a major topic for all Texans, both Anglo and Tejano. The United States government had twice rejected proposals for Texas statehood, in 1836 and June 1844, because of opposition to adding another slave state to the Union. Nevertheless, it was an idea whose time had come. In the 1844 election, U.S. citizens effectively voted to admit Texas by electing James K. Polk, who ran on a platform of annexing Texas and expanding claims in Oregon. Supporters brought the annexation issue before the United States Congress for the third time in February 1845, at the same time that Navarro was riding home from Galveston. The U.S. Congress passed a joint annexation resolution and, with the signature of President Polk on March 1, the United States handed Texas a formal invitation to join the Union.[4]

President Jones of Texas responded to the popular sentiment for annexation by calling for a convention to meet at Austin on July 4, 1845, for the purpose of writing a state constitution as necessary for admission to the United States. Bexar County voters chose José Antonio Navarro and Volney E. Howard to serve as their delegates to the convention. Howard, a native of Maine, was a lawyer and newspaper editor who had just arrived in San Antonio in December 1844.[5] The selection of Navarro had far-reaching consequences that would benefit his fellow Tejanos. He was the only Tejano member of the 1845 Convention and as such would exert a moderating influence at a time when general animosity toward Tejanos was intense. Without Navarro's presence, that rancor could easily have been written into the articles of the new state constitution and into the laws that would derive from it.

Navarro left San Antonio toward the end of June. Approaching Austin he crossed Onion Creek and perhaps paused to gaze at the property he had sold for a pittance to John Caldwell, who had also been elected to the 1845 Convention. Navarro should have had little regret—it had been unimaginable twelve years earlier that the capital would be established just a few miles to the north and thus greatly increase the value of the land. When he arrived in Austin around the first of July, Navarro found living accommodations to be primitive, as they had been at Washington-on-the-Brazos when he last participated in writing a constitution for Texas. After the Mexican raids of 1842, President Sam Houston had repeatedly attempted to remove the capital to Houston, and Austin had languished. Buildings deteriorated, and the population had fallen to about 200.[6]

Despite his four-year absence, Navarro was well known, if not famous, because of his imprisonment in Mexico. His reputation as a hero and patriot who had suffered for Texas preceded him. All the delegates knew about him, though few had made his acquaintance and even fewer could communicate with him in Spanish. But there were two men— George Fisher and Henry L. Kinney—who spoke Spanish well and had been energetic participants in Texas affairs for several years. Navarro would rely upon them as friends and allies throughout the convention.

On Friday, July 4, the convention was called to order. Fifty-five delegates from thirty-five counties presented their credentials and answered the roll call. Navarro was present, and Howard joined him the next day. Thomas J. Rusk was elected president of the convention, and the United States resolution of annexation was read into the record. Navarro probably had received a copy for review prior to the convention. Of particular interest to him would have been a provision in the second section that concerned public lands. It said that the Republic of Texas was to cede its public property to the United States, with the momentous exception of "all the vacant and unappropriated lands lying within its limits." Sale of this land was to be used to pay Texas's existing debts, but after that, every acre that remained would belong to the state of Texas. Navarro must have smiled broadly at this because he knew the enormous land holdings of the state would benefit its people far into the future. In these few words, the United States permitted the state of Texas to retain its priceless land heritage. In contrast to the vast federal holdings in western states, the only land the United States government would own in Texas would be what it purchased. Just exactly where the boundaries of Texas lay, however, had not yet been determined. Many delegates had arrived after the first roll call and a total of sixty-one signed their acceptance of the resolution. There was only one dissenting vote. The day's session ended with a resolution for the delegates to wear black crepe on their arms for one month to honor the recently deceased Andrew Jackson, who had been the equivalent of a patron saint for Anglo frontiersmen and westerners.[7]

On Monday July 7, President Rusk announced the members chosen for the six standing committees. Navarro and eight others were picked for the Executive Committee. Their purpose was to define the responsibilities, powers, and limitations of the state executive—the governor. Navarro then reported that he had selected Fisher as his translator, as authorized by the convention. With the main preliminary and procedural matters resolved, the convention began its substantive considerations. The first item on the agenda was a communication from Andrew J. Donelson, chargé d'affaires for the United States. Donelson reported that steps had already been taken by the United States to protect Texas from Mexican and Indian attacks if it accepted annexation. No one knew better than Navarro that defense was of paramount importance. A draft resolution was quickly prepared asking President Polk to send troops without delay and establish posts "upon the frontier and exposed positions of this Republic." Navarro moved to delete the word "frontier" from the proposal, perhaps thinking that San Antonio would not be considered frontier and would be excluded. His motion was defeated, but he subsequently voted with the majority for the measure.[8]

Navarro wanted his Tejano constituents kept informed of the convention's progress. At his request, Howard introduced a resolution calling for Spanish translations of both the request for military protection and the ordinance approving annexation. The two delegates from San Antonio declared that if Texas-Mexican people "understand correctly the true bearing of these measures, we should find them with little or no division in favor of annexation." The resolution passed and Fisher translated both documents into Spanish. One thousand copies were ordered printed in Spanish on a motion by Kinney, who as the delegate from San Patricio County in South Texas also represented many Tejanos.[9]

Despite these provisions for Tejanos, it remained an open question as to how the convention would treat the rights of Tejanos. Despite widespread prejudice and de facto discrimination, legal discrimination against people of Mexican descent had not been written into the 1836 Constitution, in part because of respect for the services of Navarro, Lorenzo de Zavala, Juan N. Seguín, and others. The 1836 Constitution did exclude from citizenship Africans, descendants of Africans, and Indians, which threatened the status of many Tejanos. Because many had ancestors who were Indians or Africans, they could potentially be denied citizenship. Moreover, their rights were endangered because of provisions in the 1836 Constitution that could dispossess them of land and citizenship for being disloyal to the Republic. The loyalties of almost all Tejanos were highly suspect after the Mexican raids of 1842; among those accused of complicity in the attacks was Seguín, who was living in exile in Mexico when the 1845 Convention met.

The 1845 Constitution did not directly address the rights of Tejanos. However, the record of the debates shows that the delegates were very concerned about race and the status of the Mexican population of Texas. These were subjects Navarro repeatedly sought to bring to the forefront for clarification. His participation influenced both the substance and the outcome of issues of importance to Tejanos. His imposing authority, keen comments, and forceful arguments during debates help to explain the absence of legal racial discrimination against Mexicans in the Texas Constitution at a time when most Anglo Texans, including many convention members, subscribed to racist ideas and attitudes.[10]

Navarro answered the delegate roll call on Monday, July 14. If his attention wandered during routine motions and resolutions, he must have focused sharply when Fisher translated for him a troubling resolution introduced by Abel S. Cunningham, who wanted "the judiciary committee be instructed to . . . enquire into, and cause to be brought before the district court all cases in their respective districts, of land titles forfeited under laws of Coahuila and Texas, as well as all *lands escheated under any of the laws hereinfore existing* [emphasis added] within the territory of Texas." This was a direct attack on the land rights of Tejanos who could be accused of being disloyal during the Texas Revolution.[11] Cunningham had a particular interest in the subject of forfeitures. As a delegate from Victoria, he represented constituents who were involved in attempts to take the lands of the Martín De León family based on allegations of disloyalty to the Republic. Forfeitures and escheats were a critical topic on which Navarro would exert his influence on behalf of Tejanos as the convention progressed. Cunningham's proposed resolution was tabled and not discussed until the following month. A clear distinction was made between forfeitures, which served as a penalty, and escheats, which concerned property of persons who died without heirs or a will, but the two concepts would later be lumped together by the first legislature, an error that Navarro would rectify.

Another presentation made on July 14 also must have galvanized Navarro. Since citizenship in the state of Texas was to be defined by United States law, the main concern of convention members was not defining citizenship, but determining who could vote. Hiram G. Runnels, of the Legislative Committee, presented a long report, one section of which defined "qualified electors," or those who could vote. Several conditions were enumerated, including being a "Free white male person," having United States or Republic of Texas citizenship, and satisfying a residency requirement. Specifically excluded were "Indians not taxed, Africans and descendants of Africans." Runnels's proposal differed significantly from the 1836 Constitution, which excluded *all* Indians. The distinction between Indians who paid taxes (meaning those who had substantially assimilated into U.S. society) and Indians not taxed (meaning, essentially, Indians living in tribal societies) was already in Article I of the United States Constitution. When a motion was made to strike Runnels's wording, he objected that "there might be many Indians taxed who were intelligent men and good citizens." President Rusk observed that the term should remain because it was in the United States Constitution, even though in his opinion there would be few Indians taxed. The motion was withdrawn. Navarro must have followed the debate closely because the inclusion of the words "Indians not taxed" had important implications for Tejanos of Indian ancestry: the rights of those who paid taxes could not be legally denied on the basis of parentage.[12] Thus a broad foundation was laid to strengthen the civil rights of many Tejanos. But the issue of African ancestry still remained. The presence of the word "white" in Runnels's report was

Portrait of José Antonio Navarro. Gift of Joseph Elicson, the Daughters of the Republic of Texas Library, #SC96.247, San Antonio.

deeply troubling to Navarro and concerned other members. This ill-de-
fined term allowed for conflicting interpretations, and it would be debated in later sessions.

Meanwhile, a debate regarding the powers of the governor moved
Navarro to make an impassioned speech in defense of his heritage. For
several days, he and other members of the Executive Committee met to
discuss the issue and prepare a report on whether the secretary of state
should be chosen by popular election or appointment by the governor.
During the session of July 18, the subject came before the convention.
In his opening statement James Davis, chair of the Executive Committee, declared that he opposed the governor appointing any officer
whatsoever. Runnels quickly countered by presenting an amendment
"that there shall be a Secretary of State, who shall be appointed by the
Governor, by the advice and consent of the Senate." Davis and three
other members spoke at length in opposition to Runnels. They argued
that his proposal would give the governor too much power, that the
people could better exercise the choice, and that nine times out of ten
the secretary, if appointed, would be a mere tool of the governor. Davis
did not stop with these conventional arguments. He advanced an insulting comparison of Anglos and Mexicans: "I know that in many governments the people are incapable of self government: for example, in the
government upon our western border. But what is the reason? The want
of intelligence, of education, and of virtue." He added that this was not
the case with the Anglo-Saxon race, "who have shown their capacity for
self government."[13]

Navarro's hackles rose at these coarse references to Mexican inferi-
ority, and he immediately entered the debate. He said that, within the
Executive Committee, he alone supported the principle that the secretary of state should be appointed by the governor and confirmed by
the Senate. Then with unmistakable scorn, he said that he understood
Davis's remarks to mean, "in plain words, that the Mexicans are not
always right in the selection of their functionaries, whilst these people
of the Anglo American race are fully capable of selecting individuals
in whose capacity and integrity full confidence can be placed." Navarro
told the convention that he was "very much grieved by these remarks."
He said that he would be happy to vote for Runnels's amendment, not
because of the high intelligence of the people of Texas or their superiority in selecting their officers, but because of the example of the
United States. Americans, he said with scathing irony, conform to the
antiquated system of the stupid people of Mexico by authorizing their
president to appoint his ministers or the members of his cabinet. Upon

that principle, and that alone, Navarro said he would vote for it. After that admonishment, Navarro's fellow delegates realized they were going to have to watch their language. Rusk observed that Navarro's argument was so forceful that he felt compelled to repeat it, and to agree. Navarro's view prevailed, and the secretary of state was made an appointee of the governor. [14]

On July 21, the convention again considered Runnels's Legislative Committee report, focusing on whether to include or exclude the crucial word "white." Oliver Jones's move to strike the word lost without the votes being recorded, but the matter was far from being resolved. Later that day Isaac Van Zandt moved to reconsider, and a stormy debate ensued. Navarro watched while the debate ran its course. Rusk, Runnels, Kinney, and Joseph L. Hogg all spoke. Rusk at first wanted the word included because it was in the United States Constitution, but later changed his mind. Runnels said the word was intended to include Mexicans and thus he saw no need to delete it. Kinney disagreed strongly. He said he had seen occasions where persons known to have been citizens, who had served the country well and had repeatedly taken the oath of allegiance, were denied the privilege of voting when "the only objection made was, that they could not be considered white persons; they were Mexicans." Jones reaffirmed his previous motion, saying he also had seen objections made to Mexicans, Indians, and persons of dark complexion caused by the heat of the sun. As a result of these arguments, the question on striking the word was reconsidered. Hogg renewed the debate. He argued that the word should be included because, besides being in the U.S. Constitution, it was important to retain it in order to exclude men of mixed race. Warming to the idea of disenfranchisement, Hogg said that inclusion of the word "white" would require anyone "deeply tainted with African blood . . . to go back and prove his pedigree." Moreover, he added, most members who had spoken said the word was immaterial. [15]

Navarro bided his time during the debate, listening carefully to Fisher's translations of what was being said and composing his thoughts. He waited while the main arguments were presented, looking for the most opportune moment to join the fray. When Hogg finished with his talk of pedigrees and tainted blood, Navarro took the floor and made his most important speech of the convention. The legal fate of many Tejanos turned upon the inclusion or exclusion of the word "white" in the Texas Constitution. Navarro first attacked the alleged "immateriality" of the word. He pointed out "that if the word *white* means anything at all it means a great deal, and if it does not mean anything at all it is

entire superfluous, as well as odious, and, if you please, ridiculous."
He added that this issue had great relevance to Tejanos because "they
are unquestionably entitled to vote." Confronting the racism of the delegates, Navarro pushed for an exception for "descendants of Africans"
who were white or nearly so. These were the persons whom Hogg had
said were "tainted with African blood." Navarro's words on this issue are
worth quoting in their entirety:

> By application of the word white, certain persons may be qualified, &
> cet,—and others, although as white as snow yet not white by descent,
> be disqualified. That is to say, white negroes or the descendants of
> Africans, who, in the course of time become so nearly white that no
> distinction or scarcely any can be made.

Thus Navarro advanced the cause of suffrage not only for Tejanos with
Indian parentage, but also of persons who had some African parentage.
Clearly he wanted to ensure that a Tejano who fit this description would
not have to "prove his pedigree" in the way Hogg urged.[16]

Navarro's efforts at the convention reflect his concern for his constituents of mixed race regardless of variation. As we have seen already,
a community tolerant of mixed-race persons was a social reality in the
Tejano regions of Texas. But this was not usually the case in the United
States, especially in the South, where many Anglo immigrants to Texas
had come from. Because Tejanos generally accepted persons of mixed-
race ancestry, Anglo slave owners developed an intense suspicion of
Tejanos and because of their alleged willingness to assist escaped slaves
make their way to Mexico. During his visit to San Antonio in 1854,
Fredrick Law Olmsted observed, "They consort freely with the negroes,
making no distinction from pride of race." Based on conversations he
had with a runaway slave in Piedras Negras, Coahuila. Olmsted wrote
that blacks had more freedom and opportunities to better themselves in
Mexico than in the United States—including the North.[17]

In contrast, a commitment to white supremacy was widely seen as
crucial to maintaining social order in the United States during the mid-
nineteenth century, and even opponents of slavery toed the line. Abraham
Lincoln expressed this reality in one of his famous debates with Stephen
A. Douglas in 1858. Although Lincoln abhorred slavery and opposed its
expansion, he made it clear he did not support social or political equality
for African Americans: "I am not, nor have I ever been in favor bringing
about in any way the social and political equality of the white and black
races, [applause]—that I am not nor have been in favor of making voters
or jurors of negros, nor of qualifying them to hold office."[18]

Navarro knew well that black slaves and their black descendants had no hope of voting rights in a society dominated by migrants from the United States. In the same manner as Lincoln, Navarro assured the convention that he was as opposed as anyone to giving the right of suffrage to Africans or their descendants. However, as noted above, he advocated that an exception be made for "descendants of Africans" who were white or nearly so, as applicable to those Tejanos whose ancestry included Europeans, American Indians, as well as Africans. Demonstrating a more open and tolerant attitude than was common in the United States, Navarro declared that he hoped the delegates would be convinced to strike out the word "white." It was "odious, captious, and redundant; and may be the means at elections of disqualifying persons who are legal voters, but who perhaps by arbitrary judges may not be considered white."[19]

Henry J. Jewett spoke in support of Navarro, noting that a large class of Tejanos might not be considered white by election judges, even though all lawyers would agree that they were. The outcome of the issue demonstrated a measure of the liberality of many convention delegates. When the question was put to a final vote on July 23, the word "white" was deleted by a vote of forty-two to fourteen. As a result, the 1845 Constitution did not use the word "white" in defining voter qualifications. Elimination of that word was Navarro's greatest accomplishment at the convention. His leadership secured the voting rights of Tejanos, whether of European, Indian, or partial African descent, or any mixtures thereof. Arnoldo De León expressed a view held by many contemporary historians when he wrote that Navarro almost singlehandedly prevented the possible constitutional disenfranchisement of Mexican Americans.[20]

The issue of whiteness had not quite been laid to rest. It reared its head again when the question arose of how to determine the number of representatives each county would have in the state legislature. Were they to be determined by the number of qualified voters in the counties, or by the total number of free citizens? Navarro did not attend this debate because he was ill. Delegates presented arguments for both methods. Howard criticized the view, expressed by Francis Moore Jr., an influential newspaperman from Houston, that apportionment should be based upon the number of qualified voters, and argued for representation based upon the free population. The question of the representation of immigrants prior to naturalization was raised, and Runnels remarked that it was understood that "the country was destined to have a considerable influx of foreign population."[21] Moore could scarcely contain his rage, and at the next opportunity he seized the floor again to press for apportionment by qualified voters. Apparently still smarting over elimination of the word "white" from the voter qualifications, and taking advantage of Navarro's absence, he then unleashed an inflammatory diatribe, attempting to generate fear about a massive Mexican migration into Texas.

Moore directed many angry comments at "the gentleman from Bexar" (probably Navarro), who apparently had accused Moore of conjuring up the image of foreigners as a "bugbear," and had referred to Moore as a "fugleman," meaning the ringleader of a faction. Moore responded by reviving the issue of whiteness. Noting that he had no fear of European immigration, he predicted that the result of eliminating whiteness as a qualification for voting would bring disaster:

> Hordes of Mexican Indians may come here from the West, and may be more formidable than the enemy you have vanquished. Silently they will come moving in; they may come back in thousands to Béxar, in thousands to Goliad, and perhaps to Nacogdoches and what will be the consequence? Ten, twenty, thirty, forty, fifty thousand may come in here and vanquish you at the ballot box, though you are invincible in arms. This is no idle dream; no bugbear; it is the truth.

Moore then launched a vitriolic attack on Tejanos and Mexicans, whom he described as the "descendants of the degraded and despicable race which Cortez conquered." This racist attack continued into the following day, and it sparked considerable debate, both pro and con. Moore went too far in his denunciations, however, when he raged on the convention floor about the dangers of allowing the "mean, groveling yellow race of Mexico" to live in equality with the "free born races of Europe." Kinney defended the Tejanos, saying they had done as much to sustain the Republic as anyone. Other members such William B. Ochiltree, Nicholas H. Darnell, and John M. Lewis were unimpressed with Moore's demagoguery and voiced their support. The word white remained excluded from the 1845 Constitution.[22]

Although Navarro was confined to his sickbed during Moore's two days of rage, Fisher and other friends certainly told him about Moore's slanderous condemnations and Kinney's spirited refutation. Navarro returned to the sessions on July 31 after a one-week absence. He did not comment on Moore's remarks. A week had passed, Kinney and others had already confronted Moore, and Navarro saw no need to revisit the subject. He was probably pleased by the results of the apportionment vote. Moore's racist fulminations helped doom his cause for apportionment by qualified voters. The final outcome was for representation in the counties, cities, and towns to be based on the free population, to be determined by a periodic census. Thus the founding document of the state of Texas, its constitution, did not exclude Tejanos from voting and apportioned representation based upon free population, which was reassuring to large communities of Tejanos such as existed in San Antonio. While the efforts of Navarro, Kinney, and others at the convention did not prevent many Texans from regarding Tejanos as a separate race of colored people and most Tejanos continued to be treated as inferiors well into the twentieth century, there was a constitutional rejection of inequality on which later reforms could be initiated.[23] And Navarro was largely responsible for that.

On Tuesday, August 5, the convention continued deliberations about sections to be included in Article VII of the Constitution. Cunningham again submitted an additional section that stirred up a hornet's nest concerning land forfeitures, a subject he had first broached in mid-July. Paraphrasing Section 8 of the General Provisions of the 1836 Constitution, he proposed that

> All persons who left the country for the purpose of evading a participation in the Revolution of 1836, or who refused to participate in it, or who aided or assisted the Mexican enemy, shall forfeit all rights of citizenship, and such lands as they may hold in the republic.

Although the proposal was expressed in general terms that would apply to all, Tejanos were the ones most likely to be harmed by it. An example of this had occurred the previous year when the Houston *Morning Star* assailed the De León family. An editorial declared that since the De León family had "[taken] up arms against Texas and joined Santa Anna during the revolution, their property was considered as forfeited." Newly arrived settlers believed the newspaper account and began to settle on De León lands. How should the convention treat the property rights of accused Tejanos like the De León's, or those who might be accused in the future? This was a contentious and emotional subject that delegates from the southwestern region of Texas debated at length.[24]

Cunningham represented the interests of Anglos such as those who sought to take De León land. He justified his proposal by saying that when the Mexican army invaded Texas, a large proportion of the citizens of Goliad and Victoria either joined the enemy or abandoned Texas when their services were needed. He referred to the aid that several Tejanos provided to General José de Urrea's army in 1836. Adding avarice to his argument, Cunningham contended that the land, if freed of Tejano ownership, would enrich the state treasury, as they had "millions of acres, worth millions of dollars." Cunningham's idea generated angry opposition because of its potential for future injustice. Several delegates even expressed regret for past abuses. Also undermining Cunningham's proposal was the fact that, according to Rusk, the Republic had evidently taken no property from Tejanos or anyone else as a result of legal proceedings under Section 8.[25]

Kinney, Navarro's ally, spoke against Cunningham on behalf of his constituents in the trans-Nueces region. As the operator of a trading post on Corpus Christi Bay since the late 1830s, Kinney knew that Tejano ranchers had to cooperate with Mexican officials to survive. With absolute clarity he discussed Mexicans, Indians, and Anglos who at one time or another had confronted him at his isolated trading post on the Nueces in threatening numbers. He recalled that, "I have been in such a situation myself, and when Mr. Mexican came, I treated him with a great deal of politeness, especially if he had me in his power; and when Mr. American came, I did the same with him; and when Mr. Indian came, I was also very frequently disposed to make a compromise with him." Because of such compromises, Kinney had been accused of treason, and he described in compelling terms the particular empathy he felt for the plight of Tejanos, past and present. Kinney asserted that the value of the lands held by Mexican grantees provided no reason to strip this property from them. Rather than having abandoned Texas, many were driven off during the conflict. Kinney said that even the families of Mexicans who had died in the service of Texas had been left in destitution and want while newcomers took their lands. Kinney summarized his position on Tejanos by saying, "I am for giving all their rights. If Mexicans, let them be called white or black, have rights with us, let them have those rights. I will say here that I have had as good and faithful soldiers who were Mexicans as I have had of the Americans."[26]

Other delegates added persuasive support to Kinney's argument. John Caldwell, to whom Navarro had sold his seven leagues on the Colorado River, said that Texas had never offered protection to the people along the Rio Grande, so that "The inhabitants of that region scarcely know that we claim that country." To survive they aided the enemy by selling him provisions. Caldwell asked, "Are they now to forfeit their rights because this government has never been able to exercise jurisdiction over them?" Albert C. Horton described the horrendous situation of Tejanos in the Victoria area after 1836. He said his own countrymen had stolen vast herds of their cattle and driven them east. To the accusation that they had taken up arms, he asked against whom had they taken up arms? Against robbers and bandits, he said, and they should not be blamed for protecting their property and persons. He added, "Not only have they been despoiled of their property but, I am ashamed to repeat it, such violations as have been committed upon females there, fix a blot upon the American character."[27]

Rusk joined in the challenge to delegates who spoke harshly against Tejanos and wanted to confiscate land because of supposed disloyalty. He noted that because some had taken up arms against Texas, "now the whole indignation of this Convention is aroused to punish [them all] and enrich the treasury." Cunningham's proposal, he said, "embraces nothing" and "does not carry out the principles of justice." Instead, it would result in "serious injustice, and, I am afraid, injure the cause of Texas." Rusk said that he had as good an "appreciation of the Mexican character as any gentleman here," for he had seen good and bad. As a newly appointed general, with headquarters in Victoria, he had struggled unsuccessfully to stop his men from sacking Tejano homes. He recalled that during the Texas Revolution "many a Mexican . . . stood by us, and battled bravely with us in favor of the principles of civil and religious liberty." Rusk then challenged his fellow delegates: "Will this convention, now in a time of peace and quiet, when the country is rejoicing in prosperity and about to enter the glorious American Union, descend from its high functions, to wreak the vengeance of the State upon these poor people?"[28]

Having listened to the various arguments, Navarro rose from his chair and spoke in support of Rusk:

> I have listened with attention to, and have heard with pleasure the remarks made by the gentleman from Nacogdoches, General Rusk. The eloquent speech of that gentleman in relation to the matter now under discussion is founded upon the rock of eternal truth, as regards general rules, because they are expedient, suitable, and consistent with the rules of national polity; and more than all this, because, in my humble opinion, they do honor to the magnanimity of that gentleman, and to the generous character of the Anglo Saxon race, from which he claims his descent. The reasoning of that gentleman, cleanse[s], in my humble estimation, in their equitable sense that blot which from time to time has soiled the rich drapery of the Mexican character, and provide amply for the exigencies of Texas for the time to come.
>
> Therefore, Mr. President, and for want of an adequate mastery to the task, to embellish, nay, even to add any one single reason to the support of the premises so forcibly demonstrated, and so graphically depicted by the gentleman from Nacogdoches [Rusk], I declare in

behalf of my constituents of the county of Bexar, in the face of this
Convention, and before the civilized world, that I adhere to the doc-
trine laid down by the said gentleman, and will vote with him on this
question, and thus give an evidence of the old and generally accepted
maxim that "facts speak louder than words."

It must have been difficult for Navarro to focus on the positive aspects
of Rusk's speech and ignore the nasty, and inaccurate, remarks of other
delegates. William C. Young, for example, had asked whether even "traitors like the 'celebrated gentleman named Seguin'" would be allowed to
keep their rights in Texas? Young thought this made no sense, and that
lands taken from such people could be sold for a lot of money to benefit
the public treasury.[29] Navarro could only have remained silent with great
difficulty in the face of this attack on a fellow Bexareño who had lost his
lands to squatters under the threat of violence, not laws.

In the wake of these impassioned speeches it must have been easy
to forget that the original question had been whether or not to refer the
Cunningham proposal to the Judiciary Committee for review, which is
what Navarro wanted. Without the debate, however, a vote of the entire
convention might have approved a measure that would have jeopardized
Tejano land interests. Delegate opinion on the matter was closely divided. Later that day, by a vote of twenty-eight to twenty-six, the proposal
went to the Judiciary Committee. The result was that Cunningham's
effort to preserve the draconian language of Section 8 of the 1836 Constitution was rejected. The committee decided to leave investigations
of such forfeitures to "the ordinary powers of legislation." Nevertheless, many Tejanos, like the De Leóns, continued to fight expensive legal
battles for several years to win clear title to their lands. Tejanos who
could not afford lawyers and legal fees lost their lands. Speaking from
experience, Seguín wrote that lawsuits arose in the 1850s that were intended to invalidate the land titles of individuals who were wrongfully
accused of being "enemy aliens." Seguín, in his 1858 memoir, claimed
that these lawsuits were ongoing and "anyone who has listened to the
evidence elicited in cases such as this will readily discover the base
means adopted to deprive rightful owners of their property."[30]

During the last days of the convention, with most of the substantive
work done, two eleventh-hour gambits were made to undermine the validity of Spanish and Mexican land titles. John Hemphill and the ubiquitous Cunningham proposed that Spanish and Mexican land grants
would have to be officially recorded within one year of the first legislature, upon penalty of forfeiture. Lemuel D. Evans demanded harsher

measures to invalidate titles issued by Spanish or Mexican law, which would have had the ludicrous effect of nullifying every land grant made in Texas prior to its admission as a state to the Union. Jones ridiculed Evans's proposal by offering an amendment that all land grants located in Texas prior to approval by the United States of the new state constitution would be rendered null and void. Navarro could not resist the chance to add to Jones's burlesque and to further mock the advocates of these ridiculous proposals by offering one even more absurd. He offered as a substitute amendment:

> That, in order to eliminate all difficulties with old titles and land grants that, every settler who may have located his claim upon any grants heretofore made by the former governments of Spain and Mexico, shall be bound within the term of two years from the date of the adoption of this Constitution, to enclose the same with a stone wall on all sides, of eight yards height at least. The obligation shall devolve upon his heirs and assigns, on pain, in case of not complying with it, or in case of neglect to keep said wall in constant repair, so that there never shall be a breach in it to the extent of one yard, then, and in those cases, he shall forfeit all his claim to said land; and the grant, title or claim to the said land shall be null and void, and the said land shall be declared vacant and subject to new location, and subject to the same conditions and penalties.

There was little more to be said. On August 28, 1845, the convention members met for the last time and voted unanimously to approve their work. Copies were ordered sent to President Polk of the United States and President Anson Jones of the Republic of Texas. Navarro packed his things and rode south toward San Antonio and his San Geronimo Ranch.[31]

The 1845 Constitutional Convention members had begun by honoring Andrew Jackson. Thus it is fitting that they produced a constitution that was decidedly Jacksonian in nature in that it encouraged popular participation in government and opposed excessive concentration of power. This is seen in the limits placed on the power and tenure of the governor, the requirement for a two-thirds vote of both legislative chambers to charter corporations, and the prohibition of legislation to allow banking. The convention produced a straightforward, intelligible document that led some national politicians to remark that it was the best of all of the state constitutions. The historic importance of the work of José Antonio Navarro and his fellow delegates was that they created a fundamental legal framework for Texas as it became one of the United States.

Many of the concepts they included in the 1845 Constitution would appear in subsequent state charters.[32] Perhaps of greatest significance to Navarro and his constituents was that their constitution contained no discriminatory provisions against Tejanos.

The final steps to bring Texas into the United States proceeded rapidly. In October, Texan voters approved their new constitution. The United States Congress voted its approval on the annexation resolution in December and President Polk signed it on December 29, 1845, the legal date of Texas's entry into the Union.[33] The formalities of the transfer of authority, however, were postponed until the beginning of the first state legislature in February. Meanwhile, President Polk fulfilled his campaign promise of territorial expansion by asserting Texas's claim to the land south of the Nueces River. On January 1, 1846, he ordered General Zachary Taylor to take troops to the mouth of the Nueces, establish a base, and march south to the Rio Grande.

Navarro's work during the Constitutional Convention apparently pleased the people of San Antonio. He had scarcely returned from Austin when the voters elected him to be their senator in the first state legislature. Volney Howard and Duncan C. Ogden were selected as state representatives. During the first weeks of 1846, the Republic of Texas flag continued to wave over the wooden building that would serve as the state capitol in Austin. Anson Jones, the last president of the Republic of Texas, convened the legislature on February 16. Navarro and seventeen other senators answered the roll call, were sworn in, and took their seats. They elected Edward Burleson as the president pro tem, while Navarro selected Reuben M. Potter as his interpreter. On February 19, a large, jubilant crowd gathered to witness the ceremony formalizing the end of the Republic. Navarro watched as Jones relinquished his authority to the first governor of the state of Texas, J. Pinckney Henderson, with the famous declaration, "The final act in this great drama is now performed: the Republic of Texas is no more."[34] Navarro and his fellow Tejanos knew without a doubt that they were now officially citizens of the United States. The question remained, however, about the status of Hispanics living in other areas claimed by Texas since 1837, but not occupied or governed by Texans. The war with Mexico and the treaty of Guadalupe Hidalgo in 1848 would answer that question.

The Republic of Texas had always claimed political borders far beyond its long-established boundaries under Spain and Mexico. These far-flung boundaries were accepted by the United States upon annexation. These included Texas's long-standing claims to the lands south of the Nueces River and to all of New Mexico east of the Rio Grande, from Santa Fe to

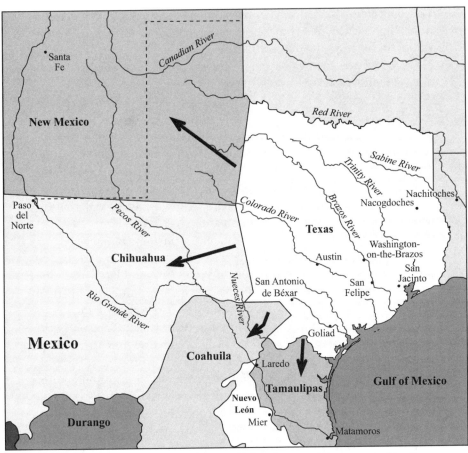

By the terms of the Treaty of Guadalupe Hidalgo, the state of Texas acquired territory that had been part of four separate political jurisdictions under Mexico. Many years passed before these areas, now in West and South Texas, become culturally and economically integrated with the rest of the state.

El Paso. Inhabitants of these distant lands had never been a part of the jurisdiction of Texas under Spain and Mexico, and they did not necessarily share Tejano traditions, which had their distinctive cultural roots in the earliest settlements of Spanish Texas. Tejanos who lived within the traditional boundaries of Texas that included San Antonio, Goliad, and Nacogdoches had over the years come to terms with the political changes imposed by the Republic and had even participated in the new system. While Texas did not get to keep all the land it claimed, many inhabitants of other regions became "Tejanos" suddenly as a result of war.

This shift in jurisdiction was imposed upon distinct, close-knit communities that had different traditions, cultures, and governments. As a result of this change, the trauma of the war between the United States and Mexico, and geographical isolation, the people of the lower Rio Grande did not identify themselves with Texas for many years.[35]

Navarro reached the high point of his political career in the first state legislature. At age fifty-one, he brought experience gained through twenty years of political service. During the three months of senate sessions, Navarro's work focused on three main issues. He settled an important election dispute; he introduced a bill, which passed into law, that provided for arbitration as an alternative to expensive lawsuits; and he put his primary focus on the thorny matter of forfeitures and escheats, which occupied most of his attention and effort.

On the day after Texas became a state, the business of the legislature began in earnest. Standing committees were appointed and Navarro became a member of the Committee on Privileges and Elections. A controversial issue immediately came before this committee: the petition of Cornelius McAnelly who was protesting the close election for senator of Harris County that he had lost to Isaac W. Brashear. The committee entrusted Navarro with the sensitive assignment of settling the disputed election. He closely studied the returns and determined that the votes cast in nine of thirteen Harris County precincts were invalid because of procedural errors. In a lengthy, meticulous analysis he reported that, "the only course which can justly be recommended to the Senate is to require a new election." The next day, committee chairman Benjamin R. Wallace conveyed the substance of Navarro's report to President Pro Tem Burleson. The Senate agreed with Navarro and declared Brashear's seat to be vacant, although he ultimately retained his position.[36]

One of Navarro's proposals, to "Establish Courts of Conciliation," became a state law that benefited everyday citizens. This bill seems to have incorporated his experience with the conciliatory hearings and judgments over which he had presided in 1822. He likely saw a need for an efficient method of conflict resolution using arbitrators to avoid the expense of time-consuming litigation. This would have been more available and comprehensible to many Tejanos, who could not afford lawsuits. Acting on Navarro's proposal, the legislature on April 25, 1846, approved a law entitled "An Act to Authorize the Settlement of Disputes Through Conciliation or Arbitration."[37]

The journals of the first legislature reveal that Navarro made good use of his expertise in land law in the most challenging issue that he confronted. The sanctity of land titles was threatened by provisions for forfeitures that had originated in the 1835 Consultation and gone un-changed in the 1845 Convention; this was an issue of great importance to Navarro and his constituents. Legislators at first merged the legal processes of forfeitures and escheats in their deliberations. Navarro was quick to make the distinction between forfeitures, which served as a penalty, and escheats, which concerned the property of persons dying without heirs or a will. Navarro's devotion to these legal concerns would strengthen the existing land-ownership rights of all Texans, both Anglo American and Mexican American.

Navarro carefully examined and recommended changes to bills per-taining to Bexar County boundaries, which in 1846 extended far to the north and west of present-day lines. The Senate implemented his amendments regarding a survey of the border between Bexar and Bas-trop counties, and he also devoted much attention to defining the limits of Comal County, Bexar's neighbor to the north.[38] But titles remained his greatest concern.

The 1845 Constitution specifically charged the legislature with re-sponsibility for writing laws pertaining to fines, forfeiture, and escheats. Navarro was appointed to a select committee of six senators to write this legislation. It would be his most important assignment during the first legislature. The instruction to the committee was "to take into consid-eration the latter clause of Sec. 4, Article 13 of the 1845 Constitution, to wit: 'All fines, penalties, forfeitures, and escheats which have accrued to the Republic of Texas under the Constitution and laws, shall accrue to the State of Texas *and the legislature shall by law provide a method for determining what lands may have been forfeited or escheated* [emphasis added]'"[39] The committee would find it very difficult to reach an agree-ment. Deliberations about the issue led to a quagmire, complicated by the related issues of alien land ownership and treason. Virtually single-handedly, Navarro clarified and sorted the parts of the matter, facilitat-ing the creation of a practical law. His opinions were a force within the committee that prevented it from recommending bills unfavorable to Tejano or Anglo holders of Mexican land grants.

The committee deliberated through February and March, reviewing the provisions of the 1835 San Felipe Consultation and the 1836 Con-stitutional Convention. Navarro became more and more dissatisfied with a proposal devised by the other committee members regarding escheats. His examination of the document in English revealed certain defects to him, and he wanted a translation in order to study it in de-tail. Before this could be provided, the committee in a majority opinion submitted the bill as it was to the Senate. Navarro persisted in an effort to fully understand and critique the bill. On March 23, he provided a detailed, dissenting report to Burleson. He expressed concern that the submitted bill was defective because of its vagueness and specifically addressed several points. The first was to distinguish between escheats and forfeitures. Navarro said it was his impression "that those lands only, which revert to the State from the lack of heirs, or devises [wills], can be considered as escheated, and that those which so revert from inability in the owner to hold them, are to be classed among the forfeited."[40] Navarro was absolutely correct to tell his fellow senators in his minority report that the two issues, escheats and forfeitures, were not directly related in the law and should be addressed in separate bills, which would be done eventually.

The committee's majority report also addressed land forfeitures in relation to aliens and treason. In his dissenting report, Navarro dealt with the alien land rights of both Hispanic and Anglo immigrants. He quoted the provision in the 1836 Constitution that said, "No alien shall hold land in Texas, except by titles emanating directly from the Government of the Republic, &c.," which was a threatening cloud hanging over Tejanos and Anglos alike. He advanced the principle that in all enlightened communities

> neither conquest nor division of empire can annul vested individual rights of property; hence a person who held real estate in Texas when it separated from Mexico, although he has not since become a citizen of Texas, has still, during his life, a vested right to that property, which the mere change of government has not impaired. . . . If the alien of a certain class has in law and equity a peculiar vested right he cannot be divested of it merely as an alien.

He advocated for alien land owners to be allowed ample time to dispose of property or to qualify for possessing it, and that all the conditions and specifications for ownership should be included in the new act, rather than being left to be inferred from other laws.[41]

Navarro also insisted that another class of landowners should be addressed in the bill. These were persons who came from the United States and purchased land in good faith both before and after Texas independence, but had been citizens of neither Mexico nor the Republic of Texas. Navarro noted that legal deficiencies caused by their ignorance of the laws, illiteracy, mishandling by incompetent agents, or accidental reasons could endanger their ownership. He declared that in the interest of justice a generous extension of time should be provided to those who had acquired an equitable, if not actually legal, right to Texas land.

To counter the defects he saw in the bill, he offered a substitute for the first section of the bill, from which succeeding sections were derived.[42]

Entries in senate journals show that the committee incorporated part of Navarro's substitute into a revised draft. The senators also approved other amendments offered by Navarro, the most important of which was "the time required for naturalization shall be allowed, and after taking the oath of allegiance, the title to such lands shall be decreed." This would allow immigrants to obtain citizenship and then receive grants.

Four days later, the committee again presented its majority report. Responding to Navarro's critique, it now proposed two separate bills based on Navarro's definitions, one for escheats and one for forfeitures. The debates within the committee had dragged on for nearly two months. Navarro held the committee's feet to the fire all the way in order to get the best interpretation for Tejanos and others whose land ownership was at risk. Henry J. Jewett, as chair, obviously wanted to be freed from the controversial issue. Concluding the committee's report he wrote, "we submit the following bills to the Senate, and ask to be discharged from the further consideration of the subject."[43] But Navarro was not yet satisfied and demanded further consideration.

Three days later, on April 13, Navarro sent a second report to Burleson, pointing out where he differed from the committee majority and offering several more amendments. He insisted that consideration should be provided for aliens who had in good faith acquired land in Texas, as well as for those who legally owned land in Texas but became aliens when the Republic separated from Mexico. Then he addressed the issue of treason. He agreed that the legislature had a duty to enforce "forfeitures of those who, while owing allegiance, were guilty of treason against the Republic of Texas." But he insisted that the law should be specific on two critical points, "the time when that allegiance [to the Republic of Texas] commenced and the circumstances under which charge of treason to it would lie." He explained that

> No person can be guilty of treason to a new and revolutionary government which he has never acknowledged, nor does he incur the guilt of treason by any compulsory aid rendered to a government hostile to his own, nor by submission for the time being, to a government de facto in his own country, though it be not founded on legitimate right. As little can any man be justly charged with treason for non-compliance with a constitution which had not been promulgated, or which, though officially published, is still incomplete from lack of its needful ratification.[44]

Navarro reminded the Senate about the confusion and uncertainty that had existed in 1836, and which for a considerable time kept most people, Anglo and Tejano, from knowing what political authority was truly in power.

Speaking as one of the participants, he explained to the senators, most of whom had not been in Texas in 1836, that the Constitution of the Republic had been written under conditions of increasing panic and fear of Santa Anna's approach. The convention at Washington-on-the-Brazos disintegrated and took flight "almost before the ink of the signatures was dry, and before the instrument was signed by all who had voted on it." Moreover, he recalled that the original document was lost in the confusion and had to be recreated "imperfectly, from written and remembered fragments of the missing document." Given these facts, Navarro asserted that it would be a mockery to assert that the Republic of Texas had any constitution legally in force until much later, after it was accepted and approved by the people. He then made an astonishing comparison regarding the validity of charges of treason, showing what false conclusion could be made by disregarding the circumstances brought about by a violent revolution, and then judging peoples' actions from the comfortable view of hindsight. He said that

> If treason can be committed against an unpromulgated law, woe to the memory of Travis. On the 2nd of March at Washington, was solemnized that declaration of Texian Independence, which they of the Alamo were destined never to hear. On the 6th of March they died in arms for the Mexican Federation, and the banner which there fell only with its last defender, was the tri-color of 1824.[45]

The senate journals do not record any reaction to Navarro's use of Travis as an example of unconscious treason, but certainly he realized the likely impact of this borderline blasphemy.

Navarro next turned to another key issue: the role of district attorneys in land forfeitures. He underscored his opposition to the provision of the proposal that left the initiation of suits for forfeiture to the discretion of district attorneys. He had argued this same point at the Constitutional Convention the previous year, asserting that matters of confiscation were inherently liable to abuse. Navarro reasoned that the office of district attorney was generally conferred on young advocates, who were "liable to that lack of mature instruction and judgment which might lead them to abuse any great discretionary power, especially when urged on by a desire of distinction or emolument." He asked that the power of district attorneys be limited to *identifying* cases where confiscation might be ordered, investigating the circumstances, and referring such cases to higher authorities.[46] The bill, with Navarro's recommendations, was sent to the Judiciary Committee for its consideration—to the great relief, no doubt, of the select committee members who had wrestled with the forfeiture issue for two months. Jewett, however, could not escape this difficult issue since he served on both committees. On April 25, Jewett reported that most of the Judiciary Committee recommended separate bills for civil and criminal forfeitures. Navarro's influence was obvious. Regarding forfeitures, district attorneys would only have jurisdiction over forfeitures related to criminal behavior, while another procedure would be provided for civil forfeitures. Four days later, when the full Senate took up the matter of forfeiture again, Navarro offered yet another amendment to limit district attorney participation in civil forfeitures: "Strike out 'District Attorney shall file a petition.'" A motion was made to table the bill, which passed.[47]

On May 2, 1846, the Senate again considered a bill on forfeiture that had been made the special order of the day, but it became hopelessly bogged down. The issues of treason and alien land ownership during the early Republic of Texas remained divisive, and arguments often focused on Tejanos. Navarro offered one more amendment to read, "all alien friends shall have five years from and after the passage of this act, to dispose of [lands]." When the Senate rejected the amendment by a vote of 10 to 6, fifty copies of the bill were ordered printed, and it was made the special order of the day for the next session. The troublesome measure was taken up on Monday, May 4, but it was again postponed to be the special order of the following day.[48]

On Tuesday, a forfeiture bill came before the Senate for the sixteenth time since the special committee had been appointed on February 25, 1846. After a lengthy debate, the senators again could not come to a clear agreement. As a result, a proposal was made to forward the bill to the next legislature. This passed, eight to seven. Navarro voted in the affirmative, even though his vote meant that the objectionable provision, Section 8 of the 1836 Constitution, would remain in effect for the time being. He understood that the tenacious Section 8 might later be used in attempts to take over the property of others under the guise of legality.[49] But he also knew that the legislature was only a few days away from adjournment and still faced a busy agenda. Thus no conclusion on the critical bill could be reached that would not be not hasty and ill-conceived. Sadly, while he proved correct about Section 8, he had little choice but to support the status quo as the session came to an end.

Another important issue dealt with by the 1845 Constitutional Convention and the first state legislature was the property rights of women, which were woven into the fabric of colonial Texas through Spanish laws dating from medieval times. Navarro in a speech to the House of Representatives in 1839 had demonstrated his knowledge of these laws, known as the *Siete Partidas*. Among other provisions, this meticulous compilation protected a wife's right to her separate property owned before marriage or received as a gift or inheritance during her marriage, and rights to common property acquired during marriage. Under the Republic, similar provisions had been codified in January 1840 that allowed a wife to retain ownership of her separate property, which was limited to land and slaves, but a husband maintained the right to manage it during the marriage. The 1845 Constitution expanded the wife's separate property to include real property and all types of personal property, but it called for registration of such property. Pursuant to this mandate, during the first state legislature, a bill defining the registration, protection, and conveyance of property in which the wife had an interest was referred to the Senate Judiciary Committee. The committee recommended against the bill, saying that existing laws on the subject were sufficient, but the legislature as a whole advanced the bill. Navarro supported this bill's passage and even offered an amendment, the details of which are unknown. Two days later the bill passed sixteen to four, and Navarro voted with the majority.[50]

The bill was signed into law on April 29, 1846. It outlined registration procedures and specifically shielded a wife's registered, separate property from being seized by her husband's creditors. Perhaps more important, it gave the wife an equal say before common property, such as a homestead, could be sold. Not only did she have to sign the deed, a notary or judge had to certify that she understood the significance of the transaction and had given her consent without her husband present. This measure greatly expanded a wife's control of her ownership interest in community property as compared with the 1840 law, which permitted the husband to sell such property without the wife's permission. It is no accident that states formerly under Spanish and Mexican rule have community property laws.[51] This continuity of a woman's right to property can be seen as an integral part of a long-standing tradition of rights under Spain and Mexico, as Navarro so eloquently argued in support of Tejanos. Anglo settlers in Texas had lived under and adapted to these provisions after many years, and statehood offered no compelling reason to upset the status quo.

Senators attended to mostly routine matters during their last week, which ended on May 13. President Pro Tem Burleson briefly addressed them with words of gratitude, and the first Texas State Senate adjourned. Navarro had fought hard against laws that would facilitate land forfeitures and inhibit alien land ownership, both of which were issues of vital importance to Tejanos, because many had lost property or were threatened with losses. Even as he spoke, challenges to Tejano claims were occurring in Victoria County with the lands of the De León family and Carlos de la Garza. Nevertheless, Navarro's fellow senators respected his achievements, as was evident when the legislature passed a bill creating Navarro County.[52] Bordering the Brazos River south of Dallas County, it was carved out of the western part of Robinson County and named in honor of José Antonio Navarro. The county seat was named Corsicana to honor his Corsican heritage.

With the close of the legislature, Navarro was ready to devote time and energy to his long neglected business interests and property. He owned nearly 42,000 acres in the vicinity of San Antonio, plus at least ten lots in town. His rural properties needed to be checked to ensure encroachments were not taking place, while his lots probably needed rental arrangements. He still had one headright claim for a labor located on the Frio River that required his attention in order to obtain a title. Navarro also began to revive his mercantile operation. By early June, he had returned to San Antonio and written to Potter, his Senate translator, directing him to send money to New Orleans suppliers. A month passed and Navarro received no reply. In July he wrote again to Potter, expressing concern. Chidingly, Navarro wrote, "I would not even presume to think that you would lose your activity and diligence for me." He added, "You will not forget to send me as soon as possible the cider of which we spoke, and I hope to learn that Messrs. Potter and Millard are in receipt of that money." Navarro probably did receive the cider or its value in other merchandise. This transaction, however, seems to mark the end of his merchant career, for no further record of mercantile activity has been found. Having lost five years, he was behind the curve. Competition from experienced traders with well-established connections probably made merchandising difficult for him. Moreover, he probably did not need mercantile profits. After statehood, Texas enjoyed an economic boom, and he was well positioned to profit from his land holdings. It is evident that beginning around 1847, and for the rest of his life, Navarro's income came primarily from rents and land sales.[53]

In the fall of 1846, Josiah Gregg visited Navarro. They had much in common as both were experienced merchants; Gregg was one of the best-known of the Santa Fe Trail traders and Navarro had long experience with the New Orleans trade. Gregg recorded details of the meeting in his diary, and his notes are a valuable addition to the many generalized descriptions of Navarro's character. Navarro's passion for conversation and his articulate speech impressed Gregg, who wrote,

> I found him reclined upon a rude sofa, with his lame leg elevated. Supposing he spoke English, I accosted him in that tongue, but he at once requested I should converse in Spanish, as he spoke very little English. He appeared a very agreeable man, and of far greater intelligence, than is usual among the Mexicans of this region. He conversed with much volubility, and expatieted [sic] particularly upon the ways of Texas. He with much justice condemned the wonted temerity of the Texans, which as he remarked, had cost them a great deal of blood and most of their defeats. He instanced, in particular, the affair of the Alamo, where 180 odd men undertook to defend it against several thousand. He asserted that Santa Anna at all times left the eastern side of the fortification free, in hopes the Texans would escape—preferring to let them to go in peace to a victory over them which he knew must cost him dearly.[54]

Gregg's notes provide rare, firsthand observations of Navarro's personality. They also reveal the severity of his lameness, his outspoken opinions about the battle of the Alamo, and his perspectives on Anglo Texans, which were not always positive.

While Navarro settled his business affairs and tended to his properties, he did not rebuild his ranch home on the Atascosa River, which was in ruins and must have been a sad sight for him. He would have seen what a visitor passing through the area had seen and recorded in November 1847 when his group "arrived at the site of the Navaro [sic] ranch." They knew that "this ranch had been destroyed by the Indians seven years ago," but "one still sees the mounds over those who are buried here—the Mexicans who were slain by the marauding Indians—marked by a cross at their feet." Augustin Treviño, "who had lived at this ranch for three years," was with the visitors and probably provided the details of the site's history.[55]

The problem of what to do with the Atascosa Ranch would have to wait. Earlier in 1847, San Antonio citizens had reelected Navarro to represent them in the Texas State Senate's second meeting, which convened on Monday, December 13, 1847. Two days later, Navarro and the other senators joined the members of the Texas House of Representatives to hear a message from Governor J. Pinckney Henderson. The governor addressed numerous subjects of interest to Navarro, including the Texan claim to New Mexico territory and land forfeitures. But, most important, Henderson reported several successful battles in the war against Mexico, noting that the army of General Winfield Scott had taken Mexico City. Henderson's satisfaction with these achievements, however, was overshadowed by the threat to Texas's claims of territory in New Mexico, resulting from the U.S. occupation of Santa Fe by General Stephen Kearny. He expressed alarm that federal military forces "had established a territorial government [of New Mexico] within the limits of the State of Texas," and that the United States Congress seemed to have questioned Texas's right to it.[56]

After the governor's address, Senate and House members cooperated in the election of a senator to represent Texas in the United States Congress, a process that briefly turned the spotlight on Navarro. Sam Houston was the only nominee for the Senate seat, but when the roll was called in the Texas Senate, Burleson, who had a long-standing feud with Houston, voted for Navarro as a protest. Houston, of course, won the election, and served in the United States Senate for the next thirteen years. Ironically, within a few days of Houston's election Navarro's seat in the Texas Senate was contested. No record was found of who disputed his election or why, but the challenge was referred to the Committee on Apportionment, Privileges and Elections. On January 4, the committee reported its conclusion that, by law and based on the evidence submitted, "José Antonio Navarro is entitled to the seat, and [we] would recommend that he be confirmed in the same." By that time, Navarro had already been assigned to three standing committees—on the judiciary, county boundaries, and education—and funds had been approved to pay for an unnamed interpreter for him.[57]

Henderson raised the deferred question of forfeitures and escheats, complaining about the failure of the previous legislature to resolve the issue and asking the senators finally "to prescribe the rules which are to govern the Executive in remitting fines and forfeitures." The bill concerning escheats that had been the subject of so much debate in the first legislature passed the second with no significant objection. This was probably because Navarro had become the dominant member of the Judiciary Committee; only one other member, Alexander H. Phillips, had been on the committee the previous year. The escheated property bill, as old business carried over from the first legislature, was among the first to be referred to the Judiciary Committee. There Navarro made sure it conformed to his specifications. On January 20, 1848, the committee considered the bill for the last time. The members made numerous changes, and then the Senate approved the measure. Within a few days it was reported as "correctly engrossed," meaning it was ready for the governor's signature.[58]

Still unresolved was the problem of land forfeitures. The Judiciary Committee prepared a bill and presented it to the Senate on February 14, when it was read for the third time and passed. Navarro must have felt a quiet sense of accomplishment to see that the draconian land forfeiture provisions to which he had objected in the previous term had disappeared. His influence and convincing arguments against forfeitures related to aliens and treason had prevailed. As a result of his tenacity and decisive arguments, the final bill specified strict procedures for handling funds resulting from forfeiture. The governor could not freely use such money, and any disposition made of such cases had to be reported to the legislature.[59] Obviously all forfeitures would be carried out under the watchful eyes of the Texas House and Senate. Having the legislature as a watchdog over land forfeitures represented another victory for Navarro. His concerns expressed during the first legislature about possible excesses of rogue district attorneys or courts had been reflected in the law.

Thus one possible abuse of land confiscations had been averted, but another stood unrecognized except by the devious minds of greedy predators, as Navarro would soon learn. Working at the same time as the legislature, the Texas Supreme Court had its say in the matter of forfeitures in a decision that would threaten some property owners. Immediately before the legislature's forfeiture act passed, the court rendered a landmark decision that allowed certain land titles acquired as Mexican grants to be challenged.[60] The following year Navarro would use his influence against unscrupulous persons attempting to use this ruling and some technicalities in the colonization laws of Coahuila and Texas to rob early settlers of their land.

Meanwhile, one of the most important issues that came before the Senate was the establishment of a public school system. As a result of unsuccessful attempts to establish schools in Béxar under Mexican rule, Navarro knew well the daunting challenges of this undertaking. He and other members of the Education Committee studied a proposal that came to them in the form of "A Bill to be Entitled an Act for the Establishment of Free Public Schools." On March 16 the committee submitted its report, recommending that the bill be postponed. The members explained that despite the need for education and the state's obligation to provide it they were "fearful that it is too early to attempt a plan of free schools for the state." They identified two insurmountable obstacles: insufficient funds and incomplete county organization.

Despite the land set aside for education under the Republic, there was only a modest school in the state treasury; if it was distributed among the organized counties, most would receive a sum too small to be of any service. Indeed, the state treasury was almost empty. The Finance Committee worried that there were scarcely enough funds to pay the expenses of the legislature. While waiting for more funds and better county organization, the Education Committee suggested that it would be wise to inquire into "the operation and details of the policy of States where systems of free public instruction are established, before attempting one of our own organization."[61]

In the second session, Navarro rose to speak on behalf of one of his prominent constituents. He presented a petition from Samuel Maverick requesting title to five leagues of land he purchased before the Texas Revolution. It was referred to the Committee on Private Land Claims, but to no avail. The committee refused the petition, explaining that the General Land Office had no legal basis to issue patents for his purchases. Always attentive to issues pertaining to land, Navarro expressed dissatisfaction about the wording of a bill to define the boundary of Comal County, which adjoined Bexar County. He had objected to the measure when it first appeared in the previous legislature, perhaps because it would change the border between Bexar and Comal counties to the detriment of some of his constituents. On his motion, the bill was indefinitely postponed. In one of his last actions, he challenged amendments made to a tax bill, with the result that the Senate backed down: "On motion of Mr. Navarro, The Senate receded from their amendments to a bill to be entitled an act to provide for the more certain collection of Taxes for the years 1846 and 1847."[62]

The senators gathered for the last session of the second legislature on March 20, 1848. Navarro then walked out of the senate chambers for the last time at the zenith of his political career, having served in three legislative bodies under three different national governments between 1827 and 1848. He would remain an influential public figure with enduring political influence through his personal contacts and published writings. More than twenty years later, friends wrote: "we can assure that his return to private life has made him a greater man than fame would have made of him in the spacious halls of the [U.S.] senate." Potter, who served as Navarro's translator, spoke highly of his ability. Had he been able to speak English, Potter wrote, "He would not only have been a star in the Congress of Texas, but [would] have passed from it to that of the United States."[63]

Navarro returned to his San Geronimo Ranch, where he lived for the next five years as a gentleman rancher. Although retired from public office, he kept up with current affairs by reading newspapers. He reportedly read English well, though he spoke it brokenly. Of the various Texas publications available, Navarro had access to the Houston *Democratic Telegraph and Texas Register*, and in early August 1848, what he saw in it changed his focus from Tejanos to Anglos. In the July 20 edition he read with concern two articles that expressed alarm about challenges to the ownership of lands that had been granted under the Mexican government. The targets of these attacks were grants made to Anglos in Austin's Colony. In the first article Guy M. Bryan, state representative from Brazoria County, wrote that recent decisions by the Texas Supreme Court "created the impression in the minds of many that the titles of many of the old grants are defective and subject to relocation." That is, if the court invalidated a grant, it would be considered in the public domain and available to be filed upon by anyone possessing a headright certificate, land scrip, or other claims. Such filings were made by unscrupulous men, known as "Land Jackalls," whose stock in trade was to "relocate" new claims on land that had originally been claimed by some of the first colonists, going back to 1824. Bryan indicated that "Old Settlers" feared that their grants were in danger of being invalidated because Land Jackalls alleged noncompliance with Mexican colonization laws, which remained in effect under the Texas Constitutions of 1836 and 1845.[64]

The Texas Supreme Court decision that threatened the old settlers was almost certainly in the case of the *Heirs of Kinchen Holliman v. Robert Peebles*. Prior to an appeal to the state supreme court, the Fort Bend County district court had ruled that a league granted to Holliman in 1824 was forfeit. When the court agreed, consternation spread across the area that had been Austin's Colony. Asa Townsend, representing some citizens in Colorado County, also wrote an article in the same July 20 edition of the Houston *Democratic Telegraph and Texas Register*. In it, he included a petition they had sent to Governor Henderson asking for his support. The petition expanded on Bryan's concern about the court's decision, complaining that "many locations [claims] have been made upon the lands of many of the oldest and best citizens of the State." The motivation to file on old settlers' land was strong since the public domain had shrunk and the choicest lands were taken. Colorado County residents implored the governor to immediately call a special session of the legislature to confirm Mexican grants and also all sales and transactions that proceeded in good faith from those grants. In conclusion, they warned of "violent animosities," declaring that an end had to be put "to the piratical speculations that are now going on" to "prevent the effusion of blood."[65]

Navarro sympathized wholeheartedly with the landowners. He agreed that many holders, purchasers, and heirs of Mexican grants were on the brink of disaster. On August 12, he completed a letter in support of the grant owners, which was translated by George Fisher and published in the November 30 issue of the *Democratic Telegraph and Texas Register*. Navarro said that he was writing "with a desire to some extent, to serve the cause of the old settlers of Texas." He wanted it well known "how much I deplore the great calamity, which a few ambitious men are about to bring upon our beloved country." Drawing on his knowledge of the Coahuila and Texas colonization law, Navarro refuted, one by one, the pretexts given for the invalidation of grants. He began by pointing out the potential for abuse of Section 8 of the 1836 Constitution. While the problem with Section 8 had been resolved by the second legislature, Navarro insisted that "what in 1836 appeared a necessary justice, in 1848, and in the future, will appear a public dishonor, and a crime against the sound intentions of the community." He angrily added, "there is no further necessity of the application of this political caustic of the 8th Section of said Constitution, which lay buried in the tomb of a departed Government."[66]

Moving on from the 1836 Constitution, Navarro observed that, since Texas independence, courts had been unwilling or unable to invalidate the land titles of early settlers. He wrote that "neither the people nor the press of the country have agitated the same," and explained that this was true "because the majority of the old settlers of Texas consist of honest men." Quoting U.S. Senator Reverdy Johnson, he added, "To seize and confiscate individual property is abhorrent to every sense of justice, which would be an act of barbarism, a dishonor to the age in which we live, and a stain upon our national character." Navarro railed against the Land Jackalls and ridiculed those who looked for technical improprieties in land grants, sarcastically calling them "moralized defenders of the fulfillment of Mexican law." He pointed out the absurd burden of proof imposed on old settlers to produce documentation from the Mexican period:

> Dare you to invalidate the titles barred for a series of years, by the various laws of limitation, under the ridiculous pretext that you have not known the Commissioner who issued them, the witnesses, the hand writing in which they are written, or the language in which they are framed. If such subterfuges were admitted in our Courts of justice, it would be necessary to repudiate the jurisprudence of all nations.[67]

Navarro thus demonstrated the folly of legalistic challenges to land ownership that make claims based on the laws of governments that no longer existed.

Navarro spelled out in clear terms, understandable to the general reader, why titles to Mexican land grants should be respected. His views must have resonated with every Texan landowner who had worked years to clear land, cultivate fields, and build a home in the wilderness. His letter had the effect of mobilizing the fear and anger that had brought tempers to the boiling point. Several landowners on the Colorado, Trinity, and Brazos rivers met with Fisher in Houston, where they made plans for a meeting of old settlers in early March 1849 "to take into consideration the subject matter, set forth in Mr. Navarro's communication." Fisher accepted a leadership role in organizing public resistance to speculators' claims made through legal efforts. He sent a copy of Navarro's letter to Samuel May Williams in Galveston, telling him, "it is the ground work upon which subsequent measures are contemplated to be predicated." He asked Williams to obtain permission from Thomas F. McKinney, Michael B. Menard, and other members of Stephen F. Austin's "first 300 families" to use their names to promote the meeting.[68] He also arranged for the printing of 1,000 circulars to announce it.

The efforts of Navarro, Fisher, and concerned colonists in Colorado County probably blunted the impact of the Texas Supreme Court's decision in *Holliman v. Peebles.* As a result, the feared "Land Jackalls" did not overrun long-established old settler claims. Their efforts in other areas, however, did not stop. In 1853, citizens of Refugio complained that the cost of defending their claims to Mexican grants presented an intolerable burden. They asked the state government for relief, but also took direct action, pledging mutual assistance to eject trespassing land locaters.[69] Cases as late as the 1870s were still citing *Holliman v. Peebles* as a precedent. The attempts to file on early grants seem to have been resolved less by legislation and more by the legal expenses born by claimants, not to mention the overt threats of violence asserted by Colorado County citizens in 1848 and Refugio citizens in 1853. Meanwhile, after Navarro expressed his views in his letter to the *Democratic Telegraph and Texas Register,* he returned to his ranch operations. If he made further efforts on behalf of the old settlers, no record of it has been found. But his intervention on their behalf against the speculators, along with his defense of the voting rights of his mixed-race constituents in 1845, demonstrates his respect for the rule of law regardless of race and social standing.

In late 1849, probably in December, a long anticipated, joyous homecoming took place. This was the return of Ángel Navarro, who had just finished his legal studies at Harvard College. It was unprecedented at the time that a Tejano family, or indeed any family of any ethnic group in Texas, would send a son to Harvard to complete his education. It was an example of the high value that José Antonio Navarro placed on education. No letters that Ángel wrote to his family were found, but he had announced his imminent return to Texas in a letter to a friend in October 1849. Although he found Harvard "a delightful place to study," he was pleased that he was leaving the extreme cold and boredom of Cambridge, Massachusetts, Ángel declared, "I don't think I could persuade myself to live here on [*sic*] any conditions." Later, in the summer of 1850, it was reported to the President and Fellows of Harvard by his professors that Ángel Navarro had passed his examinations satisfactorily. On July 29, 1850, he was awarded the A. B. degree in law.[70]

While all the Navarro children were literate, Ángel must have demonstrated a special aptitude that persuaded his father to pay the extra expense of law school at a time when the family had a large amount of land but received little income from it. No matter what the destiny of Texas would be, José Antonio Navarro knew full well that to have a son schooled at a prestigious college would benefit both the family and the community at large. It was an obvious step in fulfilling the American Dream.

During the years he lived at the San Geronimo Ranch, José Antonio made his money from rents and cattle. Among the tenants on his other properties, records show he leased the house at Flores and Commerce streets to the San Antonio *Ledger*. The ranch operation prospered and José Antonio, along with his sons Sixto and Celso, registered brands and earmarks in 1848; the brands of the sons closely resembled the father's.[71]

Three laborers from Mexico joined Jose Antonio, his wife, Margarita, and their two sons at the ranch. One boy, fourteen-year-old Adriano Rubio, was evidently the son of Navarro's deceased overseer, Ramón Rubio. The 1850 census also shows an additional worker—a twelve-year-old male slave. This young man may have been Henry Navarro, who remained with the Navarros until all Texas slaves were emancipated in 1865 (see Appendix Two).[72]

Navarro continued to follow political events through newspapers and visits to San Antonio. During 1853, he was deeply troubled by political developments he saw among Tejanos. Almost certainly what he observed was the growth of the American Party, or Know-Nothing Party as it was popularly called. Preparing for a governor's election to be held in November 1854, Know-Nothing adherents made inroads among Te-

Guadalupe County Brands of the Navarro Family, 1848

José Antonio Navarro

Antonio George Navarro

Sixto Navarro

Celso Navarro

José Antonio and three sons registered their brands in Guadalupe County in 1848 while living at the San Geronimo Ranch.

janos by means of deception. Navarro's apprehension grew with each report he heard or read, and at what he probably witnessed firsthand. Attempts were made to win Tejano votes by staging fandangos with free coffee and liquor. From his San Geronimo Ranch, Navarro wrote to the editor of the San Antonio *Ledger* expressing his concern about the "political frenzy in Bexar County." He described a malevolent political scene, referring to precipitous footsteps, livid and menacing semblances, and the use of coercion and venality to steal votes. Navarro expressed the need to oppose this invasion saying, "[T]hese events affect me intimately, as one of the elders of the country, and as one interested in the best for my country and for the honor of my preferred county." He evidently hoped to inspire *Ledger* editors to publish more articles against the Know-Nothings, rather than have to use his influence directly. Rather than print his letter, he asked them to publish an article he had enclosed entitled "Freedom and Patriotism." Although Texas voters chose Democrat Elisha Pease for governor in November 1854, Know-Nothing candidates "swept the San Antonio city elections."[73] At that point Navarro spoke out against them publicly.

Another matter besides the Know-Nothing Party captured Navarro's attention in 1853. While reading the San Antonio *Ledger* on September 15, he noticed an article purporting to describe the early history of San Antonio. It contained substantial errors and omissions that he could not bear. Setting pen to paper, Navarro composed a lengthy and detailed response that the *Ledger* published in two installments during December. His son Ángel may have taken time from his law practice to translate the two pieces into English.

In them, the elder Navarro refuted an assertion in the September 15 article that the "blood of martyrs was not spilled in Texas until the Battle of the Alamo." He expressed esteem for the Tejano martyrs who, years before the Alamo, sacrificed their lives and property to win independence from Spain. Writing as an eyewitness, he vividly described the events of the revolution against Spain as they occurred in San Antonio from 1811 to 1813. He described in detail how the struggle for independence was lost at the Battle of Medina. Navarro recalled that years later, after Mexico became independent, Governor José Felix Trespalacios gathered bones from the battlefield and buried them with military honors. Navarro wrote, "I distinctly remember the following inscription written on a square of wood which was on the trunk of an oak tree:

> Here lies the brave Mexicans,
> Who sacrificed their wealth and lives
> Fighting ceaselessly against tyrants.[74]

Navarro suggested that he might continue his writing about Texas independence at a later date. This is indeed what happened, and he concluded his historical writings in 1857. An interesting, anonymous article that was evidently written by Navarro appeared in the Seguin *Mercury* in October 1853—the period during which he was writing his response to the San Antonio *Ledger* article. The Seguin *Mercury* article concerned Navarro family history. Entitled "Accident Determines Human Destiny," it related how in 1813 Lieutenant Antonio López de Santa Anna was "engaged to a young lady, a member of a family distinguished in the Texan struggle for independence [the Navarro family]." Santa Anna was caught in the act of forging an order for payment and punished; as a result of this disgrace the engagement was broken. The writer speculated that if Santa Anna had consummated the marriage, he would have been united with a family that contributed materially to the independence of Texas and thus he might have found himself on the side of liberty and the "Lone Star" instead of leading the armies of Mexico. Thus for a trifling sum of money, Santa Anna became a military despot. This account is very close to that recorded by Reuben M. Potter many years later in his sketch of José Antonio Navarro.[75] Potter undoubtedly heard Navarro tell this story while he served as Navarro's interpreter during the first legislature.

Toward the end of 1853, Navarro decided to sell his San Geronimo Ranch. It had been his family's primary residence since 1841 and included some of the best land in the area. Perhaps one reason for selling was the rising antagonism against Tejanos in the region. While Navarro would not have been a target of such hostility, the condemnations of his fellow Tejanos could not have been easy to endure. Monetary gain was no doubt another reason for selling. Navarro had already sold several portions of the ranch, and at the time of the final sale 6,509 acres remained from his original purchase of 8,856 acres. On December 19, 1853, Navarro sold the property to Alexander Ewing for $16,000, "in hand paid."[76] He had bought the two leagues in 1834 for 250 pesos; thus in nineteen years the land had increased handsomely in value.

What to do with the $16,000 in cash must have been a problem, because no banks existed in San Antonio at the time. Some mercantile stores provided banking services, and Navarro may have deposited the money in one of them for safekeeping. But, regardless of where he kept the money, Navarro was rich. Finally, thirty-seven years after returning penniless from exile in Louisiana, he had accomplished one of his primary goals: financial well-being.

Tax records for the year 1853 establish a benchmark for Navarro's wealth and allow for comparisons with other years. After the sale of the San Geronimo Ranch, the records show he still owned 23,970 acres of rural land plus nine town lots and one slave. The majority of the land lay in the four-league grant (17,712 acres) along the Atascosa River that he had obtained in 1832. Added to this were 6,258 acres acquired by headright claims and purchases. He also owned another tract of 4,605 acres on the Atascosa River, close to the Atascosa Ranch, and 1,653 acres on the Frio River. The tax collector listed Navarro's total assessed property value as $18,690, for which he paid $79.73 in county and state taxes.[77]

In 1854, while making the transition from the San Geronimo Ranch, Navarro made his last contribution as an elected official. Voters elected him as alderman to the San Antonio city council, where he served on the local ways and means committee. He offered resolutions for collecting delinquent taxes and, with another alderman, petitioned to have cer-

José Antonio Navarro's San Geronimo Ranch house, (circa 1930) located about seven miles north of Seguin, Texas. Courtesy of the Leon Studio Photo Collection, Seguin Heritage Museum.

tain streets opened. Sometime after 1847, Navarro's workers and sons had built a new house at the Atascosa Ranch to replace the one that had been destroyed by the Indian attack in 1840. Beginning in 1854, while Navarro maintained his home in San Antonio, he began spending more time at the ranch. In May, he registered his Atascosa Ranch brand at the Bexar County courthouse because Atascosa County was not yet organized.[78] Six years later, the census taker listed the Atascosa Ranch as Navarro's primary residence. Once more, he had found another venue for the American Dream, one where he confidently expected to enjoy a lengthy retirement as a respected statesman and businessman.

CHAPTER EIGHT

Elder Statesman, 1853–71

DESPITE HIS INTENTIONS, José Antonio Navarro remained active in public affairs until the end of his life, becoming deeply involved in the evolution of modern politics in the Lone Star State. Political parties—as statewide organizations linked through committees, with stated principles, and periodic conventions for the purpose of selecting and promoting candidates—did not emerge in Texas until the 1850s. Parties began to develop during the period 1853–57 in response to the Know-Nothing movement and the rise of slavery as an issue in Texas as a result of the passage of the 1854 Kansas-Nebraska Act. Because Democrats in the United States had approved annexation and they generally supported slavery, Texans felt a natural alignment with them. One political leader made it clear as early as 1845 that "We are all Democrats in Texas." But campaigns, more often than not, still proceeded on the basis of personalities rather than party in Texas, as they had since independence.[1]

The fears Navarro expressed in his 1853 letter reflected a political reality that the unorganized Democrats were slow to accept. Texans elected Elisha M. Pease governor that year, but not as a Democrat. In fact, some Democratic candidates withdrew so that Pease would have a better chance of defeating Know-Nothing and Whig candidates. The Know-Nothing Party won several seats in the legislature and a majority of the positions on the San Antonio city council. Many complacent Democrats continued to underrate the threat of the Know-Nothing Party, which they would come to identify with abolitionist agitation. But as the gubernatorial election of 1855 approached, they finally realized the danger and mobilized in preparation for the August election. More that twenty county conventions condemned the Know-Nothings and affirmed Democratic principles.[2]

While the Know-Nothings were indeed anti-Catholic and anti-Democrat, their members included some distinguished Anglo Texans. In their view, the party "stood for the preservation and perpetuation of the constitution and the federal union; opposed the formation of sectional parties; and believed in a strict construction of the constitution and the preservation of the rights of the states." Sam Houston and many other Unionists in Texas supported it for a time. In response, proclaiming a states' rights platform, the Democratic Party convention chose Pease to run for reelection against the Know-Nothing candidate, David G. Dickson. The Austin *Texas State Times* drew clear lines supporting the Democrats. In Bexar County, the pages of the San Antonio *Ledger* were filled with articles endorsing the Democratic ticket and denouncing Dickson and other Know-Nothings. Both the Democrats and Know-Nothings attempted to win the Tejano vote, and the Know-Nothings sponsored fandangos providing free coffee and liquor to further their effort. In response, Democrats reportedly told the Tejano community that voting for the Know-Nothing Party candidates was to risk excommunication and denial of burial in consecrated ground.[3]

Amid the angry turmoil, San Antonio leaders met to establish the Bexar County Democratic Party. Navarro was named to the organizing committee. The election fervor had the effect in San Antonio of unifying Anglos and Tejanos against a common enemy that was anti-Democrat and anti-Catholic. On June 30, 1855, "Democratic Mexico-Texans" approved ten resolutions supporting the Democratic Party and its candidates. They resolved "as native born Texans, members of the Catholic Church, and citizens of the United States" to oppose the "Know-Nothings" and all secret political associations. In an eloquent affirmation of political equality, they declared "That we neither seek nor desire for ourselves as Catholic citizens more rights than are enjoyed by others, we can not consent to have less." One of the resolutions of the "Mexico Texans" dated the first appearance of the Know-Nothings in Texas to as early as 1851 when it said, "The greater number of [them] are strangers of not over four years residence in our State."[4]

Eight well-known Tejanos signed these resolutions, and a committee of twelve Tejanos was appointed to go among the people of their community as advocates for the Democrats. Narciso Leal, who chaired the Tejano meeting, translated the resolutions and sent them to Samuel A. Maverick, chairman of the Democratic Committee of Bexar County to be read at a party meeting that same day in front of the courthouse on Main Plaza. The rally began at dusk. Various motions were read and petitions against the Know-Nothing Party were addressed to Governor Pease. One speaker at the rally mentioned Navarro's captivity in Mexico in his speech against anti-Catholicism. James C. Wilson, a prominent former legislator who had also been imprisoned in Mexico after the

Mier Expedition, said he had once seen an old man, looking through dungeon bars, who had struggled for the liberty Texans enjoyed. He said, "There pined Antonio Navarro, who cared naught for that priestly influence which you [the Know-Nothings] appear so much to dread." But unlike the Know-Nothings, "Even his enemies did not ask him to forsake his religion."[5]

While the politicking raged in San Antonio, Navarro sat at a table at his Atascosa Ranch and composed a passionate speech denouncing the Know-Nothing Party. While he focused on Tejanos, he intended the speech to be read by Anglo Americans as well. He did not present the speech in person; it was read on July 12 before a meeting of the Democratic "Mexico Texans of Béxar." The eloquent speech expressed great pleasure with the political awakening of Navarro's fellow Tejanos, and emphasized the themes of unity, pride in being citizens of the United States, devotion to the Catholic faith, and optimism for the future. They were some of Navarro's most moving words:

Fellow Citizens:—

At last you have arisen from the slumber of indifference! At last you have remembered that you are the sons of those Hispanic Mexican builders who founded our lovely city and erected the venerable church in which you manifest your adoration to God.

Divine Providence and momentous events have determined that this land, cleared by the venerable work of our ancestors, would now be part of another government of a remarkable people in the social order of human events.

This was not our fault, nor is it our misfortune. It was one of those dispositions from on High beyond our power to avert, wrapped within a mysterious favor, by which we became the adopted sons of a great and free nation.

You understand very well, my fellow citizens, that we could not be rebuked then, nor should we now be disloyal and ungrateful for the glorious results of our present favorable social condition.

Let us, then, be true Americans because of clear reason and our interests.

Let us discard all prior distinctions of foreignness. Let us forget ignoble jealousies of old nationalities. We live here; our firesides are here. This Government protects and supports us, provides and defends our rights.

A new and ominous party has raised its head to shame liberty. They call themselves *Know Nothing*, which motto signifies that they

Photograph of José Antonio Navarro. Courtesy of Casa Navarro State Historic Site.

do not understand just and generous sentiments; that they do not know other than thrusting a fratricidal knife in the breasts of those who made them free Americans.

The die is cast; the Mexico-Texans are Catholics and should be proud of the faith of their fathers and defend it inch by inch against such infamous aggression.[6]

Certainly no other Tejano leader could have expressed their position better.

Perhaps Navarro's old leg injury prevented him from traveling the thirty miles from his Atascosa Ranch to present the speech in person. Possibly preparations for the wedding of his daughter Josefa Elena to Daniel J. Tobin on July 30 prevented him from attending. Nevertheless, the passion of his words electrified the crowd and it was met with "thunderous applause." The San Antonio *Ledger* initially published the English version of the speech on the 14th. On July 21, the Spanish language newspaper, *El Bexareño*, printed the speech in Spanish while the *Ledger*, at the request of Navarro's friends, republished its version that same day.[7] It was an important speech that mobilized emotions just prior to the election; it emphasized reconciliation and setting aside past bitterness, and it appealed for unity against a common political opponent.

Beginning at eight o'clock on the evening of Saturday, August 4, San Antonio Democrats held a final rally before the election. An estimated 1,200–1,500 enthusiastic supporters gathered in Alamo Plaza with Maverick as master of ceremonies. Speeches were presented in English, Spanish, and German, while "music and enthusiastic cheering enlivened the scene. Seldom, if ever, has a political party gone into an election with more spirit, or come out of one with more quiet courtesy." About eleven o'clock, after musicians performed the *Star Spangled Banner*, the crowd dispersed.[8]

The San Antonio *Ledger* published the early Bexar County election returns on Saturday, August 11. Democrats enjoyed a comfortable lead in almost all precincts. More complete results followed a week later from the twenty-seven precincts across the county, from Cibolo to Fort Chadbourne, more than 200 miles to the northwest. Democrats swept the election, winning all contests by a margin of more than two to one in Bexar County. Of the several ranches that served as polling places, 63 votes, all for Democrats, were cast at the "Navarro Rancho" and about 125 at the Seguín ranch. After another week, with the vote counted from other counties, the San Antonio *Ledger* headline shouted "VICTORY!

Victory! Victory!" The final statewide vote for governor was 26,336 for the Democrat, Pease, and 17,965 for the Know-Nothing, Dickson. While Know-Nothings won several seats in the state legislature, secured the General Land Commissioner's office, and sent one member to Congress, the election of 1855 marked the beginning of the end of their party, which declined in both Texas and the nation. After 1857, it named no candidates for Texas state offices. Although the party remained a residual force in Texas politics for several years, its members eventually drifted away and joined the Democrats or, later, the emerging Republican Party.[9]

To celebrate their resounding victory, Democrats hosted a "Mammoth Barbecue and Mass Meeting of the Democracy" at Austin in early November 1855. The *Ledger* listed the names of about 200 invitees from Bexar County, including José Antonio Navarro and his son José Antonio George, Juan N. Seguín, and about fifty other Tejanos. The *Ledger* also extended a peace offering to the defeated Know-Nothings by saying, "Those who in the mean time, *secede* [emphasis added] from the secret conclaves are invited to attend." That is to say, those who abandoned their Know-Nothing affiliation would be welcomed. Misinterpretation of the word *secede*, as used in this article, led to a gross misunderstanding of José Antonio Navarro's views on secession. Naomi Fritz, in her master's thesis wrote: "José Antonio George, Navarro's oldest son, accompanied his father to the mass meeting held in Austin, to encourage secession from the Union." Fritz's thesis has been extensively quoted as support for the erroneous view that Navarro was a secessionist—but nothing could be further from the truth. As the *Ledger* stated, the purpose of the "Mammoth Barbecue" was to celebrate an election victory, not to agitate for secession. Although the Know-Nothings were a Unionist party, secession was not a critical issue in Texas at that time.[10]

Navarro in fact supported the Union. His speech against the Know-Nothing Party urged political unity and lauded fidelity to the "American banner." He opposed the Know-Nothings primarily because of their anti-Catholicism. He expressed his true views about secession again four years later, when it had indeed become a burning issue. In the 1859 election, Sam Houston was running for governor on the Constitutional Union ticket (also called the Independent Party or Union Democratic Party). No other prominent politician in Texas was a greater supporter of keeping Texas in the Union than Houston, and Navarro wholeheartedly supported these pro-Union views and denounced secessionists. Navarro contributed to Houston's cause by writing a letter of support on July 21 from the Atascosa Ranch. Addressed to Maverick, it was one of Navarro's last known written political statements; the San Antonio *Ledger* published an English translation in the July 26, 1859, issue:

> I VOTE FOR SAM HOUSTON—down with the demagogues who wish to destroy the American Union—down with the extreemists [*sic*] who wish to make every thing subserve [*sic*] their own ambitions, views, and personal hatreds. This is my faith: this is and shall ever be my wish. I remain your very ob't. servant, J. ANTONIO NAVARRO

He undoubtedly was referring to Governor Hardin R. Runnels, who was seeking reelection and Francis R. Lubbock, a candidate for lieutenant governor. Both of them advocated proslavery and anti-Union doctrines. Like many other Texans, Navarro obviously took offence at the firebrand rhetoric of these two men and other Democratic demagogues. Showing his disdain for such leaders, he wrote, "I do not wish to be a Democrat nor any other kind of revolutionary devil, but simply *a good American conservator of the Union* as admonished by the virtuous Washington [italics in the original]."[11]

Houston ran on his reputation as a hero of San Jacinto and a protégé of Andrew Jackson. He vowed to protect the western frontier against Indian attacks that occurred under Governor Runnels, and he won the 1859 election despite the damage done to the Union cause by John Brown's attack on Harper's Ferry that October. His election, however, was not a victory for Unionism, but simply a resurgence of the "personalism" that had often dominated Texas politics. His tenure as governor would be brief. After the election of Abraham Lincoln, southern states began to secede and initiate the armed rebellion against the United States that led to the Civil War. During February 1861 the Secession Convention in Austin voted to secede from the Union and Governor Houston was impeached. Neither José Antonio Navarro nor any other Navarros are listed as Bexar County delegates to the 1861 Texas Secession Convention. However, Ángel Navarro endorsed the Secession Ordinance as a member of the Texas House of Representatives, and he continued to serve in the House for another term after Texas joined the Confederate States of America. He later became the captain of Company H in the 8th Texas Infantry. In the same company were his brothers Celso Cornelio and Sixto Eusebio, a sergeant and a lieutenant respectively. José Antonio George served in a state unit at San Antonio for the Confederacy. So, while Houston refused to take an oath of loyalty to the Confederacy, Jose Antonio Navarro's son was among the legislators who removed him from office, and all four of his sons served in the

Photograph of José Antonio George Navarro (1819–99), published courtesy of Casa Navarro State Historic Site.

military forces of the Confederacy.[12] It must have been a hard time for the aging Tejano.

While secession and war must have been sources of much distress for Navarro, his personal life was quite comfortable. When in 1856 Atascosa County was created by the legislature, his son-in-law Daniel J. Tobin was elected as the first county clerk. Navarro donated land for

In 1855, José Antonio Navarro registered this cattle brand in Bexar County when he began operations at the Atascosa Ranch.

a county seat near present-day Amphion, to be called "Navatasco," a name combining Navarro and Atascosa. A temporary courthouse of adobe was ordered built, but within a year the county seat was moved to Pleasanton.

Headings on Navarro's letters indicate that he alternated between residing at the Atascosa Ranch and in San Antonio. George W. Kendall, his Santa Fe Expedition companion, visited him in 1856 and wrote to a friend that Navarro was living in "a new and tidy house he has constructed. His affairs prosper . . . and I can assure you he looks just as young as when you last saw him in Mexico." The "new and tidy house" was built next to a two-story building, which was likely one of his rental properties.[13] Despite the availability of this new house in town, the evidence indicates that Navarro spent much if not most of his time at his Atascosa Ranch.

During this time, Navarro changed his fundamental ranch operation. When he sold the San Geronimo Ranch, he discontinued the use of Mexican workers and bought more slaves. Atascosa County tax assessments show that Navarro owned from six to nine slaves from 1856 through 1864. Tax records for Bexar County demonstrate that few Tejanos owned slaves. Those who did included José Antonio Navarro, his brother Luciano, Erasmo Seguín, and Miguel Iturri. As previously noted, in 1850 Navarro owned one black youth at the San Geronimo Ranch, therefore the work of the ranch did not depend on slave labor. In addition to this slave, the San Geronimo workers included his sons Celso and Sixto, three adult laborers from Mexico, and Adriano Rubio, age fourteen. In comparison, Navarro's brother Luciano owned a nearby ranch that had three slaves in 1850: a male, age forty-five, a female, age forty-three, and an infant girl.[14]

By 1856, Navarro had acquired six "Negroes." Church records for that year include the baptisms of two daughters of a woman named Patsy, "a Negro of Don Antonio Navarro." Jesusa Patsy was six years old and María Patsy was born November 7, 1856. The baptismal records show that Navarro's wife, Margarita de la Garza, was godmother to both girls. Four years later another Navarro slave, Rosa Navarro, was baptized at the age of 32 at Atascosa Ranch.[15] In addition to the religious implications, the baptisms show that Navarro continued to honor the Catholic tradition in which he was born and raised, which acknowledged the basic humanity of persons of whatever racial combination, free or slave. In fact, Patsy was probably the wife of Henry, the slave that Navarro had apparently owned since he was a child at the San Geronimo Ranch.

The 1860 census provided a general overview for Atascosa County. A total of 103 slaves are listed, six of whom belonged to the Navarros. Only two other Tejanos in the county owned slaves. Navarro had one adult male slave, age twenty-two, who was almost certainly the man known after emancipation as Henry Navarro. He was the only male slave at Navarro's ranch in 1860; there were three females, who ranged in age from twenty-one to thirty, and three children, ages seven, three, and one. The ranch clearly was not a plantation such as those devoted to cotton found in other parts of the South. The slaves must have been dedicated primarily to basic farm tasks, such as caring for small livestock, milking cows, churning butter, and chores around the house. Sixty acres of land had been cleared for crops. Records for 1860 suggest the extent of the farm based on the resources Navarro owned: 100 milk cows, 12 oxen, 200 swine, and $100 worth of farming equipment.[16] As documented by various records, the farm produced corn, butter, and sweet potatoes.

It is not possible to know what the working and living conditions were for Navarro's slaves, but it is likely that he followed the somewhat lenient Spanish traditions described by Frederick Law Olmsted and Judge Jose María Rodríguez. Rodríguez was a Tejano who owned slaves. In his memoirs he claimed that "In this particular section of the state, there were not many slaves, because Mexican people as a rule do not believe in slavery. My family owned some slaves, but we worked them as [the] other servants and treated them kindly." Olmsted recorded similar evidence of in his dialog with an "Old Negro Man" near Seguin in 1857. He said he was born in Maryland and was taken to South Carolina, Tennessee, Arkansas, and finally Texas, where he was treated better than anywhere else he had lived:

> How did you like San Antonio?
> I never lived no-where I liked so well as San Antone.
> How did you get on with the Mexicans and Germans?
> Oh, very well; they're very civil people and always treated me well.

Anecdotal evidence notwithstanding, whatever humane treatment some slaves may have experienced, they suffered as a result of being deprived of the freedom to make basic choices in their own interest. Even slaves who were well treated sometimes ran away. It was often argued, before the Civil War and into the twentieth century, that slaves were essentially no worse off being in bondage than being free. Scholarly works expressing this viewpoint came to an abrupt end in 1956 with the publication of Kenneth Stampp's classic work, *The Peculiar Institution*, which demolished views of slavery as a paternalistic, benign system.[17]

At the same time Navarro was dedicating more attention his Atascosa Ranch, he returned to the historical writing he began four years before. At the end of his first venture into published historical writing in October 1853 Navarro wrote, "Perhaps later on this same subject may be continued." He felt compelled to resume his writing in order to confront growing disdain and violence toward Tejanos. With the authority of his knowledge and influence he reached out to Anglos to show them that they were building upon the foundation of independence won by earlier Tejano struggles. Navarro demanded respect for the descendants of the heroes who, two generations before, had sacrificed their lives and property fighting for freedom. His reading of Henderson K. Yoakum's 1856 *History of Texas* also motivated him to write. Yoakum cited him as a source, but he found various errors in this work that displeased him and wanted to make corrections. Navarro's second installment as a writer reveals a change in his attitude toward Anglos. In 1853 he was generally conciliatory and upbeat, as he was in his 1855 speech against the Know-Nothings. His stated purpose then was to inform recently arrived Anglos about Tejano history. In 1857, he denounced the intolerable outrages committed against Mexican Americans and lashed out at callous and murderous Anglo Americans.[18]

Navarro's expression of indignation was addressed to those Anglo Americans he thought would be receptive to his message.

> I do not write for the heartless nor for the egoists—to whom the glories and misfortunes of men of another origin and language matter little or not at all. I do it for the humanitarian and cultured who understand how to respect and sympathize with the tribulations of a valiant people who have struggled, in the midst of their own ignorance guided only by an instinct for their liberty. . . . I write in order to inform our Americans, however indignant some of them among us may be, who with base aggressive pretexts want to uproot from this classic land its legitimate people who are descendants of those [earlier generations of Tejanos].

He was enraged by the "aggressive pretexts" used to commit injustices and the violence that had occurred between 1855 and 1857, which had resulted from what was known as the Cart War. Aggressive Anglo American teamsters used intimidation and violence to force Tejano cart men out of the lucrative business of transporting goods between the Gulf Coast and interior settlements. One particular atrocity Navarro condemned was the murder of Antonio Delgado, who was "riddled by bullets from the rifle of an American bastard." Delgado, a veteran of the Battle of Medina and the Siege of Béxar, was a victim of the Cart War. Another tragic death Navarro lamented was the murder of Consolación Leal, "a heroine of those days, [who] died a few months ago killed by a Spaniard." Leal was murdered at Graytown, Texas, on May 28, 1857.[19] Navarro's reference to her as a "heroine of those days" suggests that she was one of the women who had been held in La Quinta in 1813.

Navarro concluded with a poignant appeal for appreciation and understanding of the sacrifices and losses of the Tejanos who fought for Texas and won its independence, only to see it taken over by foreigners who knew little or nothing of their struggles. The corollary to Navarro's rage was his sense of profound loss: "To complete the picture of misfortune, the few descendants who survive in San Antonio are disappearing, murdered in full view of a people who boast of their justice and excellence." He expressed hope that his work would stir Anglo Americans "to treat with more respect this race of men who, as the legitimate proprietor of this land, lost it together with their lives and their hopes, to follow in the footsteps of those very ones who enjoy the land in the midst of peace and abundance."[20]

Navarro's *Apuntes Históricos*, as they were entitled, qualify him as the first Tejano historian. His work preceded memoirs written by Juan N. Seguín and Antonio Menchaca.[21] While Navarro's writing resembles a memoir, it is truly a history: a disciplined study of past events focused on the revolutionary years of 1810 to 1813. A study of the text shows that for source material he used his own experiences, first- and secondhand accounts told to him, and documentary sources. He concentrated on the details of a critical period of Tejano history that was of little concern to historians until much later when pioneers such as Herbert Eugene Bolton, Carlos E. Castañeda, and Alessio Robles began to write extensively about the history of Texas under Spain and Mexico.

Despite the outrage expressed in his *Apuntes*, in early March of 1859 Navarro traveled from his Atascosa Ranch to San Antonio to take part in the Texas Independence Day celebration. He and Antonio Menchaca were given seats of honor on the platform where Maverick read aloud the Texas Declaration of Independence. Then I. L. Hewitt gave a speech

that was interrupted by applause when he referred to the two Tejano heroes. It was a dubious tribute, for they suffered in silence when Hewitt
also made derogatory comments about Mexicans in general.[22]

Navarro had been retired from political office for several years,
spending much of his time in seclusion at his ranch. Nonetheless, his
reputation continued to be well known on both sides of the border. In
the spring of 1860, while staying in San Antonio, he received a letter from Santiago Vidaurri, governor of Nuevo León, asking for help.
Vidaurri's letter has not been found, but the reply indicates that Vidaurri wanted closer relations with Texas. Navarro politely declined to
assist for various practical reasons: "I cannot have the pleasure to offer
you my services because my age, incapacity, the distance, and my nationality form a quadruple alliance against my desires [to help you]." But
Navarro, showing fondness for his former country, did add that if he
were able to do anything to aid its progress, he would happily do so.[23]

Life was not always peaceful at Atascosa Ranch; the potential for
Indian raids was a constant source of worry. Early in 1861, Indian
raids threatened the residents of Atascosa County. Navarro, supported
by other citizens, sent the following desperate appeal for help to San
Antonio on March 12: "We are satisfied that they intend to descend
upon us, and as we are entirely unprepared to meet them and the consequences may be fearful." He added, "We are without horses, arms
and ammunition. Give us them, if you cannot come to our assistance,
we ask in the name of humanity." On the same day, Navarro sent a
letter to "My dear son Ángel," saying that "We are in eminent peril."
Describing Atascosa County residents, he said, "a complete stupor and
a cold indifference seems to prevail here amongst our people such as I
had never seen before." He emphasized the urgency of the threat and
asked for Ángel's help in mobilizing assistance. "If a patriotic effort is
not made speedily to chastise these Indians in their first incursions," he
concluded, "all Western Texas will be ruined, and those that survive will
witness a fearful and destructive Indian War." It does not appear that
the feared attacks took place, but the threat was real. The San Antonio
Alamo Express published many articles during March about Indian attacks to the west of San Antonio near Bandera and Uvalde. On the same
day that Navarro's warning was published, another article reported that
people were fleeing the western settlements and that "Never was in the
whole history of the frontier so great a panic." A party of ten Indians
was seen in Atascosa County in April 1861, but no attacks on persons or
livestock were reported.[24]

While Navarro and other Atascosa County residents worried about

*Ángel Navarro (1827–76), son
of José Antonio Navarro. Prints
and Photographs, #1991/1337-102,
Texas Album Collection, courtesy
Texas State Library & Archives
Commission.*

*Photograph of Wenseslao
Eusebio "Sixto" Navarro
(1833–1905), published
courtesy of Casa Navarro
State Historic Site.*

Indian attacks, leaders in Austin and San Antonio committed Texas to war. The legislature approved the Secession Convention, and when it submitted an ordinance of secession to a popular vote on February 23, the measure passed by an overall margin of three to one. Bexar County voters were less supportive of disunion, approving it by a narrower vote of 919 to 730; in Atascosa County, secession passed 145 to 91. Heavily armed Texans led by Benjamin McCulloch rode into San Antonio and surrounded the Alamo, which was being used as a federal armory. Without firing a shot, General David E. Twiggs surrendered to McCulloch, and within days a Confederate flag was hoisted over the Alamo. Six weeks later, news arrived of the rebel attack on Fort Sumter in South Carolina that precipitated the Civil War.[25]

Three of José Antonio Navarro's sons served in the Confederate army. José Antonio George remained in San Antonio as a member of the militia. Ángel Navarro entered the Confederate army as a captain even though he had been a member of the Union Democratic Party that opposed secession. His service was brief, however, for he became enmeshed in a conflict that was evidently based on discrimination against Mexican Americans. Colonel Andrew G. Dickinson brought charges against Ángel and scheduled him to be court marshaled in Houston on November 27, 1863.[26] Ángel did not wait for Confederate justice. He fled San Antonio and traveled to San Fernando de Rosas (present-day Melchor Múzquiz) in Coahuila, from where he wrote to Governor Santiago Vidaurri of Nuevo León. He explained that he had abandoned Texas because of unjust treatment by Confederate authorities, who treated Tejanos unfairly, and he declared his intent to settle in Mexico. Governor Vidaurri replied with a brief note expressing pleasure that Ángel had come to live south of the Rio Grande. Ángel was fortunate to cross the border ahead of Confederate vigilantes, like those who in August 1862 killed a number of fleeing German Texans near Comfort, Texas, and summarily executed others during the succeeding months. Interestingly, Ángel's brother Sixto was promoted from lieutenant to succeed him as the captain of Company H, in which their younger brother Celso also served as a sergeant. Later, both Sixto and Celso joined Colonel Santos Benavides's Confederate regiment on the Rio Grande.[27]

As enthusiasm for the Civil War was just gathering steam in San Antonio, Margarita de la Garza's health began to fail. She suffered several periods of sickness, and in June 1861 she became seriously ill. In addition to illness, she must have been saddened to see her sons Sixto, Celso, and Ángel enlist in the Confederate army, preparing to march to faraway battlefields. Realizing that she would probably not recover, Margarita sent for family members to witness her verbal testament. Luciano Navarro, his wife Teodora, their daughter Angela Navarro Cooke, and others gathered around Margarita's bedside around June 24. Luciano stated that the declaration took place at two o'clock in the afternoon "at her usual residence on Laredo Street." She died two weeks later, during the oppressive heat of the San Antonio summer. It is easy to imagine family members taking turns cooling her with fans during these last days. On August 2, Luciano, Teodora, and Angela appeared in a Bexar County court and testified under oath about Margarita's disposition of property. With Ángel Navarro acting as their translator, they stated that Margarita had declared that her husband, José Antonio Navarro, was her sole heir, and they added that she believed all her children were well satisfied with this disposition. Demonstrating trust in her husband, she said "she and they had full confidence in their father who has always

Luciano Navarro (right), brother of José Antonio, with his wife, Teodora, and daughter Amelia. Courtesy of Barbara Dove.

treated them well and provided well for them."[28] Margarita was one of the first to be buried in the San Fernando Cemetery Number One just west of the city. Evidently the Campo Santo, located three blocks north of her residence, was full. Navarro's undoubtedly great sorrow at the passing of his wife of forty-five years must be left to the imagination.

The fact that Navarro apparently wrote nothing until five years after Margarita's death suggests that he lived quietly on his ranch during the Civil War. This is confirmed by the account of a nearby rancher. This rancher was a former Texas Ranger whose ranch was also located on the Atascosa River. He often visited with Navarro and later wrote a memoir, in which he noted that

> Navarro spent much of his time at his ranch on the Atascosa [during the Civil War]. It was about three miles below my ranch and I became a frequent guest at his house and never tired of listening to the stories he told me of his early life and of early days in Texas. He was finely educated and though he could read English and understood it thoroughly, he spoke the language brokenly and always conversed in Spanish unless it was necessary to speak English.[29]

Although San Antonio functioned as a center of Confederate activity in Texas, it was untouched by the clash of armies. In fact, little military action took place in Texas during the Civil War other than skirmishes in South Texas and on the blockaded coast. Confederate Texas supplied soldiers and cattle for the war effort rather than battlefields. After the war ended, Navarro was fortunate to see his three sons return unharmed. Sixto and Celso, who had moved his family to Atascosa County before the war began, probably returned to Atascosa Ranch to resume their work as stock raisers. By September 1865, Ángel Navarro had returned from exile in Mexico and been reunited with his wife and children. Taking advantage of President Andrew Johnson's general amnesty of the previous May, which restored the rights of citizenship to many who simply took an oath of loyalty to the United States Constitution and its laws, Ángel applied for and was granted permission to resume his law practice.[30]

The Atascosa Ranch produced not only livestock, but also substantial amounts of crops such as corn and sweet potatoes on its sixty acres of improved land. These harvests enabled the ranch to be largely self sufficient. Because he owned a vast amount of land devoted to cattle raising, area residents recognized Navarro as one of Atascosa County's most prominent ranchers. His sons, however, oversaw the routine management of the livestock. While Navarro did supervise the farm operations,

Photograph of Celso Cornelio Navarro (1830–1903), published courtesy of Casa Navarro State Historic Site.

he also owned rental properties in San Antonio that required regular attention. Thus he wore two hats, as a gentleman rancher and as a respected San Antonio landlord, and he moved easily between these two worlds. A letter written in spring 1866 reveals how he managed his priorities at a time when his attention was needed both at the ranch and in town. Cash rents on his properties were due at the beginning of April. In addition, he wanted to increase some of the rents, which required negotiations, and some repairs were needed. At the same time, early April was the prime time for planting crops. Navarro placed a higher priority on overseeing the crucial farm work and delegated the rental management for that month to his nephew Alejandro Ruiz in exchange for a small commission.[31]

Navarro's instructions to Ruiz reveal that he was still sharp and active at age seventy-one. On April 5, he wrote to Ruiz asking him to collect the rents, explaining that he was too busy to come to town because "[a]t the present time I am engaged in the weeding and the planting." Navarro knew to the penny the amount of rents due: $114.00. "This will be $102.60, after having deducted your percentage which will be $11.40." He conveyed very detailed instructions to Ruiz but also allowed him to make judgment calls:

> You should understand, and keep in mind, that Mr. E. F. Gilbert (the one in the store on the corner) was paying me, according to our agreement, $25.00 rent only until the end of March, now just finished. Consequently, if you find that rents are increasing you will formally notify him that, now and in the future, he will have to pay five or ten dollars more according to what you decide. But if you see that there is no demand for rental buildings, and that it is doubtful that there will be better rents and leasing, then you will let him continue the $25.00. I will be content with what you decide to do.

Navarro urged Ruiz to raise the rent on another renter, Frances Zaguán, who was paying the "pittance of eight pesos per month." He also gave Ruiz clear instructions about how to repair falling boards in the back room of Gilbert's house.[32] Sixto carried the letter to Ruiz from the ranch, with instructions to turn the rent money over to him.

After the Civil War, Navarro seemed to be little concerned about participating in the political events of Reconstruction. The war's end apparently had little impact on stock raising and farming at the Atascosa Ranch, and political conflict was minimal. At the beginning of Reconstruction, President Andrew Johnson, following the example of Abraham Lincoln, hoping for a peaceful reconciliation, provided for lenient treatment of former Confederates but also continued to support emancipation. After the Emancipation Proclamation was implemented in Texas on June 19, 1865, Navarro likely negotiated with his former slaves to remain at the ranch and work for wages or for shares of crops, beef, pork, and other farm products. One former slave, Henry Navarro, was listed among other Navarros at the ranch in Atascosa County in 1866, where he and his family evidently remained for two or three years after emancipation. By and large, life at the Atascosa Ranch probably went on with little change in operation. The experience of Felix Haywood, who worked on a San Antonio area ranch as a slave and a freedman, was likely similar to that of Navarro's former slaves. He said that after emancipation, "The ranch went on just like it always had before the war."[33] Navarro, at age seventy-one, with freedmen for workers, had little motivation to be engaged in politics in order to deal with postwar issues.

But during the next two years, while Navarro managed his workers at the ranch, events in the larger world moved swiftly and would eventually lure him back into the political arena. The lenient policies of President Johnson ended when Republicans committed to fundamental changes in the South became a majority in Congress. Under Johnson, many Texans with conservative views had been elected to the state legislature. They wanted Texas restored to the Union with as little change as possible from the status quo antebellum. A series of bills from the legislature denied civil rights to the freedmen, including the right to vote, hold office, serve on juries, testify in court against whites, or attend public schools. This was challenged in 1867 when Radical Republicans came to power in Congress in numbers sufficient to override any presidential veto. In an era known as "Radical Reconstruction" they imposed military rule and disfranchised all voters, candidates, and public office holders unless they could meet conditions set by the "Ironclad Oath," which required that one had never participated directly or indirectly in the "Rebellion." Under these terms Texans elected to public office under the previous general amnesty were removed, and the electorate that had been restored by the amnesty was abolished in one stroke.[34] Stunned by this turn of events—that their former slaves could vote while they could not—conservatives began to mobilize to oppose these measures.

While these events transpired, Navarro moved to San Antonio, where he found himself closer to the political action. Around 1868, he had given up the pastoral life he obviously enjoyed so much, left the ranch house in the care of Sixto, and moved to his house on Laredo Street.[35] A combination of reasons probably forced this decision: age, health issues, and the fact that his long-time ranch workers, the Henry Navarro family, were beginning to work for themselves. He returned to San Antonio at a time when Texas conservatives of various factions were in the process of reforming the Democratic Party, which had been torn asunder by the war and Reconstruction. Opposition to Radical Republican measures came from several disunited conservative groups that would subsequently unite with the national Democratic Party. Navarro lent his support as an elder statesman to one of these groups, a loosely knit ad hoc movement that assembled in San Antonio to campaign for candidates to represent them in the impending constitutional convention, set for June 1868.

Navarro joined a conservative faction led by Samuel A. Maverick, who organized them in accord with a movement begun in Galveston and Houston and calling itself the Conservative Union Reconstructionists. The first meeting in San Antonio took place at the end of January 1868. Maverick was elected chairman, and Navarro was chosen as one of numerous vice presidents, as a member of the election committee, and as a senior member of the executive committee. In their discussions, the members did not adhere to the usual conservative hard-line position that denied rights and suffrage to freedmen. Among other considerations, they asserted, "That while we are unalterably opposed to negro supremacy, we are in favor of securing to them the full protection of all their rights of person and property, under just laws bearing equally on all." They unanimously approved six resolutions, to be designated the party's county platform, and announced the selection of two candidates to represent Bexar and nine nearby counties. The two were Charles F. Fisher and A. E. Carothers, "original Union men . . . who can take the Iron Clad test Oath." Fisher in fact had served on the city council during and after the war, which excluded him under the terms of the oath. Apparently that did not matter to his fellow conservatives, who were much more interested in the fact that both of their candidates "believe in the supremacy of the white race—they wish to see the reins of government retained in the hands of white men."[36]

To advertise the conservative position, a circular was published under the names of Navarro and others on February 4th and 5th. It urged voters to support their candidates, who were "uncompromisingly opposed to negro supremacy and the degradation of the white man." The circular maintained that Conservative Union Reconstructionists did not dispute the right of freedmen to vote; after all, "by enactment of Congress he is at present in possession of the elective franchise." Instead, it elaborated upon the accomplishments of white men, starting with the Revo-

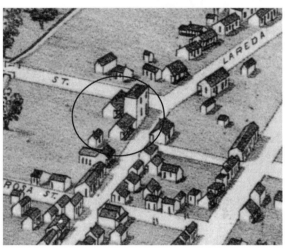

ABOVE: *Section from a 1872 bird's eye view map of San Antonio. The buildings of the old Navarro House, probable birthplace of José Antonio Navarro, were located at the lower-left corner of Military Plaza. See detail below. Courtesy of the Witte Museum, San Antonio, Texas.*

LEFT: *This detail from the 1872 Koch map of San Antonio shows the buildings of the Navarro home site much as they exist at present. Courtesy of the Witte Museum, San Antonio, Texas.*

lutionary War, and forecast the troubles that would come "if negro-rule predominates." They feared being permanently reduced to a political rank below blacks, and thus their main purpose was to elect delegates to the convention who would resist the continued disenfranchisement of former Confederates. To challenge them, San Antonio Republicans nominated James P. Newcomb and Edward Degener, who opposed any constitutional provision that did not disfranchise former Confederates. Moreover, both had an axe to grind. Newcomb had been forced to flee

San Antonio during the war, while Degener had been jailed for his dissent. They had no sympathy for conservative anxieties. In addition, the Radical Republicans included several Tejanos, notably, E. Mondragón and Juan A. F. Chávez, a former legislator. The election, held in mid-February, resulted in a resounding defeat for the conservatives. In Bexar County, Newcomb and Degener received 1,552 votes to the 557 cast for the Conservative Union Reconstructionists.[37] This effectively ended the Conservative Union Reconstructionists as an active political entity.

The various political parties active in Reconstruction Texas vied with each other to shape the political future of the state, and the stakes were highest when it came time to draft a new state constitution, which Texans were obligated to do as a condition of rejoining the Union. The Constitutional Convention met in June 1868; of the ninety delegates, most represented various Republican interests and opposed conservatives. Having been largely shut out of the Constitutional Convention, conservatives held their own political convention at Waco in July, when the Conservative Union Reconstructionists officially joined with the national Democratic Party. In a public declaration they said that Texas conservatives believed the National Democratic Party guaranteed constitutional liberties and avoided "radical rule, anarchy, and despotism."[38] The conservative faction that Navarro joined had in less than a year merged into the mainstream Democratic Party.

During the 1868 Constitutional Convention, acrimonious conflicts erupted that divided the Republican Party and prevented the convention from completing its task. When the delegates reassembled in December, they considered problems of lawlessness and railroads, but the question of dividing the state also emerged as a focus of debate. Navarro's stand on this issue was to be the final political effort of his career. Hundreds of plantations had flourished in East Texas, which was thus populated, in the opinion of many, with a multitude of uncompromising rebels. For this reason Radical Republicans, like Degener, fervently sought the creation of a state of West Texas with San Antonio as its capital. Various proposals for dividing the state were advanced, including using the Colorado River as the boundary between east and west. The strategy behind the division plan was to integrate the state of West Texas into the United States and prevent the return of East Texas to the Union for as long as possible.[39]

Republicans at the Constitutional Convention selected six commissioners to go to Washington to advocate for the division of Texas. The proponents of the idea had even drafted a constitution for West Texas.

Democrats in San Antonio organized to oppose them and held a public meeting to consider the issue of dividing the state on February 9, 1869. Navarro and others spoke against division; no one spoke in favor. Resolutions approved at the meeting questioned the credentials of the Republican commissioners, and the Democrats appointed Alexander Rossy as their own representative to go to Washington and oppose the division of Texas. Two days later Navarro "addressed the Mexican population . . . and heartily opposed the division scheme." This was the last known public speech of Navarro's long political career. In the end, a coalition of conservative and moderate Republicans defeated the radicals in the Convention, and so the 1869 Constitution had no provisions for dividing the state, disenfranchising former Confederates, or other measures favored by the radicals.[40]

Historian Arnoldo De León considered Navarro's role with the conservatives and evaluated his career concerning civil rights and slavery. He noted Navarro's support for slave owners in the Coahuila and Texas legislature of 1827, his successful effort for Tejano voting rights in 1845, and his ownership of slaves. In an attempt to resolve the apparent contradictions in Navarro's long career, De León justifiably described him as a complex figure who could assume diverse roles, depending on the circumstances. He asserted that depictions of Navarro as an American hero by some or as an "Uncle Tom" by others, were erroneous. However, after examining newspaper articles pertaining to Conservative Union Reconstructionists, De León concluded that Navarro "sent his boys to fight for the Confederacy, and emerged as a leading white supremacist in the San Antonio area during Reconstruction."[41]

This viewpoint is not an accurate characterization of José Antonio and greatly overstates the case of his sons' military service. A more critical analysis of the newspaper evidence cited by De Léon leads to different conclusions. For one thing, Navarro did not "send his sons off to war." The Confederate conscription law of 1862 required all men between the ages of eighteen and thirty-five to enlist for three years of active service, and the upper age limit was eventually extended. The Navarro brothers were men of military age who made their own decisions within the context of clearly defined rules. Moreover, one son, Ángel, deserted the Confederate army and fled to Mexico. José Antonio Navarro did support a conservative faction, all the members of which no doubt presumed the superiority of the white race. However, to characterize him as a "leading white supremacist" as a result of his brief participation in the electioneering by the Conservative Union Reconstructionists is grossly misleading. No evidence has been found to suggest that Navarro was ever a zealous racist, or that he (or other members of the group) participated in or supported the racial violence prevalent elsewhere in Texas. The primary purpose of the Conservative Unionists was to elect delegates in an effort to regain the vote for disenfranchised former Confederates, not to deny civil rights to blacks. Navarro grew up and lived among persons of mixed race and free blacks on the basis of political equality. They were citizens endowed with civil rights under Spanish and Mexican governments. He vigorously sought the right to vote for his constituents who were persons of color in 1845. The portrayal of Navarro as a white supremacist fails in the face of these facts.

Navarro's reputation among the people of San Antonio remained undiminished in his old age. In the fall of 1869, a number of citizens published a newspaper article asking him to run for state senator. Evidently, they hoped for an experienced, trustworthy man to represent them in the political turbulence for which there was no end in sight. The following day, Navarro answered in the same newspaper by thanking his fellow citizens for their confidence and support, but he declined the honor, saying that his old age and chronic illnesses would prevent him from serving. In fact, Navarro was still active in mind and body. In the summer of 1869, Narciso Leal and other friends wrote a vivid description of the venerable seventy-four–year-old statesman:

> To see José Antonio, at the age at which we write these paragraphs, is to recall the saying: "So young, so old." His appearance is of the Spanish type. He has an aquiline nose, a pure ruddy color of face, and the uniform whiteness of his complete head of hair delicately frames his wide forehead. But nothing of his physiognomy shows the excesses of premature age. To the contrary, his sane judgment and his intelligence—clear and quick to perceive—his natural voice, energetic and sonorous when he raises it, with its facile action and accent, enables the least observant person to see that José Antonio Navarro is in the prime of his old age. Consequently he possesses a high level of energy needed to develop himself with more perfected regularity—amazing results of a frugal life balanced by wholesome customs.

In addition to his frugal life the writers referred to his "scrupulous modesty," which suggests that his household furnishings were correspondingly modest. Indeed, they said that to look at Navarro's furnishings was to see immediately that he was "a man of simple and unchanging customs whose life embodied both knowledge and recreation such that he enjoyed without conflict the dry austerity of science and lively friendships." [42]

Navarro did not spend his last years alone. His youngest daughter, Josefa, cared for him at the house on Laredo Street during his last years. In June 1870, a census taker visited the house and recorded its inhabitants: Josefa, her husband, Daniel J. Tobin, their three children, and seventy-four-year-old "Josari," probably an affectionate, familiar name for Navarro. In 1869, Luciano died, leaving José Antonio Navarro as the last family member who had lived through the political and social changes Texas had experienced from the days of the revolution against Spain in 1811 through the end of Reconstruction and the readmission of Texas to the Union. He stood alone as the Navarro family patriarch, the last pilgrim who followed the trail of Texas from Spanish times through five changes in government, during which he exerted his leadership and influence on behalf of all the people of Texas. As a dedicated Unionist, Navarro was undoubtedly pleased to see Texas readmitted to the United States in March 1870.

Toward the end of Navarro's life, both Tejanos and Anglos honored him. The Alamo Literary Society praised him at their November 1870 meeting after paying tribute to David Crockett and William B. Travis. They said, "none shines brighter, or has left a more enduring record, than one of the sons of the Alamo city—Don Antonio Navarro. The welfare of our city seems to have been the pole star of this great man's thoughts and actions, and it matters not whether amidst the council halls of the Texas Republic or spending his days in the dungeon of a Mexican prison, he was always our firm and faithful friend."[43]

Early in 1870, Navarro began to verbally assign portions of the Atascosa Ranch to his sons and then began formalizing the distribution of his estate in a will. Of his seven children, two daughters—María Casimira and María Gertrudis—had already died. He wrote the main part of his will during February 1870, distributing his ranch and town properties among the five surviving children: José Antonio George, Sixto, Celso, Ángel, and Josefa. The ranch land totaled 19,898 acres, which included land on the Medina and Uvalde rivers. Navarro gave each of his sons equal, undivided portions of this acreage, less 606 acres for Josefa. While each son received 4,823 acres, this was determined by simple division; the brothers would have to negotiate among themselves to determine exactly which part of the land went to whom. Navarro left the house on Laredo Street, its furnishings, a kitchen, and other adjacent buildings to Josefa. He gave the other town properties to his sons, again in equal, undivided shares. He was particularly concerned about the old Navarro house on Flores Street. He no doubt felt a particular emotional attachment to it because it was probably his birthplace. Nevertheless, Navarro appealed to his sons on a business basis. He implored them not to sell the house for at least eight to ten years since it would probably double in value. Finally, he named his five children as executors of the will, in the hope that they would work harmoniously in the division of the estate. [44]

Navarro knew his indeterminate land division could lead to an unseemly squabble over property. A conflict seems have surfaced right away over which son would get the part of the Atascosa ranch containing the house and farm. Navarro suggested the simple solution of drawing lots; the winner would have to reimburse the other three for their portions of its value. He repeatedly enjoined the children to treat each other in a brotherly manner so as to show respect for the memory of their father. Not content with mere verbal appeals for brotherly comportment, Navarro put some teeth in his will. He pointedly emphasized, with a not very subtle threat, that he was not yet signing it so that he would have "the option that I will be able to remove, add, or rewrite the clauses that I have already written."[45]

Navarro's health deteriorated and it is clear that he suffered a serious affliction of the mouth. On September 24, he decided to sign his will, noting, "I fear that the results of this surgical operation that Dr. [Ferdinand L.] Herff will perform on my mouth may be fatal. Thus [my will] will take effect if God does not wish to prolong the days of my life." Again he added ominously that he might "decide to write a new disposition of my said testament." Although his health was steadily becoming worse, he nevertheless had the energy in November 1870 to complete an agreement with Fritz Schreiner for renting the old Navarro house, at the corner of Flores and Commerce streets, for two years at $75 per month. Navarro also had a long memory when it came to debts owed. A few days later he filed a claim for $113 on behalf of his brother-in-law, Mateo Ahumada, a debt that dated from 1837. The state auditor approved the claim on the day it was received.[46]

Disagreement among his children over the land distribution, in fact, did emerge. Josefa wanted her 606 acres to be located on Agua Negra Creek on the north side of the property, which one or more of her brothers evidently opposed. The conflict was sufficiently troublesome that on December 27 Navarro added a final clause to his will, writing, "I am dying. I care . . . about your honor, your obedience and affection for

Anonymous photograph of Josefa Elena Navarro de Tobin family. From right to left:
Josefa Elena Navarro de Tobin (1835–1913); Josefa's daughter, María Inez Tobin de
Cass; Maria Inez's daughter, Celina Gertrudes Cass de Carillo; Celina's daughter, Ester.
Published courtesy of Casa Navarro State Historic Site (donated by Marie Smith).

your father. I order, beg, and hope that you do not speak or murmur any words about my final determination." He affirmed that Josefa indeed was to have the land that she wanted: "I now declare by this clause that she may take these 606 acres, I repeat that she may take them, right in the said springs of the Agua Negra. I have assigned it to her, and between noble brothers and sister there is no need for differences [of opinion]. I order it like this so that it will be accomplished." Then before seven witnesses Navarro signed the addendum to his will and entrusted it to Josefa to keep "until the time it is needed." His weak handwriting in this final clause is witness to his rapidly faltering health as he lay on his deathbed.[47]

On Saturday, January 14, 1871, at fifteen minutes past one o'clock in the morning, José Antonio Navarro passed away. Preparations had already been made. On the morning of his death a requiem mass, for the repose of his soul, was celebrated in San Fernando Cathedral at ten o'clock. The funeral was conducted at his Laredo Street house at four o'clock in the afternoon of the same day. His obituary in the San Antonio *Herald,* published the next day, read:

> It is with profound regret that we announce the death of Don José Antonio Navarro, the venerable citizen, the revered patriot, and the honest man, who expired at his residence in this city on yesterday (Saturday) morning 14th last, at fifteen minutes past one o'clock, aged 76 years.
>
> To none of her greatest statesmen, nor to her many eminent patriots, is Texas more indebted for her existence as a Republic, than Don José Antonio Navarro, who ever retiring in his manners, but ever firm and unflinching, and always honest, unselfish and unswerving in his devotion to the course of Texas Independence proved in his support a tower of strength.

The San Antonio *Herald* obituary continued, saying Navarro lived and died a true Democrat, that his death brought the deepest sorrow across the community, and that his memory would be honored with the deepest respect. Observers reported Navarro's funeral procession to be one of the largest ever seen in San Antonio.[48] The funeral cortège made its way through Laredito to Cemetery Number One, east of San Antonio, where he was laid to rest next to his wife, Margarita de la Garza.

Within a generation of Navarro's death, his children sold most of the land they inherited and all but Celso moved away from San Antonio. Josefa, widowed in 1871, sold the house in Laredito in 1876

José Antonio Navarro and Margarita de la Garza gravestone, San Fernando Cemetery No. 1, San Antonio, Texas. Courtesy of Alvin Gerdes.

and moved to Arizona with her three children. From Arizona she relocated to Los Angeles, where she died in 1912 or 1913. Ángel moved to Laredo, where he was active as a lawyer and judge. He was assassinated in 1876. José Antonio George settled in Zapata County around 1879, after the death of his wife, Juana. He became a county judge and lived close to his Navarro relatives, including his daughter Isidora and her husband, until his death in the 1890s. In 1894, Sixto sold the part of the Atascosa Ranch on which his father's house stood and moved to Laredo. Apparently he later returned to San Antonio, where he died in 1905, two years after Celso had passed away.[49] By the time of the death of his children, the land legacy of José Antonio Navarro had dissipated. None of the land of the Atascosa Ranch is known to remain in the possession of any descendants.

The death of José Antonio Navarro marked the end of an extraordinary era during which the destiny of Texas was determined. It would be fair to say that in Texas, for Tejanos, the fifty years from 1821–71 was the Age of Navarro. More than any other Texan, he was a continuous, influential participant in the history of Texas as a Spanish colony, as part of Coahuila and Texas, as a republic, and as a state in the United States. A wealth of Texas history was written from his memories of more than sixty years of experience as observant youth, merchant, political figure, influential citizen, and rancher. Navarro left a priceless legacy in the form of his legislative record, his personal and political correspondence, and his published writings. A tangible legacy of Navarro preserved for all to see is his former home in San Antonio at 228 South Laredo Street. In 1960, the San Antonio Conservation Society saved it from demolition and restored it. The three limestone and adobe structures that comprise the site are now preserved as Casa Navarro State Historic Site, operated and maintained by the Texas State Historical Commission.

Navarro never swerved from his decision to support Texas independence nor his resolve to maintain Texas in the Union. He extolled the virtues of statehood and hoped for a future that would open the way to the American Dream for all Texans. At the same time, he never deviated from his adherence to the language, culture, and values of his Mexican origin. To the end he was a true Mexican American who sought for and reached the American Dream—not as a goal reached and then conspicuously displayed like a prize, but as a continuing struggle in the face of innumerable obstacles. He declined the ordinary roles society expected of Tejanos of his place and time, shaped his own life, and became the man he was meant to be. Navarro's life and accomplishments have often been reduced to designating him as a signer of the Texas Declaration of Independence, as though that single fact is sufficient to secure his place in Texas history. A more fitting summation of Navarro's life can be found in the writing of Narciso Leal, his friend and biographer. Paraphrasing Leal, Navarro's epitaph might well read:

From the time of Santa Anna to the end of his life
in the United States
José Antonio Navarro was the strongest champion of the people.[50]

Appendices

Appendix One: Margarita de la Garza

Conflicting evidence has caused considerable confusion about the identity of José Antonio Navarro's wife, Margarita de la Garza. The purpose of this appendix is to examine and resolve these conflicts in order to establish the basic facts of her identity. Numerous documents show that Margarita de la Garza was the wife of José Antonio Navarro although they were not married in the Catholic Church.

Baptismal records establish beyond any doubt the birthdate, birthplace, and parentage of Navarro's wife. San Fernando Church baptismal records document the baptism of Juana Margarita Modesta, a natural child, five days old, on February 2, 1795. It lists Xaviera Flores as the mother and the father as unknown. The godparents were Mauricio de Muy and María de la Garza. Twenty-two years later another baptismal record reports that this same Juana Modesta Margarita and José Antonio Navarro brought their first child into the world. She was María Casimira del Carmen, baptized on March 5, 1817, "natural child of Don José Antonio Navarro and Doña Margarita de la Garza . . . Maternal Grandparents: Eusebio de la Garza and Doña Xaviera Flores."[1] This baptismal record identifies Eusebio de la Garza as Margarita's father and confirms that her mother was Xaviera Flores. Thus the conjunction of Xaviera Flores as the mother in two baptismal records corroborates that Margarita de la Garza, Navarro's wife, was clearly one and the same person whose birth was recorded in Béxar in 1795, as noted above.

Two other sources, apparently authoritative, show different birthdates for Margarita. On José Antonio Navarro's tombstone, her birthday is shown to be October 17, 1801. In addition, Mormon genealogical files show Margarita de la Garza was born at Mier, Tamaulipas, in 1797; however, there is no source given for this statement. Such an anonymous report cannot be accepted as authoritative when other documented, verifiable evidence is readily available—thus this claim regarding Margarita must be dismissed. The origin of the information about Margarita on her husband's tombstone can be determined. It came from José Antonio Navarro III, the son of Sixto Navarro and namesake of his grandfather. Pursuant to the 1936 Texas Centennial, granite tombstones were erected at state expense for signers of the Texas Declaration of Independence and other Texas heroes. José Antonio Navarro III wrote to Louis W. Kemp, historian for the Texas Centennial Commission, inquiring about a marker for his grandfather. Kemp returned Navarro's letter with a short note saying it would be placed and asking "when Mrs. Navarro was born and when she died." The information about Margarita that Navarro III sent to Kemp is reflected in the undated tombstone text, on State of Texas Centennial letterhead, evidently submitted for Navarro's approval. About Margarita, it said: "HIS WIFE MARGARITA DE LA GARZA NAVARRO BORN OCTOBER 17, 1801, DIED JULY 8, 1861." This information was engraved on José Antonio Navarro's tombstone, which still stands at his grave. In 1930, Navarro's grandson wrote that José Antonio Navarro married Margarita de la Garza of Mier. Eight years later, he applied for membership in a historical organization and repeated that Margarita's birthplace was Mier and that her birthday was October 17, 1801.[2] He is mistaken in his assertions about his grandmother, whose birthdate and place are clearly found in the baptismal records of San Fernando.

Appendix Two: Henry Navarro

THE CASE OF FREEDMAN HENRY NAVARRO is worth examining in detail because the relationship he had with the José Antonio Navarro family may provide some insight on Tejano perspectives concerning slavery. In 1860, Henry was twenty-two years old and the only adult male among the Navarro slaves, which also included three adult women and three children.[3] Atascosa County tax records for 1864 show that José Antonio Navarro owned six slaves, which evidently constituted a family with Henry as head of household. Two years later, Henry is listed as a freedman in the Atascosa County tax records and was listed along with the sons of José Antonio Navarro.[4] Evidence shows that Henry remained at the Navarro Ranch for several years, probably having arranged to work for José Antonio Navarro for wages or as a sharecropper.

Henry did not remain a hired hand for long. He had the determination, ambition, and opportunity to take advantage of his new freedom, and he quickly began to improve living conditions for himself and his family. The property he acquired demonstrates this. In 1867, Henry owned three horses; the next year he was taxed for four horses, twenty cows, and forty-five dollars worth of equipment. In 1869 Henry became a landowner. He claimed 160 acres of land on which he had settled with the understanding that it was vacant and unclaimed. This kind of concession was called a preemption grant and resulted from legislation originally passed in 1845 and renewed in 1866. Henry was illiterate, and to obtain a preemption grant required the ability to navigate the necessary bureaucratic procedures. José Antonio Navarro's influence probably assisted him in the process. Abraham G. Martin, who had been married to Navarro's niece, directly assisted freedman Navarro. In support of the grant, Martin, as the Atascosa County District Clerk, certified that Navarro was a credible and trustworthy citizen.[5]

The census taker visited the Henry Navarro farm in 1870 and found a household of ten persons: Henry, age thirty-five; Patsy, age thirty-eight; and five children, ages eleven to three. The latter's names were Henry Jr., Lucinda, Mary, Edmund, and Rose. Also present was a black "housekeeper," Malie Richards, age fifty. Completing the household were Susan Ford and Sarah Cox, ages eighteen and thirteen, both listed as mulattos. It is interesting to note that Henry is listed as a United States citizen, born in Louisiana, but the census taker marked the box next to Henry Jr. that indicated his mother was of foreign birth, as was the father of Susan Ford. Henry Sr., Patsy, Susan Ford, and Malie Richards were all recorded as illiterate, and only Sarah Cox attended school that year. There also seems to be a correlation not just between Patsy and the woman of the same name whose children were baptized by the Navarros in 1856, but also the two young mulatto women. They are the right ages, but do not have the right names, to be the children who were actually baptized in 1856. Too, Patsy and Susan were born in Arkansas, and Sarah in Texas, which would support the idea that they are the three involved in the baptisms.[6] Thus with Navarro family assistance, Henry successfully made the transition from slave to head of a free household that included several former Navarro slaves.

By 1871, Henry improved his circumstances even more. He held title to 260 acres of land with twelve horses and 110 head of cattle. He continued to acquire land. In 1872, José Antonio George Navarro and Sixto Navarro sold Henry 277 acres—more evidence that the family had an ongoing relationship with Henry. In 1881, for $75 he bought 160 acres that had been a preemption grant. In 1885, tax assessments show that he had succeeded in increasing his Atascosa land holdings to a total of 520 acres. A community of African Americans, called Mata Mosa (later renamed Ditto), flourished in the area where he and Patsy lived, just north of the Atascosa Ranch. Around 1884, they donated an acre to the Methodist Episcopal Church that became a graveyard for African Americans, known to the present day as the Black Brite Cemetery.[7]

Appendix Three: Will of José Antonio Navarro

Dated December 27, 1870 (Navarro died January 14, 1871)
Filed January 16, 1871, Béxar County Courthouse, San Antonio, Texas
Navarro Collection, Spanish Archives (BCC)

In the city of San Antonio de Béxar, on the fifteenth day of February of our Lord, eighteen hundred and seventy, I, José Antonio Navarro, fearing that I may be surprised by the hour of my death, which is a common debt to all mortals; and that my five children who will survive me, who are José Antonio Geo., Celso Cornelio, Ángel, Sixto E. and Josefa, will know, comply, and conform without complaint with this last will of their father, I am writing in my own hand these notes, or better said, this my codicil and testament, which is the only and the last that I will leave written, to make you aware of what I own to this date, and so you can divide it, in a brotherly way with complete conformity, as I have here ordered and disposed.

First of all my rural properties are the following: four leagues that the Government of Coahuila and Texas granted me on the Atascosa [River], 3,272 acres of which were sold to Don José María Rodríguez, 200 acres to Don Matías Díaz, and 600 acres to Don Luís García; therefore the remainder is: 13,640 acres

I have a league and a labor bought from Francisco Garza

4,605

On the Medina and Uvalde Rivers I bought one third of a league from Juan Fernández

1,476

Also on the Medina and Uvalde I bought one labor from Leonardo Gil

177

Total 19,898 acres

Thus, as is evident, I have nineteen thousand eight hundred and ninety-eight acres of rural land which will be divided among my five said children in the following way:

To Antonio George, in addition to the acres I have previously allocated, there will be added the amount to make 4,823 acres, whether it is the land on the Atascosa, the third of a league, or the labor on the Medina and Uvalde, in which case his said total in cited acres is

4,823 acres

To Celso Navarro, including [the land] which I have previously given him, in the same way his total will be increased to

4,823 acres

To Ángel Navarro, to whom until now I have not designated any land to, he will have a total of

4,823 acres

To Sixto E. Navarro, including the acres that I previously allocated, there will be added the amount to make a total of

4,823 acres

To my daughter Josefa Elena, there will be given only the place where she previously had her ranch: six hundred and six acres

606 acres

which is the 19,898 acres

I command that these said acres of land be divided in the manner which I have stated above; that my children be in accord like good brothers, respecting the memory of their father and his disposition of the division of the land of the Atascosa, as well as that on the Medina and Uvalde; in which case, everyone will receive the number of acres that I have indicated.

Some of my four sons may wish to keep the house where I have my ranch. In that case it will be necessary that the said house be appraised by the said four men. With the value determined by agreement or conciliation, the cost will be divided among the four said sons.

I have not mentioned Josefa Elena because of all the land that I own, and what I have at Atascosa, I do not leave any for her except for the already mentioned six hundred and six acres of land. Keep this in mind.

I also command that all the cattle, the horses that I may have, goats, and pigs, if there are any, that all these animals should be equally divided among my four sons, Antonio, Celso, Ángel, and Sixto. Gathering the stock to the best of your ability, can trade among yourselves, land for cattle or vice versa; in which case each one must receive their equal part.

With this, I conclude the disposition of my rural properties and I now turn to distribute the urban property.

Urban Property

My house on the corner of Flores Street, also known as the *Navarro House*], I leave to my four sons: Antonio, Celso, Ángel, and Sixto Navarro so that they may enjoy their own equal portions. I ask and beg my sons not do anything foolish like sell the house until after eight to ten years. Instead, one of them should take charge of collecting monthly rent; that money should be used for any renovating that may be needed, and the remaining balance should be equally divided monthly by my four sons. Presently, the house is earning seventy-five pesos rent which will be paid in advance monthly by the renter; consequently, each one of my four sons will be entitled to eighteen pesos six reales each month, except when you have to pay taxes or when you do some necessary renovating. In any event, I hope that you preserve the house well so that when you do get ready to sell the house it will be worth double the amount of what it is worth today.

I have arranged and I order that my house in Laredito, where I actually live, entirely as it is from the rooms on the corner of Nueva Street to its boundary at the fence on the north, that is to say all the enclosed land of my house, for which the deed exists, absolutely all the house [premises] I bequeath to my daughter, Josefa Elena, presently married to Daniel Tobin.

I order and declare that all of the furniture and accessories of this said house exactly like it is and how it will be found after my death, I leave to my said daughter to use to her advantage, without anyone asking for anything or removing anything that may be inside the said house and kitchen except for some books that may belong to my son Ángel and my papers and important documents which are in a black leather trunk.

I declare that I leave this said house to Josefa in consideration that she is the only daughter, and besides I am not leaving leave her anything else but this said house and six hundred and six acres of land on the Atascosa—in case she would need to go and live there using it as a ranch and at even rent the house I am leaving her. I am confident that my four remaining children will understand that [even] if I do not leave them well off, at least I am giving them all the properties that I own up to this day.

I also declare that I have a lot which borders to the North with the house of my son Antonio. Considering that he presently possesses and is cultivating it, I bequeath the lot to my said son that he may enjoy it as his own.

Also, on Flores Street, I have to the north of this city of San Antonio some small portions of lots, as shown by the deeds among my papers. These fractions are presently unfenced, cultivated land. I leave them to be divided equally among my three sons: Celso Cornelio, Ángel, and Sixto E. Navarro. If they wish to build houses, that would be very advantageous; if not, they could benefit by selling them to arriving immigrants, who will want property close to town.

I declare that I have loaned Mr. Captain Durán the ranch site where he lives. You know this very well, as do Don Tomás Rodríguez, Don José María Cárdenas and many others from Atascosa. If Mr. Durán wishes to buy land from you, it is my desire for you to sell him from 100 to 200 acres at an equitable price, for he has been settling the land in my name and with my knowledge.

All my rural and urban properties are divided as well as the cattle, horses, and the rest of the animals that appear to come from my property. If before I die, I do not amend, lengthen, or shorten, my testament in any way, such that nothing is added or removed, it is to be carried out according to my disposition, as is stated by my own hand, free will, and in good judgment. I entrust my soul to the will of God obtain His forgiveness and mercy, and my body to the earth so that my children may modestly bury me.

I declare that I do not owe anyone anything, either money or objects whatever. Nor does there exist any obligation or any documentation written in my hand. The newspapers that I receive are paid up a year in advance, as can be seen in the receipts which I have organized in my trunk.

I enjoin my children to never deviate from paying all their taxes, as I have carefully done. It is a good citizen's obligation and will prevent difficulties with officials of the government. Meanwhile, the properties which I leave you that are not yet divided must be taken care of by making arrangements to pay taxes among yourselves. In my file you will find the memoranda on how I keep records of my inventory.

You may find among my papers some notes of accounts or memoranda of cattle, oxen, or money that I may have been able and have wanted to give to each of my sons or daughter from time to time more or less in conformity with I have been able and have wanted to give. However, I definitively declare by this clause that the figures or memoranda that you may find are not worth anything, nor will they have a negative effect towards my children because I do not take into account any cattle, oxen, or money that I may have given them before this disposition. Even though the land cited for Antonio, Celso, and Sixto at Atascosa Ranch may seem to be a loan, these said acres belong to each one as I have stated above. They have compared and taken into account in order to complete the 4,823 acres of land that I have assigned to each one through my testament. I repeatedly declare this so you will understand and be comfortable with my decision.

I name my said five children as executors of my will so that when they come together they will divide everything that I leave them through my will. In the event that all five children are not able to meet at the same time, I order that the three, being the majority, can carry out the justifications and distributions of what each is entitled to; however, if all my children gather or just three, I order and declare that my son Sixto Navarro be present to adjudicate the distributions or divisions that will be done.

Regarding what is done for my daughter, Josefa Elena, even though she may not be present, like I said before I have given her the house in Laredito with all its objects, furniture, and belongings of all kinds which are found in the said house, in addition to the six hundred and six acres of land that she will receive at Atascosa. As a result, nothing is to be spoken of or touched with respect to this said house of Laredito, other than to make application to its boundaries from North to South as it is today, where my ownership is recognized.

I beg, enjoin and order that all and each and every one of my children make these divisions with a noble and generous fraternal spirit without provoking any pressured words or displeasure because it is unworthy of children with noble hearts to object or rebel against a father who believes he has done the best he can to leave you the little he was able to acquire. I believe that you can very well distribute [your inheritance] in a judicious manner because you are all adults and you do not have any debts; but if you feel that it is convenient, you may place my testament in an archive, after you have done all the distributions according to my disposition.

Although as one can see, I began to write this testament on the 15th day of February of the present year 1870, I am leaving it without a conclusion so that I will be able to remove, add, or rewrite the clauses that I have already written. If I should die by accident without being able to complete and sign my said testament, as I intend to do, I declare by this same clause to order and to plead for all my children to fulfill and be satisfied with all of what I have written. For even if it is not signed by my own hand and pen, you will recognize my handwriting and know that all was done by my own will in accord with the conscience and love that I have for each and all of you, motives for which my testamentary disposition will have its force, validation, and fulfilled effect.

I have already stated that the house in Laredito I have left for and belongs to my said daughter Josefa Elena, with all the furniture that the house encloses, without anyone attempting to remove anything, for whatever reason. It remains for me to state and declare what is in the house at my ranch at Atascosa, left in the care of my son Sixto. There is some furniture, such as beds, mattresses, one dozen of silver spoons both large and small, farming tools, kitchen dishes, and some other small things that I cannot recall. All is to be divided equally among my four sons, Antonio, Celso, Ángel, and Sixto. However, if you know that this furniture is not worth much you can leave it all to Sixto, who has been taking care of it.

Today the 24th of September of the said year of 1870, fearing a fatal result from a surgical operation that Dr. Herff is to perform on my mouth, I think it well to sign this my testamentary disposition so it will have its needed effect if God is not served to prolong the days of my life—or if I decide to write a new disposition of my said testament, or if I should add a new disposition to the testament.

[Signed] José Antonio Navarro

Special Clause: I am dying. I care for your honor, your obedience, and affection for your father.

I order, beg, and hope that you do not speak or murmur any words about my determinations. Your little sister Josefa Elena now wants her six hundred and six acres, that I left her at Atascosa, on the Agua Negra [Creek]. I now declare by this clause that she may take these 606 acres, I repeat that she may take them on the spring waters of the said Agua Negra Creek. So I have assigned it to her, and between noble brothers and sister there should be no differences. I order it done thus so it will be accomplished.

Secret Testament
Clause 12 and last

Done by the will, pen, and hand of the undersigned José Antonio Navarro before these seven good witnesses who observed the signing and themselves signed for further confirmation of this act on the 27th December of A.D. eighteen hundred and seventy, in conclusion of the said secret testament, which was sealed and delivered to Doña Josefa Elena de Tobin for her to keep it until the time that it is needed.

San Antonio December 27, 1870

[Signed] José Antonio Navarro

Witnesses

P[eter] Scheiner, Fritz Schreiner, Jacob F. Inselman, Agustin Barrera, Juan José Moll [?], María Antoni M-es, José M. Cortina.

Notes

Abbreviations

AGEC: Archivo General del Estado de Coahuila
BA: Béxar Archives, Microfilm, Texana Department, San Antonio Public Library, San Antonio, Texas
BCC: Bexar County Courthouse
BCAH: Dolph Briscoe Center for American History, University of Texas at Austin
DRT: Daughters of the Republic of Texas Library, San Antonio, Texas
GLO: Archives and Records Division, Texas General Land Office, Austin, Texas
QTSHA: Quarterly of the Texas State Historical Association
SWHQ: Southwestern Historical Quarterly
TSL: Texas State Library and Archives, Austin

Notes to Introduction

1. José Antonio Navarro to Antonio López de Santa Anna, n.d., Santa Fe Expedition Scrapbook, Vol. 338, p. 16, Box 2Q175 (BCAH).

2. Lewis F. Fisher, *Saving San Antonio: The Precarious Preservation of a Heritage* (Lubbock: Texas Tech University Press, 1996), 240, 242, 245.

3. David McDonald, "José Antonio Navarro State Historical Park." *The Handbook of Texas Online* <http://www.tshaonline.org/handbook/online/articles/JJ/ghj1.html> [Accessed June 5, 2010].

4. Jesús F. de la Teja, "San Fernando de Béxar," *The Handbook of Texas Online*, <http://www.tshaonline.org/handbook/online/articles/SS/hvs16.html> [Accessed Mar. 24, 2010].

5. Ana Carolina Castillo Crimm, *De León: A Tejano Family History* (Austin: University of Texas Press, 2003).

6. Guillermo Colín Sánchez, *Ignacio Zaragoza; Evocación de un Héroe* (México, D.F.: Editorial Porrúa, 1966); and Joseph E. Chance, *José María de Jesús Carvajal: The Life and Times of a Mexican Revolutionary* (San Antonio: Trinity University Press, 2006).

7. Jacob De Cordova, *Texas: Her Resources and Her Public Men* (1858; reprint, Waco: Texian Press, 1969), 145–153.

8. An Old Texan [Narciso Leal, et al.], *José Antonio Navarro* (Houston: Telegraph Steam Printing House, 1876).

9. Naomi Fritz, "José Antonio Navarro" (master's thesis, St. Mary's University of San Antonio, 1941).

10. Joseph M. Dawson, *José Antonio Navarro: Co-Creator of Texas* (Waco: Baylor University Press, 1969)

11. James E. Crisp, "Anglo-Texan Attitudes toward the Mexican, 1821–1845" (PhD diss., Yale University, 1976).

12. Crisp, "José Antonio Navarro: the Problem of Tejano Powerlessness," in *Tejano Leadership in Mexican and Revolutionary Texas*, ed. Jesús F. de la Teja (College Station: Texas A&M University Press, 2010), 146–168.

13. Anastacio Bueno, "In Storms of Fortune: José Antonio Navarro of Texas, 1821–1846" (master's thesis, University of Texas at San Antonio, 1978).

14. José Antonio Navarro, *Defending Mexican Valor in Texas: the Historical Writings of José Antonio Navarro, 1853–1857*, ed. David R. McDonald and Timothy Matovina (Austin: State House Press, 1995).

15. Andrés Reséndez (ed. and trans.), *A Texas Patriot on Trial in Mexico: José Antonio Navarro and the Texan Santa Fe Expedition* (Dallas: DeGolyer Library, William P. Clements Center for Southwest Studies Southern Methodist University, 2005).

16. Patsy McDonald Spaw (ed.), *The Texas State Senate: Republic to Civil War, 1836–1861* (College Station: Texas A&M University Press, 1990), 170.

17. "Remember the Alamo," *The American Experience*, DVD, directed by Joseph Tovares (Boston: WGBH Educational Foundation, 2004). At the beginning of this segment the narrator says, "One hundred and fifty miles from the Alamo, a group of prominent Texans was gathering to sign a Declaration of Independence. Among them, was an ambitious merchant and idealistic politician who had been pushing for Texas independence for much of his life. No one had more to gain, or to lose, from the fight for Texas than José Antonio Navarro." The transcript for this segment is available at: http://www.pbs.org/wgbh/amex/alamo/filmmore/pt.html.

18. For Navarro's election, see "Cuartel del Alamo," Feb 1. 1836, BA, roll 167, frames 484–500.

19. Arnoldo De Léon, *The Tejano Community, 1836–1900* (Albuquerque: University of New Mexico Press, 1982), 28.

20. Jose Antonio Navarro, *Apuntes Históricos Interesantes de San Antonio de Béxar, San Antonio: Publicado por Varios de sus Amigos* (San Antonio: [Augustus Siemering], 1869). A facsimile of *Apuntes* and new, annotated translation of them by David McDonald are in Navarro, *Defending Mexican Valor in Texas.*

21. James Truslow Adams, *The Epic of America* (18th ed.; Boston: Little, Brown, and Company, 1933), 414.

NOTES TO CHAPTER ONE

1. Ángel Navarro to Governor [Manuel Muñoz], May 14, 1792, BA, roll 22, frame 370. Early published accounts of the life of Ángel Navarro exaggerate his origins, usually claiming that he was a military officer who came to colonial Mexico in the service of the king of Spain. Frederick C. Chabot introduced a major error about Ángel's life when he mistakenly wrote that he left Corsica in 1772 instead of 1762. Frederick C. Chabot, *With the Makers of San Antonio* (San Antonio: Artes Graficas, 1937), 202. Subsequent authors perpetuated Chabot's error and drew incorrect conclusions based upon it. The authority of Navarro's sketch of his origins, however, must supersede all other accounts of his life.

2. Ángel Navarro to Governor [Manuel Muñoz], May 14, 1792, BA, roll 22, frame 370. The town of Vallecillo still exists in Nuevo León.

3. Bexár Census, 1779, Archivo General de las Indias (hereafter cited as AGI), Guadalajara 283; Ángel Navarro to Bartolo Seguín, Aug. 31, 1780, Land Grants and Sales, No. 613 (Spanish Archives, BCC); Ángel Navarro, document inventory, [Dec.] 1781, BA, roll 14, frame 896. Although the two Navarros may have been in communication during Ángel's first years in New Spain, they did not arrive in San Antonio together; however, to have two persons born in Corsica, which had never been a Spanish territory, living so near each on the far northern frontier of New Spain seems unlikely to be solely due to chance.

4. Navarro to [Muñoz], May 14, 1792, BA, roll 22, frame 370; Emily Cooley, "A Retrospect of San Antonio," *QTSHA* 4 (July 1901): 54–56. John O. Leal (comp.), "San Fernando Baptismals," Book 1775–1793 (typescript), 74: 1183 (Texana Department, San Antonio Public Library, San Antonio).

5. Old Texan, *José Antonio Navarro*, 4; *Expediente Formado para el Remate de los Generos Extrangeros en Publica Subasta*, Nov. 7, 1792, BA, roll 22, frame 842. Regarding Ángel Navarro's slaves, see Carmela Leal (comp.), *Residents of Texas, 1782–1836* (3 vols; St. Louis: Ingmire Publications, 1984), I, censuses of 1790 (p. 61), 1792 (p. 76), 1793 (p. 124), 1795 (p. 206), 1797 (p. 265), and 1803 (p. 327).

6. Receipt signed by Ángel Navarro and Friar Manuel Pedrajo, Jan. 15, 1796, BA, roll 25, frame 446.

7. There is no exact English translation for the term *alcalde*, the name for the chief municipal officer in colonial and Mexican San Antonio. The alcalde incorporated the functions of mayor and judge, presided over the city council, and reported to the governor; "Alcalde," *The Handbook of Texas Online*, <http://www.tshaonline.org/handbook/online/articles/AA/nfa1.html> [Accessed May 26, 2010]. References to Ángel Navarro as alcalde and alderman are found in BA roll 14, frame 896; BA, roll 15, frames 124–125; BA, roll 23, frames 310–318; BA, roll 27, frames 107 and 410–412; BA, roll 29, frames 260–261; BA, roll 36, frames 488–496; and BA, roll 170, frames 408–412.

8. The 1795 Béxar Census erroneously shows the Navarro family to have a twelve *and* a thirteen-year-old son (Carmela Leal (comp.), *Residents of Texas*, I: 206, 168. Baptismal records and other censuses show that the Navarros had only one son in this age range, José de los Ángeles. For José Antonio Navarro's baptism, see John O. Leal (comp.), "San Fernando Baptismals," Book 1793–1812 (typescript), 14, no. 161.

9. Real Street was also known as Calle (street) de las Flores as early as 1797; subsequently it became known simply as Flores Street. See will of Juan Manuel Ruiz, July 28, 1797, Wills and Estates Book 93–66, p. 4, no. 94, Spanish Archives (BCC). The Ruiz house would eventually become the main Navarro residence. In 1803, however, the Navarros lived separately from the Ruiz family, evidently on the lot Ángel Navarro had purchased from Bartolo Seguín in 1781. See Ángel Navarro to Bartolo Seguín, Aug. 31, 1780, Land Grants and Sales, 613 (Spanish Archives, BCC).

10. José Francisco de la Mata to the *Cabildo*, May 1789, BA, roll 19, frames 768–700.

11. Old Texan, *José Antonio Navarro*, 8; I. J. Cox, "Educational Efforts in San Fernando de Béxar," *QTSHA* 6 (July 1902): 27–35; Juan Bautista Elguézabal to Nemesio Salcedo, Oct. 12, 1803, BA, roll 31, frames 390–391. Cox reported (p. 29) that the *cabildo* appointed Ruiz as schoolmaster, citing an "Act of the Cabildo, January 20, 1803, Béxar Archives," but this document could not be located in the microfilm version nor in the manuscripts of the Béxar Archives. Elguezábal does not name Ruiz, but refers to a "youth [*mozo*] who could read and do arithmetic and had an appropriate house." In *The Men Who Made Texas Free* (Houston: Texas Historical Publication Company, 1924), 314, Sam Houston Dixon reported that both José Francisco Ruiz and José Antonio Navarro were educated in Spain. Dixon seems to have been the first to publish this implausible assertion, which has been cited by many writers. Contrary to Dixon's claim, it is evident that Ruiz and Navarro were educated in Texas and Coahuila, not in Spain.

12. *Enciclopedia de México* (12 vols.; México, D.F.: Instituto de la Enciclopedia de México, 1966–1977), II: 492; Miguel Ramos Arizpe (quotation), cited in Alessio Robles, *Coahuila y Tejas en la Epoca Colonial* (México, D.F.: Editorial Porrua, 1978), 624–625.

13. José Antonio Navarro, "Autobiographical Notes," in *The Papers of Mirabeau Buonaparte Lamar*, eds. Charles Gulick, Harriet Smither, et al. (6 vols., Austin: Texas State Library, 1920–27; reprint, Austin: Pemberton Press, 1968), III: 597–598.

14. Old Texan, *José Antonio Navarro*, 5, 9 (quotations); José Antonio Navarro, in the

Ledger (San Antonio), Dec. 12, 1857, in McDonald and Matovina (eds.), *Defending Mexican Valor in Texas*, 64. In his letter to President of the Republic [Antonio López de Santa Anna], Sept. 26, 1843 (Santa Fe Expedition Scrapbook, Vol. 338, pp. 50–52, Box 2Q175 (BCAH), Navarro indicated that the injury to his leg happened in 1808.

15. John O. Leal (comp.), "Campo Santo: An Ancient Burial Ground of San Antonio, Texas, 1808–1860" (typescript), 1 (Texana Department, San Antonio Public Library). At the death of their father, there were six surviving Navarro children: José Ángel, age 25; María Josefa Candida Gertrudis, 16, José Antonio, 13; María Antonia, 11; José Luciano, 8; and José Eugenio, 5.

16. Reuben M. Potter writes that Navarro was "educated for an advocate" but he never practiced law. Other reports have Navarro studying law in New Orleans as a young man. See Potter, The Texas Revolution: Distinguished Mexicans Who Took Part in the Revolution of Texas with Glances at Early Events," *Magazine of American History* (October 1878): 17. No supporting evidence to support these claims was found, and it is clear that they are incorrect; Navarro's legal study was done informally in San Antonio, and he received on-the-job legal training as a delegate and legislator.

17. José Antonio Navarro to the Speaker [John M. Hansford of the House of Representatives], Jan. 26, 1839, in Houston *Telegraph and Texas Register*, Jan. 29, 1839, p. 5; Gulick, Smither, et al. (eds.), *Lamar Papers*, III: 525–527; Juan Martín de Veramendi, Estate Inventories, Sept. 26, 1833, BA, roll 158, frame 593; Navarro, in the *Ledger* (San Antonio), Dec. 19, 1857, and Jan. 2, 1858, in McDonald and Matovina (eds.), *Defending Mexican Valor in Texas*, 69, 73, 75; José Antonio Navarro to Stephen F. Austin, July 7, 1831, Samuel May Williams Collection, 23-0751 (Rosenberg Library, Galveston, Texas). Leonidas was the Spartan king who, with other Greeks, died heroically defending the pass of Thermopylae in 480 BC.

18. Although no marriage record for the Navarro-Veramendi wedding has been found, an 1811 census reports notes that Juan Martín de Veramendi was married to Josefa Navarro; see Carmela Leal (comp.), *Residents of Texas*, II, 69.

19. David R. McDonald, "Juan Martín de Veramendi: Political and Business Leader," in Jesús F. de la Teja, ed., *Tejano Leadership in Mexican and Revolutionary Texas* (College Station: Texas A&M University Press, 2010), 29–43; Veramendi's power of attorney to José Antonio Navarro, May 16, 1825, Book PA 71–84, pp. 1–4 (Spanish Archives, BCC). José Antonio Navarro referred to Veramendi as his "*Hermano político*" (political brother), which is synonymous with "brother-in-law."

20. Navarro, "Autobiographical Notes," 597.

21. José Ángel Navarro, Member of the San Carlos de Parras Company, Jan. 1, 1807 (Archives, University of Texas Institute of Texan Cultures, San Antonio); Carmela Leal (comp.), *Residents of Texas*, II: 4; Josefa Ruiz and Erlinda Bustillos, petition to Gov. Antonio Cordero, Nov. 7, 1810, Fondo Presidencia Municipal, caja 59, expediente 11 (Archivo Municipal de Saltillo, Saltillo, Coahuila). According to José Antonio Navarro, José Ángel served as a lieutenant in the army of General Joaquín de Arredondo, see "Autobiographical Notes," 598.

22. Félix D. Almaráz, *Tragic Cavalier: Governor Manuel Salcedo of Texas, 1808–1813* (Austin: University of Texas Press, 1971), 25.

23. Navarro, in the *Ledger* (San Antonio), Dec. 12, 1857, in McDonald and Matovina (eds.), *Defending Mexican Valor in Texas*, 64.

24. Almaráz, *Tragic Cavalier*, 78–79.

25. Manuel Salcedo, Proclamation of Oct. 5, 1809, Nacogdoches Archives, box 2Q294, vol. 180, pp. 5–7 (BCAH). The San Antonio de Béxar presidio was named after the Duke of Béxar, brother of Viceroy Marques de Valero, who authorized its establishment in 1718. An informal community of civilians grew around the presidio, which they called

Béxar. In 1731, the settlement was formally named "San Fernando de Austria." The name did not stick, however, and people continued to call the town Béxar.

26. Almaráz, *Tragic Cavalier*, 104–116; Navarro, in the *Ledger* (San Antonio), Dec. 19, 1857, in McDonald and Matovina (eds.), *Defending Mexican Valor in Texas*, 70.

27. Navarro, in the *Ledger* (San Antonio), Dec. 19, 1857, in McDonald and Matovina (eds.), *Defending Mexican Valor in Texas*, 67–68. Navarro consistently overstates the number of troops throughout his narrative. Juan Bautista de las Casas would probably have had about 150 to 200 men.

28. Almaráz, *Tragic Cavalier*, 118; Navarro, in the *Ledger* (San Antonio), Dec. 19, 1857, in McDonald and Matovina (eds.), *Defending Mexican Valor in Texas*, 68.

29. Almaráz, *Tragic Cavalier*, 118–120; Navarro, in the *Ledger* (San Antonio), Dec. 19, 1857, in McDonald and Matovina (eds.), *Defending Mexican Valor in Texas*, 69.

30. J. Villasana Haggard, "The Counter-Revolution of Béxar, 1811," *SWHQ* 43 (July 1939): 226, 229.

31. Almaráz, *Tragic Cavalier*, 120–121; Haggard, "The Counter-Revolution of Béxar, 226, 229.

32. Navarro, in the *Ledger* (San Antonio), Dec. 19, 1857, in McDonald and Matovina (eds.), *Defending Mexican Valor in Texas*, 69.

33. Navarro, in the *Ledger* (San Antonio), Jan. 2, 1858, in McDonald and Matovina (eds.), *Defending Mexican Valor in Texas*, 70–71. Frederick C. Chabot, *Texas in 1811: The Las Casas and Sambrano Revolutions* (San Antonio: Yanaguana Society, 1941), 32.

34. Almaráz, *Tragic Cavalier*, 124–125.

35. Navarro, in the *Western Texan* (San Antonio), Dec. 1, 1853, in McDonald and Matovina (eds.), *Defending Mexican Valor in Texas*, 46.

36. Almaráz, *Tragic Cavalier*, 168–169.

37. Chabot, *Makers of San Antonio*, 240–241; Almaráz, *Tragic Cavalier*, 124–125, Navarro, in the *Western Texan* (San Antonio), Dec. 1, 1853, in McDonald and Matovina (eds.), *Defending Mexican Valor in Texas*, 47–48 (quotation).

38. Navarro, in the *Western Texan* (San Antonio), Dec. 1, 1853, in McDonald and Matovina (eds.), *Defending Mexican Valor in Texas*, 48–49 (quotation).

39. Ibid., 51–52. Arredondo reported that he brought a total of 1,830 men: 695 infantry and 1095 cavalry. See Mattie Austin Hatcher (trans.), "Joaquin de Arredondo's Report of the Battle of Medina, August 18, 1813," *QTSHA* 11 (January 1908): 225.

40. "Arredondo, Joaquín de," *The Handbook of Texas Online*, <http://www.tshaonline. org/handbook/online/articles/AA/far18.html> [Accessed Jan. 5, 2010]; "Gutiérrez de Lara, José Bernardo Maximiliano," *The Handbook of Texas Online*, <http://www.tshaonline.org/handbook/online/articles/GG/fgu11.html> [Accessed Jan. 5, 2010];. "Medina, Battle of" *The Handbook of Texas Online*, <http://www.tshaonline.org/handbook/online/articles/MM/qfm1.html> [Accessed Jan 5, 2010]; "Toledo y Dubois, José Álvarez de," *The Handbook of Texas Online*, <http://www.tshaonline.org/handbook/online/articles/TT/fto10.html> [Accessed Jan. 5, 2010); Navarro, "Autobiographical notes," 597–598.

41. Ted Schwarz and Robert H. Thonhoff (eds.), *Forgotten Battlefield of the First Texas Revolution: The Battle of Medina, August 18, 1813* (Austin: Eakin Press, 1985), 102.

42. Navarro, in the *Western Texan* (San Antonio), Dec. 1, 1853, in McDonald and Matovina (eds.), *Defending Mexican Valor in Texas*, 53.

43. Ibid., 54; Hatcher, "Arredondo's Report," 225. José Antonio Navarro had to have been referring to cannons that fired four- to eight-pound balls. Sources locate the battle south of the Medina River, but an exact location has not been determined, according to Schwarz and Thonhoff (eds.), *Forgotten Battlefield*, 146.

44. Navarro, in the *Western Texan* (San Antonio), Dec. 1, 1853, in McDonald and Mato-

vina (eds.), *Defending Mexican Valor in Texas*, 54; Schwarz and Thonhoff (eds.), *Forgotten Battlefield*, 64, 102. Arredondo later revised the number of men his troops had slain to "about a thousand." See Hatcher, "Arredondo's Report," 225.

45. Father J. M. Rodríguez, "Notes Regarding the Insurgent invasion of Texas, 1812–1813" (microfilm; Special Collections, University of Texas at San Antonio). "Gachupín" was a derogatory term for a Spaniard born in Spain.

46. Navarro, "Autobiographical Notes," III, 597 (quotations). José Antonio's brother, José Ángel, was not exiled in 1813 but rather remained a royalist in good standing with Arredondo. In 1841, when Navarro wrote this passage in his autobiographical sketch, he was probably less concerned with historical accuracy and more interested in presenting a public image of his family as one that was united from the beginning in its support for republican principles. The erroneous idea that José Ángel Navarro had to flee from Arredondo has persisted in other historical writings about him.

47. While visiting San Antonio in 1828, Jean-Louis Berlandier, the French naturalist, recorded the account of "La Bexareña" along with others in his "Notes sur [deleted] la revolution de Texas en 1813—Fournis par une femme de Béxar victime des exces des royalistes Espagnols" (microfilm; Special Collections, University of Texas at San Antonio). The *Quinta* was located on the south side of Main Plaza.

48. Schwarz and Thonhoff, *Forgotten Battlefield*, 123. Agustín Soto, *alcalde* of Laredo, related this account as told by his father, who was a lieutenant with Santa Anna under Arredondo in the 1813 campaign. See Gulick, Smither, et al. (eds.), *Lamar Papers*, VI: 118–119.

49. Testimony of Bernardo Benítes, Oct. 18, 1814, BA, roll 54, frames 322–331; Francisco Martínez to Francisco Llorens, Sept. 29, 1815, Nacogdoches Archives, box 2Q299, vol. 186, pp. 17–29 (BCAH); Navarro, "Autobiographical Notes," 598. Naomi Fritz, in her master's thesis, "José Antonio Navarro", cites Navarro's "Autobiographical Notes" and Chabot, *Makers of San Antonio*, p. 203, in support of the conclusion that Navarro stayed in New Orleans (p. 14). Navarro actually wrote in his "Autobiographical Notes" that he and family members were "wandering in the state of Louisiana"; he does not mention New Orleans. The reference in Chabot states that after the death of his father, Navarro went to Louisiana to work in a mercantile establishment. It is most unlikely that his family sent the thirteen-year-old José Antonio to work in Louisiana. As noted above, if Navarro worked anywhere at that time it would have been in the family business in Béxar, not in Louisiana. And Chabot's statement does not indicate where Navarro was during the period of his exile. Evidence noted above indicates that Navarro stayed in the Natchitoches area during his exile. In another view of Navarro's pardon, Jacob R. De Cordova, in *Texas: Her Resources and Her Public Men* (Philadelphia: Lippincott, 1858), 146, says that José Antonio's mother, Josefa, secured the royal pardon, which allowed him to return home. This seems most unlikely.

50. McDonald, "Veramendi: Tejano Political and Business Leader," in *Tejano Leadership in Mexican and Revolutionary Texas*, ed. Jesús F. de la Teja (College Station: Texas A&M University Press, 2010), 33. Details regarding José Ángel Navarro's tenure as councilman can be found in BA, roll 56, frames 159–160 and 494.

NOTES TO CHAPTER TWO

1. City Council to Mariano Varela, Feb. 1, 1816, BA, roll 56, frames 259–260.

2. Donald E. Chipman, *Spanish Texas, 1519–1821* (Austin: University of Texas Press, 1992), 240–241; David J. Weber, *The Mexican Frontier, 1821–1846* (Albuquerque: University of New Mexico Press, 1982), 177. Weber estimated the 1836 Tejano population of Texas at 3,500.

3. [Ignacio Pérez] to Joaquín de Arredondo, Nov. 11, 1816, BA, roll 57, frame 402.

4. Navarro, in the *Ledger* (San Antonio), Dec. 12, 1857, in McDonald and Matovina (eds.), *Defending Mexican Valor in Texas*, 63.

5. San Fernando Burial Records show 551 burials, beginning with Ángel Navarro in 1808 to the end of 1815. John O. Leal (comp.), "Campo Santo: An Ancient Burial Ground of San Antonio, Texas, 1808–1860" (typescript), 1–28.

6. General Census Report of the City of Béxar and its Missions: Barrios Valero, Sur, Norte, Laredo, Jan. 1, 1820, in Carmela Leal (comp.), *Residents of Texas*, II, 153–184.

7. Carmela Leal (comp.), *Residents of Texas*, II, 121, no. 166; personal communication from Alvin Gerdes to the author, Nov. 22, 2009, with genealogical data from Alvin and Angie Gerdes (eds. and comps.), "A Navarro Family Heritage: Their Kith and Kin, 2009" (San Antonio: privately printed, 2008).

8. Deed Record, vol. H-1, 350–351, Mar. 20, 1849 (BCC).

9. "Dawn at the Alamo: Celso Navarro to McArdle," <http://www.tsl.tx.us/mcardle/alamo/alamo83.html> [Accessed Mar. 31, 2010].

10. María Casimira del Carmen, three days old, natural child of José Antonio Navarro and Margarita de la Garza, was baptized at San Fernando Church on March 5, 1817. John O. Leal (comp.), "San Fernando Church Baptismals," Book 1812–1825 (typescript), 48: no 416.

11. Carmela Leal (comp.), *Residents of Texas*, II, censuses of 1817 (pp. 120–121), 1819 (pp. 136, 141), 1820 (pp. 170, 176), 1826 (pp. 205–206), 1829 (pp. 244, 249), 1831 (293, 305), 1832 (pp. 324–325).

12. Asunción Lavrin, "Women in Colonial Mexico," in *The Oxford History of Mexico*, ed. Michael C. Meyer and William H. Beezley (New York: Oxford University Press, 2000), 261.

13. John O. Leal (comp.), "San Fernando Church Baptismals," Book 1812–1825 (typescript), 48, no. 416 (María Casimira del Carmen Navarro), 61, no. 542 (José Antonio George Navarro) , 82, no. 761 (María Gertrudes Josefa Navarro); John O. Leal (comp.)," San Fernando Church Baptismals," Book 1826–1843 (typescript), 22, no. 254 (Celso Corenelio Navarro), 25, no. 408 (Wenseslao Eusebio Sixto Navarro).

14. John O. Leal (comp.), "San Fernando Church Baptismals," Book 1812–1825 (typescript), 48, no. 364.

15. It must be noted that Navarro's grandson, José Antonio Navarro III, maintained that José Antonio Navarro and Margarita de la Garza did marry. In his application for membership in the Signers of the Declaration organization he stated the José Antonio and Margarita were married at Mier, Tamaulipas, on an unknown date. See José Antonio Navarro III's application for membership to the Descendants of the Signers of the Texas Declaration of Independence, DRT, Navarro Collection. Genealogists Alvin Gerdes and Illene Treviño Villareal have searched the Mier Church archives, but found no record of the marriage. While José Antonio Navarro III left an extensive and valuable legacy of writing about his grandfather, in this case the evidence found in the Béxar baptismal records shows Margarita de la Garza was born in Béxar in 1795 and supersedes all contrary assertions. A detailed examination of the facts regarding the identity of Margarita is presented in Appendix One to demonstrate the author's conclusions.

16. Antonio Martínez to Juan Ruiz de Apodaca, Dec. 18, 1817, BA, roll 59, frames 439–440 (quotation); Salvador Carrasco, inventory of contraband, Dec. 31, 1817, BA, roll 59, frames 447–451.

17. Martínez to [Béxar] *Ayuntamiento*, Oct. 21, 1818, BA, roll 62, frames 4–5.

18. For more on the Baron de Bastrop, a native of Dutch Guiana whose real name was Philip Hendrick Nering Bögel, see "Bastrop, Baron de," *The Handbook of Texas Online*, <http://www.tshaonline.org/handbook/online/articles/BB/fbaae.html> [Accessed

Jan. 11, 2010]. The declaration Navarro wrote and signed on behalf of his mother states her losses as "32 pesos for 800 posts of good wood taken from my garden and burned 1,820 pesos for 260 cows, at 7 pesos each, at the ranch I abandoned 270 pesos for 27 tame horses, 2,126 Pesos Total." That Josefa Navarro listed no merchandise as lost property indicates that her family was out of the mercantile business by 1813. The "ranch" was on León Creek ("S. Antonio de León"), a tributary of the San Antonio River located west of Béxar. See José Antonio Navarro, Declaration, Nov. 11, 1818, BA, roll 62, frame 277.

19. María Josefa Navarro de Veramendi's declaration, Oct. 20, 1818, BA, roll 61, frames 1021–1023. While José Antonio Navarro did not sign this declaration, it is clearly written in his distinctive hand.

20. Martínez to Antonio de Puertas, May 6, 1819, BA, roll 62, frame 950.

21. Copia del Sumario Ynstruido en el Presidio de la Bahía p.r el Ten.te D. Fran.co García contra el Ten.te Coronel D. Juan Man.l Zambrano, BA, roll 62,frame 897 (henreafter cited as Zambrano Sumario).

22. Martínez to Arredondo, Feb. 4, 1819, Nacogdoches Archives, box 2Q295, vol. 181, p. 465, no. 427 (BCAH).

23. Navarro wrote about Zambrano: "Gigantic and obese, arrogant in manner, dynamic and volatile as mercury, he possessed a special talent for total disorder." Navarro, in the *Ledger* (San Antonio), Dec. 19, 1857, in McDonald and Matovina (eds.), *Defending Mexican Valor in Texas*, 70.

24. Martínez to Puertas, May 6, 1819, BA, roll 62, frame 950.

25. Antonio Fernández de Córdova to Martínez, Sept. 20, 1818, BA, roll 61, frames 826–827.

26. Zambrano Sumario, BA, roll 62, frames 878–904.

27. José Ángel Navarro and Veramendi volunteered for a military expedition to rid Galveston of pirates and filibusterers. Request of Veramendi and José Ángel Navarro, Sept. 16, 1818, BA, roll 61, frame 802.

28. [Martínez] to Arredondo, Feb. 4, 1819 (quotation), Nacogdoches Archives, box 2Q295, vol. 181, p. 464, no. 425 (BCAH).

29. Puertas to Martínez, Mar. 16, 1819, BA, roll 62, frame 794; Zambrano Sumario, BA, roll 62, frame 897.

30. Sumario Ynformacion contra los Vecinos D.n José Antonio Navarro, Manuel Carabajal, Nicolas Carabajal, Damian Rodríguez, y Norato de Luna por el delito de haverse pasado al Ynterior con el pretexto de haver sacado licenisa [sic] para pasar a la costa del Rio Grande, Fondo Colonial, caja 34, año 1819, expediente 12, AGEC, 560, 570–571, 573, 580 (cited hereafter as Navarro Sumario). This document consists of thirty-four pages of testimony rich in details about the contraband trip. A faded, difficult-to-read copy of it can be found in the Carlos Castañeda Photostats (vol. 14) at the Center for Mexican American Studies & Research, Our Lady of the Lake University, San Antonio.

31. Navarro Sumario, 560, 580, 592.

32. Navarro Sumario, 563–565, 569; Ignacio Pérez to Martínez, Apr. 5, 1819, BA, roll 60, frames 793–794. La Sal del Rey is a saline lake from which salt was quarried. It is located twenty-eight miles northeast of McAllen, Texas.

33. Martínez to Arredondo, May 5, 1819, Nacogdoches Archives, box 2Q295, vol. 181, pp. 497–501 (BCAH); Zambrano Sumario, BA, roll 62, frames 878–904; Navarro Sumario, 566, 592.

34. Ibid., 566–579. Many other people in Béxar suffered from the same poverty that drove José Antonio Navarro up the contraband trail. The desperation of soldiers, for example, was particularly evident. Early in 1820, eight soldiers were accused of having

butchered an ox and a cow that belonged to private individuals. Nicolás Morales, one of the accused, confessed that his great need obliged him commit the crime of killing the ox. See Sumario of Nicolás Morales et al., Feb. 9, 1820, BA, roll 63, frames 875–888.

35. Navarro Sumario, 566–579, 581.

36. Ibid., 582–583.

37. Ibid., 584.

38. Ibid., 593.

39. Ibid., 594. The office of assessor-auditor of war represented the judicial arm of the *Commandancia General*. Its decrees exercised great clout and legal force, especially on the northern frontier. Charles R. Clutter, *The Legal Culture of Northern New Spain* (Albuquerque: University of New Mexico Press, 1995), 54–55.

40. Navarro, "Autobiographical Notes," 598.

41. Martínez to Arredondo, July 8, 1819, Nacogdoches Archives, box 2Q295, vol. 182, pp. 527–531, no. 432 (BCAH); Martínez to Arredondo, July 8, 1819, Nacogdoches Archives, box 2Q296, vol. 187, pp. 148–154, no. 105 (BCAH). A list of Béxar flood deaths can be found in BA, roll 64, frames 706–707.

42. Puertas to Martínez, July 21, 1819, BA, roll 63, frames 120–21; Puertas to Martínez, July 25, 1819, BA, roll 63, frames 145–147. Numerous documents, beginning in 1819, show that Puertas was a special investigator sent by Arredondo to oversee Martínez. This clearly indicates Arredondo's lack of confidence in the Governor. For examples, see BA, rolls 62, frames 786–787; BA, roll 62, frames 794 and 796, and BA roll 62, frame 812.

43. This petition was not found. Navarro quotes from it in his petition, José Antonio Navarro to Martínez, Dec. 28, 1820, Castañeda Photostats, vol. 14, pp. 24–25 (Center for Mexican American Studies & Research Our Lady of the Lake University, San Antonio).

44. José Antonio Navarro to Arredondo, June 18, 1821, Castañeda Photostats, vol. 15, p. 21.

45. José Antonio Navarro to Martínez, July 12, 1821, Castañeda Photostats, vol. 15, p. 16.

46. Spanish Minutes Book One (1815–1820) of the San Antonio City Council (hereafter cited as SB1), section 38, June 26, 1820, pp. 186–187, English translation (microfilm; Texana Department, San Antonio Public Library, San Antonio). The minutes of the San Antonio City Council, cited here, are stored in the city clerk's office. Typed copies in Spanish and English translation, which were used in this study, are available on microfilm at the San Antonio Public Library. A brief explanation of these records is needed since many of the pages are very hard to read and the organization is complex; thus sometimes the Spanish transcripts are cited, other times the English translations. The council minutes are contained in three books entitled Spanish Minute Book One, Spanish Minute Book Two, and Journal A. The books are divided arbitrarily into sections of Spanish and English translations with page numbers and dates. Spanish Minute Book Two is designated as SB2, and Journal A as JA and follow the same format as SB1. The notations SB1, SB2, and JA are necessary to navigate through the microfilm source.

47. SB1, section 40, June 23, 1820, pp. 189–190, English translation (microfilm). The other electors were Juan José María Erasmo de Jesús Seguín, José Antonio Saucedo, Vicente Gortari, José Gaspar María Flores de Abrego, Francisco Montes de Oca, Luís Galán, Manuel Barrera, and José Antonio de la Garza.

48. Ibid.; Martínez, Election Results, July 25, 1820, BA, roll 64, frames 862–863. Note that the junta elected three of its own members: Erasmo Seguín, José Flores, and Vicente Gortari.

49. Refugio de la Garza to Martínez, June 22, 1820, BA, roll 64, frame 584; Martínez to Arredondo, May 9, 1819, Nacogdoches Archives, box 2Q295, vol. 181, pp. 497–99, no. 483 (BCAH).

50. Navarro to Martínez, Dec. 28, 1820, Castañeda Photostats, vol. 15, pp. 24–25.

51. Martínez to Arredondo, Dec. 31, 1820, Castañeda Photostats, vol. 15, p. 23; Arredondo to Martínez, Feb. 13, 1821, BA, roll 66, frames 625–626.

52. Expediente formado sobre el pago de los travajos expendidos por los vicinos de la Villa de S.n Fernando y Presidio de S.n Antonio de Béxar in la obra de las Casas Reales [del Ayuntamiento] de esta Villa, Apr. 11, 1793, BA roll 23, frames 310–318.

53. Arredondo to Martínez, Feb. 14, 1821, BA, roll 66, frame 434–435; Martínez to Ambrosio María Aldasorio, Feb. 6, 1821 (quotation), BA, roll 66, frame 557–579.

54. Año de 1822: Cargos contra el fondo de Propios [y fondo mesteño], BA, roll 70, frames 613, 614, and 623. These receipts provide valuable documentation of the value of labor and building materials.

55. Martínez to First Alcalde [José Ángel Navarro], July 16, 1821, BA, roll 57, frame 980; Béxar Ayuntamiento Minutes, July 16, 1821, BA, roll 66, frames 302–303. Those attending this historic meeting were Gov. Antonio Martínez, presiding; Alcaldes José Ángel Navarro and José Manuel Granados; regidores Manuel Barrera, Gaspar Flores, Francisco Flores de Abrego, Pablo Salinas, Francisco Bustillos, and Juan Ignacio Chávez; and Síndico Procurador Francisco Montes de Oca. Regidor Juan Martín de Veramendi was absent. Father Refugio de la Garza's full name was Jose Refugio Guadalupe de la Garza. See "Garza, José Refugio Guadalupe de la," *The Handbook of Texas Online*, <http://www.tshaonline.org/handbook/online/articles/GG/fga69.html> [Accessed Jan. 11, 2010].

56. José Ángel Navarro to Martínez, July 18, 1821, and José Vivero to Martínez, July 18, 1821, BA, roll 67, frames 995–996; Béxar Ayuntamiento Minutes, July 16, 19, 1821, BA, roll 66, frames 301–302, 306.

57. Félix D. Almaráz Jr., "Governor Antonio Martínez and Mexican Independence in Texas: An Orderly Transition," *The Permian Historical Annual* XV (December 1975): 44–55; Martínez to V.E. [Gaspar López], Sept. 18, 1821 (quotation), BA, roll 68, frames 362–364.

58. Weber, *Mexican Frontier,* 159–160.

59. Provincial Deputation [of Monterrey] to [Béxar] City Council, Feb. 1, 1821, BA, roll 66, frame 291; Andrés Tijerina, *Tejanos & Texas under the Mexican Flag, 1821–1836* (College Station: Texas A&M University Press, 1994), 37.

60. Bueno, "In Storms of Fortune," 45.

61. Martínez to Félix Trudeaux, Feb. 26, 1821, BA, roll 66, frames 778–789; Erasmo Seguín to Martínez, June 23, 1821 (quotation), Nacogdoches Archives, box 2Q296, vol. 189, pp. 180–182 (BCAH).

62. Gregg Cantrell, *Stephen F. Austin: Empresario of Texas* (New Haven: Yale University Press, 1999), 89.

63. Eugene C. Barker (ed.), "Journal of Stephen F. Austin on His First Trip to Texas, 1821," *QTSHA* 7 (April 1904): 286–307.

64. Thomas Buentello to Martínez, Sept. 12, 1821, BA, roll 68, frames 338–339; Martínez to [La Bahía Alcalde], Nov. 11, 1821, BA, roll 68, frames 971–972.

65. Veramendi to [Martínez], Jan. 31, 1822, BA, roll 70, frame 503; Gaspar López to Interim Custom Collector, Feb. 27, 1822, BA, roll 70, frames 859–860; José Ángel Navarro to Francisco Bustillos, Dec. 24, 1821, BA, roll 69, frame 647.

66. Martínez to Béxar Ayuntamiento, Dec. 24, 1821, BA, roll 66, frame 323. The complete roster of council members elected were: José María de Jesús Salinas, first alcalde; Juan José Flores, second alcalde; councilmen [regidores], in order of rank, José Antonio Navarro, Clemente Delgado, Vicente Treviño, José Miguel de Arciniega, Manuel Yturri Castillo, José Gomes, Eugenio Flores, and José Darío Zambrano. Síndico procuradores were Ignacio Villaseñor and Juan Manuel Montes. Various sources have erroneously reported that José Antonio Navarro was elected alcalde in 1822. He did, however, serve as

acting or interim alcalde in 1822, during the absence of the first and second alcalde.

67. Béxar Ayuntamiento Minutes, Jan. 16, 1822, BA, roll 66, frames 236–237.

68. Béxar Ayuntamiento Minutes, Jan. 16, 1822, BA, roll 66, frame 236; López to Béxar Ayuntamiento, Mar. 5, 1822, BA, roll 70, frames 921–922; López to Martínez, Jan. 16, 1822, BA, roll 70, frame 281; Clemente Delgado to José Félix Trespalacios, Aug. 26, 1822, BA, roll 72, frames 649–665.

69. Béxar Ayuntamiento Minutes, Dec. 27, 1821, Jan. 28, 1822, BA, roll 66, frames 324, 327–328; Béxar Ayuntamiento, Instructions to the Deputy of the Province of Texas who is to attend the Constituent Congress of the Cortes of the Mexican Empire, Jan. 30, 1822, Nacogdoches Archives, box 2Q297, vol. 189, pp. 8–17 (BCAH); Refugio de la Garza, receipt to [Béxar] Ayuntamiento, Feb. 2, 1822, BA, roll 70, frame 526; [Béxar] Ayuntamiento to Provincial Deputation, Quaderno de Oficios, Año de 1822, Feb. 3, 1822, Béxar Archives, box 2S142 (BCAH).

70. Béxar Ayuntamiento to Martínez, Feb. 22, 1821, BA, roll 66, frame 293; Béxar Ayuntamiento Minutes, Jan. 10 and 31, Mar. 7, 1822, BA, roll 66, frames 325–326, 328–330.

71. Béxar Ayuntamiento Minutes, Aug. 4, 1822, Bexar Archives, box 2S135 (BCAH); Béxar Ayuntamiento to Martínez, Mar. 28, 1822, BA, roll 71, frames 222–224; Francisco García to Martínez, Mar. 1, 1822, BA, roll 70, frame 896.

72. Libro de Judicios Consiliatorios del Año de 1822, 1823, 1824, and 1825, BA, roll 71, frames 786–814; Libro de Judicios Consiliatorios: Juan Manuel Sambrano vs. Vicente Alderete, Apr. 10, 1822, BA, roll 71, frame 806; Tijerina, *Tejanos & Texas*, 40; Clutter, *Legal Culture of Northern Spain*, 143; Jesús F. de la Teja, "Tejano Profile," in Gerald E. Poyo and Gilberto M. Hinojosa (eds.), *Tejano Origins in Eighteenth-Century San Antonio* (Austin: University of Texas Press, 1991), 8–9.

73. Libro de Judicios Consiliatorios: *Juana Francisca de los Santos Coy v. Miguel Martínez*, June 4, 1822, BA, roll 71, frame 787.

74. Libro de Judicios Consiliatorios: *Leonarda Vázquez v. Xaviera Flores*, July 22, 1822, BA, roll 71, frame 790.

75. Béxar Ayuntamiento Minutes, Aug. 4, 1822, Béxar Archives, box 2S135 (BCAH); Libro de Judicios Consiliatorios: *José Antonio Navarro v. Josepha de la Garza*, Jan. 9, 1823, BA, roll 71, frame 793. The case of Rocque Charles illustrates the blurred line that separated contractual, voluntary servitude and slavery. The conciliatory judgment system remained in effect until February 1824. It illustrates an aspect of the Spanish constitution that, like the provision for parish electors, decentralized decision making and facilitated rapid resolutions to local disputes based on a legal process that Bexareños considered desirable and fair. The use of the conciliatory system is evidence of the relevance of the Spanish Constitution up to the time when the 1824 Mexican constitution went into effect.

76. José Antonio Navarro to Martínez, Mar. 29 and 30, 1822, BA, roll 71, frames 244, 258–259.

77. Salinas to Martínez, June 28, 1822, BA, roll 71, frames 1,055–1,057; Béxar Ayuntamiento Minutes, June 18, 1822, Béxar Archives, box 2S135 (BCAH); Correspondence Between Trespalacios and Martínez, Aug. 24, 1822, BA, roll 72, frames 609–629.

78. Noticia de las guias que da esta administracion de Extrangeras para lo Interior desde 1.0 de Septiembre, Sept. 5, 1822, BA, 67, frames 882–883; Béxar Ayuntamiento Minutes, Nov. 28, 1822, Béxar Archives, box 2S135 (BCAH).

79. Béxar Ayuntamiento Minutes, Nov. 21, 1822, BA, roll 66, frames 352–353; Timothy M. Matovina, *Guadalupe and Her Faithful: Latino Catholics in San Antonio from Colonial Origins to the Present* (Baltimore: John Hopkins University Press, 2005), 53–56; Elliot

Coues, *The Expeditions of Zebulon Montgomery Pike* (3 vols.; New York: Francis P. Parker, 1895), II: 694.

80. Refugio de la Garza to Béxar Ayuntamiento, Apr. 30, 1822, BA, roll 71, 494–496.

81. John O. Leal (comp.), "San Fernando Baptismals," 1812–1825 (typescript), 82, no. 761.

NOTES TO CHAPTER THREE

1. Béxar Ayuntamiento Minutes, Jan. 2, 1823, BA, roll 74, frames 356–357.

2. Justo Sierra, *The Political Evolution of the Mexican People*, trans. Charles Ramsdell (Austin: University of Texas Press, 1969), 185; Nettie Lee Benson, "The Plan of Casa Mata," *Hispanic American Historical Review* 25 (February 1945): 45–56.

3. Tijerina, *Tejanos & Texas*, 37. Béxar representative Refugio de la Garza was a little behind the curve in Mexico City. On March 12, 1823, he wrote to the Béxar city council that Iturbide had prevailed and Congress had given him the title of "Liberator." Iturbide abdicated a week later.

4. Antonio López de Santa Anna's Proclamation to the Northern Provinces (English translation), Mar. 31, 1823, Nacogdoches Archives, box 2Q297, vol. 190, pp. 162–164 (BCAH).

5. Trespalacios to López, Mar. 31, 1823, BA, roll 74, frames 423–424.

6. Béxar Ayuntamiento to the *Junta Provincial Gubernativa de Monterrey*, Mar. 22, 1823, BA, roll 74, frame 431; Statement by La Bahía Ayuntamiento et al., Mar. 24, 1823, BA, roll 74, frames 434–435.

7. Béxar Junta Gubernativa to Béxar Ayuntamiento; Juan Manuel Zambrano to Junta Gubernativa, Apr. 19, 1823, BA, roll 74, frames 601–603.

8. José Miguel Alderete to Trespalacios, Apr. 20 1823 (1st quotation), BA, roll 74, frame 610; La Bahía Ayuntamiento Minutes, May 25, 1823 BA, roll 74, frame 848; La Bahía Ayuntamiento to Francisco García, Apr. 24, 1823 (2nd quotation), BA, roll 74, frames 631–633.

9. Mariano Gonzales Laris to Monterrey representatives (English translation), May 14, 1823, Nacogdoches Archives box 2Q297, vol. 190, pp. 167–170 (BCAH); Santa Anna to Trespalacios (English translation), May 6, 1823, Nacogdoches Archives, box 2Q297, vol. 190, p. 11 (BCAH).

10. Béxar Junta Gubernativa to Béxar Ayuntamiento, June 6, 1823, BA, roll 74, frames 948–949.

11. Refugio de la Garza to Béxar Ayuntamiento, May 21, 1823, Nacogdoches Archives, box 2Q297, vol. 190, pp. 172–173 (BCAH).

12. Béxar Junta Gubernativa to Santa Anna, June 11, 1823, BA, roll 75, frame 10.

13. José Ignacio García Illueca to Representatives of Nuevo León (English translation), Apr. 28, 1823 (1st quotation), Nacogdoches Archives, box 2Q297, vol. 190, pp. 165–166 (BCAH); Béxar Junta Gubernativa to Illueca, June 11, 1823 (2nd, 3rd, and 4th quotations), transcribed in Vito Alessio Robles, *Coahuila y Tejas Desde la Consumacíon de la Independencia hasta el Ttratado de Paz de Guadalupe Hidalgo*, 2nd ed. (2 vols.; México, D.F.: Editorial Porrua, 1978), I: 426–429.

14. *Quaderno de Oficios Corridor*, July 22, 1823, BA, box 2S142 (BCAH).

15. Veramendi to Luciano García, July 8, 1823, BA, roll 75, frame 169; Alessio Robles, *Coahuila y Tejas*, I: 429. After 1824, Texas ceased to be an independent province and became a department of the new state of Coahuila and Texas. The *jefe politico* (political chief) was the top civil official in the department, and he reported to the governor in the capital at Saltillo.

16. Cantrell, *Stephen F. Austin*, 134–135.

17. Luciano García to Béxar Ayuntamiento, Sept. 25, 1823, BA, roll 75, frames 591–592.

18. Carlos E. Castañeda, *Our Catholic Heritage in Texas, 1519–1936* (7 vols.; Austin: Von Boeckmann-Jones Company, 1936), VI, 310.

19. José Antonio Navarro to Jefe Politico [José Antonio Saucedo] on behalf of José Ángel Navarro, Nov. 11, 1823, Mission Records, no. 80 (Spanish Archives, BCC); José Antonio Navarro and Veramendi on behalf of José Francisco Ruiz to Jefe Politico [Saucedo], Nov. 11, 1823, Deed Record, vol. F-1, pp. 57–60 (BCC); Veramendi, power of attorney to José Antonio Navarro, May 16, 1825, Book PA 71–84, pp. 1–4 (Spanish Archives, BCC); Eugenio Navarro to Administrator [Veramendi], Oct. 1, 1823, BA, 75, frames 636–637. It was perhaps at this time that Veramendi decided to locate a ranch on the road linking the port of Copano to Refugio and thence onward to La Bahía. This strategic location would have facilitated the import and export of goods.

20. Election of the 1825 [Béxar] Ayuntamiento, Dec. 24, 1824, BA, roll 73, frame 776. In 1824, the election of members was held at the end of December in the same manner as it had been since 1820. In fact, pending official implementation of the new constitution, provisions of the 1812 Spanish Constitution continued to be observed, as demonstrated by a reference to "compliance with Article 49 of the Constitution still in effect."

21. Election of the 1825 [Béxar] Ayuntamiento, Dec. 24, 1824, BA roll 73, frame 776; Béxar Ayuntamiento to the Governor [Rafael González], *Quaderno de Oficios Borradores*, Feb. 3, 1825, Béxar Archives, box 2S142 (BCAH). Rafael González to Ayuntamiento, Mar. 23, 1825, BA, roll 80, frames 142–45.

22. José Antonio Saucedo to Rafael González, Apr. 21, 23, and 24, 1825, BA, roll 80, frame 682; Governor [Gonzales] to Béxar Ayuntamiento, June 8, 1825, BA, roll 81, frame 762–764.

23. Veramendi to Jefe Politico [Saucedo], Sept. 30, 1825, BA, roll 83, frame 937–938. Eugenio Navarro, José Antonio's brother, substituted for Veramendi in charge of the foreigners fund, that is, collection of duties on imports. See Veramendi to Béxar Ayuntamiento, July 24, 1825, BA, roll 82, frames 925–926.

24. "Fredonian Rebellion," The Handbook of Texas Online, <http://www.tshaonline. org/handbook/online/articles/FF/jcf1.html> [Accessed May 27, 2010]; T. R. Fehrenbach, *Lone Star: A History of Texas and the Texans* (Cambridge, Mass.: Da Capo Press, 2000), 163.

25. José Antonio Navarro to Inhabitants of Nacogdoches, Dec. 28, 1826, Nacogdoches Archives, box 2Q299, vol. 31. pp. 175–176 (BCAH).

26. Austin to José Antonio Navarro, Feb. 27, 1827, in *The Austin Papers*, ed. Eugene C. Barker (3 vols.; Washington: Government Publishing Office, 1924–1928), I: 1,609–1,610. This is the first correspondence found between Austin and Navarro.

27. Tijerina, *Tejanos & Texas*, 113; Cantrell, *Stephen F. Austin*, 192–193.

28. Tijerina, *Tejanos & Texas*, 115.

29. Saucedo to Austin, July 27, 1826, in Barker (ed.), *Austin Papers*, I: 1,166.

30. Cantrell, *Stephen F. Austin*, 9.

31. John O. Leal (comp.)," San Fernando Baptismals", Book 1793–1812 (typescript), 14: 159.

32. Pedro López Prieto to Gov. Antonio Cordero, Jan. 21, 1808, BA, roll 37, frames 495–496).

33. Randolph B. Campbell, *Gone to Texas: a History of the Lone Star State* (New York: Oxford University Press, 2003), 226.

34. John O. Leal (comp.), "San Fernando Baptismals," Book 1793–1812 (typescript), pp. 13–19.

35. Jesús F. de la Teja, "Why Urbano and María Trinidad Can't Get Married: Social Relations in Late Colonial San Antonio," *SWHQ* 112 (October 2008): 128.

36. The 1824 Constitution of Mexico divided the state of Coahuila and Texas into three departments, or jurisdictions: Saltillo, Monclova, and Béxar. Within a few years the indeterminate location of the state capital would lead to a fierce competition between Saltillo and Monclova.

37. Election of Legislative Deputies, May 27, 1827, Nacogdoches Archives, box 2Q299, vol. 32, pp. 124–127 (BCAH); José Salinas to Political Chief, Department of Texas [Saucedo], June 14, 1827, BA, roll 104, frames 398–399; Anastacio Bustamante to Antonio Elozúa, June 20, 1827, Elozúa to Mateo Ahumada, June 28, 1827, BA, roll 104, frame 789; *Actas del Primer Congreso Constitutional del Estado Libre de Coahuila y Tejas*, box 2Q228, vol. 703, p. 640 (BCAH).

38. Interrogation of Celestin Forrestal, July 5, 1827, BA, roll 105, frames 5–6; José Antonio Navarro to Saucedo, July 13, 1827, BA, roll 105, frames 347–348; Cantrell, *Stephen F. Austin*, 198.

39. Cantrell, *Stephen F. Austin*, 198; Saucedo to Alcalde, Aug. 23, 1827, BA, roll 106, frames 616–617; Ahumada to Political Chief, Department of Texas [Saucedo], Aug. 29, 1827, BA, roll 106, frames 636–637; Old Texan, *José Antonio Navarro*, 10; Laredo Military Commandant to Commandant General [Mateo Ahumada], Sept. 10, 1827, BA, roll 107: frame 71; Vicente Arreola to Elozúa, Sept. 11, 1827, BA, roll 107, frames 107–108; *Actas del Primer Congreso*, box 2Q228, vol. 703, p. 707 (BCAH).

40. The sitting legislators at the time of Navarro's arrival were Ramón García Rojas, president; Father Juan Antonio González, 1st Deputy Secretary (D.S.); José Miguel de Arciniega, 2nd D.S.; José María Echaiz; José Francisco Madero; José Antonio Tijerina; Father José Ignacio Sánchez Navarro; José María Valdés Recio; and José Manuel Cárdenas. See *Actas del Primer Congreso*, box 2Q228, vol. 703, pp. 708ff (BCAH).

41. Ibid., 708–709.

42. José Antonio Navarro to Austin, May 17, 1827 [1828], in Barker (ed.), *Austin Papers*, II: 40–41.

43. H. P. N. Gammel (comp.), *The Laws of Texas, 1822–1897* (10 vols.; Austin: Gammel Book Company, 1898–1902), I: 178–179.

44. *Actas del Primer Congreso*, box 2Q228, vol. 703, p. 686 (BCAH).

45. Ibid., 720.

46. Ibid., 722–723.

47. Sierra, *Political Evolution of the Mexican People*, 189, 194; Gammel (comp.), *Laws of Texas*, I: 204–205; *Actas del Primer Congreso*, box 2Q228, vol. 703, p. 757 (BCAH); Harold D. Sims, *The Expulsion of Mexico's Spaniards, 1821–1836* (Pittsburgh: University of Pittsburgh Press, 1990), 37.

48. Gammel (comp.), *Laws of Texas*, I: 195–198, 450–451.

49. Alessio Robles, *Coahuila y Tejas*, II: 251; Gammel (comp.), *Laws of Texas*, I: 1,314.

50. *Actas del Primer Congreso*, box 2Q228, vol. 703, p. 816 (BCAH).

51. *Actas del Primer Congreso*, box 2Q228, vol. 703, pp. 818–821.

52. *Actas del Primer Congreso*, box 2Q228, vol. 703, pp. 866, 868; Gammel (comp.), *Laws of Texas*, I: 211–212.

53. Gammel (comp.), *Laws of Texas*, I: 212, 424.

54. Austin to José Antonio Navarro, July 23, 1829, in Barker (ed.), *Austin Papers*, II: 234; Bueno, "In Storms of Fortune," 45.

55. Gammel (comp.), *Laws of Texas*, I: 188–189, 202.

56. Lester G. Bugbee, "Slavery in Early Texas," *The Political Science Quarterly* 13 (September 1898): 389–412; Juan Antonio Padilla to Austin, June 18, 1825, in Barker (ed.),

Austin Papers, I: 1,135–1,137. For the state colonization law, see Gammel (comp.), *Laws of Texas*, I: 99–107. Its only reference to slavery, Article 46, says: "As regards the introduction of slaves, the new settlers shall obey the laws already established, and which hereafter may be established on the subject" (p. 105).

57. Peter Ellis Bean to Austin, July 5, 1826, in Barker (ed.), *Austin Papers*, : 1,367–1,368; *Actas del Primer Congreso*, box 2Q228, vol. 703, p. 898 (BCAH); Eugene C. Barker, (ed.), "Minutes of the Ayuntamiento of San Felipe de Austin, 1828–1832," *SWHQ* 21 (January 1918): 311.

58. *Actas del Primer Congreso*, box 2Q228, vol. 703, p. 900 (BCAH).

59. *Actas del Primer Congreso*, box 2Q228, vol. 703, pp. 900–901 (BCAH); Gammel (comp.), *Laws of Texas*, I: 213.

60. Ramón Músquiz to Austin (1st quotation), May 15, 1827, and José Antonio Navarro to Austin, May 17, 1828 (2nd and 3rd quotation), in Barker (ed.), *Austin Papers*, II: 38–41.

61. José Miguel de Arciniega to Austin, May 17, 1828, in Barker (ed.), *Austin Papers*, II: 41–42.

62. Eugene C. Barker, *The Life of Stephen F. Austin* (Austin: University of Texas Press, 1925), 210.

63. José Francisco Ruiz to Austin, July 23, 1829, in Barker (ed.), *Austin Papers*, II: 232–233; Tijerina, *Tejanos & Texas*, 117.

64. *Actas del Primer Congreso*, box 2Q228, vol. 703, p. 912 (BCAH).

65. Gammel (comp.), *Laws of Texas*, I: 82. The election of the first president, Guadalupe Victoria, with Nicolás Bravo as vice-president, took place in October 1824, after passage of the federal constitution.

66. Jan Bazant, *A Concise History of Mexico from Hidalgo to Cárdenas, 1805–1940* (Cambridge, UK: Cambridge University Press, 1990), 41; Sierra, *Political Evolution of the Mexican People*, 194–195.

67. Padilla to Austin, Jan. 26, 1828, in Barker (ed.), *Austin Papers*, II: 10–11; *Actas del Primer Congreso*, box 2Q228, vol. 703, pp. 925–926 (BCAH); Gammel (comp.), *Laws of Texas*, I: 217.

68. Bueno, "In Storms of Fortune," 40–41; personal conversations with Adela M. Navarro, 1979.

69. Gammel (comp.), *Laws of Texas*, I: 220–221; "Homestead Law," *The Handbook of Texas Online*, <http://www.tshaonline.org/handbook/online/articles/HH/mlh2.html> [Accessed Jan. 11, 2010]; Barker, *The Life of Stephen F. Austin*, 196–197. The Laws of the Indies included a decree issued by Ferdinand and Isabella in 1476 prohibiting the confiscation of work animals and the tools of trade of laborers because of debt, except for debts owed to the sovereigns, or overlords.

70. Old Texan, *Jose Antonio Navarro*, 11.

71. De Cordova, *Texas: Her Resources and Her Public Men*, 147.

72. Deed Record, vol. C-1, p. 7 (BCC).

73. Alessio Robles, *Coahuila y Tejas*, I: 265.

NOTES TO CHAPTER FOUR

1. José Antonio Navarro to Austin, Nov. 27, 1828 in Barker (ed.), *Austin Papers*, II: 147–148; Deed Record, vol. C-1, pp. 9–10 (BCC). A league of land (4,428 acres) is often referred to as a *sitio*—the two terms are synonymous. For clarity, sitios will henceforth be designated as leagues.

2. José Antonio Navarro to Austin, Nov. 27, 1828, in Barker (ed.), *Austin Papers*, II: 147–148. An *arroba* was a measure of weight equal to twenty-five pounds.

3. José Antonio Navarro to Austin, Jan. 8, 1829, in Barker (ed.), *Austin Papers* II: 156–157. A fanega was a measure of volume equal to about 2.6 bushels.

4. Thomas F. Leaming to Austin, May 28, 1828, Ruiz to Austin, July 23, 1829, Austin to José Antonio Navarro, July 23, 1829 (quotations), in Barker, *Austin Papers*, II: 7, 232–235. Austin's map of Texas can be viewed at <http://www.bcah.utexas.edu/collections/maps.php> [Accessed Aug. 22, 2009].

5. Austin to José Antonio Navarro, Oct. 19, 1829, in Barker (ed.), *Austin Papers*, II: 271–273.

6. "Guerrero Decree," <http://web.me.com/joelarkin/MontereyDemographicHistory/_Guerrero_2.html> [Accessed Aug. 27, 2009]; Austin to José Antonio Navarro, Oct. 19, 1829 (quotations), in Barker, *Austin Papers*, II: 271–273.

7. Spanish Minutes Book Two (1830–1835) of the San Antonio City Council (hereafter cited as SB2), section 1, Jan. 7, 1830, p. 1, English translations (microfilm; Texana Department, San Antonio Public Library, San Antonio);"Síndico Procurador," *The Handbook of Texas Online*, <http://www.tshaonline.org/handbook/online/articles/SS/nfs1.html> [Accessed Jan. 11, 2010].

8. *Jefetura* [Ramón Músquiz] to José Antonio Navarro, Feb. 18, 1830, Notice of farmland, with its corresponding water in the Barrio de Valero, Feb. 18, 1830, BA, roll 128, frames 560–563.

9. Austin to José Antonio Navarro, Oct. 19, 1829, in Barker (ed.), *Austin Papers*, II: 271–273. A translation in English of this letter is in Gulick, Smither, et al. (eds.), *Lamar Papers*, V: 39–40.

10. José Antonio Navarro to Austin, Oct. 29, 1829, in Barker (ed.), *Austin Papers*, II: 276–278; José Antonio Navarro to Governor [José María Viesca], Jan. 16, 1830, Travis County Deeds, vol. A, p. 316 (Travis County Courthouse, Austin, Texas; manuscript copy filed for record on Apr. 2, 1841).

11. Governor [José María Viesca] to José Antonio Navarro, Feb. 2, 1830, Travis County Deeds, vol. A, p. 316 (Travis County Courthouse, Austin, Texas); José Antonio Navarro to Austin, Feb. 18, 1830 (quotation), in Barker (ed.), *Austin Papers*, II: 333–334.

12. José Antonio Navarro to Austin, Feb. 18, 1830 (1st quotation), in Barker (ed.), *Austin Papers*, II; Austin to José Antonio Navarro (2nd and 3rd quotations), Mar. 23, 1830, in Gulick. Smither, et al. (eds.), *Lamar Papers*, VI: 48–49. Years later, tobacco of excellent quality was reportedly grown at Castroville. See *Ledger* (San Antonio), Mar. 21, 1857, p. 2.

13. José Antonio Navarro to Austin, Mar. 24, 1830, Stephen F. Austin Papers, series IV, box 2Q414 (BCAH).

14. SB2, section 20, Apr. 1, 1830, p. 25, English translation (microfilm); Ruiz to Austin, Apr. 11, 1830, in Barker (ed.), *Austin Papers*, II: 367–368; Campbell, *Gone to Texas*, 116–127.

15. The second state legislature of Coahuila y Tejas in 1829 changed the name of La Bahía to Goliad, an anagram of the name Hidalgo—the "H" being omitted, since it is silent in Spanish. "Goliad, Texas," *The Handbook of Texas Online*, <http://www.tshaonline.org/handbook/online/articles/GG/hjg5.html> [Accessed Jan. 11, 2010].

16. José Antonio Navarro, Invoice of Goods, June 10, 1830, BA, roll 131, frame 464–466.

17. Milam, Benjamin Rush," *The Handbook of Texas Online*, <http://www.tshaonline.org/handbook/online/articles/MM/fmi3.html> [Accessed Jan. 5, 2010]; "Wavell, Arthur Goodall," *The Handbook of Texas Online*, <http://www.tshaonline.org/handbook/online/articles/WW/fwa77.html> [Accessed Jan. 5, 2010].

18. Austin to José Antonio Navarro, May 31, 1830 (quotations), in Barker (ed.), *Austin Pa-*

pers, II: 404; "Genealogia de Mexico," http://genealogia-mexico.blogspot.com/2009/05/genealogiaorgmx-22947-re-francisco-de.html [Accessed Aug. 27, 2009].

19. José Antonio Navarro to Austin, June 24, 1830, Spanish Collection, Boxed and Bound Material, box 29/6 (GLO).

20. Deed Record, Vol. C-1, pp. 10–12 (BCC). The Béxar city council found that José Luís Carvajal and Manuel Zepeda had already claimed the area at the Gachupin Trail and the Agua Negra Spring.

21. José Antonio Navarro to Governor [José María Viesca], July 19, 1830, Arthur G. Wavell Papers, pp. 214–217 (Catholic Archives of Texas, Austin).

22. Robert W. Amsler, "General Arthur G. Wavell, A Soldier of Fortune in Texas [Part One]," *SWHQ* 49 (July 1965): 15–16.

23. J. M. J. Carvajal to Austin (quotation), Sept. 1, 1830, in Barker (ed.), *Austin Papers*, II: 475–477; Receipt from José Antonio Navarro, Sept. 17, 1830, José Antonio Navarro, Draft of Recommendations for Political Chief, Sept. 22, 1830, BA roll 134, frames 477, 604–606; SB2, section 55, Sept. 23, 1830, p. 73, Spanish transcripts (microfilm).

24. José Antonio Navarro, invoice, Nov. 1, 1830, BA, roll 135, frame 916: Michel B. Menard to Austin, Nov. 27, 1830, in Barker (ed.), *Austin Papers*, II: 543–544.

25. Robert W. Amsler, "General Arthur G. Wavell, A Soldier of Fortune in Texas [Part Two]," *SWHQ* 49 (October 1965): 191. Manuel de Mier y Terán was Commandant General of the Eastern Interior Provinces, which included Coahuila y Tejas, from 1830 to 1832. His full name was José Manuel Rafael Simeón de Mier y Terán. See "Mier y Terán, Manuel de," *The Handbook of Texas Online* <http://www.tshaonline.org/handbook/online/articles/MM/fmi2.html> [Accessed Jan. 11, 2010].

26. José Antonio Navarro to Músquiz, Dec. 2, 1830, quoted in Bueno, "Storms of Fortune," 57–58.

27. José de la Piedras to Antonio Elozúa, Jan. 3, 1831, Spanish Collection, Boxed and Bound Material, box 127/5, p. 23 (GLO).

28. Piedras to Austin, Jan. 3, 1831 (Williams Collection, 23-0531, Rosenberg Library, Galveston); Ramón Múzquiz to governor, Dec. 30, 1830, in Joseph W. Dawson, *José Antonio Navarro: Co-Creator of Texas* (Waco: Baylor University Press, 1969), 51–52; [Múzquiz to governor] Jan 2., 1831, copy to José Antonio Navarro, Ibid.

29. José Antonio Navarro to Williams, Feb. 3, 1831, Williams Collection, 23-0562 (Rosenberg Library, Galveston).

30. José Antonio Navarro to Williams, Feb. 17, 1831, Williams Collection, 23-0576 (Rosenberg Library, Galveston). See also BA, roll 138, frames 66–67.

31. José Antonio Navarro to Governor [José María Viesca], Mar. 14, 1831, Wavell Papers, 208–209 (Catholic Archives of Texas, Austin).

32. José Antonio Navarro to Williams, Mar. 31, 1831 Williams Collection, 23-0624 (Rosenberg Library, Galveston). The wedding on January 9, 1831 was a "December-May wedding." José Ángel Navarro's age was listed as forty-six; Juana was fourteen.

33. R. M. [Ramón Músquiz] to José Antonio Navarro, Apr. 4 and 6, 1831, José Antonio Navarro to Músquiz, Apr. 4, 1831, Spanish Collection, Boxed and Bound Material, box 126/22, pp. 221–222, 224 (GLO). José Salinas was married to Margila Chirino, a half-sister of Navarro's wife. He had been granted two leagues of land in 1827, which he wanted to locate at the junction of the San Marcos and Guadalupe rivers in the DeWitt colony. He died in 1830 and his widow had the grant located and later sold it to Navarro. See "DeWitt Colonists 1828 Biographical Sketches," <http://www.tamu.edu/ccbn/dewitt/1828census3.htm> [Accessed Aug. 23, 2009).

34. José Antonio Navarro to Williams, Apr. 14, 1831 (quotation), Williams Collection, 23-0642 (Rosenberg Library, Galveston); Statement by José Antonio Navarro, Apr. 14,

1831, Spanish Collection, Boxed and Bound Material, box 34/31, pp. 807, 825 (GLO); San Fernando Marriage Records, pp. 178–179, no. 338 (microfilm; Texana Department, San Antonio Public Library); Chabot, *Makers of San Antonio,* 247. Navarro's reply to Williams also reveals that he continued his mercantile efforts while serving as a land commissioner. He sent his reply to Williams with Geronimo Santos and José María Jimenez and asked Williams to let the pair stay at his house and advise them so that in Brazoria they would not be cheated in what they were to buy.

35. Músquiz to Elozúa, May 26, 1831, Elozúa to Músquiz, May 27, 1831, José Antonio Navarro to [Músquiz], June 7, 1831, Spanish Collection, Boxed and Bound Material, box 126/23, pp. 232, 234 (GLO); Músquiz to José Antonio Navarro, Apr. 14, 1831, BA, roll 140, frame 144; José Antonio Navarro to Political Chief [Músquiz], Apr. 30, 1831, Austin Papers, series IV, box 2Q414, p. 248 (BCAH); José Antonio Navarro to Austin, July 7, 1831, Williams Collection, 23-0751 (Rosenberg Library, Galveston).

36. Ethel Zivley Rather, "DeWitt's Colony," *QTSHA* 8 (October 1904): 108; Músquiz to José Antonio Navarro, Aug. 11 and 17, 1831, Spanish Collection, Boxed and Bound Material, box 125/20, p. 238, and Box 126/23, p. 233 (GLO); Governor [José María Letona] to José Antonio Navarro, Apr. 15, 1831, Wavell Papers, 210–122 (Catholic Archives of Texas, Austin). Apparently José Maria Salinas was not related to José Salinas. See "DeWitt Colonists 1828 Biographical Sketches," http://www.tamu.edu/ccbn/dewitt/1828census3.htm [Accessed Aug. 23, 2009]. José María Letona succeeded José María Viesca as governor of Coahuila y Tejas on April 5, 1831. See "Letona, José María," The Handbook of Texas Online, <http://www.tshaonline.org/handbook/online/articles/LL/fle35.html> [Accessed Jan. 11, 2010].

37. José Antonio Navarro to Williams, May 14, 1831, Williams Collection, 23-0696 (Rosenberg Library, Galveston).

38. José Antonio Navarro to Williams, May 16, 1831, Williams Collection, 23-0699 (Rosenberg Library, Galveston).

39. José Antonio Navarro to Williams, May 27, 1831, Williams Collection, 23-0713 (Rosenberg Library, Galveston).

40. José Antonio Navarro to Williams, June 6, 1831, José Antonio Navarro to Austin, July 7, 1831, Williams Collection, 23-0728 and 0751 (Rosenberg Library, Galveston).

41. José Antonio Navarro to Stephen F. Austin, July 7, 1831, Williams Collection, 23-0751 (Rosenberg Library, Galveston). *Poleo,* or pennyroyal, is an aromatic mint that yields an oil used in folk medicine.

42. José Ángel Navarro, List of Goods, June 25, 1831, BA, roll 142, frames 298–300; José Antonio Navarro to Stephen F. Austin, July 7, 1831, José Antonio Navarro to Williams, August 8, 1831, Williams Collection, 23-0751 and 0774 (Rosenberg Library, Galveston).

43. José Antonio Navarro to Constitutional Alcalde [José María Salinas], Oct. 2, 1831, Deed Record, vol. C-1, pp. 7–8; José María Carvajal survey, Oct. 4, 1831, Deed Record, vol. C-1, pp. 14, 18 (BCC); Original Grantee Map of Atascosa County, Abstract No. A-42, p. 97 (GLO). As Navarro had previously requested, the east side of the land lay along the Gachupin Trail, which was also known as part of the southern route to Presidio Rio Grande. The tract straddled the Atascosa River, and included a section of the Agua Negra Creek. The bulk of the land formed of a rectangle 5.81 miles in length and 4.60 in width. On the north side a "panhandle," roughly a mile square, projected so as to include water from the Agua Negra Creek. At 4,428 acres per league, the four leagues equaled to 17,712 acres—one hundred million square varas. The northeast corner of the property was contiguous with the present-day town of Poteet. Modern roads correspond closely to all of the boundaries of the property. Highway 476 lies along the north border; Highway 2146 passes just inside of and parallel to the eastern boundary.

44. Veramendi to Músquiz, Sept. 22, 1831, Músquiz to José Antonio Navarro, Sept. 23, 1831, Spanish Collection, Box 126/24, pp. 250–252 (GLO); Veramendi to José Antonio Navarro, Nov. 11, 1831, Deed Record, vol. C-1, p. 64 (BCC). Veramendi, as a Mexican citizen, was entitled to six additional leagues, and he asked that these be given to him from the vacant lands of the defunct Mission Refugio. As he explained in his September 1831 petition to Músquiz, as soon as the legislature had opened these lands to private applicants, "I presented myself to the alcalde (the only one of the Villa of Goliad) so that he could put me in possession of the six cited leagues." Veramendi "built a house there, corrals and other improvements, so as to be able to bring down my remaining possessions. The rest of this is to be taken on the other side toward the port [of Copano] because they are now vacant . . . [and] I consider myself to be the owner of them." His petition for the six leagues was granted in the form of an *amparo*, which gave him a claim but not a title. Despite the fact that this land was listed on the inventory of his estate, no evidence has been found of a title issued to him or his heirs.

45. María Josefa Rodríguez (alias Chefa Romano), Jan. 11, 1832, Deed Record, vol. C-1, pp. 90–92 (Spanish Archives, BCC); María Loreto de Castañeda, sale to José Antonio Navarro, Apr. 16, 1832, Deed Record, vol. C-1, pp. 93–95 (BCC). What Navarro did with this property before using it for personal purposes is not certain, but it can safely be assumed that he did not let it just sit. Most likely he put it to immediate use as a rental property.

46. Margila Chirino to DeWitt Land Commissioner [José Antonio Navarro], Mar. 1, 1832, Deed Record, vol. 185, pp. 388–389, 391–392 (Guadalupe County Courthouse, Seguin, Texas). The designation "Tio" Geronimo and "San" Geronimo were both used. The name Tio Geronimo goes back at least to 1781, when a reference was made to the *Paso de Tio Geronimo*, or Tio Geronimo crossing; see BA, roll 14, frame 752. However, the following year (Sept. 30, 1782) a soldier reported an attack on an encampment on San Geronimo Creek; see BA, roll 15, frame 8. San Geronimo will be used here because that was the usage in Navarro's time. The present-day name is Geronimo Creek.

47. Músquiz to José Antonio Navarro, Jan. 30, 1832, Spanish Collection, box 126/24, p. 254 (GLO).

48. José Antonio Navarro to Williams, Feb. 1, 1832, Williams Collection, 23-0879 (Rosenberg Library, Galveston).

49. Austin to Williams, Mar. 21, 1832, in Barker (ed.), *Austin Papers*, II: 758–759. Regarding personal and political matters, Austin wrote in this letter to Williams that someone was trying to make James Bowie his enemy. There was also concern at Béxar over affairs at Brazoria, not only because of a memorial that the ayuntamiento had produced but also because two cannon had turned up there in an unexplained manner. It was feared that the memorial would cause Santa Anna to regard the colonists as enemies. To keep more Mexican troops from being sent to Texas, Austin said that "dead calm" was needed. It was in the true interest of Texas that "we never separate from Mexico," keep encouraging immigration, and make it a state separate from Coahuila. If immigration from the United States ceased, Austin believed, then Indians would take possession of Texas and all would be lost.

50. José Antonio Navarro to Williams, Apr. 12, 1832, Williams Collection, 23-0923 (Rosenberg Library, Galveston). Navarro's allegorical reference is to two ancient centers of learning: the Sorbonne, or University, in Paris and the University of Salamanca, the oldest such institution in Spain. His awareness of these two universities is another indicator of his broad knowledge of significant places and events.

51. Margaret Swett Henson, *Samuel May Williams: Early Texas Entrepreneur* (College Station: Texas A&M University Press, 1976), 47; José Antonio Navarro to Jefe Politico [Ramón Músquiz], May 13, 1832, Arciniega [to José Antonio Navarro], July 10, 1832, Deed

Record, vol. A, pp. 317, 319–320 (Travis County Courthouse, Austin, Texas); José Antonio Navarro, Title for Seven Leagues, July 10, 1832, Spanish Collection, 134/5 (GLO). The land was in present-day Travis and Bastrop counties; see Travis County Abstract A-18 and Bastrop County Abstract A-53. A map of original grantees in the Map Collection of the Texas State Library and Archives in Austin shows the land was titled on July 16, 1833 (Travis County, vol. 41, p. 64, and Bastrop County, vol. 2, p. 52). All monetary figures are rounded off to the nearest peso.

52. Arciniega [to José Antonio Navarro], July 10, 1832, Travis County Deed, vol. A, 321 (Travis County Courthouse, Austin, Texas).

53. Crimm, *De León*, 112; J. F. Madero to Williams, Apr. 14, 1832, Williams Collection, 23-0927 (Rosenberg Library, Galveston) José Antonio Navarro, notes, n.d., José Antonio Navarro III Collection 904, folder 18 (DRT).

54. José Antonio Navarro, List of colonists granted land in DeWitt's colony, Nov. 9, 1832 (quotation), Spanish Collection, box 34/32 (GLO); Béxar Political Chief [Músquiz] to Governor [Veramendi], Dec. 1, 1832, BA, roll 154, frames 168–169; Crimm, *De León*, 113; Galen Greaser, Texas General Land Office Archivist, personal conversation with the author, April 15, 2005. Five pages in chart format, written in Navarro's neat handwriting, contain the names of the grantees, their civil status, number of persons in each family, amount and classification of the land granted, and the payments due.

55. Carmela Leal (comp.), *Residents of Texas*, II: 325.

56. David J. Weber (ed.), *Troubles in Texas, 1832: A Tejano View Point from San Antonio* (Dallas: DeGolyer Library of the Southern Methodist University, 1983), 1; Austin to Williams, Dec. 6, 1832 (quotation), Williams Collection, 23-1025 (Rosenberg Library, Galveston).

57. Weber, *Troubles in Texas*, 4; Austin to Williams, Dec. 6, 1832 (quotations), Williams Collection, 23-1025 (Rosenberg Library, Galveston). Among the remedies proposed was to move the state capital from Saltillo to Monclova, which Navarro and Miguel Arciniega had supported in the first legislature.

58. Austin to Williams, Dec. 6, 1832 (quotations), Williams Collection, 23-105 (Rosenberg Library, Galveston); Alessio Robles, *Coahuila y Tejas*, I: 913.

59. Austin to Williams, Mar. 21, 1832, in Barker (ed.), *Austin Papers*, II: 758–759; Músquiz to Governor [Veramendi], Jan. 10, 1833, in Barker, *Austin Papers*, II: 912–913; Miguel Soto, "La Disputa entre Monclova y Saltillo y la Independencia de Texas," in María Elena Santoscoy, Arturo Eduardo Villarreal, and Miguel Soto, *La Independencia y el Problema de Texas: Dos Eventos en Coahuila* (Saltillo, Coahuila: Archivo Municipal de Saltillo, 1997), 48. The Plan of Veracruz was a modified version of Santa Anna's Plan of Casa Mata.

60. Veramendi in *Béxar Administrador de Rentas*, Dec. 24, 1833, BA, roll 153, frames 396–397; *Acts of the Fourth State Congress*, Mar. 2, 1833, box 2Q229, vol. 707, pp. 1,678, 1,687–1,688 (BCAH); Gammel (comp.), *Laws of Texas*, I: 317; Tijerina, *Tejanos & Texas*, 134; Lúcas Martínez Sánchez, *Monclova: Hechos Históricos del Siglo XIX* (Monclova, Coahuila: Editorial del Valle de Cándamo 2004), 57.

61. [Elozúa] to Veramendi, Jan. 18, 1833 (quotation), Bexar Archives, box 2S295 (BCAH); Santiago Navayra to Elozúa, Jan. 18, 1833, BA, roll 154, frame 682; Elozúa to Miguel García, Apr. 19, 1833, BA, roll 156, frame 58; De Cordova, *Texas: Her Resources and Her Public Men*, 148; Old Texan, *José Antonio Navarro*, 13.

62. Cantrell, *Stephen F. Austin*, 267–68; José Antonio Navarro to Austin, July 8, 1833, Williams Collection, 23-0751 (Rosenberg Library, Galveston).

63. Miguel García to Elozúa, March 1833, BA, roll 155, frames 647–648; notice to Miguel García that José Antonio Navarro had received 1,200 pesos from Antonio Menchaca, Apr. 19, 1833, BA, roll 156 frame 58; Gifford White, *1830 Citizens of Texas* (Austin: Eakin Press,

1983), 105; John O. Leal (comp.) "San Fernando Church Baptismals," Book 1826–1842,p. 22, no. 254; Lauretta Russell (comp.), *1850 Census of Béxar County, Texas* (San Antonio: San Antonio Genealogical and Historical Society, 1983), 64, no. 642; Cipriano Ramírez, certification of taxes paid by José Antonio Navarro, June 29, 1833, José Antonio Navarro, valuation of listed imports, June 29, 1833, BA, roll 158, frames 463–464. By this time, Navarro's six children were María del Carmen, José Antonio George, María Gertrudis, José Ángel, Celso Cornelio, and Wenseslao Eusebio ("Sixto").

64. Alejandro Treviño to Elozúa, July 2, 1833, Elozúa to Erasmo Seguín, Aug. 1, 1833 (quotation), BA, roll 157, frames 151, 708–709; [Department Chief of Béxar] to Veramendi, Jan. 18, 1833, BA, box 2S295 (BCAH); Alessio Robles, *Coahuila y Tejas*, I: 455.

65. Santiago del Valle to Béxar Political Chief [Músquiz], Aug. 13, 1833, BA, roll 158, frames 141–142; Actas de la Diputación Permanente, vol. 709, pp. 54–55 (BCAH); Martínez Sánchez, *Monclova: Hechos Históricos*, 62–63; Lúcas Martínez Sánchez, speech to San Antonio Genealogical Society, May 7, 2005, San Antonio, Texas.

66. José Antonio Navarro to Williams, Sept. 11, 1833, Williams Collection, 23-1206 (Rosenberg Library, Galveston). Laudanum was solution of opium in alcohol, commonly used in the nineteenth century for the relief of pain. This may have been a remedy Navarro used when his leg was inflamed.

67. José Antonio Navarro to Williams, Sept. 26, 1833, Williams Collection, 23-1212 (Rosenberg Library, Galveston); María Josefa Ruiz de Navarro to Béxar Alcalde [Músquiz], Sept. 26, 1833, BA, roll 158, frames 548–539. Despite various published reports, it appears James Bowie and Ursula de Veramendi did not have children. Amelia Williams published a mistranslation of Navarro's Sept. 26, 1833, letter to Williams, saying that Navarro reported that Bowie's "children" died with Ursula, in "A Critical Study of the Siege of the Alamo and the Personnel of its Defenders [Chapter 1]," *SWHQ* 36 (April 1933): 251–287. An entry in the Mormon listings show a James Bowie, born in 1831, at Saltillo, son of James Bowie and María Ursulita de Veramendi. This cannot be correct. The couple married in Béxar in April 1831, and records show Bowie to have been in Texas through December 1831.

68. José Antonio Navarro to Luciano Navarro, Deed Record, vol. F-1, pp. 15–18 (BCC). These pages are copies of the original records, made when the deeds were re-recorded in San Antonio in 1838 under the Republic of Texas government.

69. José Antonio Navarro, Declaration, Jan. 10, 1858, <http://tslarc.tsl.state.tx.us/repclaims/256/25600084.pdf> [accessed Aug. 29, 2009]; Gus L. Ford, *Texas Cattle Brands: A Catalog of the Texas Centennial Exposition Exhibit, 1936* (Dallas: Clyde C. Cockrell Company, 1936), 3. Ford noted that the Navarro brand and date shown were provided by A. N. Langston of Devine, Texas. No documentary record of Navarro's brand was found in the Béxar Archives or other primary sources. He certainly had a brand as early as 1831, as evidenced by his reference to it being stolen (José Antonio Navarro to Williams, Aug. 8, 1831, Williams Collection, 23-0774, Rosenberg Library, Galveston). The earliest documented record of Navarro's brand was in Guadalupe County in 1847; its shape is very similar to what Ford presented.

70. Cantrell, *Stephen F. Austin*, 277.

71. Jesús F. de la Teja (ed.), *A Revolution Remembered: the Memoirs and Selected Correspondence of Juan N. Seguín* (Austin: State House Press, 1991), 125–127; José Antonio Navarro to Williams, Feb. 26, 1834 (quotations), Williams Collection, 23-1274 (Rosenberg Library, Galveston).

72. John O. Leal (comp.), "San Fernando Church Burials" (typescript) p. 68, no. 1546; José Antonio Navarro to Williams, Oct. 8, 1834, Williams Collection, 23-1363 (Rosenberg Library, Galveston).

73. Gerdes, "Navarro Family Heritage"; Músquiz to Béxar Ayuntamiento, Mar. 27,

1834, BA, roll 160, frames 888–891; José Antonio Navarro and Ignacio Herrera, Permit to transport goods, Dec. 15, 1834, BA, roll 163, frames 518–520. Navarro paid Margila Chirino 250 pesos for her two leagues of land on Geronimo Creek, a tributary of the Guadalupe.

74. José Antonio Navarro, receipt to John Smith, Nov. 28, 1838, Jose Antonio Navarro III Collection (DRT).

75. Juan N. Seguín, list of prisoners and their assignees, Apr. 29, 1834, BA, roll 161, frames 285–286 (see also frames 219–220, 226, and 633–634); Pedro Flores to Judge to the First Instance, June 23, 1834, BA, roll 162, frames 135–136.

76. De la Teja (ed.), *Revolution Remembered*, 21; Alessio Robles, *Coahuila y Tejas*, II: 508.

77. Santoscoy, Villareal, and Soto, *La Independencia y el Problema*, 50; Weber, *Mexican Frontier*, 254.

78. Bexareño petition, Oct. 7, 1834 (quotation), Nacogdoches Archives, box 2Q308, vol. 241, pp. 113–116 (BCAH). For an English translation and further discussion of this document, see Jack Jackson and John Wheat (eds.), *Almonte's Texas: Juan N. Almonte's 1834 Inspection, Secret Report & Role in the 1836 Campaign* (Austin: Texas State Historical Association, 2003), 294–296.

79. José Antonio Navarro to Williams, Oct. 8, 1834, Williams Collection, 23-1363, (Rosenberg Library, Galveston).

80. De la Teja (ed.), *Revolution Remembered*, 134; Franklin Madis, *The Taking of Texas: A Documentary History* (Austin: Eakin Press, 2002), 59. See Robert García and Sylvia Jean de Jesús García, *Tejano Participants in the Texas Revolution of 1835–1837* (San Antonio: Los Bexareños Genealogical Society, 2005) for numerous statements by Tejanos, recruited by Juan N. Seguín in 1835, who subsequently applied to the Texas state government for pensions for their service during the Texas Revolution.

81. José Antonio Navarro, list of merchandise, March 8, 1835, BA, roll 164, frame 362; Veramendi estate papers, Sept. 26, 1833, BA, roll 158, frames 538–620; Luciano Navarro, tax receipt, Feb. 25, 1835, José Antonio Navarro III Collection (DRT); Luciano Navarro, List of property lost and confiscated from him at the Veramendi House during the siege of Béxar, July 28, 1837, Luciano Navarro Collection (TSL). Additional records relating to the Veramendi estate are in Proceedings on the Inventories in the Probate Court in the Estate of Juan Martín de Veramendi and his Wife María Josefa Navarro . . . who died Intestate in the City of Monclova, probate record, H-833, Jan. 1, 1839 (Spanish Archives, BCC).

82. Austin to Williams, Mar. 21, 1835, in Barker (ed.), *Austin Papers* III: 50–52; Cantrell, *Stephen F. Austin*, 357.

83. Cantrell, *Stephen F. Austin*, 357; José Antonio Navarro to Secretaries of the [Monclova] Congress of the State of Coahuila y Tejas, Apr. 6, 1835, José Antonio Navarro III Collection (DRT).

84. Old Texan, *José Antonio Navarro*, 15–16.

85. José Ángel Navarro to *Administrator de Rentas* [Gaspar Flores], May 30, 1835, Gaspar Flores to José Antonio Navarro, Nov. 11, 1835, BA, roll 165, frames 372–373, 412–412; Alessio Robles, *Coahuila y Tejas*, I: 536.

86. Receipt signed by Agustín Moral and José Antonio Navarro, June 6 and June 8, 1835, List of money paid by José Antonio Navarro to Williams, June 26, 1835, Jose Antonio Navarro III Collection, (DRT); [Domingo de Ugartechea] to Commandant General [Martín Perfecto de Cos], June 15, 21, 1835. BA, roll 165, frames 616–617.

87. Mier y Terán to Elozúa, Apr. 18, 1831, BA, roll 140, frames 167–168; José Antonio Navarro to Rodríguez, June 29, 1833, BA, roll 158, frame 463ff. At one time or another, all four of the Navarro brothers participated in the merchant trade. For example, in Au-

gust 1829, José Ángel Navarro returned from New Orleans on the ship *Pomona*, along with José Cassiano, who had a load of merchandise as no doubt José Ángel did as well.

88. Budget for September 16th celebration, signed by Ugartechea and [José Ángel] Navarro, Sept. 7, 1835, BA, roll 166, frame 645.

89. Store taxes, January 1824, BA, roll 76, frame 286; seven dance taxes, February 1824, BA, roll 76, frames 318–324.

Notes to Chapter Five

1. José Ángel Navarro to *Alcalde* of Gonzales [Andrew Ponton], Sept. 21, 1835, BA roll 166, frames 778–779; Francisco Castañeda to Ugartechea, Oct. 10, 1835, in John J. Jenkins, *Papers of the Texas Revolution, 1835–1836* (9 vols.; Austin: Presidial Press, 1973), II: 33–36. This interesting narrative contains a detailed, day-by-day, account of Castañeda's actions and that of the colonists.

2. Reséndez (ed.), *A Texas Patriot on Trial in Mexico*, 80–81; Rafael Eca y Músquiz to Political Chief of Béxar [José Ángel Navarro], Oct. 24, 1835, BA, roll 167, frame 379.

3. "Texas Declaration of Causes for Taking up Arms Against Santa Anna," Nov. 7, 1835 (1st, 2nd, and 3rd quotations), in., *Documents of Texas History*, ed. Ernest Wallace, David M. Vigness, and George B. Ward (2nd ed.; Austin: State House Press, 1994), 91; Todd Hansen (ed.), *The Alamo Reader: A Study in History* (Mechanicsburg, Pa.: Stackpole Books), 638 (4th quotation); Luciano Navarro, Petition to the Republic of Texas to Recover Losses Incurred during the Siege of Béxar, July 28, 1837 (4th quotation), Luciano Navarro Collection (TSL). Francis W. Johnson's battle report to Gen. Edward Burleson said the Navarro house had been an advanced and important position close to the square. The capitulation document was signed in a small building in La Villita, preserved by the City of San Antonio as "the Cos House." The Republic of Texas legislature changed the name of San Fernando de Béxar to San Antonio in December 1837.

4. Hansen (ed.), *Alamo Reader*, 652, 658–659 (quotations); [José Antonio Navarro III], "Señor Navarro Tells the Story of His Grandfather," in Howard R. Driggs and Sarah S. King, *Rise of the Lone Star: A Story of Texas Told by its Pioneers* (New York: Frederick & Stokes Co., 1936), 268, 272. In the petition cited above, Luciano Navarro made it clear that Francis W. Johnson confiscated his supplies, and he tried for the next thirty years to gain reimbursement for both the goods taken and the damage that the rebels did to the interior of his house.

5. Béxar Election Results, Feb. 1, 1836, BA, 167, frames 484–500; Juan N. Seguín to Francisco Ruiz, Feb. 10, 1836, in De la Teja (ed.), *Revolution Remembered*, 135–136.

6. Blas Herrera, Pension Application, Nov. 3, 1874, <http://tslarc.tsl.state.tx.us/repclaims/220/22000246.pdf> [Accessed Sept. 6, 2009]; Reséndez (ed.), *Texas Patriot on Trial*, 59; William F. Gray, *From Virginia to Texas, 1835* (Houston: Gray, Dillaye & Co., 1909; reprint, Houston: Fletcher Young Publishing Company, 1965), 120.

7. Gray, *From Virginia to Texas*, 121.

8. Gammel (comp.), *Laws of Texas*, I: 823–828; Gray, *Virginia to Texas*, 120–122, lists fifty-seven "Members-Elect of the New Convention." Not all of these were present on March 1, 1836. Evidently his was a preliminary list of elected delegates, since he names many who did not attend or arrived after March 1.

9. Gray, *Virginia to Texas*, 123. Historians believe that George C. Childress was the primary author of the Texas Declaration of Independence and already had a draft when he arrived at Washington-on-the-Brazos. He probably used the declaration of causes for taking up arms against Mexico, adopted by the Consultation at San Felipe in December 1835. See "Childress, George Campbell," *The Handbook of Texas Online*, <http://www.tshaonline.org/handbook/online/articles/CC/fch28.html> [Accessed Jan. 11, 2009].

10. Gammel (comp.), *Laws of Texas*, I: 834–838, 847, 848, 879; Gray, *Virginia to Texas*, 124; De Cordova, *Texas: Her Resources and Her Public Men*, 150 (1st quotation); Old Texan, *José Antonio Navarro*, 16–17 (block quotation); Potter, *Texas Revolution*, 9 (3rd quotation). Late-arriving members added their signatures: Maverick and James Woods on the 6th, and Andrew Briscoe by the 9th. Their later arrival is reflected in the fact that their names were the last signed to the manuscript, some too late to be shown on the printed copies of the Declaration of Independence. The manuscript of the Declaration of Independence is preserved in the Texas State Library and Archives at Austin. None of the enlarged copies have been found.

11. Gray, *Virginia to Texas*, 124.

12. Gammel (comp.), *Laws of Texas*, I: 265; Gray, *Virginia to Texas* (quotation), 127–128.

13. Gray, *Virginia to Texas*, 128; Edward L. Miller, *New Orleans and the Texas Revolution* (College Station: Texas A&M University Press, 2004), 49; "Burnley, Albert Triplett," *The Handbook of Texas Online*, <http://www.tshaonline.org/handbook/online/articles/BB/fbu53.html> [Accessed Jan. 11, 2010]; "Gray, William Fairfax" *The Handbook of Texas Online*, <http://www.tshaonline.org/handbook/online/articles/GG/fgr27.html> [Accessed Jan. 11, 2010]; "Green, Thomas Jefferson," *The Handbook of Texas Online*, <http://www.tshaonline.org/handbook/online/articles/GG/fgr39.html> [Accessed Jan. 11, 2010]. No record was found in the Bexar County deed records for Navarro's purchase or sale of these five leagues.

14. Gammel (comp.), *Laws of Texas*, I: 834, 856 (quotation); Rupert N. Richardson, "Framing the Constitution of the Republic of Texas," *SWHQ* 31 (January 1928): 199.

15. Miller, *New Orleans and the Texas Revolution*, 49; "The Constitution of the Republic of Texas," in Wallace, Vigness, and Ward (eds.), *Documents of Texas History*, 104; Gammel (comp.), *Laws of Texas*, I: 867; Galen D. Greaser, *Catalogue of the Spanish Collection of the Texas General Land Office* (2 vols.; Austin: General Land Office, 2003), I: 4.

16. "The Constitution of the Republic of Texas," in Wallace, Vigness, and Ward (eds.), *Documents of Texas History*, 104; Gray, *Virginia to Texas*, 131. A cursory comparison shows a close similarity between the March 9 draft of the Constitution in Gammel (comp.), *Laws of Texas*, I: 859–872, and the final version, as published in Wallace, Vigness, and Ward (eds.), *Documents of Texas History*, 98–106. On March 14, Gray noted that the delegates received news from Gen. Sam Houston of the fall of the Alamo, and that a letter from "John Seguín, at Gonzales, to Ruis and Navarro, brought the same account." Further confirmation of the fall of the Alamo arrived the next day.

17. Gray, *Virginia to Texas*, 132; *Journals of the Senate of the Republic of Texas, First Congress* (Columbia, Tex.: G. &. T. H. Borden, Public Printers, 1836), 204 (quotation). What became of the original Constitution after the 1836 Convention ended remains a mystery. During the frenzied departure and subsequent turmoil, the document that was completed and signed at Washington-on-the-Brazos disappeared and has never been found. Evidently the manuscript was taken to Nashville and was printed in a newspaper there. It was reprinted in a Cincinnati paper, and from there it was copied by the *Texas Telegraph* on August 3, 1836. This version subsequently was accepted as official. See Richardson, "Framing the Constitution of the Republic of Texas," 215. An interesting document has been found recently that appears to be a draft of the 1836 Constitution. Jerry C. Drake, Director of the Archives of the Texas General Land Office (GLO), presented a paper online in 2006 about the discovery and analysis of a document, entitled "Constitution of the Republic of Texas," which was found in the GLO archives. While he says that this draft is not the missing final copy of the Republic of Texas Constitution, there is "a strong if not conclusive case that the GLO document is a draft of the Republic of Texas

constitution presented at the convention on March 7." He also says handwriting analysis illustrates that "the GLO draft of the Republic of Texas Constitution was created at the . . . convention of 1836." Drake, "Draft—Texas Constitution," <http://74.125.45.104/search?q=cache:mUlYIfmwqHoJ:www.sanjacintosrt.org/ConstitutionRTF.rtf+Jerry+c.+drake+1836+constitution&hl=en&ct=clnk&cd=1&gl=us&client=safari> [Accessed Sept. 6, 2009].

18. Dixon, *Men Who Made Texas Free*, 243–244 (quotation); Richardson, "Framing the Constitution of the Republic of Texas," 197. The journal of the Convention lists voters by name for only six issues. Navarro's vote is recorded in only one of these, on an amendment to a bill regarding land titles and surveys. See Gammel (comp.), *Laws of Texas*, I: 883–884, 898, 900, 901.

19. Gray, *Virginia to Texas*, 132, 134–137. Jared E. Groce and his son, Leonard W. Groce, farmed a huge estate with the assistance of more than a hundred slaves.

20. Stephen L. Hardin, *Texian Iliad: A Military History of the Texas Revolution* (Austin: University of Texas Press, 1994), 187; Gray, *Virginia to Texas*, 135.

21. Hardin, *Texian Iliad*, 188; De la Teja (ed.), *Revolution Remembered*, 136.

22. Hobard Huson (ed.), *Dr. J. H. Barnard's Journal* ([n.p.], 1950), 44-45. Hydrothorax is a condition resulting from an excess of serous fluid in the pleural cavity. José Ángel Navarro died on June 11, 1836. San Fernando Church burial records show that he was interred on June 13. See John O. Leal (comp.), "San Fernando Church Burials" (typescript), p. 69, no. 1569.

23. Juan N. Seguín in De la Teja (ed.), *Revolution Remembered*, 140, 143 (1st quotation); Gray, *Virginia to Texas* (2nd, 3rd, and 4th quotations), 180, 184. Gray refers only to "Seguín," which must be Erasmo, since his son Juan was in Texas during May 1836.

24. List of merchandise [*Factura de los efectos que le vinieron del Nueva Orleans a D.a Juana Ramírez*], Oct. 27, 1836 [copied by José Antonio Navarro on Oct. 17, 1837], J. A. Navarro Documents, box 2-23/1099 (TSL); Juan José Galván to Jesús de la Garza, Nov. 16, 1836 (quotation), in Madis, *Taking of Texas*, 83–84. Navarro's list of goods is particularly interesting because it shows the cost of insuring the cargo (10 percent of its value), the cost of transferring the cargo from ship to shore, and the cost of carting the merchandise from the coast to Béxar.

25. Bueno, "In Storms of Fortune," 90, 126; *Journal of the First Senate of the Republic of Texas*, 3–4; Gammel (comp.), *Laws of Texas*, I: 1,193–1,194; Galen Greaser of the Texas General Land Office, in conversation with the author, Jan. 26, 2006.

26. Cantrell, *Stephen F. Austin*, 350–352, 363; José Antonio Navarro to Austin, July 7, 1831 (quotation), Williams Collection, 23-0751 (Rosenberg Library, Galveston). Francisco Ruiz remained in Columbia a few days after the close of Congress and was there when Austin died. That same day he wrote to his son-in-law Blas Herrera about his concern for the situation in Béxar. Ruiz recognized the finality of the change in Texas's government. He advised Herrera that Mexican military forces were advancing and warned him not to take up arms against the Texans, saying "Only God could return Texas to the Mexican government." Most likely, he sent the sad news of Austin's passing to José Antonio Navarro about the same time. See José Francisco Ruiz to Blas Herrera, Dec. 27, 1835, in James W. Knight and Richard Santos (comps.), *Letter from Columbia, Texas, December 27, 1836, Addressed to Blas Herrera* (San Antonio: privately published, 1966). James W. Knight was the Béxar County Clerk, Richard Santos was the County Archivist.

27. José Ángel Navarro Will, Inventories and Estate Distribution, Wills and Estates, Book WE, vol. 16, p. 76 (Spanish Archives, BCC).

28. Juan N. Seguín, in De la Teja (ed.), *Revolution Remembered*, 148–151 (block quotation). Years later, Juan N. Seguín wrote that the remains were placed in an urn and

buried in San Fernando Cathedral near the "presviterio" in front of the banister. Juan N. Seguín to Hamilton P. Bee, Mar. 28, 1889, in Frederick C. Chabot, *Texas Letters* (San Antonio: Yanaguana Society, 1940), 77.

29. Juan N. Seguín, Certificate, Feb. 11, 1837, <http://tslarc.tsl.state.tx.us/repclaims/77/07700036.pdf> [Accessed Sept. 7, 2009]; De la Teja (ed.), *Revolution Remembered*, 87; Andrew Forest Muir (ed.), *Texas in 1837: An Anonymous, Contemporary Narrative* (Austin: University of Texas Press, 1986), 99; José Antonio Navarro to Houston, Mar. 23, 1837, Andrew J. Houston Collection, 2-22/159 (TSL).

30. José Antonio Navarro to Houston, Mar. 23, 1837 (quotations), Andrew J. Houston Collection, 2-22/159 (TSL); José Antonio Navarro, Claim for Reimbursement, Mar. 30, 1837, <http://tslarc.tsl.state.tx.us/repclaims/77/07700022.pdf> [Accessed Sept. 7, 2009].

31. José Antonio Navarro, Claim for Reimbursement, Mar. 30, 1837, <http://tslarc.tsl.state.tx.us/repclaims/77/07700022.pdf> [Accessed Sept. 7, 2009]; Sam Houston to Henry W. Karnes, Mar. 31, 1837 (quotations), in Amelia W. Williams and Eugene C. Barker (eds.), *The Writings of Sam Houston, 1813–1863* (8 vols,; Austin: University of Texas Press, 1939), II: 77–78.

32. Deed Record, vol. A-2, p. 1 (BCC).

33. Deed Record, vol. A-2, p. 1 (BCC). For examples of José Antonio Navarro's activities as associate judge, see the order of José Antonio Navarro and Ignacio Cháves, as probate judges, for the admission of the will of Alex Leroy de Chaumont, dated Oct. 24, 1837, José Antonio Navarro Papers, Box Z-23/950 (TSL).

34. See José Antonio Navarro's certification that Dolores García did not "mix" against the Republic of Texas, dated Dec. 6, 1837, José Antonio Navarro III Collection (DRT).

35. Journal A (1837–1849) of the Minutes of the San Antonio City Council (hereafter cited as JA), section 2, Sept. 16, 1837, p. 471, Spanish transcript (Texana Department, San Antonio Public Library).

36. Bexar County Tax Rolls, 1837, reel 1, no. 3030 (microfilm; TSL).

37. See many claims of José Antonio Navarro indexed at Republic of Texas Claims, TSL, <http://www.tsl.state.tx.us/arc/repclaims/index.php> [Accessed Sept. 7, 2009]. For the terms of headrights, see "The Constitution of the Republic of Texas," in Wallace, Vigness, and Ward (eds.), *Documents of Texas History*, 104.

38. De la Teja (ed.), *Revolution Remembered*, 154–155.

39. John Bost Pitts III, "Speculation in Headright Land Grants in San Antonio From 1837 to 1842" (master's. thesis, Trinity University of San Antonio, 1966), 14, 23, 54–56, 63–64, 112. In April 1837, seventy Bexareños sold their rights for 259,690 acres to the partnership of Ludovic Colquhoun and William Steele. Another speculator who bought headrights was William Richardson. He contracted to purchase fifty-six claims from Bexareños during May and June 1837 that totaled 211,122 acres, for a total price of about $36,000. The Bexar County General [Direct] Index to Deeds (BCC) shows that 154 Bexareños got headright certificates. The Texas General Land Offices' online index, however, shows that only five received titles: Domingo Bustillos, Jeronimo Leal, Luzgardo Martínez, Rafael Martínez, and Pedro Treviño.

40. E. T. Miller, "The Money of the Republic of Texas," *SWHQ* 52 (January 1949): 294–295; Inventory of the Estate of Eugenio Navarro, May 24, 1838, wills and estates, book EN-38, p. 17 (Spanish Archives, BCC). "Texas paper" probably refers to "Star Dollars," the paper currency issued by the Republic beginning in the fall of 1837. Until the mid-nineteenth century, the Mexican peso was circulated widely in the United States. The U.S. dollar and the Mexican silver peso were equivalent in weight and value; the equivalence was set by the United States in 1789. The peso was the first monetary de-

nomination to use the $ sign. The United States also minted dollars in gold coins begin-
ning in 1795. Thus sums expressed in transactions with the $ sign may be American
dollars or Mexican pesos.

41. Deed Record, vol. D-1, pp. 132–133 (BCC), shows that José Antonio Navarro purchased the rights to a league and labor from Francisco Flores for seventy-five dollars.
Flores, however, was a single man and was entitled to only one-third league, which is
what Navarro eventually obtained a headright certificate for (No. 448), which he sold to
John Twohig on April 10, 1841; see Patents, Francisco Flores File, Béxar 1-453, GLO. Just
what "current money of the Republic" Navarro referred to is puzzling because the first
Texas paper currency, known as "Star Dollars," was not issued until later in the year. At
least nine Bexareños, including Navarro, acquired tens of thousands of acres by completing the lengthy process that led from the granting of a headright to obtaining a title.
Information on Francisco de la Garza's relationship with Navarro comes from author's
conversation with Alvin Gerdes, Navarro genealogist, Mar. 8, 2006.

42. James E. Crisp, "Anglo-Texan Attitudes Toward the Mexican, 1821–1845" (Ph.D.
diss., Yale University, 1976), 348.

43. An example of the procedure in acquiring a headright is found in Pitts, "Speculation in Headright Land Grants," 15–18, but it does not follow through the process of
actually getting the patent, or title.

44. Deed Record, vol. D-1, pp. 131–132 (BCC). Leonardo Gil's declaration, edited for
clarity and to remove redundancies, reads as follows: "Republic of Texas, County of
Béxar. Know all men by these presents that I Leonardo Gil for and in consideration of the
sum of seventy dollars, in hand paid, do bargain and sell unto José Antonio Navarro, his
heirs, and assigns forever all of my rights which I have for one league and labor of land
as a native citizen of the Republic of Texas previous to the Declaration of Independence.
This claim is evidenced by my application and affidavit herein annexed and I do hereby
authorize José Antonio Navarro to select such location for this land as he may deem best.
. . . Witness my hand and seal this 18th day of May, A.D. one thousand eight hundred
thirty seven Leonardo Gil (his mark)"

45. Patents, Leonardo Gil File, Béxar-1, 292 (GLO). Certificate 292 reads, "This is to
certify that José Antonio Navarro assignee of Leonardo Gil appeared before the Board
of Land Commissioners for the County of Béxar and proved according to law that said
Gil as a native citizen of Texas a married man and entitled to one league and labor of
land upon condition of paying at the rate of $3.50 for every labor of irrigatible [*sic*] land
and $2.50 for every labor of temporal or arable land and $1.20 for every labor of pasture
land which may be contained on the survey secured to said Gil or his assigns by this
certificate."

46. Bexar County Tax Rolls, 1837 (microfilm; TSL).

47. Béxar County Tax Rolls, 1837; Inventory of the Belongings of José Ángel Navarro,
1830–1840 (typescript), wills and estates-76, pp. 1–6, 30 (Spanish Archives, BCC).

48. Béxar County Tax Rolls, 1837.

49. Conversation between author and Alvin Gerdes, Navarro genealogist, April
2007.

50. José Antonio Navarro to C[ornelius] Van Ness, Mar. 19, 1838, Jose Antonio Navarro
III Collection (DRT). Van Ness's letter was not found, but Navarro conveyed its import
in the text of his reply.

51. José Antonio Navarro to Van Ness, Mar. 19, 1838 (quotation), Jose Antonio Navarro
III Coll.Collection (DRT); Bexar County Tax Rolls, 1837. This servant may have been
Meralla, the *criada* Navarro was renting to John W. Smith four years earlier. The differ-
ence between slavery and indentured servitude was evidently clear. Navarro referred to

the many contractual servants in the county, but the 1837 tax rolls for Bexar County list only three slaves: two for a James Harris, and one for Erasmo Seguín.

52. José Antonio Navarro to Van Ness, Mar. 19, 1838, Jose Antonio Navarro III Collection (DRT). Navarro's reference to "property" seems to refer to his contractual rights to her services rather than outright ownership as with a slave. There is a question whether she was legally a chattel when Navarro allowed her to leave. Had he been more familiar with the United States Constitution, Navarro might have bolstered his legal argument by pointing out Article IV, Section 2, which says that, "No Person held to Service or Labour in one State, under the Laws thereof, escaping into another, shall, in Consequence of any Law or Regulation therein, be discharged from such Service or Labour, but shall be delivered up on Claim of the Party to whom such Service is due."

53. José Antonio Navarro to Van Ness, Mar. 19, 1838, Jose Antonio Navarro III Collection (DRT); JA, section 8, Oct. 8, 1837, English translation (microfilm).

54. The identity of Tinsley has not been determined. He probably was not James W. Tinsley, who fought at San Jacinto, commanded a cavalry regiment in San Antonio in 1838, and was killed there in a duel with another officer that same year. See "Tinsley, James W.," *The Handbook of Texas Online*, <http://www.tshaonline.org/handbook/online/articles/TT/fti3.html> [Accessed Jan. 11, 2010]. Tinsley is listed as receiving a headright certificate on July 25, 1838, but this may have been granted to his estate. See the Bexar County General [Direct] Index to Deeds, A–G, p. 461 (BCC).

55. Inventory of the Estate of Eugenio Navarro, May 24, 1838, wills and estates, book EN-38, pp. 13, 28 (Spanish Archives, BCC).

56. Rafael Aldrete interview, *San Antonio Daily Express*, Sept. 21, 1891, p. 2. The Texana Department of the San Antonio Public Library has a typescript of this fragile article. Another account of Eugenio's death is found in the 1856 "Diary of Eliza (Mrs. Albert Sidney) Johnston," eds. Charles P. Roland and Richard C. Robbins, *SWHQ* 60 (April 1957): 498–499. She refers to Eugenio's killer as "officer Tinsley." The Eliza Johnston account briefly tells the basic story of the fatal fight, but differs in many essential details from Aldrete's.

57. Rafael Aldrete interview, *San Antonio Daily Express*, Sept. 21, 1891, p. 2.

58. David Bowser, *West of the Creek: Murder, Mayhem and Vice in Old San Antonio* (San Antonio: Maverick Publishing Co., 2003), 65. The Spanish text of the plaque in San Fernando Church reads, "Aqui Yace Eugenio Navarro Originario de esta Ciudad de Bejar muerto a los 34 años 5 meses 21 dias de su edad el dia seis de mayo de 1838. Acabo victima de su inocencia al tiro de pistola de un vengativo adversario que también sucumbia al puñar del bravo defensor de su honor y persona."

59. Distribution of Eugenio Navarro Estate, wills and estates, book EN-38, pp. 57, 182 (Spanish Archives, BCC). When appraisers assessed this estate, the value of Eugenio Navarro's merchandise alone was set at $9,468.37. After deductions for debts and fees were made, the net appraised value of was $23,363.25. It was divided equally into five bequests: Heirs of José Ángel Navarro, Heirs of Josefa Navarro, José Antonio Navarro, María Antonia Navarro, and José Luciano Navarro. Josefa was the sister who had married Juan Martín de Veramendi, while Maria is the sister who married Col. Mateo Ahumada. José Antonio Navarro sold his certificate to the 295 acres of land to John W. Smith for $100 in August 1838, before he had officially received it. See Sale to Smith, August 1938, in José Antonio Navarro III Collection, DRT.

60. List of an Election held at the Courthouse in and for the County of Bexar, Sept. 3, 1838, Inventory of Republic of Texas Returns, 1835–1845, Bexar County, 1838, Secretary of State Records, Election Division, RG 307 (Archives Division, Texas State Library, Austin).

61. William E. Howth to José Antonio Navarro, Sept. 10, 1838, <http://www.thehisto-ryshop.com/documents/Navarro.htm> [Accessed Sept. 7, 2009]. This site also provides a brief biography of Howth.

62. List of an Election held at the Courthouse in and for the County of Bexar, Sept. 3, 1838, Inventory of Republic of Texas Returns, 1835–1845, Bexar County, 1838, Secretary of State Records, Election Division, RG 307 (Archives Division, Texas State Library, Austin).

63. Castañeda, *Our Catholic Heritage in Texas*, VII: 19.

64. Bueno, "In Storms of Fortune," 93; *Journal of the House of Representatives of the Republic of Texas, Regular Session of Third Congress, Nov. 5, 1838* (Houston: S. Whiting, printer, 1839), 4.

65. The deliberations recorded in the 400-plus pages of the journal of the third House of Representatives are difficult to assess, because it is often unclear which topic the members are discussing. More clear and direct are the acts and resolutions actually passed and signed into law, which can be found in Gammel (comp.), *Laws of Texas*, II: 2–118.

66. Ibid., II: 75–76, 125–126; Jonathan W. Jordan, *Lone Star Navy: Texas, The Fight for the Gulf of Mexico, and the Shaping of the American West* (Washington, D.C.: Potomac Books, 2006), 122–123.

67. *José de la Garza v. John W. Smith et al.*, Oct. 23, 1838, Map Collection, no. 14560, and Patents, José de la Garza File (GLO).

68. *De la Garza v. Smith et al.*, Oct. 23, 1838, Map Collection, no. 14560, and Patents, José de la Garza File (GLO). It is interesting to note that Judge James Robinson took an entirely opposite view of the De León family in Victoria. Ana Carolina Castillo Crimm found Robinson "to be his [Fernando de León's] most determined enemy" in supporting claims against De León property. But then, De León was accused of providing supplies to Mexican forces during the Texas Revolution. See Crimm, *De León*, 172.

69. José Antonio Navarro to the Speaker of the House [John M. Hansford], Jan. 26, 1839, in *Telegraph and Texas Register* (Houston), Jan. 29, 1839, p. 5.

70. Ibid.

71. Ibid.

72. Cherokee Indian land, secured for the tribe by Sam Houston, was also attacked on the same basis of incomplete titles. President Lamar made this clear in his first address to Congress in 1839. He contended that the Cherokees had never received complete titles to their lands whether under the governments of Spain, Mexico, or the Republic of Texas, and that the various treaties pertaining to land ownership had never been ratified. The implication was clear: Cherokee lands were subject to being taken with no compensation. Like the lands of many Tejanos, they would no doubt become available to headright hunters by the rule that lands claimed with imperfect titles reverted to the public domain. See Stanley E. Siegel, *The Poet President of Texas: The Life of Mirabeau B. Lamar, President of the Republic of Texas* (Austin: Jenkins Publishing Company, 1977), 53.

73. *Telegraph and Texas Register* (Houston), Jan. 29, 1839. Rotation in office, or term limits, dates back to the American Revolution and to antiquity.

74. Timothy M. Matovina, *Tejano Religion and Ethnicity: San Antonio, 1821–1860* (Austin: University of Texas Press, 1995), 41–43; Castañeda, *Our Catholic Heritage in Texas*, VII: 20.

75. Castañeda, *Our Catholic Heritage in Texas*, VII: 26–27; De la Teja (ed.), *Revolution Remembered*, 172; Thomas L. Miller, *The Public Lands of Texas, 1519–1970* (Norman: University of Oklahoma Press, 1972), 116; Robert E. Wright, O.M.I., "Father Refugio de la Garza," in De la Teja (ed.), *Tejano Leadership in Mexican and Revolutionary Texas*, 84–87.

76. *Members of the Texas Congress, 1836–1845* (Austin: Senate Engrossing and Enrolling Office and Senate Reproduction, 1992), 9–10; De la Teja (ed.), *Revolution Remembered*, 173–174; José Antonio Navarro to Austin, Nov. 27, 1829, in Barker, *Austin Papers*, II: 147–148.

77. JA, section 57, Jan 8, 1839, p. 28, English translation (microfilm).

78. Rena Maverick Green, *Samuel Maverick, Texan: 1803–1870* (San Antonio: privately printed, 1952), 99; José Antonio Navarro to Lamar in Gulick, Smither, et al. (eds.), *Lamar Papers*, III: 321. Lamar probably had gained Navarro's appreciation, along with that of other Bexareños, for moving the capital of the Republic from Houston to Austin, located only eighty miles from Béxar.

79. Francisco de la Garza, headright survey and plat, Apr. 14, 1839, patents, Bexar-1, no. 226 (GLO).

80. John W. Wilbarger, *Indian Depredations in Texas* (Austin: Hutchings Printing House, 1889; reprint, Austin: Eakin Press, 1985), 605–606; William Cazneau, Promissory Note to José Antonio Navarro, Oct. 28, 1840, and José Antonio Navarro's Receipt for Payment, Nov. 28, 1840 (Star of the Republic Museum, Washington, Texas); José Antonio Navarro, Certificate, Jan. 10, 1858, <http://tslarc.tsl.state.tx.us/repclaims/256/25600084. pdf> [accessed Sept. 7, 2009]. In his 1858 certificate, among other things, Navarro attested that "Ramon Rubio," while in his employment, was killed by Comanche Indians near the San Geronimo Ranch in 1845.

81. Dorothy Kendall and Carmen Perry, *Gentilz: Artist of the Old Southwest* (Austin University of Texas Press, 1974), 114.

82. JA, section 2, Jan. 6, 1840, Spanish transcript (microfilm); Jose Antonio Navarro, Certificate, Oct. 1, 1840 <http://tslarc.tsl.state.tx.us/repclaims/77/07700056.pdf> [Accessed Sept. 7, 2009].

83. San Fernando Burials, Book D, 1817–60, p. no. 1. The cause of José Francisco Ruiz's death was *ydropecia*, or *hydropecia*: hydropsy, an older term for edema. A portrait of Ruiz, painted while he was on his death bed according to family tradition, is preserved at the Daughters of the Republic Library in San Antonio, Texas.

84. *Catalogue, St. Vincent's College Cape Girardeau, Missouri, 1843–1908* (n.p., n.d), 3–4; *Daily Express* (San Antonio) Dec. 22, 1907, p. 11. On Aug. 12, 1995, Rev. Louis J. Derbes, C. M., Archivist for St. Mary's of the Barrens, Perryville, Mo., provided the author with copies from the St. Vincent's College booklet as well as copies of records pertaining to Ángel Navarro's and Luciano Cornelio Navarro's studies. Luciano Cornelio was the son of José Luciano Navarro, and therefore was Ángel's first cousin. These copies are filed at the Casa Navarro State Historical Park in San Antonio, Texas. Note that Father John Timon, whom José Antonio Navarro met while he was a member of the Texas Congress, belonged to the Vicentian Order.

Notes to Chapter Six

1. Jesús Cárdenas to José Antonio Navarro, Feb. 29, 1840, and José Antonio Navarro to Cárdenas, Mar. 15, 1840, in *City Gazette* (Austin), May 13, 1840, pp. 4–5; David M. Vigness, "Relations of the Republic of Texas and the Republic of the Río Grande," *SWHQ* 57 (January 1954): 317–318. George Fisher, a native of Hungary, had been active in Mexican and Texas political affairs for more than twenty years. "Fisher, George," *The Handbook of Texas Online*, <http://www.tshaonline.org/handbook/online/articles/FF/ffi16.html> [Accessed Jan. 11, 2010].

2. Vigness, "Relations of the Republic of Texas and the Republic of the Rio Grande," 313.

3. Noel M. Loomis, *The Texan-Santa Fe Pioneers* (Norman: University of Oklahoma Press, 1958), 6; Miller, "Money of the Republic of Texas," 294.

4. Miller, "Money of the Republic of Texas," 54–55; Weber, *The Mexican Frontier*, 57, 125ff.

5. Weber, *The Mexican Frontier*, 55; Siegel, *Poet President of Texas*, 105 (quotation). Reports such as William G. Dryden's, while greatly exaggerated, did reflect dissatisfaction among many New Mexicans, which worried the governor, Manuel Armijo. He learned of the planned expedition and expressed his concern to the Mexican Minister of War, José María Tornel, saying, "Many of the people expect better conditions from the Texans and thus refuse to help defend this land." Armijo's alarm was enhanced by the fact that New Mexico had come to rely for goods more by trade with the United States over the Santa Fe Trail than from Mexican supply lines to the south. See Charles R. McClure, "The Texan-Santa Fé Expedition," *New Mexico Historical Review* 48 (January 1973): 47–48; Marc Simmons, *New Mexico: A Bicentennial History* (New York: W. W. Norton & Co., 1977), 114–115.

6. Reséndez (ed.), *Texas Patriot on Trial*, 3–5.

7. Hugh McLeod to Lamar, Aug. 28, 1840 (quotation), in Gulick, Smither, et al. (eds.), *Lamar Papers*, III: 439; Deed Record, vol. E-1, pp. 386–387 (BCC).

8. H. Bailey Carroll, *Texan Santa Fe Trail* (Canyon, Tex.: Panhandle Plains Historical Society, 1951), 13 (quotation). Edward Burleson was later replaced by Richard F. Brenham; see "Brenham, Richard Fox," *The Handbook of Texas Online*, http://www.tshaonline.org/handbook/online/articles/BB/fbr41.html [Accessed Jan. 11, 2010].

9. JA, section 120, May 13, 1841, English translation (microfilm). Lamar's visit was the social highlight of the year. Mary A. Maverick recorded that the "grand ball" was held in his honor in the long room of the Miguel de Yturri house, which was decorated with flags and flowers. Prominent citizens of San Antonio attended, including the Seguíns, Arciniegas, Mavericks, and undoubtedly the Navarros. She noted that while Lamar was a gallant man, a poet, and a first rate conversationalist, he acquitted himself poorly as a dancer. Navarro may have been amused by the spectacle of three of Lamar's entourage who, having but one dress coat among them, used it in turn for the dances so as to keep up proper appearances. See Rena Maverick Green (ed.), *Memoirs of Mary A. Maverick* (Lincoln: University of Nebraska Press, 1989), 49–50. Maverick's recollection that the ball occurred in June 1841 must be an error. Inclusions in Gulick, Smither, et al. (ed.), *Lamar Papers*, III: 531–543, show that Lamar remained in Austin during that month. Thus the ball took place in May, as Seguín's note indicates.

10. José Antonio Navarro to Manuel Armijo, Oct. 11, 1841 (quotation), Santa Fe Expedition Scrapbook, H. B. Carroll Papers, box 2Q175, vol. 338, pp. 102–103 (BCAH); *City Gazette* (Austin), May 26, 1841, p. 2.

11. José Antonio Navarro to Lamar, May 18, 1841 (quotations), in Gulick, Smither, et al. (ed.), *Lamar Papers*, III: 524–527, 597–598; Old Texan, *José Antonio Navarro*, 9. That Lamar never returned the Austin letters no doubt pained Navarro, but it ensured their survival. They can be found in the Texas State Library and Archives and have been published, where the descendants of José Antonio Navarro can peruse them as he had wished. Only a few documents from Navarro's personal archives are preserved; most of those were donated by José Antonio Navarro III to the Daughters of the Republic of Texas Library in San Antonio.

12. José Antonio Navarro, Certificate, June 12, 1850, <http://tslarc.tsl.state.tx.us/repclaims/162/16200643.pdf> [Accessed Sept. 12, 2009]; Reuben M. Potter to Lamar, June 5, 1841, in Gulick, Smither, et al. (eds.), *Lamar Papers*, III: 532–33.

13. Potter to Lamar, June 5, 1841 (1st quotation), in Gulick, Smither et al. (eds), *Lamar Papers*, III: 532–33; Reséndez, *Texas Patriot on Trial*, 7–24; [Mirabeau B. Lamar], Proclamation to the Inhabitants of Santa Fé, ca. 1841 (block quotation), Jose Antonio Navarro III Collection (DRT). Historian Andrés Reséndez notes that the translation was faithful

to the English and was done by a well-educated man. See Reséndez (ed.), *Texas Patriot on Trial*, 119. Further evidence that Navarro was the principal translator is provided by the fact that the document uses the second-person, plural, familiar "*vosotros*" form, which was not commonly used in Texas.

14. Weber, *Mexican Frontier*, 267.

15. *City Gazette* (Austin), May 26, 1841, p. 2 (quotation), June 9, 1841, p.1; Loomis, *Texan-Santa Fe Pioneers*, 15–16.

16. Carroll, *Texan Santa Fe Trail*, 85; Paul N. Spellman, *Forgotten Texas Leader: Hugh McLeod and the Texas Santa Fe Expedition* (College Station: Texas A&M University Press, 1999), 62, 78; George W. Kendall, *Narrative of an Expedition Across the Great South-Western Prairies* (2 vols.; London: David Bogue, 1845; reprint, New York: Readex Microprint Corp., 1966), I: 63, 72. Kendall, owner of the *Picayune* (New Orleans), probably wrote his account from his letters, which were published in his paper, since his notes were confiscated. Two other valuable sources are journals kept by Thomas Falconer and Peter Gallagher, both of whom evidently managed to keep or recover their written notes.

17. Spellman, *Forgotten Texas Leader*, 63.

18. Loomis, *Texan Santa Fe Pioneers*, 30; Carroll, *Texan Santa Fe Trail*, 170.

19. Thomas Falconer, *Letters and Notes on the Texan Santa Fé Expedition, 1841–1842* (New York: Dauber & Pine Bookshops, 1930), 80, 126; Loomis, *Texan-Santa Fe Pioneers*, 43; Carroll, *Texan Santa Fe Trail*, 171; Kendall, *Across the Great South-Western Prairies*, II: 121–122; Spellman, *Forgotten Texas Leader*, 74–75. The location of the expedition at the time of Falconer's observations, which he admitted might not be reliable, was 33 degrees, 35 minutes north latitude, and 97 degrees, 44 minutes west longitude, which is in the vicinity of the present-day town of Bowie.

20. Spellman, *Forgotten Texas Leader*, 77.

21. Carroll, *Texan Santa Fé Trail*, 85, 95, 172. This town, which was more accurately known as San Miguel del Vado, lay on the Santa Fe Trail about twenty-five miles southwest of Las Vegas, New Mexico. What remains, including the church, is listed on the National Register of Historic Places.

22. Ibid., 80–81, 173. Llano Estacado (literally "Staked Plain") refers to the High Plains located between Texas and New Mexico. It was discovered and named by the Coronado Expedition in 1541.

23. Spellman, *Forgotten Texas Leader*, 86–87; Ford Dixon, "Cayton Erhard's Reminiscences of the Texan Santa Fe Expedition, 1841, Part II," *SWHQ* 66 (April 1963): 547–548; Kendall, *Across the Great South-Western Prairies*, I: 289, 290, 293–299 (quotations).

24. Spellman, *Forgotten Texas Leader*, 88–91; Kendall, *Across the Great South-Western Prairies*, I: 240 (quotation), 281; Falconer, *Letters and Notes*, 111; Dixon, "Erhard's Reminiscences, Part II," 548.

25. Falconer, *Letters and Notes*, 114 (1st quotation); Old Texan, *José Antonio Navarro*, 19–20 (2nd quotation); De Cordova, *Texas: Her Resources and Her Public Men*, 152 (3rd quotation). Old Texan, in *José Antonio Navarro*, quotes Navarro as saying I have sworn to be a free Texan and it is my custom to respect my oath."

26. Falconer, *Letters and Notes*, 115; Spellman, *Forgotten Texas Leader*, 92.

27. Falconer, *Letters and Notes*, 45, 115–116; Spellman, *Forgotten Texas Leader*, 92; Andrés Archuleta, Report, Oct. 5, 1841, with endorsement of Manuel Armijo, Oct. 6, 1841, Santa Fe Expedition Scrapbook, vol. 340, pp. 47–48. This is a copy of Archuleta's report, which was actually made in Santa Fe on October 1, 1842. It has been translated by the author.

28. Falconer, *Letters and Notes*, 135; Kendall, *Across the Great South-Western Prairies* II: 331–332.

29. José Antonio Navarro to Armijo, Oct. 11, 1841, in Reséndez (ed.), *Texas Patriot on Trial*, 32.

30. Spellman presents a comprehensive discussion about the reasons for the failure of the expedition in *Forgotten Texas Leader*, 93–104.

31. José Antonio Navarro to José Leyva, Oct. 14, 1841 (1st, 2nd, and 3rd quotations), Santa Fe Expedition Scrapbook, vol. 338, 57–58; Peter Gallagher, Journal of the Santa Fe Expedition, cited in Carroll, *Santa Fe Trail*, 178 (4th quotation); Armijo to Ministro de Guerra y Marina [José María Tornel], Oct. 22, 1841 (5th quotation), Santa Fe Expedition Scrapbook, vol. 338, 69–72. "Don Juan Begil" is probably [Juan] Gregorio Vigil, a rancher who befriended some of the Texas prisoners. The story of the expedition quickly entered the realm of New Mexican popular culture. An anonymous writer or writers gathered details about the event and fashioned them into a folk play that expressed a defiant attitude toward the defeated Texans, inflamed by the rumors spread by Armijo that they were "blood-thirsty cannibals" who came to rob, slay, and pillage. The principal characters were Navarro, McLeod, an Indian, and Don Jorge, a New Mexican. Accurately reflecting the rumors that had been spread, the Indian said that he heard that the Texans "were coming here to steal . . . to rob the churches and the rich people. Murderers he said you were!" The play mocked the Texans as gullible and easily tricked into falling into the hands of the Mexican army. When the Texans captured Don Jorge, he offered to betray Armijo—but in fact he deceived the Texans and betrayed them. Don Jorge, in the final verse, says "Die, you dog! Now you are going to pay for all the evil you had planned against my general! This will teach you not to trust the New Mexicans. Whenever you hear them bark at foreigners they always bite them. There is no doubt about it." If Navarro saw the play, he certainly must not have enjoyed being one of its stars. See Kendall, *Across the Great South-Western Prairies*, II: 290, 360; Aurelio M. Espinosa and J. Manuel Espinosa (eds.), "The Texans: a New Mexican Spanish Folk Play of the Middle Nineteenth Century," *New Mexico Quarterly* 13 (Autumn 1943): 308.

32. Falconer, *Letters and Notes*, 50 (quotation).

33. See Kendall, *Across the Great South-Western Prairies*, I: 395–397, 399; Carroll, *Texan Santa Fe Trail*, 179. Col. José María Elias González considered Salazar to be a brute and subsequently, at a court-martial, testified against him for his abusive treatment of the prisoners. Spellman, *Forgotten Texas Leader*, 110.

34. Kendall, *Across the Great South-Western Prairies*, II: 30–32, 44.

35. Kendall, *Across the Great South-Western Prairies*, II: 67–68, 70, 72 (quotation); Falconer, *Letters and Notes*, 137.

36. Loomis, *Texan Santa Fe Pioneers*, 267; Kendall, *Across the Great South-Western Prairies*, II: 85, 91(1st and 2nd quotations); Dixon, *Men Who Made Texas Free*, 247; Williams and Barker, *Writings of Sam Houston*, II: 435.

37. Kendall, *Across the Great South-Western Prairies*, II: 86, 92 (quotation). Col. Mateo Ahumada married María Antonia, José Antonio Navarro's younger sister, on Sept. 14, 1826. See Gerdes, "Navarro Family Heritage."

38. Kendall, *Across the Great South-Western Prairies*, II: 99 (quotations).

39. Loomis, *Texan Santa Fe Pioneers*, 128 (1st quotation); Potter, *Texas Revolution*, 22 (2nd quotation); Kendall, *Across the Great South-Western Prairies*, II: 99 (3rd quotation). The escape plot shows that Navarro was willing to single-handedly trump the reckless plans of his fellows for their benefit, even though he must have known they would condemn him for it. These accounts demonstrate key features of Navarro's character—his self-confidence, decisiveness, and willingness to go against the grain when he knew he was right.

40. Kendall, *Across the Great South-Western Prairies*, II: 151, 154.

41. José Antonio Navarro to Williams, Feb. 26, 1834, Williams Collection, 23–1274 (Rosenberg Library, Galveston).

42. Kendall, *Across the Great South-Western Prairies*, II: 211.

43. Oakah L. Jones Jr., *Santa Anna* (New York: Twayne Publishers, Inc., 1968) 83–85 (quotation); Robert L. Scheina, *Santa Anna: A Curse upon Mexico* (Washington, D.C.: Brassey's Inc., 2002), 42; Will Fowler, *Santa Anna of Mexico* (Lincoln: University of Nebraska Press, 2007), 226–227.

44. Minister of War [José María Tornel] to Commandant General of Mexico [Juan José Andrade], Feb. 4, 1842, Gabriel Venucia [Valencia] to Minister of War [Tornel], Feb. 4, 1842, [Minister of War Tornel] to Commandant General of Mexico [Andrade], Feb. 5, 1842, Andrade to Gen. Mariano Morlet, Feb. 9, 1842 (quotation), Santa Fe Expedition Scrapbook, vol. 338, 59–61, 64, 96–97; Reséndez (ed.), *Texas Patriot on Trial*, 99.

45. Reséndez (ed.), *Texas Patriot on Trial*, 35–37, 41.

46. Ibid., 54–55. As one might expect, Navarro downplayed his role in the Texas Revolution and emphasized the services he had rendered to Mexico. He maintained that circumstances obliged him to side with the rebels and that he really had no choice but to represent the wishes of the citizens who had elected him to both the Convention of 1836 and the Texas Congress in 1838. He likewise portrayed his role as a commissioner for the Santa Fe Expedition as peaceful and one he could not avoid. Navarro's insinuation of being in danger had some basis. Amos Pollard reflected the views of many Anglos when he wrote that he intended to warn the two Béxar representatives to the 1836 Convention (José Antonio Navarro and José Francisco Ruiz) that if they did not vote for Texas independence, "they will have to be very careful on returning here." See Amos Pollard to Henry Smith, Feb. 13, 1836, in Hansen (ed.), *Alamo Reader*, 673.

47. Ibid., 58, 60–61.

48. Ibid., 49, 50 (1st quotation), 58 (2nd quotation). Nepumuceno Navarro was listed by Juan N. Seguín in De la Teja (ed.), *Revolution Remembered*, 136.

49. Reséndez (ed.), *Texas Patriot on Trial*, 57.

50. Ibid, 55 (quotations).

51. Ibid., 56 (quotations).

52. Ibid., 60.

53. Ibid., 76 (1st quotation), 80 (2nd quotation).

54. Ibid., 81–82.

55. Kendall, *Across the Great South-Western Prairies*, II: 331–332, 380, 383.

56. Ibid., 380–384, 435–436.

57. Reséndez (ed.), *Texas Patriot on Trial*, 83–85.

58. Ibid., 87 (quotation), 90.

59. Ibid., 91–92. Because Navarro's earlier testimony provided similar arguments, it appears that he and Linaste developed this defense prior to his interview.

60. Ibid., 93–94 (quotations).

61. Ibid., 98.

62. Ibid., 98–100.

63. José Manuel Zozaya to Commandant General [Juan José Andrade], May 31, 1842, in Ibid., 102–103 (quotations), 111; Andrade to Minister of War [Tornel], Aug. 25, 1842, Santa Fe Expedition Scrapbook, vol. 338, p. 48.

64. Andrade to Minister of War [Tornel], Aug. 25, 1842, Melchor Álvarez to Tornel, Aug. 29, 1842, Santa Fe Expedition Scrapbook, vol. 338, pp. 48–49 (quotation).

65. Álvarez et al., Judgment of Military Supreme Court, Sept. 24, 1842 (quotation), Santa Fe Expedition Scrapbook, vol. 338, pp. 55–56.

66. *Mosquito Mexicano*, Sept. 27, 1842.

67. José María Tornel to Juan José Andrade, Oct. 22, 1842, in Reséndez (ed.), *Texas Patriot on Trial*, 103–107 (quotations); Sierra, *Political Evolution of the Mexican People*, 224, 228.

68. Reséndez (ed.), *Texas Patriot on Trial*, 106–107.

69. Ibid., 111, 114.

70. José Antonio Navarro to Santa Anna, Sept. 19, 1843, Santa Fe Expedition Scrapbook, vol. 338, pp. 14–17.

71. Ibid.

72. Ibid.; Valentín Canalizo to Minister of War [Tornel], Sept. 20, 1843, Jose Antonio Navarro to Santa Anna, Sept. 26, 1843 (quotations), Santa Fe Expedition Scrapbook, vol. 338, pp. 18, 51–52; Jones, *Santa Anna*, 87–88; Scheina, *Santa Anna*, 44.

73. Manuel Rincón to Minister of War [Tornel], Oct. 14, 1843, [D. Benito] Quijano to Minister of War [Tornel], Oct. 26, 1843 (quotation), Santa Fe Expedition Scrapbook, vol. 338, pp. 22, 24.

74. Loomis, *Texan-Santa Fe Pioneers*, 242–243; Commandant General [Quijano] to Santa Anna, Feb. 16, 1844, Santa Fe Expedition Scrapbook, vol. 338, p. 40; Ruiz to Herrera, Dec. 27, 1835 (quotation), in Knight and Santos (comps.), *Letter from Columbia*.

75. Commandant General [Quijano] to Santa Anna, Feb. 16, 1844 (1st quotation); Santa Anna to Commandant General [Quijano], Feb. 19, 1844 (2nd and 3rd quotations), Santa Fe Expedition, vol. 338, pp. 39–40.

76. A. N. Langston, Navarro's great grandson, told the story of the ring to Gus L. Ford, but the latter discovered that Navarro's brand was registered in November 1833 and already had this ring, a common feature on many Tejano brands. See Ford, *Texas Cattle Brands*, 3.

77. Old Texan, *José Antonio Navarro*, 23–25 (1st quotation); A. J. Sowell, *Early Settlers and Indian Fighters of Southwest Texas* (Austin: B. C. Jones and Co., 1900; reprint, Austin: State House Press, 1986), 250 (2nd quotation).

78. Quijano to Tornel, Oct. 23, 1843, Santa Fe Expedition Scrapbook, vol. 338, p. 23; Potter, *Texas Revolution*, 24 (quotations). For addition accounts of Santa Anna's alleged overtures to Navarro, see Old Texan, *José Antonio Navarro*, 23–25, and De Cordova, *Texas: Her Resources and Her Public Men*, 152. Interestingly, only Potter places the Santa Anna overture at San Juan de Ulúa; De Cordova and the Old Texan say this occurred in the Acordada—and by means of emissaries, not by Santa Anna personally.

79. Potter, *Texas Revolution*, 24 (quotations); José Antonio Navarro to Santa Anna, Sept. 19 and 26, 1843, Santa Fe Expedition Scrapbook, vol. 338, pp. 14–17, 51–52.

80. Jones, *Santa Anna*, 87, 90–91.

81. José Isidro Reyes to Commandant of Veracruz [Quijano], Aug. 20, José Juan Clandero to Minister of War [Reyes]; Aug. 26, 1844 (quotation), Santa Fe Expedition Scrapbook, vol. 338, pp. 26, 38.

82. Jones, *Santa Anna*, 91–93.

83. McLeod to Charles Elliot, Nov. 26, 1843 (1st quotation), in Ephraim D. Adams (ed.), "British Correspondence Concerning Texas, Part X" *SWHQ* 17 (April 1914): 425; Luís María Aguilar to the Council of Government, Jan. 4, 1845 (2nd quotation), Santa Fe Expedition Scrapbook, vol. 338, 3–5.

84. José Antonio Navarro to Pres. José Joaquín de Herrera, Jan. 16, 1845 (1st quotation), Ignacio de Mora y Villamil to Minister of War [Pedro María Anaya], Feb. 1, 1845 (2nd quotation), José Rincon to Minister of War [Anaya], Feb. 10, 1845 (Santa Fe Expedition Scrapbook, vol. 338, pp. 28–29, 34–37; Sierra, *Political Evolution of the Mexican People*, 23; Jones, *Santa Anna*, 94.

85. José Antonio Navarro to William G. Cooke, Jan. 18, 1845 (quotations), in *Northern Standard* (Clarksville, Tex.), Feb. 20, 1845. Cooke had married Navarro's niece Angela the previous year.

86. Old Texan, *José Antonio Navarro*, 82 (1st quotation); *Democratic Telegraph and Texas Register* (Houston), Jan. 29, and Feb. 5, 1845; *Morning Star* (Houston), Feb. 6, 1845, cited

in James E. Crisp, "Anglo-Texan Attitudes Toward the Mexican, 1821–1845" (Ph.D. Diss., Yale University, 1976), 401 (2nd quotation).

Notes to Chapter Seven

1. José Antonio Navarro, Certificate, Jan. 10, 1858, <http://tslarc.tsl.state.tx.us/rep-claims/256/25600084.pdf> [Accessed Sept. 15, 2009].

2. *The Civilian and Galveston Gazette*, quoted in the *Northern Standard* (Clarksville, Tex.), Mar. 6, 1845, cited by Crisp, "Anglo-Texan Attitudes," 402.

3. Gammel (comp.), *Laws of Texas*, II: 1,142; Crisp, "Anglo-Texan Attitudes"" 402; José Antonio Navarro III, "Story of His Grandfather," 268, 287–288 (quotations). What compensation was awarded to Navarro has not been determined, but in an era when many Tejanos suffered losses, tax records show that he did not lose his land and he was not charged taxes during his absence. While his youngest sons, Sixto and Celso, may have not progressed in their education, the same is not true of José Antonio George. Letters, legal documents, and records of his employment as a city tax collector in the 1850s all reveal a high level of literacy. And Ángel Navarro as a student at St. Vincent's College in Missouri must have learned something of the classics.

4. *Journals of the Convention, Assembled at the City of Austin on the Fourth of July, 1845, fortThe Purpose of Framing a Constitution for the State of Texas* (Austin: Miner & Cruger, 1845; reprint, Austin: Shoal Creek Publishers, 1974), 9–10. This can be found online at http://tarlton.law.utexas.edu/constitutions/pdf/images/index1845.html [Accessed Sept. 15, 2009].

5. Crisp, "Anglo-Texan Attitudes," 406; Zachary T. Fulmore, "General Erskine Howard," *QTSHA*, 14 (October 1910): 146–147; "Convention of 1845," *The Handbook of Texas Online*, <http://www.tshaonline.org/handbook/online/articles/CC/mjc13.html> [Accessed Jan. 11, 2010]; "Howard, Volney Erskine," *The Handbook of Texas Online*, <http://www.tshaonline.org/handbook/online/articles/HH/fho80.html> [Accessed Jan. 11, 2010].

6. "Austin, Texas," *The Handbook of Texas Online*, <http://www.tshaonline.org/handbook/online/articles/AA/hda3.html> [Accessed Jan. 11, 2010].

7. *Journals of the Convention*, 9–11; William F. Weeks, (ed.), *Debates of the Texas Convention* (Houston: J. W. Cruger, 1846), 5–11. The first of the resolution's two sections accepted Texas as a state with the consent of its people, the Constitutional Convention, and the existing government of the Texas Republic. The second section contained the substance of the Resolution. It said acceptance of Texas by the United States Congress was subject to several conditions: boundary questions were to be resolved by the United States; a constitution approved by the people was to be submitted to Congress for final adoption by January 1, 1846; Texas would retain all of its public funds, taxes due, and debts; and Texas was authorized, under specified conditions, to divide itself into as many as five separate states. Two records were kept during the Constitutional Convention: the *Journals* and the *Debates*. In general, the *Debates* contain much more detail regarding the daily give and take among the delegates. Some critical information, however, such as how individuals voted, is found only in the *Journals*.

8. Weeks, *Debates of the Convention*, 17–18; *Journals of the Convention*, 21; Crisp, "Anglo-Texan Attitudes," 409.

9. Crisp, "Anglo-Texan Attitudes," 409; Weeks, *Debates of the Convention*, 85–86; *Journals of the Convention*, 70–72. Texas's claim to San Patricio County extended from the Nueces River to the Rio Grande. Both Texas and Mexico claimed this region, but neither country controlled it effectively.

10. "1836 Texas Constitution," in Wallace, Vigness, and Ward (eds.), *Documents of*

Texas History, 103–104; Crisp, "Anglo-Texan Attitudes," 338, 408. Beginning in eighteenth-century census records for Béxar and La Bahía, a variety of racial heritages combining European, Indian, and African origins were recorded. See censuses for Béxar in 1779 and La Bahía in 1780 in AGI, Audiencia de Guadalajara, Legajo 283. Copies can be found at Casa Navarro State Historical Park, San Antonio. In an article entitled "Blacks in the Mexican Mestizaje," historian Gilberto Hinojosa also noted the African input into the racial mixtures of Mexico. See the *Express-News* (San Antonio), Jan. 18, 2002.

11. *Journals of the Convention*, 52–54. Escheat means the reversion of property to the state when the owner dies without heirs or a will. The 1836 Constitution sanctioned loss of citizenship and forfeiture of property for having evaded fighting for the Revolution or having given aid or assistance to the enemy.

12. *Debates of the Convention*, 52, 156–157; Crisp, "Anglo-Texan Attitudes," 338, 407; Carey N. Vicenti, "Indians Not Taxed," *Indian Country Today*, Apr. 8, 2003, <http://www.indiancountrytoday.com/archive/28182299.html> [Accessed Sept. 15, 2009].

13. *Debates of the Convention*, 118, 120–121.

14. Ibid., 123–124. The Convention eventually restricted the powers of the executive in other respects. It rejected a term of office of four years, reducing it to two years, and made the lieutenant governor and treasurer elective offices, rather than appointees.

15. Ibid., 156–158.

16. *Debates of the Convention*, 158–159. James E. Crisp, in "Anglo-Texan Attitudes," 333, found that if Tejanos accepted persons with African ancestry as relatives and countrymen, Anglos in the Republic of Texas did not force them to comply with constitutional provisions governing free people of color in Texas.

17. Frederick Law Olmsted, *A Journey through Texas: Or, a Saddle-Trip on the Southwestern Frontier* (New York: Dix, Edwards, & Company, 1857; reprint, Austin: University of Texas Press, 1986), 65, 163, 339 (quotation).

18. Fourth Lincoln-Douglas debate, held in Charleston, Illinois, Sept. 18, 1858, cited in *Lincoln on Race and Slavery*, ed. Henry Louis Gates Jr. and Donald Yacovone (Princeton, N. J.: Princeton University Press, 2009), 157.

19. *Debates of the Convention*, 159.

20. *Journals of the Convention*, 97–98; De León, *Tejano Community*, 28. (Dr. De León credits historian James E. Crisp for this observation.)

21. *Debates of the Convention*, 232.

22. Ibid., 235–236 (quotations), 243; Crisp, "Anglo-Texan Attitudes," 427–428.

23. "1845 Constitution, Article III, Section 29," in Wallace, Vigness, and Ward (eds.), *Documents of Texas History*, 151; Arnoldo De León, *They Called Them Greasers: Anglo Attitudes Toward Mexicans in Texas, 1821–1900* (Austin: University of Texas Press, 1983), 104.

24. *Debates of the Convention*, 395 (block quotation); Houston *Morning Star*, May 2, 1844 (2nd quotation), cited in Crimm, *De León*, 180; Crisp, "Anglo-Texan Attitudes," 434–435. It is interesting to note that the state constitution of Coahuila and Texas had a similar restrictive provision that said: "Those born within the territory of the republic . . . who did not remain true to the cause of its independence, but emigrated to a foreign country, or dependency of Spain, shall neither be Coahuiltexians, nor citizens of Coahuila and Texas." See Gammel (comp.), *Laws of Texas*, I: 425.

25. *Debates of the Convention*, 377, 401 (quotation) ; Crisp, "Anglo-Texan Attitudes," 438.

26. *Debates of the Convention*, 368, 405 (1st quotation), 406 (2nd quotation); Crisp, "Anglo-Texan Attitudes" 437.

27. *Debates of the Convention*, 397 (1st and 2nd quotations), 407–408 (3rd quotation);

Crisp, "Anglo-Texan Attitudes," 341–342, 440.

28. *Debates of the Convention*, 401 (1st and 2nd quotation) 402 (3rd–5th quotations); Crisp, "Anglo-Texan Attitudes," 442; Crimm, *De León*, 165.

29. *Debates of the Convention*, 410–411 (1st quotation), 398 (2nd quotation); Crisp, "Anglo-Texan Attitudes," 441, 443.

30. *Journals of the Convention*, 190, 197 (1st quotation); Juan Seguín in De la Teja (ed.), *Revolution Remembered*, 101 (2nd quotation).

31. *Journals of the Convention*, 301, 317–318, 374; *Debates of the Convention*, 738 (quotation); Crisp, "Anglo-Texan Attitudes" 447–450. The compensation for Navarro's work at the 1845 Convention would total $187.20 (*per diem* for 56 days of $168 and $19.20 for 160 miles travel).

32. Spaw (ed.), *Texas State Senate: Republic to Civil War, 1836–1861*, 182; "Constitution of 1845," *The Handbook of Texas Online*, <http://www.tshaonline.org/handbook/online/articles/CC/mhc3.html> [Accessed Jan. 11, 2010].

33. Annie Middleton, "The Texas Convention of 1845," *SWHQ* 25 (July 1921): 59.

34. Thomas Whitehead, et al., Report, Sept. 1, 1845, Election Returns for Bexar County, 1845, box 2-9/47 (Secretary of State Records, TSL); *Journals of the Senate of the First Legislature of the State of Texas* (Clarksville, Tex.: Standard Office, 1848), 4, 15; Spaw (ed.), *Texas State Senate: Republic to Civil War, 1836–1861*, 165 (quotation). Navarro's two terms in the Texas Senate coincide with the Mexican War, but no record has been found concerning his thoughts or opinions about that conflict.

35. De León, *They Called Them Greasers*, 58; David Montejano, *Anglos and Mexicans in the Making of Texas, 1836–1986* (Austin: University of Texas Press, 1987), 25, 30. After the war with Mexico, the people of the El Paso region of southern New Mexico welcomed Texas rule, although it has retained regional characteristics up to the present day. Leaders in Santa Fe rejected being part of Texas and sent a petition to Congress saying, "We firmly protest against the dismemberment of our territory in favor of Texas or from any cause." The eventual outcome was that the United States prevented Texas from retaining its claim to New Mexico except for the El Paso region. The final boundaries of the state of Texas as they presently exist were finally defined in 1853.

36. *Journals of the First Senate*, 19, 49, 52; Opinion of the Honorable Antonio Navarro on the Contested Election in Harris County between Messrs. Brashear and McAnelly for the Senate, Feb. 24, 1845 [1846] (BCC); *Appendix to the Journals of the Senate of the First Legislature of the State of Texas* (n.p., [1848]), 105–107; Spaw (ed.), *Texas Senate: Republic to Civil War, 1836–1861*, 180.

37. *Journals of the First Senate*, 67; *Laws Passed By the First Legislature of the State of Texas* (Austin: Ford & Cronican, 1846), 127.

38. *Journals of the First Senate*, 180.

39. Ibid. 42.

40. Ibid., 107.

41. Ibid., 107.

42. Ibid., 108–109. Navarro referred to his substitute for the first section of the bill, but it was not recorded in the Senate journals.

43. Ibid., 161, 185. The texts of neither of the two bills are found in the Senate journals. The select committee's report did little more than review the provisions in the 1836 Constitution. The journals do not reveal what measures the committee had written into their proposal in order to comply with the 1845 Constitution.

44. Ibid., 203–204.

45. Ibid., 204–205.

46. Ibid., 203–205.

47. Ibid., 251, 260.

48. Ibid., 287, 296.

49. Ibid., 302. Navarro said that he had predicted this in his letter to the *Telegraph and Texas Register* (Houston), July 20, 1848, p. 1.

50. Jose Antonio Navarro to the Speaker of the House [Hansford], Jan. 26, 1839, *Telegraph and Texas Register* (Houston), Jan. 26, 1839, p. 5; Gammel (comp.), *Laws of Texas*, II: 178–180; *Journals of the First Senate*, 131, 141; Jean A. Stuntz, *Hers, His, & Theirs: Community Property Law in Spain & Early Texas* (Lubbock: Texas Tech University Press, 2005), 20 and 29. Stuntz's groundbreaking book is a comprehensive history of Texas's community property law. She provides a detailed examination of how laws to protect women's property evolved from medieval Spain to Mexico, and, through Texas's heritage of Mexican law, to be incorporated in laws of Texas. This invaluable work stands alone as the place to begin any investigation of community property law in Texas constitutional provisions and legislation.

51. Gammel (comp.), *Laws of Texas*, II: 153–154. California, Arizona, New Mexico, Texas, and Louisiana are states formerly under Spanish jurisdiction that have community property laws. Washington, Wisconsin, and Idaho also have such laws.

52. Crimm, *De León*, 190–196; Gammel (comp.), *Laws of Texas*, I: 1,483. The boundaries of Navarro County specified by the 1846 law made it much larger than the present county.

53. José Antonio Navarro to Ruffino [Rueben] Potter, July 21, 1846, Spanish Archives (BCC). More than its uncommon use as a proper name, Ruffino is widely known as a Chianti wine, for which Potter may have had a predilection, alluded to by Navarro as a joke. Concerning land transactions, Navarro in May 1847 sold to Edward Dwyer a half league (2,214 acres) on Cibolo Creek for $1,151.25. This must have been his part of a league and labor that he and José Herrera had jointly purchased in 1832 for 300 pesos, Deed Record, vol. C-1, pp. 95–97; Deed Record, Vol. Q, pp. 582–583 (Spanish Archives, BCC). In September 1847, Navarro received the title to his labor on the Frio River. This transaction completed the process of headright acquisition that he began ten years earlier, José Antonio Navarro, patent for one labor, Sept. 24, 1847, patents, Béxar 1-581 (GLO).

54. Josiah Gregg, *Diary and Letters of Josiah Gregg: Southwestern Enterprises 1840–1847*, ed. Maurice G. Fulton (Norman: University of Oklahoma Press, 1941), 231–232. No evidence was found to support Navarro's claim that Santa Anna left the east side of the Alamo undefended during the siege, hoping the defenders would try to escape. To the contrary, he was pleased that they had fallen into a trap from which no escape was possible.

55. Kendall and Perry, *Gentilz*, 114.

56. *Journals of the Senate of the State of Texas, Second Legislature* (Houston: Telegraph Office, 1848), 3, 11.

57. Ibid., 18–21, 49, 99.

58. *Journals of the Second State Senate*, 8–18, 50, 177–178, 196. There is no record of the bill being read for the first time.

59. *Journals of the Second State Senate*, 362; Gammel (comp.), *Laws of Texas*, III: 45.

60. *Heirs of Holliman vs. Peebles*, Feb. 11, 1848, Supreme Court Docket Ledger, #201-3 (TSL).

61. *Journals of the Second State Senate*, 127–128, 587, 589–590.

62. Ibid., 521, 563, 585, 618.

63. Ibid., 680–683; Anonymous, "A Brief Biographical Sketch of the Author of These Commentaries" (1st quotation), in McDonald and Matovina (eds.), *Defending Mexican Valor*, 37; Potter, *Texas Revolution*, 27 (2nd quotation).

64. Gregg, *Diary and Letters*, 90; Anonymous, "Col. José Antonio Navarro," in *The Pageant of America: The Lure of the Frontier*, ed. Ralph H. Gabriel (New Haven: Yale University Press, 1925); Guy M. Bryan to citizens of Brazoria County in *Democratic Telegraph and Texas Register* (Houston), July 20, 1848, p. 3. According to the 1836 Constitution, "all laws now in force in Texas, and not inconsistent with this constitution, shall remain in full force until declared void, repealed, altered, or expired by their own limitation." The Constitution in 1845 affirmed the same.

65. *Texas Reports: Reports of Cases Argued and Decided in the Supreme Court of the State of Texas during the December Term 1846, and Part of December Term, 1847, Volume I* (St. Louis: Gilbert Book Company, 1881), 673–722; *Democratic Telegraph and Texas Register* (Houston), July 20, 1848 (quotations), p. 6.

66. Ibid., July 20, 1848, p. 1. Section 8 of the 1836 Constitution read as follows: "All persons who shall leave the country for the purpose of evading a participation in the present struggle, or shall refuse to participate in it, or shall give aid or assistance to the present enemy, shall forfeit all rights of citizenship and such lands as they may hold in the Republic."

67. *Democratic Telegraph and Texas Register* (Houston), July 20, 1848, p. 1.

68. George Fisher to Williams, Dec. 2, 1848, Williams Collection, 23-2119 (Rosenberg Library, Galveston).

69. *Texan Mercury* (Seguin), Oct. 15, 1853, p. 2.

70. Ángel Navarro to D. J. Miller, Oct. 2, 1849 (quotation; W. D. Miller Collection, TSL); College Papers, 2nd Series, vol. 17, pp. 311–313 (Harvard University Archives, Cambridge, Mass.). Ángel Navarro enrolled at Harvard in 1848 and completed his studies there the next year. He also wrote in his letter to Miller that: "Cambridge is a delightful place to study [and] a good place to study is all that it is fit for. For in every other aspect it is a very dull place. It is very quiet and retired and very religious. To walk along the streets on a Sunday just after the bells have been ringing for an hour, you would think that the city had been deserted or that every person was dead: for every store and every private house is closed on Sunday."

71. *Ledger* (San Antonio), Jan. 9, 1851, p. 2; Vital Records, Cattle Brands, vol. 1, p. 1 (Office of the County Clerk, Guadalupe County Courthouse, Seguin, Texas). By 1841, the names of Real and Presidio streets had changed to Flores and Commerce, respectively. See *Memoirs of Mary A Maverick*, ed. Rena Maverick Green (Lincoln: University of Nebraska Press, 1989), 48.

72. United States Department of the Interior, Bureau of the Census, Seventh Census, 1850, Guadalupe County, Texas, Schedule 1: Free Inhabitants; Schedule 2: Slave Inhabitants, Record Group 29 (National Archives, Washington, D.C.). Henry took "Navarro" as his surname after emancipation, as was the case with many freedmen.

73. Donald E. Everett, *San Antonio: the Flavor of its Past* (San Antonio: Trinity University Press, 1976), 41; José Antonio Navarro in the *Ledger* (San Antonio), July 19, 1853: "American Party," *The Handbook of Texas Online*, <http://www.tshaonline.org/handbook/online/articles/AA/waa1.html> [Accessed Jan. 11, 2010]; Ralph A. Wooster, "An Analysis of the Texas Know Nothings" *SWHQ* 70 (January 1967): 414. The Know Nothing movement began on the East Coast as a secret society that called itself the American Party. In response to inquiries, its members would reply "I know nothing," and it became known as the Know Nothing Party. Fearing papal interference in American public affairs, the Know Nothings were fiercely anti-Catholic, and their attention was primarily directed against Irish Catholic immigrants, an antipathy they easily redirected against Tejanos.

74. Navarro, in the *Western Texan* (San Antonio), Dec. 1, 1853, in McDonald and Matovina (eds.), *Defending Mexican Valor in Texas*, 58.

75. *Texan Mercury* (Seguin), Oct. 1, 1853 (quotation), p. 2; Potter, *Texas Revolution*, 17.

76. José Antonio Navarro to Alexander Ewing, Dec. 19, 1853, Deed Record, vol. E, p. 137 (Office of the County Clerk, Guadalupe County Courthouse, Seguin, Texas). Among other accusations, Tejanos were accused of assisting the escape of runaway slaves; see *Texan Mercury* (Seguin), Dec. 24, 1853, p. 2. Investors had been interested in buying the San Geronimo land since 1844, probably hoping for a good price because of Navarro's imprisonment. See Nell M. Pugh, "Contemporary Comments on Texas, 1844–1847," *SWHQ* 62 (July 1958): 368–369.

77. Bexar County Tax Rolls, 1853.

78. City Council, Journal B: Jan.–June, 1854, pp. 243–286 (City Clerk's Office, San Antonio); Kendall and Perry, *Gentilz*, 114; Brands Book B, No. 798, p. 65, Antonio Navarro, Bexar County, May 18, 1855 (Spanish Archives, BCC).

Notes to Chapter Eight

1. Ernest W. Winkler, "Platforms of Political Parties in Texas," *Bulletin of the University of Texas* 53 (1916), 11, 15 (quotation); Anna Irene Sandbo, "Beginnings of the Secession Movement in Texas, *SWHQ* 18 (July 1914): 48–50. The Kansas-Nebraska Act of 1854 created these two territories and allowed settlers to decide if they would allow slavery.

2. Rupert N. Richardson, Adrian Anderson, and Ernest Wallace, *Texas: the Lone Star State* (6th ed.; Englewood Cliffs, N. J.: Prentice Hall, 1992), 161; T. R. Fehrenbach, *Lone Star: A History of Texas and the Texans* (New York: Collier Books, 1968), 333; *Ledger* (San Antonio), July 14, 1855, p.1; Sandbo, "Secession Movement," 52.

3. Ibid., 50 (quotation); *Ledger* (San Antonio), July 14, 1855, p. 3, July 7, 1855, p.1, and Aug. 25, 1855, p.3.

4. *Ledger* (San Antonio), July 7, 1855, p.1.

5. *Ledger* (San Antonio), July 7, 1855, p. 2. James C. Wilson failed to note that Navarro's enemies were themselves Catholic.

6. *El Bejareño*, July 21, 1855, pp 1–2.

7. John O. Leal (comp.), "San Fernando Marriages, Book 1798–1856" (typescript), p. 103, no. 10 (Texana Department, San Antonio Public Library); *Ledger* (San Antonio), July 14, 1855, page 2 (quotation); [San Antonio] *El Bejareño*, July 21, 1855, pp. 2–3. Because of errors in the English translation published in the *Ledger* (San Antonio), the translation provided here was made by the author using the Spanish version published in *El Bejareño*. Daniel J. Tobin and his brother William G. Tobin arrived in San Antonio in October 1853. See *Handbook of Texas Online*, "Tobin, William Gerard," <http://www.tshaonline. org/handbook/online/articles/TT/fto4.html> [Accessed Sept. 20, 2009].

8. *Ledger* (San Antonio), Aug. 11, 1855, p. 2.

9. *Ledger* (San Antonio), Aug. 11, 1855, p. 2; Aug. 18, 1855, p. 1, Aug. 25, 1855, p. 1 (quotation); Winkler, "Platforms of Political Parties," 644; "American Party," The Handbook of Texas Online, http://www.tshaonline.org/handbook/online/articles/AA/waa1.html [Accessed Jan 11, 2010]; Sandbo, "Secession Movement," 50; Wooster, "Texas Know Nothings," 417.

10. *Ledger* (San Antonio), Oct. 13, 1855, p. 3 (1st and 2nd quotations); Fritz, "José Antonio Navarro," 77 (3rd quotation). Walter L. Buenger, in *Secession and the Union in Texas* (Austin, University of Texas Press, 1984), repeats the error, initiated by Fritz, that Navarro supported secession. He says that "certain Mexicans, the most prominent of whom were José Antonio Navarro and Santos Benavides, shared southern values, were an accepted part of the economic and political life of Texas . . . had a high degree of personal loyalty of Sam Houston, usually supported the Democratic party, and conceived of Texas, not the United States, as being their homeland. Despite the personal appeals of Houston this

group was to support secession." (p. 104) In fact, during the 1859 gubernatorial election, Navarro supported Houston's candidacy as a Unionist and denounced the Democrats.

11. Jose Ántonio Navarro to Maverick, *Ledger* (San Antonio), July 26, 1855 (quotations), p. 1; Sandbo, "Secession Movement in Texas," 63; Robert A. Calvert and Arnoldo de León, *The History of Texas* (Arlington Heights, Ill.: Harlan Davidson, 1990), 117. The manuscript in Spanish of Navarro's letter to Maverick is in the Maverick Family Papers, box 2F29, folder 1858–1859 (BCAH).

12. Sandbo, "Secession Movements," 64; Ernest W. Winkler, *Journal of the Secession Convention of Texas, 1861* (Austin: Austin Printing Company, 1912), 405–408; "Muster Roll of 8th Texas Infantry," <http://www.angelfire.com/tx/RandysTexas/page219.html> [Accessed Sept. 16, 2009]. The absence of any Navarro as a delegate at the Secession Convention further contradicts Fritz's contention that José Antonio Navarro attended a meeting to encourage secession, as she asserts in "José Antonio Navarro," 77.

13. Norman F. Porter Sr., *Atascosa County History through 1912* (Pleasanton, Tex.: Galvan Creek Postcards, 2007), 45–47; George W. Kendall to Thomas Falconer, Oct. 4, 1856 (quotation), in Falconer, *Letters and Notes*, 143–144. Navarro had three structures on his Laredo Street property that have been preserved; a fourth, which was probably the detached kitchen, can be seen on the 1873 Map of San Antonio by Augustus Koch, <http://www.birdseyeviews.org/zoom.php?city=San%20Antonio&year=1873&extra_info=> [Accessed Sept. 18. 2009]. These were the square, two-story structure at the corner of Laredo and Nueva Street, the building just north of it, and a small building east of the two-story structure. It is not possible at present to determine the sequence of construction at the site. In the author's opinion, the larger buildings were constructed at different times, and the "new and tidy house" described by Kendall was the structure built next to the preexisting corner structure. This house was later designated as "the usual residence of Margarita de la Garza."

14. Bexar County Tax Rolls, 1850; Atascosa County Tax Rolls, 1856–1864 (microfilm; TSL); United States Seventh Census, 1850, Guadalupe County, Texas, Schedule 2: Slave Inhabitants.

15. Atascosa County Tax Rolls, 1856; "Baptismals of El Carmen Church of Losoya, Texas, 1855 to 1891 and 1894 to 1907," nos. 41 and 42, Dec. 28, 1856, and no. 167, Mar. 26, 1860 (Texana Department, San Antonio Public Library).

16. United States Eighth Census, 1860, Atascosa County, Texas, Schedule 2: Slave Inhabitants, Schedule 4: Agricultural Production, Record Group 29 (National Archives, Washington, D.C.). Navarro's six slaves had an assessed value of $2,800. See Atascosa County Tax Rolls, 1860.

17. Rodríguez, *Memoirs of Early Texas*, 20 (1st quotation); Olmsted, *Journey through Texas*, 229–230 (block quotation); Kenneth M. Stampp, *The Peculiar Institution: Slavery in the Antebellum South* (New York: Alfred A. Knopf, 1956), 111.

18. Henderson K. Yoakum, *History of Texas from its First Settlement in 1685 to its Annexation to the United States in 1846* (New York: J. H. Colton and Company, 1856; reprint, New York: Redfield, 1955, 176). Yoakum said he received "Navarro's account" from Francois Giraud, a prominent San Antonio surveyor and engineer.

19. Navarro, in the *Ledger* (San Antonio), Dec 12, 1857, in McDonald and Matovina (eds.), *Defending Mexican Valor*, 63 (block quotation), 76 (3rd and 4th quotations) 90–91; Robert Tarin, descendant of Joaquín Leal, personal communication with author, July 7, 1994. Antonio Delgado's obituary appears in the *Ledger* (San Antonio), Sept. 19, 1857, p. 2. Navarro's first historical writings were published in the *Ledger* in 1853, in two consecutive issues; the three installments written in 1857 were also published in the *Ledger* in December 1857 and January 1858.

20. Navarro, in the *Ledger* (San Antonio), Jan. 2, 1858, in McDonald and Matovina (eds.), *Defending Mexican Valor*, 76.

21. Antonio Menchaca, *Memoirs* (San Antonio: Yanaguana Society, 1937); De la Teja (ed.), *Revolution Remembered*.

22. Everett, *San Antonio: the Flavor of its Past*, 79.

23. Ronnie C. Tyler, *Santiago Vidaurri and the Southern Confederacy* (Austin: Texas State Historical Association, 1973), 34; José Antonio Navarro to Santiago Vidaurri, May 24, 1860 (quotation). Correspondencia Santiago Vidaurri, Asunto Morales-Maceda, 2nd sección, caja 26, expediente 891: José Antonio Navarro #14849 (Archivo General del Estado de Nuevo León, Monterrey). Thanks to Jerry D. Thompson, who referred me to this letter.

24. José Antonio Navarro, J. D. Durand, Daniel J. Tobin, Marcellus French, Joseph P. Michie, and Sixto Navarro to Citizens of San Antonio, Mar. 12, 1861 (1st and 2nd quotations), in *Ledger* (San Antonio), Mar. 13, 1861, cited in Porter, *Atascosa County*, 79–80 (3rd–5th quotations); *Alamo Express* (San Antonio), Mar. 13, 1861 (6th quotation), p. 2; Apr. 15, 1861, p. 3.

25. *Alamo Express* (San Antonio), Mar. 20, 1861, p. 3, Apr. 15, 1861, p. 3; *Alamo Express* (San Antonio), Apr. 17, 1861, p. 2.

26. Jerry D. Thompson, *Vaqueros in Blue & Gray* (Austin: State House Press, 2000), 170; *Daily Herald* (San Antonio). July 26, 1859, p. 1; *The War of the Rebellion: A Compilation of the Official Records of the Union and Confederate Armies* (130 vols.; Washington, D.C.: Government Printing Office, 1880–1902), Series I, Vol. I: 572, 635; Vol. XV: 851; and Vol. XXVI, part 2: 99, 413, 421–422.

27. Ángel Navarro to Santiago de Vidaurri, Dec. 1, 1863, Correspondencia Santiago Vidaurri, Asunto Morales-Maceda, 2nd sección, caja 26, expediente 890: Ángel Navarro, no. 14848 (Archivo General del Estado de Nuevo León, Monterrey); "Battle of the Nueces," *The Handbook of Texas Online*, <http://www.tshaonline.org/handbook/online/articles/NN/qfn1.html> [Accessed Jan. 11, 2010]; "Civil War Soldier and Sailors," <http://www.itd.nps.gov/cwss/soldiers.cfm> [Accessed Sept. 18, 2009].

28. Testimony of Luciano Navarro, Theodora Navarro, and Angela Navarro Cooke, Aug. 2, 1861, Bond Record, vol. A or B [*sic*], 130–132 (BCC). Luciano stated that Margarita made her verbal will at 2:00 p.m., about fifteen days before she died on July 8, 1861.

29. This is taken from an undated article in the *Lure of the Frontier*, a typescript of which is in the Jose Antonio Navarro III Collection, DRT. The "ex-Ranger" included some information about Navarro's early life that is wildly inaccurate. For example, he says that José Antonio Navarro was born in Corsica. Nevertheless, he provides a credible and valuable account of his personal meetings with Navarro. Andrew J. Sowell, another ex-Ranger, wrote about Navarro and other early Atascosa County settlers in an account published in the *Dallas Morning News*, May 5, 1896, p. 12; a later article by Sowell, also regarding Navarro, is in the *San Antonio Light*, Dec. 29, 1912, p. 14. The information on Navarro in these articles was taken from Sowell's book, *Early Settlers and Texas Indian Fighters of Southwest Texas*, 250.

30. Bexar County Civil Court Minutes, vol. F, p. 358, no. 198 (BCC).

31. José Antonio Navarro to Alejandro Ruiz, Apr. 5, 1866, Navarro Collection (Spanish Archives, BCC)

32. Ibid. This "store on the corner" was probably the existing two-story building at the Casa Navarro State Historical Park. Navarro did own another rental building on a corner—the old Navarro House, where he was born. Located in a pricier part of town, that building was rented to Fritz Schreiner by 1870 for $75.00 a month. Consequently, the lower priced "store on the corner" was almost certainly the present two-story building located at the corner of W. Nueva and S. Laredo.

33. Atascosa County Tax Rolls, 1866; Ronnie C. Tyler and Lawrence R. Murphy (eds.), *The Slave Narratives of Texas* (Austin: The Encino Press, 1974), 112 (quotation).

34. Campbell, *Gone to Texas*, 270–273.

35. That Sixto took possession of the ranch house is indicated in Jose Antonio Navarro, will, Dec. 27, 1870, Navarro Collection (Spanish Archives, BCC). A translation of Navarro's will is in Appendix Three.

36. *Daily Herald* (San Antonio), Jan. 31, 1868, p. 2 (1st quotation), Feb. 2, 1868, p. 2, (2nd quotation); Feb. 4, 1868 (3rd quotation). Concerning Charles F. Fisher, see "City of San Antonio Officers," <http://www.sanantonio.gov/Library/texana/cityofficers. asp?res=1680&ver=true> [Accessed Sept. 18, 2009).

37. *Daily Herald* (San Antonio), Feb. 4, 1868, p. 3 (quotations), Feb. 16, 1868, p. 3; Ernest Wallace, *The Howling of the Coyotes: Reconstruction Efforts to Divide Texas* (College Station: Texas A&M University Press, 1979), 42; De León, *They Called Them Greasers*, 57.

38. Winkler, "Political Parties in Texas," 108–109.

39. Carl H. Moneyhon, *Republicanism in Reconstruction Texas* (Austin: University of Texas Press, 1980), 98, 100–101; Wallace, *Howling of the Coyotes*, 42.

40. *Daily Herald* (San Antonio), Jan. 14, 1869, p. 2, Feb. 11, 1869, p. 22; Wallace, *Howling of the Coyotes*, 110; Campbell, *Gone to Texas*, 278.

41. De Léon, *Tejano Community*, xvi (quotation); De León, *They Called Them Greasers*, 57. Rodolfo F. Acuña repeats and cites De León's white supremacy conclusions in *Occupied America: A History of Chicanos* (6th ed.; New York: Pearson Longman, 2007), 63.

42. *Daily Herald* (San Antonio), Sept. 1, 1869, p. 3, Sept. 2, 1869, p.3; Anonymous, "A Brief Biographical Sketch of the Author of These Commentaries" in McDonald and Matovina (eds.), *Defending Mexican Valor in Texas*, 38 (quotations).

43. *Daily Express* (San Antonio), Nov. 11, 1870, p. 2.

44. José Antonio Navarro, will, Dec. 27, 1870 (quotations), Navarro Collection (Spanish Archives, BCC). Navarro's sons ignored his advice and a short time after their father's death sold the property. Navarro Brothers Sixto, Antonio George, Celso, and Angel, deed of trust to sell to Fritz Schreiner the José Antonio Navarro house at Flores and W. Commerce, Deed Record, vol. 3, p. 36 (BCC).

45. José Antonio Navarro, Will, Dec. 27, 1870, Navarro Collection (Spanish Archives, BCC).

46. Ibid. (quotation), José Antonio Navarro to Fritz Schreiner, Nov. 4, 1870, Deed Record, vol. VI, p. 585 (BCC); José Antonio Navarro, File, Nov. 28, 1870,<http://www.tsl. state.tx.us/arc/repclaims/viewdetails.php?id=57927&set=1#viewSet> [Accessed Sept. 18, 2009). Navarro's agreement with Schreiner notes that the house had nine rooms and was located on the east side of Flores Street.

47. José Antonio Navarro, will, Dec. 27, 1870, Navarro Collection (Spanish Archives, BCC).

48. *Herald* (San Antonio), Jan. 15, 1871, p. 2 (quotation), Jan. 17, 1871, p. 3. Navarro's burial site is in the lower north east area of San Fernando Cemetery No. 1, San Antonio.

49. Kay Thompson Hindes, "The José Antonio Navarro Ranch: Atascosa County, 1831–1894" (unpublished paper, University of Texas at San Antonio: Anthropology 4913 for Dr. Thomas R. Hester, filed with the Bexar County Clerk, Robert D. Green, on February 15, 1984); Gerdes, "Navarro Family Heritage;" *Express* (San Antonio), Aug. 11, 1876; *A Twentieth Century History of Southwest Texas*, (2 vols.; Chicago: Lewis Publishing Company, 1907), I: 102–105.

50. Anonymous, "A Brief Biographical Sketch of the Author of These Commentaries" in McDonald and Matovina (eds.), *Defending Mexican Valor*, 40.

NOTES TO APPENDICES

1. For Juan Margarita de la Garza's baptism, see John O. Leal (comp.) "San Fernando Baptismals," Book 1793–1812 (typescript), 14, no. 158. A reading of the baptismal manuscript from the San Fernando Church archives shows two errors in the Leal compilation: the baptism date is February 12, not February 2, and Margarita's middle name is Modesta, not "Nónica." For María Casimira Navarro's baptism, see John O. Leal (comp.), San Fernando Baptimals," Book 1812–1825 (typescript), 48, no. 416.

2. José Antonio Navarro III to Louis W. Kemp, Oct. 17, 1935 (1st quotation), José Antonio Navarro III Collection, Correspondence 1935–1938, col. 904, folder 2, item 4, (DRT). Kemp's undated, handwritten reply is on this letter, and the text for the marker is also in the file. Chabot, *With the Makers of San Antonio*, 205; José Antonio Navarro [III], application for membership to the Descendants of the Signers of the Texas Declaration of Independence, Jan. 25, 1938 (2nd quotation), José Antonio Navarro III Collection (DRT). Genealogists have examined the baptismal records at Mier, but no record of a Margarita de la Garza was found (personal conversation of Illene Villareal Treviño with the author, January 2005).

3. United States Eighth Census, 1860, Atascosa County, Texas, Schedule 2: Slave Inhabitants.

4. Atascosa County Tax Rolls, 1864, 1866.

5. Atascosa County Tax Rolls, 1867, 1869; Henry Navarro, Preemption Grant, Apr. 1, 1868, file Bexar 3-6506 (GLO); "Atascosa County Chronicles," <http://atascosacounty. blogspot.com/2008/06/abraham-geiger-martin.html> [Accessed Sept. 19, 2009].

6. United States Ninth Census, 1870, Atascosa County, Texas, Schedule 1: Population; "Baptismals of El Carmen Church of Losoya, Texas, 1855 to 1891 and 1894 to 1907," transcriptions nos. 41 and 42, Dec. 28, 1856, and Mar. 26, 1860 , no. 167 (Texana Department, San Antonio Public Library).

7. Atascosa County Tax Rolls, 1871; Sixto E. Navarro to Henry Navarro, Mar. 20, 1872, Deed Record, Book A-1, p. 87 (BCC); A. E. Thurber to Henry Navarro, Aug. 23, 1881, file Bexar Preemption-2401(GLO). Henry Navarro's death date is not known; but his presumably buried in the Black Brite Cemetery.

8. José Antonio Navarro, Will, Dec. 27, 1870, Navarro Collection (Spanish Archives, BCC). Note that Navarro began the will on February 15, 1870, signed it on September 24, 1870, and added a final signed codicil on December 27, 1870.Will translated by author.

Index

Index Note: JAN used in subheadings refers to José Antonio Navarro. *Italic* page numbers refer to illustrations.

A

Acts of the First Constitutional Congress of the Free State of Coahuila and Texas, 86

Adams, James Truslow, 10

Aguero, Seferino, 59

Aguilar, Luís María, 199–200

Agustín, Juan Antonio, 14

Ahumada, María Antonia Navarro (sister), 31, 178

Ahumada, Mateo (brother-in-law), 69–70, 74, 178, 268

Alamo, the, 35, 127–129, 133, 135, 138, 230, 255

Alamo Literary Society, 267

Alderete, José Miguel, 64

Aldrete, Rafael, 147

Andrade, Juan José, 180–182, 189, 190, 192–193

Angiano, Pascual, 118

annexation of Texas, 204–207, 220, 242

Apodaca, Juan Ruiz, 38

apportionment debate, 213–214

April 6, 1830, Law of, 94–96, 98, 113, 133

Apuntes Históricos (Navarro), 9, 19, 28–29, 253

Archer, Branch T., 167

Archuleta, Juan Andrés, 172–175, 180

Arciniega, José Miguel de, 73–79, 82–85, 100, 103, 104, 108, 140

Armijo, Manuel, 171–176, 175, 178, 182, 185, 187, 189–190, 192

Armiñán, Benito de, 31

Arredondo, Joaquín de, 17, 26–31, 33–35, 40, 43, 46–51, 166

Arredondo, Miguel de, 42, 45

Atascosa Ranch, 126–127, 158; brand registration for, 116, 250; land grants for, 96–97, 102, 105, 144; map of plat, 110; operation of, 109–110, 116, 117, 118, 144–145, 241, 250–251, 254, 258–261; will and division of, 267–270, 272, 279–280, 281, 283–284

Austin, James E. B., 66, 91

Austin, Moses, 52

Austin, Stephen F., 7, 8, 18, 66, 71; arrest of, 117; and Béxar petition for separation, 111–112; business relationships with JAN, 68, 70, 90–91, 93–94; colonization ventures and, 52–54, 138; death of, 138; friendship with JAN, 70, 74, 75, 91–92, 165–166; homestead law (Decree No. 70) and, 85–86; slavery and, 91–92; Texas statehood as objective of, 111–117

ayuntamiento: as autonomous democratic government, 49–50; role in local governance, 55–56

B

Badgett, Jesse, 128–129, 131

Baker, Joseph, 140, 143

Balmaceda, José María, 84, 111, 123

Bank of Texas, 73, 76

Barnard, Joseph H., 136

Barrios, Antonio, 189

Bastrop, Baron de, 38, 40, 54, 59, 61, 64, 65, 66, 71–72

battles. *See specific locations*

Baum, José La, 88–90

Bean, Peter Ellis, 81

Béxar, 3; federalism in, 119–120, 126; flood (1819), 46; junta, as governing body of, 24–25, 48, 64–66, 113, 182; Siege of, 121, 127, 139, 179, 183, 185, 253

Blanco, Victor, 122

Bollinger, Ephraim, 152

Bolton, Herbert Eugene, 253

Borden, John, 152

borders: maps of contested territory and undefined, 52, 201; of Republic of Texas, 220–222, 221

Bowie, James, 18, 101, 115, 122

Bowie, Ursula de Veramendi, 101, 115

Bradburn, Juan Davis, 109

brands (livestock), 116, 196, 238, 250

Brashear, Isaac W., 222

Bravo, Nicolás, 180, 187

Brenham, Richard F., 182, 186

Bryan, Guy M., 234

Bueno, Anastacio, 6

Burleson, Edward, 164, 220, 222, 224, 225, 228–229, 231

Burnet, David G., 134

Burnley, Albert T., 132

Bustamante, Anastacio, 84–85, 110

Bustillos, Domingo, 57

Bustillos, Francisco Xavier, 94

C

Calderón Bridge, Battle of, 22–23

Caldwell, John, 103, 106–108, 205, 216

Caldwell, Mathew, 168, 170

Camacho, Francisco, 182, 186

Canalizo, Valentín, 193–194, 199

Cantú, Antonia, 59

Carillo, Celina Gertrudes Cass de (great-granddaughter), 269

Carillo, Ester (great-great-granddaughter), 269

Carlos, Juan, 168

Cart War, 252–253

Carvajal, José Luis, 142

Carvajal, José María de Jesús, 4, 96, 97–98, 100, 105, 109, 121, 122

Carvajal, Manuel, 41–44, 46

Carvajal, Nicolás, 41–44, 46

Casa Navarro State Historic Site, 1–2, 3

Casas, Juan Bautista de las, 21–24

Casas Reales, 21

Cass, María Inéz Tobin de

(granddaughter), 269

Castañeda, Carlos E., 253

Castañeda, Francisco, 126–127

Castañeda, Juan de, 64, 65

Castañeda, María Loreto de, 35, 106

Castillo, Manuel Iturri, 67, 77

Catholicism. See Roman Catholic Church

Cazneau, William, 158

centralism, conservative, 72, 88, 110–111, 119, 123, 126–128, 130, 161, 191–192

Chalmers, John C., 163

Chambers, Thomas Jefferson, 107

Charles, José Rocque, 59, 118, 146

Charleston (steamship), 151

Chávez, Juan A. F., 264

Childress, George C., 129–130, 134

Chirino, Margila, 36, 101, 106, 117–118

cholera, 35, 114–115, 117

citizenship, 208; race and, 208, 211–213

Civil War, 248–249, 255–256, 265

Clandero, José Juan, 199

Coahuila and Texas, 8; Article 13 and prohibition of slavery in, 72, 79–81, 84, 91; Béxar petition for separation, 111–112; Constitution of 1827, 70; erosion of relationship with Mexico, 95; location of capital of, 85; presidential politics in, 84–85; taxes and revenues in, 78–79

Coe, Antonio, 129

colonization: colonization laws, 68–72, 80, 97, 107, 109, 137, 232, 234, 235; DeWitt's Colony, 8, 97, 100, 100–103, 106–109, 117–118, 126; Law of April 6, 1830, and immigration, 94–96, 98, 113, 133; Mexican independence as context for, 50–54; Pecan Point colony, 95–100, 105, 108, 129, 183

Conde, García, 177, 178

Confederate States of America, 6, 248–249, 255–256, 258, 265

Constitutional Union Party (Union Democratic Party), 247–248, 256

Constitution of 1812: 47–48, 55–56, 58

Constitution of 1827 (Coahuila and Texas), 70, 73, 74; Article 13 and prohibition of slavery, 72, 79–81, 84, 91

Constitution of 1836 (Republic of Texas), 2, 7–8, 128, 129–131, 134; and Declaration of Independence, 7–8, 129–131, 134; election of delegates to

convention, 128; land grant provisions in, 132–133, 137; slavery provisions in, 91, 133
Constitution of 1845 (State Constitution of Texas), 2, 6, 8, 11, 202, 204, 232–233; citizenship as defined in, 207; land forfeitures and, 215–218, 222–232; racial policy and, 207–210
Constitution of 1869 (Reconstruction), 264–265
Cooke, Angela Navarro (niece), 256
Cooke, William G., 164, 171–172, 178–179, 182, 186, 201
Cordova, Vicente, 150
Corsica and Corsican ancestry, 10–14
Cos, Martín Perfecto de, 121, 123, 127–128, 135, 183, 185–186
cotton, 70–71, 80, 81
Crisp, James E., 6
Cruz, Ermenegildo de la, 42, 45
Cunningham, Abel S., 207–208, 215–216, 217, 218
Curbelo, Antonio, 43, 44
currency, 73, 76, 142–143

D

Daingerfield, Henry, 146, 152
d'Alvimar, Octaviano, 19–20
Darnell, Nicholas H., 214
Davis, James, 210
Dawson, Joseph M., 5
Dawson Massacre, 203
Declaration of Independence, 7–8, 129–133, 134; JAN as signatory of, 130–131, 134, 196, 226, 272–273, 276
De Cordova, Jacob, 4, 86, 130
Decrees: No. 18: 18, 79; No. 30: 78, 79; No. 35: 18; No. 38: 77; No. 50: 79, 81–82; No. 52: 79; No. 56: 81–83, 91; No. 64: 85; No. 70: 85–86
Defending Mexican Valor in Texas (Matovina & McDonald), 6
Degener, Edward, 263–264
De la Garza, Refugio Guadalupe, Fr., 50, 56, 61, 63, 65, 111, 114, 155, 158
De León, Arnoldo, 265
De León family, 3–4; land forfeiture 215, 218, 229
Delgado, Antonio, 25–26, 253
del Rey, Félix María Calleja, 22–23
Democratic Party, 243, 262, 264. *See also*

Constitutional Union Party (Union Democratic Party)
DeWitt colony, 8, 97, 100–103, 106–109, 117–118, 126
Dickinson, Andrew G., 256
Dickson, David G., 243, 247
Dill, James (a.k.a. Dilmore), 150
Donelson, Andrew J., 206
Dryden, William G., 163
Dwyer, Edward, 143, 146, 202

E

Eca y Músquiz, Rafael, 127
education: colleges and universities established in Texas, 155–156; elementary school established in San Antonio, 57; JAN as proponent of, 10, 155–156, 232–233; of JAN, 9–10, 15–18; of JAN's children, 158–159, 204, 236–237; legal studies, 17; public school system in Texas, establishment of, 232–233
Edwards, Haden, 69
Elizondo, Ignacio, 26–27, 30–31
Elliot, Charles, 199–200
Ellis, Richard, 129, 132
Elozúa, Antonio, 92, 101, 113, 114
escheats, 207–208, 222–225, 231
Evans, Lemuel D., 218–219
Ewing, Alexander, 240

F

Falconer, Thomas, 169, 173, 174–175, 179
family coalition, Navarro-Ruiz-Veramendi, 3, 18–19, 31–32, 101, 106, 114–116, 117–118, 166
Farías, Eusebio, 129
Farías, Juan José, 15
Farías, Valentín Gómez, 116, 118–119
federalism: in Béxar, 63, 119–120, 126–128; JAN and, 126–128, 130, 162; Santa Anna as federalist, 62–63, 110–111, 119
Fisher, George, 161, 205, 206–207, 211, 214, 235, 236, 262
Fitzgerald, Archibald, 169–170
Flores, Francisco, 143
Flores, Gaspar, 58, 123, 128, 136
Flores, Juan José, 55, 57, 58
Flores, Xaviera, 35–36, 58, 275
forfeitures of property, 133, 208, 215–218, 222–232

Fredonian Rebellion, 67, 69, 70
Fritz, Naomi, 5, 247

G

Gallagher, Peter, 170, 176–177
Galván, Juan José, 137
García, Francisco, 43, 63, 64
García, Luciano, 66
García, Luis, 279
Garza, Felipe de la, 63, 66
Garza, Francisco, 279
Garza, Margarita de la (wife), 15, 35–37,
    40, 61, 114, 126–127, 145, 201, 204,
    237, 256, 258; gravesite of, 270, 271
Gil, Leonardo, 143, 279
Gómez, Francisco, 129
Gómez Pedraza, Manuel, 84–85
González, José María Elias, 177–178
Gortari, Vicente, 48, 92
Grant, James, 122–123
Gray, William Fairfax, 129, 131–132,
    134–135, 136
Green, Thomas J., 132, 137
Gregg, Josiah, 229–230
Groce, Jared E., 105, 135
Guadalupe Festival, 60–61
Guerrero, Enrique, 59
Guerrero, Patricio, 59
Guerrero, Vicente, 84–85, 90–92
Gutiérrez de Lara, José Bernardo
    Maximiliano, 24–27
Gutiérrez-Magee Expedition, 18, 38

H

Hamilton-Gordon, George, Earl of
    Aberdeen, 199
Haywood, Felix (freedman), 261
headrights, land grants and, 140–144,
    151–152
Hemphill, John, 218
Henderson, J. Pinckney, 220, 230–231,
    234
Herrera, Blas, 129
Herrera, Ignacio, 118
Herrera, José Joaquín de, 200
Herrera, Simón de, 22, 24–25, 32
Hewitt, I. L., 253–254
Hidalgo, Miguel, Fr.: insurrection lead by,
    21–24, 177
Hill, George W., 151
Hogg, Joseph L., 211–212

Holliman v. Pebbles, 234–235, 236
homestead law, 85–86, 151
Horton, Albert C., 216
Houston, Capitol building in, 149
Houston, Sam, 128, 129, 135–136, 138,
    139–140, 142, 162, 163, 178, 205, 231,
    243, 247–248
Howard, George T., 166
Howard, Volney, 220
Howland, John, 169
Howth, William E., 148–150

I

Illueca, José Ignacio García, 65–66
immigration: colonization laws and,
    68–69; as essential to Texas economy,
    33, 51–52; homestead law (Decree No.
    70) and, 85–86; Law of April 6, 1830,
    and, 94–96, 98, 113, 133
indenture, 14, 81, 145–147
independence, Mexican, 50–52
Indians, 61; citizenship status of, 208,
    214; as hostiles or raiders, 33, 35, 44–
    45, 150, 156, 158, 169–170, 171, 203,
    230, 248, 254–255; Lamar's anti-Indian
    policies, 156; as military or political
    allies, 24, 28–29, 135; missions and
    education of, 15; racial designation
    and, 73, 207
"In Storms of Fortune" (Bueno), 6
Iturbide, Agustín de, 50, 60–61, 62–63,
    64, 65
Iturría, Manuel María, 189
Iturría, Miguel, 250

J

Jewett, Henry J., 213, 225, 227
Joe (slave and Alamo survivor), 135
Jones, Anson, 204, 205, 219
Jones, Oliver, 211, 219
Jones, William J., 163
José Antonio Navarro: Co-Creator of Texas
    (Dawson), 5
"José Antonio Navarro" (thesis, Fritz), 5

K

Karnes, Henry W., 140
Kearney, Stephen, 231
Kendall, George W., 168, 170, 171,
    174–175, 177, 178, 179–180, 186–187,
    201–202, 250

Kinney, Henry L., 205, 207, 211, 214–215, 216

Kinney, Samuel, 140

kinship. *See* family coalition, Navarro-Ruiz-Veramendi

Kiowa Indians, 171

Know-Nothing Party (American Party), 11, 237–239, 242–247, 252

L

La Bahía de San Bernardo, port of, 52, 54–55

Lamar, Mirabeau B., 148, 154, 156

land grants. *See* property rights and land claims

"Land Jackalls," 234

language barriers, 54, 91, 129, 130–131, 151, 154, 156, 206, 211, 223, 233

la Quinta, Casa de, 31, 35, 124, 253

law and legal processes, 98, 113, 133; foundational documents of colonial legal system, 17, 57; investigation of JAN on smuggling charges, 43–49; JAN and conciliation process, 57–58, 222; JAN as city attorney, 92; JAN's early study of, 17, 47; translation of laws, 91, 151, 207. *See also* Decrees; *specific constitutions*

Law of Contracts, 81–83

Leal, Consolación, 152, 253

Leal, Francisco, 142

Leal, Narciso, 4–5, 130, 243, 266, 273

Leal family land claims, 152–154

leg injury and subsequent disability, 10, 16–17, 36, 74, 164, 168, 169, 176, 178, 182, 188–189, 194–195, 230, 246

Letona, José María, 102, 109

Lewis, John M., 214

Lewis, Nathaniel, 156

Leyva, José, 176

Linaste, Francisco, 187–189

Lipan Apache, 29

livestock: expedition to Louisiana to acquire, 41–49; roundup of wild, 55, 76

Llanos, Rafael, 46–48

Longueville, Peter, 67

López, Gaspar, 51, 52, 63

López, Ignacio, 72

López, María Claudia, 72

Louisiana Purchase, 18; map of neutral ground along border after, 53

loyalty oaths, 23, 63, 65, 140, 248–249, 258

Lubbock, Francis R., 179, 248

Luna, Norato de, 42, 43, 46

M

Madero, José Francisco, 75–76, 79, 83, 103, 108–109

Magee, Augustus W., 24

Magoffin, James W., 178

Magoffin, María Gertrudis Valdez, 178

maps: of Ángel Navarro's travels in the Mediterranean, *13*; of Atascosa Ranch, *110*; of neutral ground between Texas and Louisiana, *53*; of San Antonio de Béxar, *34, 263*; of San Geronimo Ranch, *157*; of Santa Fe expedition and journey as prisoner, *201*; of territory assigned to Texas during Treaty of Guadalupe Hidalgo, *221*; Texas map commissioned, 90–91

Martínez, Antonio, 38

Martínez, Francisco, 31

Matovina, Timothy, 6

Maverick, Samuel, 128–129, 156, 233, 243, 246, 247–248, 262

McAnelly, Cornelius, 222

McCraven, William, 152

McCulloch, Benjamin, 255

McLeod, Hugh, 164, 168–169, 171–174, 176, 177, 178, 185, 199

McMullen, John, 129

Medina, Battle of, 17–18, 19, 28–30, 135, 239, 253

Menchaca, Antonio, 253

Meralla (servant or slave in the Navarro household), 118

Mexican Revolution, 17–18, 21, 177; Battle of Medina, 28–29; executions during, 25–27; pardons granted to insurgents, 31; and self-imposed exile, 29–30

Milam, Benjamin R., 95, 97, 108, 127, 179

Monclova government, 85, 112–113; arrest of Austin, 117; collapse of, 123–124; land grants made by, 132–133, 137, 151–154; opposition to Santa Anna, 119–121, 122; troops garrisoned at Béxar, 113–114

Mondragón, E., 264

Moore, Francis, Jr., 213–214
Moreland, W., 107–108
Moreno, Geronimo, 118
Morlet, Mariano, 182, 183, 185–186, 187–189, 193
Músquiz, Melchor, 127
Músquiz, Ramón, 82, 91–92, 96–102, 105, 106, 108, 109, 111

N

Napoleon, invasion of Spain, 18
Native nations. See Indians
Navarro, Amelia (niece), 257
Navarro, Ángel (father), 2–3, 16–17; autobiographical sketch of, 14–15; education of, 15–16; emigration from Corsica by, 10–14; map of travels, 13; marriage of, 14; political career of, 15
Navarro, Celso Cornelio (son), 114, 237, 248, 250, 256, 258, 259, 267
Navarro, Eugenio (brother), 67, 68, 101, 123, 124, 128, 137, 138, 139, 142; death of, 147–148; political career of, 141; signature on document, 121
Navarro, Henry (freedman), 251, 261, 277–278
Navarro, José Ángel, III (son), 5, 10, 114, 158–160, 236–237, 239, 248–249, 254, 255, 256, 281
Navarro, José Antonio, 11, 209; as Anglo sympathizer, 7–8; biographies of, 4–7; birth of, 15; character of, 16–17, 230, 266; children of, 36–37, 40, 61, 114, 145, 158–159, 204, 270–272 (See also specific individuals); death of, 270; Declaration of Independence, signing of by, 130–131, 134, 196, 226, 272–273, 276; education of, 9; gravesite of, 271; as historian, 8–9, 19–20, 165–166, 239, 252–253; home pictured, 3; as land commissioner, 2, 8, 88, 95, 97–100, 105–106, 113, 117–118; leg injury and subsequent disability, 10, 16–17, 36, 74, 164, 168, 169, 176, 178, 182, 188–189, 194–195, 230, 246; marriage to Margarita de la Garza, 36–38; as merchant, 60, 67–68, 70, 88, 90, 94, 114, 118, 121–122, 124, 229–230; political career of (See political career of JAN); ranching and (See Atascosa Ranch; San Geronimo Ranch);

Santa Fe Expedition (See Santa Fe Expedition); signature on document, 121; as smuggler of contraband, 40–49; wealth and success of, 109, 144, 240
Navarro, José Antonio, III (grandson), 204, 276
Navarro, José Antonio George (son), 116, 145, 156, 247, 248–249, 249, 255–256, 267
Navarro, José de los Ángeles (Jose Ángel) (brother), 15, 19, 144–145; death of, 138; as mentor and ally, 37–38; signature of, 121
Navarro, Juana Chávez (daughter-in-law), 156
Navarro, Juan Antonio (kinsman), 14
Navarro, Juliana (kinswoman), 14
Navarro, Luciano (brother), 67, 120, 127, 128, 145, 156, 256; signature on document, 121
Navarro, María Antonia (sister), 31, 178
Navarro, María Gertrudis (daughter), 61, 267
Navarro, María Josefa (sister), 15, 18, 30, 115
Navarro, Nepomuceno (nephew), 184
Navarro, Teodora (sister-in-law), 96, 256, 257
Navarro, Wenseslao "Sixto" Eusebio (son), 144, 237, 248, 250, 255, 256, 258, 260, 267, 272, 276, 278; death of, 272; provisions in will for, 279–284
Navatasco (abandoned county seat), 250
Neill, James C., 128
Neill, John, 152
Newcomb, James P., 263–264
Nolan, Philip, 67

O

Ocampo, Carlos, 182, 186
Ochiltree, William B., 214
Odin, John, Fr., 158–159
Ogden, Duncan C., 166, 220
Olmsted, Frederick Law, 212, 251

P

Padilla, Antonio, 80, 83, 84
Paredes, Mariano, 199
Parmer, Martin, 132, 133
Patton, María Casimira del Cármen (daughter), 36, 145, 267, 275

Patton, Robert, 145
Pease, Elisha M., 239, 242–243, 247
Pecan Point colony, 95–100, 105, 108, 129, 183
The Peculiar Institution (Stampp), 252
Peña, Hilario de la, 67–68
Peña, Manuela de la, 14, 15, 16, 117
Peña, Petra de la (aunt), 75
Pérez, Ignacio, 61
Pesa, José María de la, 193
Phillips, Alexander H., 231
Piedras, José de las, 99
Plan de Casa Mata, 62–65
political career of JAN, 2, 6, 120–123, 266; as city attorney, 92; as city council member, 48, 55–56; as delegate to Coahuila and Texas legislature, 73–87; as delegate to Constitutional Convention of 1835, 128–131, 133–134; as legislator, 8, 10–11, 64, 66, 67–68, 148–156. *See also* Decrees
politics: Anglo colonists and political representation, 74; apportionment debate, 213–214; Béxar junta as governing body, 24–25, 48, 64–66, 113, 182; Constitutional Union Party (Union Democratic Party), 247–248, 256; Democratic Party, 243, 262, 264; election controversies and, 84–85, 149–150; Know-Nothing Party (American Party), 11, 237–239, 242–247, 252; Mexican Constitution and local governance, 70; Radical Republican Party and Radical Reconstruction, 261–264; representative government, 48, 55, 56; representative government established in, 48, 55; slavery as political issue, 72, 79–81, 84, 91. *See also* political career of JAN
Polk, James K., 204–205, 206, 219, 220
Potter, Reuben M., 130–131, 132, 166–167, 197–198, 220, 229, 233, 240
Power, James, 129
property rights and land claims: alien land owners and, 224–225; *amparos* and unspecified sites, 88; chart of Spanish and English land measures, 89; Constitution of Texas (1836), provisions in, 132–133; De León family land forfeiture, 215, 218, 229;

forfeitures and escheats, 133, 208, 215–218, 222–232; headright grants, 140–144, 151–152; *Holliman v. Pebbles* and "old settlers," 234–235, 236; homestead laws, 85–86, 151; JAN as land commissioner, 2, 8, 88, 95, 97–100, 105–106, 113, 117–118; JAN as landlord, 261; JAN's acquisition of land, 86, 87, 96–97, 106, 109, 117–118, 143, 156, 164, 229, 240; JAN's will and disposition of, 267–269, 279–285; land grants made by the Monclova government, 132–133, 137, 151–154; "Land Jackalls," 234; Leal family land claims, 152–154; legislative efforts to protect Tejano, 151–154; native Texans as *pobladors* entitled to, 92–93; Royall and Royall-Caldwell land deal, 93–94, 99–100, 103–108; speculators and, 92, 107–108, 132–133, 137, 142, 234–236; squatters and illegal settlement, 57, 93, 218; Tejano legacy land rights, 151–154, 207–208, 222–224, 227; women and, 143, 227–228
provisional government of Texas, 127–128

Q

Quijano, Benito, 195, 196, 199
Quintana, Teodora, 176–177

R

race relations, 9; *castas*, 35, 73; Indians and, 73, 207, 208, 211; racial designation and intermarriage, 73, 207, 211; "whiteness" and citizenship debate, 211–215, 213. *See also* slavery
Radical Republican Party, 261–264
Ramírez, Juana (sister-in-law), 101, 137
Ramírez, Pablo, 42–47, 45
ranching: JAN as rancher (*See* Atascosa Ranch; San Geronimo Ranch); livestock, roundup of wild, 76
Reconstruction, 260–266
Refugita (Comanche servant), 75
Republic of Texas, 8; annexation of, 220; Capitol building in Houston, 149; Lamar's Santa Fe expedition and expansionism, 162–163. *See also* Constitution of 1836 (Republic of Texas)
Republic of the Rio Grande, 161–162

Reséndez, Andrés, 6–7
revenue: customs as income source, 54–55; government operations and, 76–77; tax collection, 92, 94
Reyes, José Isidro, 199
Richardson, William, 152
Roberts, John S., 131
Roberts, Samuel, 179
Robinson, James W., 150, 152
Robles, Vito Alessio, 86–87, 253
Rodríguez, Damian, 40–42
Rodríguez, José Maria, 251, 279
Rodríguez, María Josefa, 106
Rojas, Ramón García, 75
Roman Catholic Church: anti-Catholicism, 155, 242–243, 247; legislation to promote Catholicism, 155; race relations or slavery and, 72–73, 251
Rosillo, Battle of, 24–26
Roxo, Francisco, 64
Royall, Richard R., 93–94, 99, 103–104, 106–108
Rubio, Adriano, 237, 250
Rubio, Ramón, 116, 118, 158, 203
Ruiz, Donaciano, 98
Ruiz, Francisco Antonio (cousin), 141, 156
Ruiz, José Francisco (uncle), 3, 10, 15–16, 64, 67, 84, 91, 120, 128, 159; as conspirator in Hidalgo insurrection, 21, 28, 33; death of, 126, 158; as teacher and mentor, 15–16, 17, 123
Ruiz y Peña, María Gertrudis Josefa (mother), 2–3, 6, 14, 30, 36–40, 44, 117
Runnels, Hardin R., 248
Runnels, Hiram G., 208–209, 210–211, 213
Rusk, Thomas J., 206, 208, 211, 216, 217–218

S
Sáenz, Joaquín, 43–46
Salado, Battle of, 24–26
Salazar, Dámaso, 171, 177
Salcedo, Manuel María de, 20–26, 32, 50
Salinas, José María de Jesús, 55, 60, 102, 105
Saltillo, 14, 16, 19, 67
San Antonio de Béxar, 3, 33–35; maps of, 34, 263
San Felipe convention, 111–113

San Fernando Cathedral, 27
San Fernando de Béxar, 3
San Geronimo Ranch, 241; brands used on, 238; land acquisition for, 117–118, 132, 144; operation of, 156–158, 164, 203, 233–234, 237, 250–251; plat map of, 157; sale of, 240
San Jacinto, Battle of, 121, 135, 156, 183–186, 203, 248
San Juan de Ulúa, 194; JAN as prisoner in, 193–200, 202
San Miguel del Vado, New Mexico, 173
Santa Anna, Antonío López de, 181; at Alamo, 133–134, 230; and Battle of San Jacinto, 135–136; as centralist, 110–111, 119; as despotic or tyrannical, 64–66, 84–85, 110–112, 118–123, 127, 161, 174, 180, 190–192, 195, 197–198, 240; as federalist, 62–63, 110–111, 119; JAN charged with treason and imprisoned by, 180–198; personality cult and amputated leg of, 195, 199; relations with Béxar, 64–66, 119–121; remarriage of, 198–199; scandals linked to, 198–199, 239–240; as suitor of JAN's sister, 31, 239–240; Texas independence and, 116, 128, 133; treason charges against, 199
Santa Fe Expedition, 6–7; Armijo's treatment of members, 171–176, 178, 185; capture of members of, 171; Cooke's role in, 164, 171; escape plot by, 178–179; guides for, 168, 169; as ill prepared, 168–169, 171, 172; Indians as threat to, 169–170, 171; JAN tried and sentenced for treason as member of, 180–199; JAN's role in, 166–167; map of route (including journey as prisoner), 201; McLeod's role in, 164, 172–173, 185; release of members other than JAN, 190; Santa Anna's capture and imprisonment of JAN as member of, 161, 176–180; surrender of members, 172–174, 185, 190; as trade mission, 161
Saucedo, José Antonio, 68–70, 72, 74, 84, 98
Scott, Winfield, 231
secession, 5, 8, 247–249, 255–256
Seguín, Erasmo, 6, 35, 48, 52, 56–58, 64, 65, 128, 136, 149–150, 250; as JAN's

legislative ally, 152–156; and statehood,
111–112, 120–121

Seguín, Juan N., 117, 124, 128, 203, 207,
218, 247, 253; and Battle of San Jacinto,
135–136, 183–184; burial of Alamo
defenders by, 138–139; as legislator,
150; as military leader, 135–136,
139–140, 142; opposition to Sante Fe
Expedition, 165, 166

Siegel, Stanley, 163

Siege of Béxar, 121, 127, 139, 179, 183,
185, 253

Simpson, John S., 152

Sims, Harold, 77

síndico procurador (city attorney), role of,
48, 92

slavery, 9, 15; Anglo colonization and,
70–73; Article 13 and prohibition of,
72, 79–81, 84, 91; Austin as proponent
of, 70–71, 72; Catholicism and, 72–73;
convict laborers, 118; Emancipation
Proclamation and end of, 261;
Guerrero and abolition of, 91–92;
indenture as alternative to, 81; slaves
held by Navarro family, 250–252, 265,
277

Smith, Henry, 128

Smith, John W., 118, 140–141, 150, 152

Spaniards: anti-Spanish sentiment, 77

Stampp, Kenneth, 252

Sutton, John, 171

T

Tahuancano Indians, 44

Tanner, Henry S., 90

Taylor, Charles S., 131

Taylor, Zachary, 220

Tejanos: anti-Tejano sentiment, 11,
203–204, 207–213, 216–217, 227,
240, 252–253 (*See also* Know-Nothing
Party); citizenship and voting rights of,
211–213; race relations and, 9, 72; as
Texas patriots, 216–217, 239, 253; use
of term, 8–9, 221–222

Terán, Manuel Mier y, 98–99

A Texan Patriot on Trial in Mexico
(Reséndez), 6–7

Texas: annexation of, 204–207, 220,
242; Declaration of Independence by,
7–8, 129–131, 134; independence from
Mexico, 8, 127, 129–133; proposed

division of, 264–265; provisional
government of (1835–36), 127–128;
State Constitution of 1845, 2, 6, 8, 11,
202, 204, 207–210, 215–218, 222–232,
232–233; statehood, 7, 8, 111–114, 116,
204, 208, 229, 272. *See also* Republic
of Texas

Tijerina, Andés, 72

Tinsley, _____, 147–148

Tobin, Daniel J. (son-in-law), 246, 249,
267

Tobin, Josefa Elena de Navarro (daughter),
246, 267, 269; provisions in will for,
280–284

Toledo y Dubois, José Álvarez, 27–29

Tornel, José María, 175–176, 179, 180,
182, 187–196, 191, 199

Tosta, María Dolores de, 198–199

Townsend, Asa, 234

trade: Ángel Navarro's employment as
merchant, 14–15; customs and control
of, 54–55; JAN as merchant, 60, 67–
68, 70, 88, 90, 94, 114, 118, 121–122,
124, 229–230; JAN as smuggler of
contraband, 40–49; port of La Bahía
and, 52, 54–55; Sante Fe expedition as
trade mission, 161

Travis, William B., 2, 129, 226

treasury, establishment of, 78

Treaty of Guadalupe Hidalgo, 220–221

Trespalacios, José Félix, 60, 63–65, 76,
239

Treviño, Alejandro, 114

Treviño, Augustin, 230

Treviño, Geronimo, 58

Trimble, Robert C., 152

Twiggs, David E., 255

U

Ugartechea, Domingo de, 121, 124, 126,
127, 128

Urrua, Fernando, 182–184, 186

V

Valdés, José Antonio, 155

Van Ness, Cornelius, 145–146, 148, 154

Van Ness, George, 164, 177, 195–196

Van Zandt, Isaac, 211

Vásquez, Leonarda, 58

Vásquez, Rafael, 180

Velásquez, Trinidad, 195

Veramendi, Juan Martín de (brother-in-law), 3, 31, 40, 114–115, 121–122; as conspirator in Hidalgo insurrection, 21; as mentor, 18–19, 110, 113; political career of, 55, 109, 110, 112–113
Veramendi, María Josefa Navarro (sister), 15, 18, 30, 115
Victoria, Guadalupe, 62, 65, 84–85
Vidaurri, Santiago, 254, 256
Viesca, Agustín, 123
Viesca, José María, 83, 86, 88–90, 93, 95, 97, 98, 99, 100, 101
Villarreal, Pedro, 43

W
Wallace, Benjamin R., 222
Wavell, Arthur G., 95, 97
Wavell colony. See Pecan Point colony
Weddle, Robert, 4
Williams, Samuel May, 5, 6, 91, 99–107, 109, 111, 112, 115, 117, 120, 122–124, 132, 151, 180, 236
Wilson, James C., 243–244
Woll, Adrián, 180, 203
women: imprisoned in La Quinta, 30–31, 35, 124–125, 166, 253; property rights of, 143, 227–228

Y
Yoakum, Henderson K., 252
Young, William C., 218

Z
Zambrano, José Darío, 48, 51, 58, 92
Zambrano, Juan José Manuel Vicente, 23–24, 40–43, 48–49, 64–65, 67
Zapata, María, 72
Zaragoza, Ignacio de, 4
Zavala, Lorenzo de, 84, 90, 129, 131–132, 134–135, 204, 207
Zozaya, José Manuel, 189–190, 192, 193